Labour's First Century

The Labour Party's centenary is an appropriate moment to evaluate its performance across the twentieth century and to reflect on why a party which has so many achievements to its credit has none the less spent so much of the century in opposition. This is the only book that attempts such an assessment. Duncan Tanner, Pat Thane and Nick Tiratsoo have assembled a team of acknowledged experts who cover a wide range of key issues, from economic policy to gender. The editors also provide a lucid, accessible introduction. *Labour's First Century* covers the most important areas of party policy and practice, always placing these in a broader context. Taken together, the essays provide a fundamental challenge to those who minimise the party's contribution, whilst also explaining why mistakes and weaknesses have occurred. Everyone interested in British political history – whether supporters or opponents of the Labour Party – will want to read *Labour's First Century*.

Duncan Tanner is Professor of History at the University of Wales, Bangor. His first book, *Political Change and the Labour Party 1900–1918* (1990) won the Royal Historical Society's Whitfield Prize; he has continued to publish widely, both on the Labour Party and on broader themes.

Pat Thane is Professor of Contemporary History at the University of Sussex. Her many publications include *The Foundations of the Welfare State* (1982) and *Old Age in English History: Past Experiences, Present Issues* (2000).

Nick Tiratsoo is a Senior Research Fellow at the University of Luton and Visiting Research Fellow at the London School of Economics. He has written or edited a number of books on the Labour Party's history and on post-war British business history.

Frontispiece *Labour election poster from the late 1920s*

Labour's First Century

Edited by **Duncan Tanner**
University of Wales, Bangor

Pat Thane
University of Sussex

Nick Tiratsoo
University of Luton

CAMBRIDGE
UNIVERSITY PRESS

PUBLISHED BY THE PRESS SYNDICATE OF THE UNIVERSITY OF CAMBRIDGE
The Pitt Building, Trumpington Street, Cambridge, United Kingdom

CAMBRIDGE UNIVERSITY PRESS
The Edinburgh Building, Cambridge CB2 2RU, UK   www.cup.cam.ac.uk
40 West 20th Street, New York, NY 10011-4211, USA   www.cup.org
10 Stamford Road, Oakleigh, Melbourne 3166, Australia
Ruiz de Alarcón 13, 28014 Madrid, Spain

First published 2000

Printed in the United Kingdom at the University Press, Cambridge

Typeface Monotype Imprint 9/11.5 pt.   *System* QuarkXPress™ [SE]

A catalogue record for this book is available from the British Library

ISBN 0 521 65184 0 hardback

Hardback edition
at paperback
price

Contents

Illustrations

*Illustration 2 is courtesy of the Mitchell Library,
Glasgow City Libraries and Archives; all remaining
illustrations are reproduced by permission of the
National Museum of Labour History, Manchester.*

Acknowledgements

The editors would like to record their gratitude to Stephen Bird and Phil Dunn at the National Museum of Labour History in Manchester; Richard Fisher and Elizabeth Howard at Cambridge University Press; and Martin Daunton and Steven Fielding, two colleagues who provided invaluable help in the early stages of the project.

Notes on contributors

Stefan Berger is Professor of History at the
University of Glamorgan. He has written
widely on comparative labour history and the
history of historiography. His previous
publications include *The Labour Party and the
German Social Democrats, 1900–1931* (Oxford:
Oxford University Press, 1994); *The Search for
Normality. National Identity and Historical
Consciousness in Germany since 1800* (Oxford:
Berghahn, 1997); with Angel Smith (eds.),
Labour, Nationalism and Ethnicity, 1870–1939
(Manchester: Manchester University Press,
1999); and *Social Democracy and the Working
Class in Nineteenth and Twentieth Century
Germany* (London: Longman, 1999).

Steven Fielding is a Senior Lecturer in the School
of English, Sociology, Politics and
Contemporary History and a member of the
European Studies Research Institute at the
University of Salford. He has written on
various aspects of the Labour Party, including
(with Peter Thompson and Nick Tiratsoo),
*'England Arise!' The Labour Party and Popular
Politics in 1940s Britain* (Manchester:
Manchester University Press, 1995) and *Labour:
Decline and Renewal* (Manchester: Baseline,
1999). He is presently working on a study of
how Labour responded to social change during
the 1960s for Manchester University Press.

Martin Francis is Lecturer in British and
American History at Royal Holloway and
Bedford New College, University of London.
He is the author of *Ideas and Policies under
Labour, 1945–1951* (Manchester: Manchester
University Press, 1997), and editor (with Ina
Zweiniger-Bargielowska) of *The Conservatives
and British Society, 1880–1990* (Cardiff:
University of Wales Press, 1996). He is
currently exploring codes of emotional
expression and restraint in British and
American politics in the twentieth century.

Notes on contributors

Jose Harris is Professor of Modern History in the University of Oxford, and currently holds a Leverhulme Research Professorship. She is the author of *Private Lives, Public Spirit: Britain 1870–1914* (Oxford: Oxford University Press, 1993; Penguin edition, 1994), and *William Beveridge: A Biography* (Oxford: Oxford University Press, revised edition, 1997).

Stephen Howe is Tutor in Politics at Ruskin College, Oxford, and has been a Research Fellow at Corpus Christi College, and political columnist and leader writer at the *New Statesman*. He has published *Anticolonialism in British Politics* (Oxford: Oxford University Press, 1993); *Afrocentrism* (London: Verso, 1998); *Ireland and Empire* (Oxford: Oxford University Press, 2000); and edited *Lines of Dissent* (London: Verso, 1988).

Jon Lawrence is Senior Lecturer in History at the University of Liverpool. He is the author of *Speaking for the People: Party, Language and Popular Politics in England, 1867–1914* (Cambridge: Cambridge University Press, 1998), and editor (with Miles Taylor) of *Party, State and Society: Electoral Behaviour in Britain since 1820* (Aldershot: Scolar Press, 1997). He is currently working on political disorder and the transformation of election customs in Britain between the 1860s and the Second World War.

Alastair J. Reid is a Fellow and Lecturer in History at Girton College, Cambridge. His publications include (with Henry Pelling) A *Short History of the Labour Party*, 11th edition (London: Macmillan, 1996). He is currently writing a new history of British trade unionism.

Duncan Tanner is Professor of History and Welsh History, University of Wales, Bangor. His publications include *Political Change and the Labour Party 1900–1918* (Cambridge: Cambridge University Press, 1990) and his current interests include Labour ideology and politics between the wars and women's position and contribution within the Labour Party.

Notes on contributors

Miles Taylor is a Lecturer in Modem History at King's College, London. He is the author of *The Decline of British Radicalism, 1847–1860* (Oxford: Clarendon Press, 1995) and editor (with Jon Lawrence) of *Party, State and Society: Electoral Behaviour in Britain since 1820* (Aldershot: Ashgate, 1997). He is currently completing a biography of Emest Jones, the last Chartist leader.

Pat Thane is Professor of Contemporary History at the University of Sussex. She has written extensively on the history of social welfare and other aspects of twentieth-century history. Her most recent publications are: *Foundations of the Welfare State* (London: Longman, 1984; second edition 1996); with Paul Johnson (eds.), *Old Age from Antiquity to Post-Modernity* (London: Routledge, 1998); and *Old Age in England, Past and Present* (Oxford: Oxford University Press, 2000).

Nick Tiratsoo is Senior Research Fellow at the University of Luton and Visiting Research Fellow at the Business History Unit, the London School of Economics. He has written extensively on the Labour Party and on aspects of business history, and is currently completing a study of British management after 1945.

Jim Tomlinson is Professor of Economic History and Head of the Department of Government at Brunel University. He has written widely on the history of economic policy and ideas in twentieth-century Britain. Most recently he has published *Democratic Socialism and Economic Policy: The Attlee Years 1945–1951* (Cambridge: Cambridge University Press, 1997) and (with Nick Tiratsoo), *The Conservatives and Industrial Efficiency 1951–64. Thirteen Wasted Years?* (London: Routledge/LSE, 1998).

Introduction

Duncan Tanner, Pat Thane and Nick Tiratsoo

At the end of a century in which state social-
ism has been convincingly beaten to its corner, it might be assumed that a
history of the British Labour Party would be a story of failure and ideological compromise. Few historians surveying the evolution of Europe
during the twentieth century have stressed the significance of democratic
socialist ideas and politics. Rather they identify an age of fascist aggression and Soviet expansion, of wars which left countries devastated and
the continent divided. In this story democratic socialist parties frequently appear as the poor relations, without sophisticated ideology or
clear purpose – political forces which were largely eclipsed by the
extremes.[1] Nor have these parties received much praise for their role in
the introduction of social reforms. For many years the most influential
texts argued that the growth of collectivist intervention emerged from
periods of consensus, from the demands created or unleashed by war, or
from the spread of liberal ideologies.[2] Even helpful and original studies
saw the reform process as anyway incomplete.[3] To well-regarded left-
wing polemicists, the Labour Party was particularly culpable, a pale
reflection of its allegedly more sophisticated and dynamic European
counterparts.[4] It was attacked by Marxists for its lack of socialist vigour,[5]
by Liberals for being class-based,[6] and by feminists for its neglect of

women.[7] Measured against absolute standards or the agendas of others, Labour has inevitably been regularly condemned.

This volume does not hide Labour's weaknesses. However, it does offer a more positive evaluation of the party's record, by judging Labour against its own aims and values, and against what might reasonably have been expected. Whatever its weaknesses, the party has many successes to its credit. It compares very favourably to its rivals. No party was more successful at actually delivering reforms, more feminist, more opposed to imperialism or racism, more able to deliver when given the opportunity. If ideologies are judged by what their advocates achieve, then the contribution of democratic socialism – and of the Labour Party – to the twentieth century stands close comparison to the failure of both the radical left and the conservative right.

This is not to suggest that all socialist parties in Europe have adopted the same mix of ideological aims and immediate policies, or achieved the same degree of success. The British Labour Party is more evidently part of a broader movement than many have suggested,[8] but its history and that of its counterparts elsewhere are not identical. The party has constructed its own electoral constituency, and manufactured its own agenda, in response to specifically national conditions.[9] However, in the following pages, adapting to sober views on the constraints of the immediate context or the means to achieve stated goals is seen not as 'weak' pragmatism, but as a sensible respect for what is possible; not as the consequence of consensus, but as due regard for the balance of political forces at particular moments.

In the real world of politics and economics, parties can achieve only so much through their own actions. Judging a party's performance over a complex, challenging, changing century is no easy matter. What was appropriate before 1914 was inappropriate once peace returned four years later. Labour had to shift from being a fringe party of opposition to a party of government, and also had to contend with global economic collapse, a crisis that served only extremists, as events in mainland Europe testified. During the Second World War, Labour dutifully played its part in running what was effectively a siege economy. A reforming agenda was developed, but had to be stifled.[10] After 1945, the party was forced to concentrate on reconstruction rather than socialist transformation, to recreate an active economy and to generate wealth before it could put any other policies into effect. At national and local levels it had to choose between competing needs, at times sacrificing plans for change to the immediate task of rebuilding the country.[11] More recently, a party rooted in the male trade-union movement and traditional industries has had to contend with the collapse of the manufacturing economy, the decline of trade unionism and the challenge of feminism. In such circumstances an unchanging ideology and policy would not have denoted consistency, merely atrophy.

In meeting challenges, Labour has faced a series of difficulties. The party has always been dedicated to improving poorer people's living standards – a commitment that in practical terms demanded higher taxation for the better-off and regulated pay increases. It has also tried to improve human behaviour, for example by fighting prejudice. At times, Labour has even stood for issues which the electorate firmly opposed, from the abolition of hanging to the removal of nuclear weapons, because it believed these to be morally right. All this has meant that the battle for electoral support has frequently been arduous.

Labour has on occasion been successful both at 'educating' opinion and introducing reforms despite popular opposition or indifference. But by the end of its periods in office, the party has regularly been faced with electoral unpopularity and internal discord. Persuading people to accept a planned, regulated removal of inequalities has been no easy task. Faced with the alternative promise of unbridled individual freedom, often carefully argued and popularly expressed by the Conservatives in particular,[12] the electorate has regularly voted with its feet. Moreover, some of the party's own activists have been vocal in denouncing 'betrayal'.

More often than not, then, Labour has failed to convince the country as a whole to accept a second dose of its egalitarian medicine. Following its formation as the Labour Representation Committee in February 1900, the party made little headway until after 1918, when the war reduced the Liberal Party to a less effective rival. Even in these improved circumstances, the party could only form two brief minority governments in 1924 and 1929. It was not until 1945, nearly half a century after its formation, that Labour finally achieved an overall majority. Even then it required the special circumstances generated by war to make the party's programme acceptable. Moreover, within six years, the most successful reforming government in twentieth-century British politics was voted out of office. There have been only two subsequent elections in which Labour has achieved a substantial majority – 1966 and 1997. Once elected, even apparently successful Labour governments have been rejected at the polls without achieving a second full term.

Given this legacy of electoral problems and internal divisions, Labour's capacity to implement concrete, lasting reforms is all the more remarkable. As a series of thoughtful biographies have shown, the party has been led by complex, difficult, but politically shrewd leaders.[13] Its operating principles have been defined and refined by a series of original and practical politician/thinkers, rather than abstract theoreticians.[14] Its policies in office have been constructive and often progressive.[15] Even whilst trying to devise a successful collectivist programme between the wars, the party managed to set the pace in local government and to devise housing and other policies in London and elsewhere which were models of innovation and efficiency.[16] Labour introduced the measures which effectively constructed the welfare state between 1945 and 1951. If some of the ideas came from Liberals such as Beveridge and Keynes, it was only Labour that had the drive to turn them into reality (against considerable opposition in the case of the national health service).[17] Subsequent Labour ministries introduced a range of major, lasting and significant legislation, designed to open out opportunity and correct injustice – including comprehensive education and attempts to outlaw racial and sexual discrimination – despite the mixed views within the party on such issues.[18]

All such legislation has its defects. Labour has not eradicated the inequalities of class and gender. However, to attack it for this is hardly reasonable; the causes of such prejudices are too deep, the government's powers too limited. It would be more appropriate to argue that, despite its commitment to change, the party has at times made mistakes, given some issues less attention than it might have done, ignored sound advice and good ideas, and placed obstacles in the way of progress. Institutional weaknesses have prevented ideas reaching the top, and allowed factions to obstruct change. Tensions between party leaders and colleagues have prevented the party coping as well as it might have done with crises and problems.[19] In the struggle for power within Labour cabinets, some individuals have focused on their careers rather than the quality of legis-lation.[20] The party's tendency to fratricidal conflict has devalued its standing in the eyes of electors and occasionally turned its own organisa-tions into battlegrounds. The impact of Labour's own culture – its myths and prejudices – on its capacity to generate policy suggests that an understanding of its internal history is vital to any appreciation of its viability as a vehicle for reform.

The chapters that follow build on the many excellent individual studies of Labour's policies and leaders. They reflect the existence of a substantial, still-developing and vibrant body of scholarship. Although written by leading authorities, they are not definitive works. There are still too many gaps in the literature for anyone to justify such a claim.[21] Nonetheless, they embrace interpretations, approaches and themes which make this book very different from previous histories. The authors offer views and evaluations that are often new and sometimes controversial.

This is not an official history, but neither is it – in contrast to many previous works – an assault on everything that Labour has attempted to achieve. Labour's members, activists and officials are portrayed not as flawless angels, nor as zealots, but as committed individuals, engaged in public service because of a cause in which they believe and for little tangible reward.[22] Labour's thinkers and leaders appear as more thoughtful, more intellectually coherent and consistent, more dedicated, than is sometimes the case.[23] The party's policies are shown to be more rational, more practical, more reasonable and sometimes more effective.[24] Similarly, the party as a whole is seen to be less isolated from developments in other countries, and more concerned with events abroad. From the Spanish Civil War in the 1930s, through the movements for colonial freedom in the 1950s, to the problems of Nicaragua in the 1980s, Labour members have supported the defence of liberty, reform and freedom.[25]

Changes during the century have required Labour to adapt its policies, to move with popular opinion, to embrace changing expert views, in order to create effective economic and social policies. Yet there are also many continuities, both in terms of values and specific policy areas (such as the commitments to modernise the economy and provide work rather than welfare). In 1997 a long and painful process of adaptation finally resulted in a landslide victory. This was only the latest of several reassessments which have taken place in the electoral wilderness. Once again, many of the party's key aims and values have remained intact, even though items of its traditional faith have been challenged in the process.[26]

It is perhaps surprising that Labour should end the century in office. Many of the industries that once underpinned the bulk of the party's support have disappeared. Some of the ideas it once championed have been discredited. Yet it is also appropriate. Despite the peaks and troughs in popularity, the tensions and conflicts, the moments of unfulfilled hope and of dark despair, the book tells the story of a party which has usually given of its best. The desire for socialist change has united more than it has divided; it has produced a record which contains far more success than failure, including policies which have vastly improved the lot of those Labour exists to serve. All those associated with this party should feel justly proud.

Notes

1 Eric Hobsbawm, *Age of Extremes: The Short Twentieth Century, 1914–91* (London: Michael Joseph, 1994); Donald Sassoon, *One Hundred Years of Socialism: The West European Left in the Twentieth Century* (London: Fontana Press, 1996).
2 Paul Addison, *The Road to 1945. British Politics and the Second World War* (London: Jonathan Cape, 1975).
3 Marcel van der Linden and Jurgen Rojahn (eds.), *The Formation of Labour Movements 1870–1914: An International Perspective* (New York: E. J. Brill, 1990); James E. Cronin, *The Politics of State Expansion: War, State and Society in Twentieth Century Britain* (London: Routledge, 1991).
4 Perry Anderson, 'Origins of the present crisis', *New Left Review* 23 (1964); Tom Nairn, 'The English working class', *New Left Review*, 24 (1964).
5 Ralph Milliband, *Parliamentary Socialism: A Study in the Politics of Labour* (London: Allen and Unwin, 1961); Leo Panitch, 'Ideology and integration: the case of the British Labour Party', *Political Studies* 19 (1971).
6 Peter Clarke, 'The social democratic theory of the class struggle', in Jay Winter (ed.), *The Working Class in Modern British History: Essays in Honour of Henry Pelling* (Cambridge: Cambridge University Press, 1983), pp. 3–18.
7 For a review and critique of this approach, Pat Thane, 'The women of the British Labour Party and feminism, 1906–45', in Harold Smith (ed.), *British Feminism in the Twentieth Century* (Aldershot: Edward Elgar, 1990), pp. 124–43.
8 See the argument in Duncan Tanner, 'Socialist parties and policies', in Martin Pugh (ed.), *A Companion to Modern European History 1871–1945* (Oxford: Blackwell, 1997), pp. 133–54 and Stefan Berger and David Broughton (eds.), *Force of Labour. The Western European Labour Movement and the Working Class in the Twentieth Century* (Oxford: Berg, 1995), esp. pp. 245–61.
9 See especially ch. 2 below by Tomlinson.
10 Stephen Brooke, *Labour's War: The Labour Party during the Second World War* (Oxford: Clarendon Press, 1992).
11 Jim Tomlinson, *Democratic Socialism and Economic Policy. The Attlee Years 1945–51* (Cambridge: Cambridge University Press, 1997); Nick Tiratsoo, *Reconstruction, Affluence and Labour Politics. Coventry 1945–60* (London: Routledge, 1990).
12 David Jarvis, 'The shaping of Conservative electoral hegemony, 1918–39', in Jon Lawrence and Miles Taylor (eds.), *Party, State and Society. Electoral Behaviour in Britain since 1820* (London: Scolar Press, 1997), pp. 131–52; Ina Zweiniger-Bargielowska, 'Explaining the gender gap: the Conservative Party and the women's vote, 1945–64', in Martin Francis and Ina Zweiniger-Bargielowska (eds.), *The Conservatives and British Society, 1880–1990* (Cardiff: University of Wales Press, 1996), pp. 194–224.
13 See, for example, Kenneth O. Morgan, *Keir Hardie. Radical and Socialist*

(London: Weidenfeld and Nicolson, 1975); David Marquand, *Ramsay MacDonald* (London: Jonathan Cape, 1977); Kenneth Harris, *Attlee* (London: Weidenfeld and Nicolson, 1982); Philip M. Williams, *Hugh Gaitskell* (Oxford: Oxford University Press, 1982); Ben Pimlott, *Harold Wilson* (London: HarperCollins, 1992); Kenneth O. Morgan, *Callaghan: A Life* (Oxford: Oxford University Press, 1997).

14 Elizabeth Durbin, *New Jerusalems. The Labour Party and the Economics of Democratic Socialism* (London: Routledge and Kegan Paul, 1985); Anthony Wright, *R. H. Tawney* (Manchester: Manchester University Press, 1987); Michael Freeden, *Liberalism Divided. A Study in British Political Thought 1914–39* (Oxford: Clarendon Press, 1986), pp. 294–328; Martin Francis, *Ideas and Policies under Labour 1945–51. Building a New Britain* (Manchester: Manchester University Press, 1997); Nick Ellison, *Egalitarian Thought and Labour Politics* (London: Routledge, 1994).

15 Kenneth O. Morgan, *Labour in Power 1945–1951* (Oxford: Oxford University Press, 1984); R. Coopey, S. Fielding and N. Tiratsoo (eds.), *The Wilson Governments 1964–70* (London: Pinter, 1995).

16 Andrew Thorpe, 'The consolidation of a Labour stronghold, 1926–51', in Clyde Binfield et al. (eds.), *The History of the City of Sheffield 1843–1993*, vol. I: *Politics* (Sheffield: Sheffield Academic Press, 1993); Bernard Donoughue and George Jones, *Herbert Morrison. Portrait of a Politician* (London: Weidenfeld and Nicolson, 1973), pp. 189–210.

17 Michael Foot, *Aneurin Bevan 1945–1960*, vol. II (London: Granada Publishing, 1975), esp. pp. 100–215.

18 Peter Thompson, 'Labour's "Gannex conscience"? Politics and popular attitudes in the "permissive society"', in Coopey et al., *The Wilson Governments*, pp. 136–50; Zig Layton-Henry, *The Politics of Immigration* (Oxford: Blackwell, 1992); Morgan, *Callaghan*, pp. 308–13.

19 See Duncan Tanner, *Political Change and the Labour Party 1900–18* (Cambridge: Cambridge University Press, 1990), pp. 437–41 and chs. 8 and 11 below.

20 This was particularly striking during the second Wilson government. See Pimlott, *Wilson*, ch. 19.

21 For example, there are no recent studies of the first or second Labour governments, whilst very little work has been done on Labour's achievements in local government.

22 See chs. 7 and 8 below.

23 See ch. 1 below.

24 See chs. 2 and 3 below.

25 See chs. 4 and 10 below.

26 See ch. 12 below.

1 | Labour's political and social thought

Jose Harris

> No Labour Party can hope to maintain its position unless its proposals are . . . the outcome of the best Political Science of its time.
> *Labour and the New Social Order* (1918), p. 23

In an essay published in 1894, Sidney Webb wrote of the need to generate a 'body of systematic political thought', as the prime task of those who hoped to 'teach others how practically to transform England into a Social Democratic Commonwealth'. Already, Webb believed, creeping collectivism in every sphere was replacing the 'unsystematic and empirical Individualism' that had dominated national life throughout the nineteenth century. But the development of a coherent rationale for such a change was required not merely to 'teach others', it was an essential part of the process of change itself. Lack of 'precision in our thinking' might not merely obstruct change but lead it in the wrong direction – towards either 'individualist' alternatives to collectivism (such as imperialism and protectionism) or 'spurious' rival collectivisms which ignored scientific laws and sought instant socialist Utopias.[1] Webb's essay was not merely a seminal document in English socialist thought, but a classic statement of the 'modernist' position in the social sciences – that correct theory was an essential predicate of right social action. Six years later, however, the rhetoric of the founding conference of the Labour Representation Committee (LRC) was markedly more pragmatic. Despite the demands of some delegates for a more substantive statement of purpose, the outlook of the majority echoed a position familiar in English political thought since the mid-eighteenth century. This was the view that what counted in politics was not 'principle' but 'interest' – the major problem for labour being that, while land and capital were amply represented in government, the interests of labour were not. It was this, rather than any unifying political theory, that brought together the component organisations of the LRC – many of whose members in their private capacities were quite frankly Liberals or Tories.[2]

These differing perceptions of the role of political theory, dating from the very foundation of the Labour Party, pinpoint certain issues that have remained salient in the party's history throughout the twentieth century. Was Labour's primary role that of an 'electoral machine' designed to win power at all costs within existing constitutional structures, or was it to forge a new kind of society and civic polity?[3] Was analytical 'theory' merely a polemical footnote to the business of power, or was it (as was reiterated in 1918 by *Labour and the New Social Order*) a key element in the gaining and use of that power – in the accurate interpretation of historical change, in the formulation of effective policies, and in democratic persuasion?[4] Was the purpose of a labour movement to take advantage of trends that were happening anyway – or was it to resist and reverse them? Was the onset of socialism a functional necessity of modern life, or was it driven by ethical, religious and humanitarian imperatives that overruled questions of practical utility?

Disentangling these issues is complicated by the very diverse character of Labour, both as a parliamentary party and as a wider movement. At both levels Labour was always a broad coalition (changing in precise character over different periods) between trade unionists, different brands of committed socialist, single-issue pressure-groups, and (particularly after 1918) individual men and women interested in various kinds of ethical and practical reform. Its historic roots lay not just in trade unionism and democratic socialism, but in radical republicanism and pro-Gladstonian Lib–Labism, Marxism and municipal reformism, positivism and idealism, Nonconformist and incarnationalist Christianity, anti-modernist mediaevalism and the quest for advanced 'scientific' modernity. Labour theorists, with a few notable exceptions, were much more interested in drafting programmes and policies than in clinical analysis of power structures – which means that Labour's understanding of the latter has often to be gleaned from the assumptions of the former. Throughout the party's history there has been movement in and out of more doctrinaire groups (on both left and right, and both inside and outside the Labour fold), which have attracted support from those irritated by Labour's relative lack of a sharply defined official ideology. Much of the historiography of the subject has been implicitly bound up with re-fighting old internal Labour battles, between supposedly 'conservative' trade unionists and 'radical' socialist intellectuals, between evolutionary and activist models of change, between theoretical rivalries of 'left' and 'right', and between supporters and opponents of collaboration with other parties.

Concentration on such rivalries doubtless gives a certain dramatic coherence to the party's theoretical controversies over the past hundred years. Yet the historian who bores holes into such controversies may well be struck by the artificiality of the fixed ideological lineages frequently proclaimed. Throughout the century there have been instances of Labour leftists occupying ground previously vacated by theorists of the right – and vice versa. The same has been true of many Labour ideas in relation to other parties – particularly the Liberals, out of whose 'progressive' and 'radical' wings many strands of Labour thought evolved.[5] Moreover, despite the existence of powerful local pockets of 'grass-roots' Labour culture, Labour was never a self-contained 'nation within a nation' in the way that could be said at certain periods of social-democratic movements in continental Europe. On the contrary, Labour was at all times deeply embedded in the wider society of Great Britain; and the broad spectrum of Labour's political thought both reflected and influenced wider changes in national attitudes and values. From 'New Liberal' proposals on social reform in the 1900s through to those of 'New Labour' in the 1990s; from 1930s' debates about the gold standard through to present-day controversies about a European currency; from Edwardian 'social purity' campaigns through to late twentieth-century 'libertarian' movements – in all these contexts Labour's ideas on such issues as 'social justice', state power, sovereignty and personal freedom have been part of a much broader national (and international) theatre of political opinion. And, like Liberal and Conservative thought, Labour's ideas have broadly mirrored certain supra-political philosophical trends in conceptions of how language is used and how the external world is mentally constructed: trends, for example, such as the 'idealism' of the 1900s, the 'positivist' reaction of the 1930s and 1940s, the Marxian controversies of the 1960s and 70s, and the collapse of 'meaning' into the mish-mash of relativism and postmodernism fashionable at the present day.

This chapter will therefore aim to avoid assessing Labour's political thought simply in terms of pitched battles between rival intellectual factions. Instead it will take a number of classic themes – common to theorists both British and non-British, Labour and non-Labour – conventionally found in the analysis of politics and civil society; and it will look at ways in which those themes have been handled, in different periods and contexts, by groups and individuals within the British Labour Party. Such an analysis must necessarily be skewed towards those who have written or spoken in a 'theoretical' way, and towards that tiny group of people (tiny in absolute numbers, but disproportionately large by comparison with other parties) who have functioned as 'academic' theorists. But it also draws upon the thinking of many who contributed to policy documents, spoke in Parliament, and engaged in debate and propaganda. It will include ideas about how societies and social structures change, about constitutionalism and state power, about property and welfare, freedom and morality, and about the very nature of political reasoning and social action.

Social evolution and political action

Throughout the nineteenth and early twentieth centuries European social theorists of all complexions were obsessed with the problem of identifying the balance between historical determinism on the one hand and individual and/or collective human agency on the other. Was society, like nature, something that was 'given' and regulated by 'natural' laws, or was it artificially constructed by the continuous interaction of human wills? Mass industrialisation, population explosion, Darwinian biology, all seemed to point towards vast impersonal forces outside human control; while the spread of education, science, and liberal ideas about freedom pointed in the opposite direction – towards rational human understanding, moral choice, purposive action and free will.[6] Socialist and labour theorists in all European countries were to the forefront of these debates, and many divisions within the British Labour Party have been implicitly rooted in tension between these two perspectives. Labour policy-makers have often been accused by critics of trying to do things that defied psychological or economic laws; yet from the very foundation of the LRC in 1900 many Labour intellectuals were exceptionally conscious of precisely those behavioural laws (or at least of what they understood those laws to be). Within both the Independent Labour Party (ILP) and the early Fabian Society certain key theorists were committed to a model of continuous 'social evolution', not as a mere vague analogue of evolutionary biology, but as a driving principle that universally governed all day-to-day processes of societal change. When Sidney Webb, for example, spoke of the 'inevitability of gradualness' he was not necessarily defending (as many have imagined) policies of cautious expediency and pragmatism, but rather the view that incremental change was an inexorable part of the historical process, as much a part of the natural order of things as biological growth.[7] Many of the supposed contradictions in the career of Ramsay MacDonald are explicable in terms of his commitment to a developmental model of socialism derived, not from the competitive struggle envisaged by Darwin and Marx, but from Comtean positivism and the evolutionary theories of Lamarck and Spencer.[8] That is to say, he believed that society both as an ethical unit and as a living organism was purposefully moving towards a 'higher stage' of structure and organisation, in which altruism and co-operation would displace the waste and inefficiency of self-interest and free competition. This perspective was something quite different from pragmatism, and by no means confined to those temperamentally inclined to piecemeal change. Despite its commitment to activism and militancy, the Marxian strand in the early Labour Party, represented by the Social Democratic Federation, also often expressed the view that society was unfolding in a unilinear direction and that socialism and the labour movement must necessarily be the ultimate beneficiaries of accelerated capitalist expansion.[9]

This notion that socialism and/or labourism would eventually trump capitalism, simply by virtue of superior efficiency, morality, 'modernity' and fitness for survival, was to have an enduring role in Labour thought throughout the twentieth century. An evolutionary perspective by no means implied that Labour should simply sit back and do nothing, since it was shared by many of the party's most energetic reformers, and by those who believed most strongly in the practical application of 'social science'. The Webbs' programme of 'national housekeeping', for example, envisaged continuous intervention in all areas of national life by civic representatives deploying the most advanced forms of scientific knowledge.[10] From the earliest days, however, this evolutionary vision was rivalled (often in the minds of particular individuals) by views of the opposite kind – views which were in themselves very diverse, but had in common the belief that there was *no* necessary connection between modernity and the advance of socialism, and that large-scale organisational collectivism was happening quite independently of, and often in direct opposition to, the interests of the working classes and humanity in general. Key figures behind this *anti*-evolutionary tradition were John Ruskin and William Morris, whose political writings had totally rejected any accommodation with the political economy of advanced capitalism. As Bernard Shaw once remarked, those members of the British labour movement who were inclined to root-and-branch change had no need of Karl Marx – they already had their prophet in Ruskin.[11] In place of the 'illth' generated by capitalism, Ruskin had proposed an alternative 'citizens' economy' wherein work, wages and social welfare would all be regulated by a mandatory ethic of universal 'public service'.[12] Supporters of this more 'revolutionary' view were found in all sectors of the early Labour Party, from the ILP rank and file through to guild socialists and syndicalists.[13] And within the Fabian Society, the evolutionary philosophy of the first generation of Fabians was disputed from the late 1900s by the young G. D. H. Cole, whose political thought – influenced perhaps by his study of Rousseau's 'general will' – strongly emphasised the role of popular sovereignty, face-to-face democracy and strategies of direct action.[14]

Disenchantment with 'evolutionary' socialism was greatly intensified by the industrial conflicts of the First World War, the onset of long-term depression, and the emergence of a much more 'activist' model of socialism in the wake of the Bolshevik revolution. Though never in a majority, supporters of syndicalism and the 'general strike' were now much more prominent within the trade-union movement than they had been before 1914 – a fact that persuaded Labour's 'gradualist' wing of the need for a more formal party structure. Clause Four of Labour's 1918 constitution was no mere concession to the party's small minority of advanced socialists, but an index of increasing hostility to private ownership of industry among the 'Triple Alliance' of leading trade unionists. Moreover, a similar shift could be detected among individual theorists. Sidney Webb in *Labour and the New Social Order* (1918) called for 'universal enforcement of the national minimum', 'democratic control of industry', a 'revolution in national finance', and expropriation of 'surplus wealth for the common good' – none of which sounded like the painless transition from capitalism to administrative collectivism that he had anticipated twenty years before.[15] And five years later the Webbs' book on *The Decay of Capitalist Civilization* explicitly abandoned their 'former abstention' from passing judgement on capitalism: citing the authority of Ruskin, they now portrayed private enterprise as economically inefficient, environmentally dangerous and morally corrupt.[16] Evolutionary socialism remained strong within the party leadership, particularly in the entourage of Ramsay MacDonald. But MacDonald himself fully acknowledged the changed political culture of the post-war era: 'Before the war it was sufficient to create the Socialist mind by explaining the Socialist standpoint and outlook; the war has so revolutionized people's minds and still more their methods . . . [that] the Socialist has now to prepare far more details to meet the expectation of rapid change than was necessary before 1914'.[17] Among the new generation of Labour intellectuals there was increasing pessimism about 'organic' change, and increasing resort to the language of class war. As George Lansbury declared, though 'the state of war' was 'against the system, not necessarily against individuals', those who opposed 'our efforts to create a new society must be and are counted as our enemies'.[18]

Constitutionalism, law and the state

Underpinning Labour's uncertainty about how far it should aim to impose socialist and/or labourist principles, or just wait for them to happen, was a rather fluid spectrum of ideas about the constitution and the role of the state. The founders of the LRC in 1900 were in no doubt that many aspects of existing constitutional arrangements were unfairly stacked against them – indeed the whole rationale of labour representation was to reverse what was seen as bias and injustice at the very apex of the constitution, embodied in the Taff Vale decision of the House of Lords. Early party conferences strongly supported reform or abolition of the Lords, manhood suffrage, and Irish Home Rule; while the Fabian Society's 'New Heptarchy' series called for the extension of 'home rule' to democratically elected provincial parliaments throughout Britain.[19] Among trade unionists and other working-class bodies there was a longstanding perception of structural class bias within the common law; and there was some feeling within the LRC that 'we must revolutionise Parliament itself before we got many political changes of much consequence'.[20]

Yet this was very different from believing that *all* legal and constitutional arrangements in capitalist societies were irremediably unjust (which, in theory at least, was the view of many continental socialists). Labour's enduring suspicion of the Lords only rarely extended to the monarchy, which was portrayed even on the left as an organ of national philanthropy, and 'the supreme ornament of a democratic system, as republican as any republic in the world'.[21] Beyond the demand for universal suffrage, there was very limited Labour support for more refined barometers of democracy such as referenda and proportional representation.[22] Despite endemic complaints about the law, many working-class organisations routinely used the law courts for their own day-to-day purposes; and resistance to Taff Vale itself was depicted not as defiance of the law but as its proper enforcement, against 'politically-made judges' who had themselves been 'subverting the laws of the land'.[23] And though supporters of early Labour may have been uncertain about what the overall purpose of their party really was, they had little doubt (in marked contrast to Social Democrats in Imperial Germany) that the constitution *would* allow them to form a government, in the unlikely event of their ever winning a parliamentary majority.

Nevertheless, Labour's 'constitutionalism' always bore certain hallmarks of its own internal culture. From its foundation, and throughout the twentieth century, the party's adherence to the orthodox principles of the British constitution (rooted in the sovereignty of Parliament) was to be in latent tension with its role as a popular movement (rooted in the sovereignty of the party conference).[24] The notion that, behind parliamentary sovereignty, lay the sovereignty of 'the common people' was not peculiar to Labour, but was perhaps more strongly held there than elsewhere in British politics. As with other parties, Labour's attachment to the 'national interest' always mirrored its own, often internally contested, perceptions of whom 'the nation' actually comprised. Moreover, there was a lurking suspicion, not of 'constitutionalism' *per se*, but of how the principle was interpreted by other political parties: the threatened Ulster rebellion of 1912–14 was to become a longstanding reference-point in Labour discussions of the nature and limits of orthodox 'constitutionalist' theory.[25]

Similar dichotomies governed Labour's ideas about the state and its executive organs, although it is hard to discern any conception of state power in the early period that could be identified as exclusively 'labourist' or 'socialist'. As indicated above, despite their roots in Lib–Labism, many of Labour's trade unionists were instinctive adherents of an eighteenth-century 'Tory' view that state power was primarily about domination by 'interests' (a view that had a certain tacit affinity with Marxian claims that the state by definition was always the instrument of a ruling class). Those sections of the party which had evolved out of late nineteenth-century municipal radicalism appeared more comfortable with the language of 'neighbourhood and community' than with that of state or central government.[26] And despite Sidney Webb's call for constructive 'political theory', Labour's socialist intellectuals were slow to formulate a theory about what 'the state' actually *was*, although they wrote extensively about what they thought it should be *doing*. The Webbs' own theory of the 'housekeeping state', which envisaged a national minimum of health, education and efficiency for the whole population (including a statutory minimum wage, compulsory military training, and institutional confinement for unemployables) gave little indication of how such heavyweight measures could be practically enforced. They simply assumed that the state was a useful workhorse which would do the bidding of whomsoever had control of democratic power (a view echoed by Harold Wilson half a century later).[27] When it

came to more reasoned defence of the state, Labour theorists were
inclined to fall back on the 'public-interest' and 'moral-community'
arguments employed by progressive Liberals. The socialist debt to the
liberal-idealist theory of an 'organic' community was clearly spelt out by
the Fabian philosopher, Sidney Ball, and was also latent in much of the
supposedly anti-idealist writing of MacDonald and the Webbs. Modern
political thought, wrote Ball, was 'reverting to the position of Aristotle,
that the State ought to put before itself "the good of the whole", by
interfering with the "natural" course of events in favor of collective
ends'; as a result 'the organized power of community . . . helps the individual to be not less but more of an individual, and . . . therefore more of
a definite social person'.[28]

This complex of attitudes in early Labour conceptions of the state
largely dovetailed with the 'evolutionary' view of socialism mentioned
above, and discouraged resort to political (as opposed to merely industrial) direct action. But it also contained the seeds of a very ambitious
vision of what might be done by legislation and public administration, if
only Labour could once lay its hands upon power. Prior to 1914 these
ambitious visions were most explicit among Labour's social reformers,
who did not necessarily see the trade-union-dominated Labour Party as
the most appropriate channel for their ideas.[29] The First World War,
however, greatly expanded the state's executive power *and* Labour's
understanding of that power – the latter in both a negative and a positive
direction. The industrial conflicts of wartime, together with budgetary
retrenchment after 1919, strongly reawakened older suspicions that the
state was *not* an impartial mediator of differing interests but a sinister
conglomerate of upper-class power; and despite the 1918 Representation
of the People Act there was less optimism than before the war about the
automatically 'progressive' thrust of parliamentary democracy. At the
end of the war there was much talk within the Labour movement about
the need to reinforce the traditional 'territorial' structures of representative government with 'vocational' structures that would give a more
immediate voice to citizens in their roles as 'workers by hand or by brain'.
This was a view that in various forms stretched right across the party
from guild socialists via the Fabians to Ramsay MacDonald (even so
strong an advocate of a unitary 'civic' state as MacDonald proposed that
the Lords should become a 'House of Soviets', in which peers would be
replaced by representatives of trade unions and professional organisations).[30] The General Strike of 1926 sharply divided the party into those
who insisted that the issues involved were strictly economic, and a minority who saw it as calling into question Labour's deep-seated commitment

to promoting socialism within existing political structures.[31] On the other hand, the war had also entailed large-scale 'experiments in state control' in many areas of economic and social policy. These experiments – often initiated by officials sympathetic to Labour – were gradually to transform Labour's expectations about what could be done by a dynamic central government (even among those members of the party most convinced that the state was a tool of repressive class power).

These ambiguities were to pervade Labour conceptions of state power throughout the inter-war era. Within the trade-union movement, the Trade Disputes Act of 1927 was widely seen as an act of state-oppression; yet trade unionists were now much more strongly in favour of state welfare and economic interventionism than they had been before 1914. During the course of the 1920s the rising star among Labour theorists, Harold Laski, who had earlier advanced a 'pluralist' model of the state, now shifted towards a realist, neo-Hobbesian analysis, in which sovereignty rested with whoever could command the greatest naked political force. The first edition of Laski's *A Grammar of Politics* (1925) identified a 'crisis in the theory of the state' as profound as that which had precipitated the Civil War of the seventeenth century.[32] By the early 1930s Laski was claiming that pluralism had been simply a stage on his road to Marxism, and that only a 'classless society' could dissolve 'the vast apparatus of state-coercion'.[33] Yet Laski was also a strong supporter of the kind of state social-insurance schemes that many further to the left saw as mere cosmetic surgery to the face of liberal capitalism; and his theory of revolution was in many respects not a Marxian but a Lockeian one, rooted in the notion that a government was bound by fundamental contract to 'secure to its citizens the maximum satisfaction of their wants'. Moreover, before resorting to resistance, it was a citizen's duty to 'exhaust the means placed at his disposal by the constitution of the state'.[34]

Laski's ambivalence on these issues was echoed by many younger Labour activists. Aneurin Bevan, coming to Westminster from a Welsh mining valley, initially felt totally alienated from the antique rituals of the British constitution; yet two decades later, after fingering the alternatives of communism and fascism, he had come to perceive parliamentary democracy as 'an instrument of social change' that had 'received inadequate attention from students of political theory'.[35] Conversely, the Webbs, who down to 1918 had been dedicated advocates of the constitutionalist road to socialism, were now much less assured. Their *Constitution for the Socialist Commonwealth of Great Britain*, published in 1920, was markedly *less* optimistic about established institutions than

17

their writings of before the war. They now viewed Parliament and the existing machinery of government as largely incompetent to deal with the immensely complex problems of advanced industrial society: these ancient institutions needed to be supplemented by a 'Social Parliament' with its own 'Executive', by multiple layers of civic democracy at every level of national life from empire to village street, and by mass promotion of 'the greatest attainable development of public spirit'.[36] But *The Decay of Capitalist Civilization* three years later revealed growing pessimism about whether any of this was likely to happen: in the Webbs' view, capitalism was failing not just because of economic injustice, but because the very conditions of competitive production were increasingly incapable of generating the qualities of character, personal honesty and disinterested civic virtue essential for running a well-ordered administrative state.[37] Though composed while the Webbs were still major contributors to Labour thought (indeed when Sidney was on the brink of his career as a minister), *The Decay of Capitalist Civilization* closely foreshadowed the disenchantment with evolutionary change and displacement of capitalists by virtuous commissars that were to be core themes of the Webbs' *Soviet Communism: A New Civilisation?* published twelve years later.

Private and public property

Ideas about constitutions and states were traditionally enmeshed with ideas about private property. Among orthodox constitutional theorists there were some who saw the prime rationale of the state as being the defence of property rights; others for whom the personal independence conferred by property (particularly land) was an indispensable qualification for full citizenship (lack of property being a clear token of civic incapacity). Both these views had a 'radical' past; but for much of the nineteenth century radicals and reformist liberals had argued that, far from being the sign of civic virtue, large-scale private property was a major source of injustice and civic corruption. Since 1832, property in the *political* sphere had been continually re-defined to include all settled households and rented tenements; and by 1900 the age-old link between property and voting rights had been largely whittled away for all except women and paupers (and significantly dented even for the latter). In the *economic* sphere, however, property rights were in some respects even more unfettered than they had been a century earlier, because of the continuous conversion of property in land (formerly limited by feudal and communal constraints) into a freely marketable commodity. How to deal with the economic and political implications of vast concentrations of property constituted one of the most obdurate of theoretical questions for a party committed to large-scale structural change by peaceful and constitutional processes.

The early Labour Party brought to this question a complex range of ideas, many inherited from radical liberalism, others stemming from a more peculiarly labourist or socialist perspective. Labour theorists of all complexions shared with many Liberals the Lockeian view that all property could ultimately be traced back to 'labour' as the sole source of wealth. Labour's affiliated socialist societies all endorsed the longstanding radical view that 'rent' and 'interest' were largely a function of monopoly (mere 'quasi-rent' stemming from artificial shortage of supply, which would be done away with by restoring ownership to wealth's true progenitors). Labour also shared the view of 'New Liberals' like J. A. Hobson, that wealth production was impossible without an infrastructure of 'community': the element in profit that stemmed from communal rather than private activity (e.g. from education, public order, land values) was deemed to constitute 'organic surplus value', which the community was entitled to claw back in the form of taxation.[38] Most Labour theorists likewise endorsed the long-established Liberal (and Aristotelian) view that some minimum of personal property was essential for individual freedom: and Ramsay MacDonald went so far as to suggest that socialism, not capitalism, was the *true* creed of property because only 'the socialisation of certain forms of property' would allow for its 'general diffusion' among all citizens.[39] Labour theorists differed from most Liberals, however, in declining to differentiate between large-scale *landed* property (as a largely illegitimate expropriation of communally created wealth) and commercial and industrial *capital* (which many Liberals viewed as a just reward for entrepreneurial effort). And there were a few voices, mainly within the Ruskinian tradition, who saw wealth production of all kinds as not just enhanced by community support but inherently communal – and therefore all distribution, even of goods for personal consumption, as properly stemming solely from 'the community'. Within such a framework, property was not a *right* that existed prior to communal life but a *trust* that followed from it. Such views were strongest in the various strands of 'Christian socialism', which from Ruskin and Hastings Rashdall through to Keir Hardie, George Lansbury and Archbishop William Temple nourished a vision of 'socialist fellowship' where, though 'use' might be personal, property in the literal sense would have given way to the vesting of ownership in an organic popular commonwealth.[40]

Practical debates about property within Edwardian Labour largely focused upon the distributional question of how resources might be allocated more 'justly' and 'efficiently' in a society where 1 per cent of the nation owned nearly 70 per cent of capital wealth, while 10 per cent lived in 'absolute want' and 30 per cent in 'secondary poverty'. Pre-war Labour intellectuals envisaged a radical programme (largely shared with advanced Liberals) of publicly enforced development of uncultivated estates, taxation of 'unearned increment', and steeply progressive taxes on rentier incomes and wealth passing at death.[41] Such concerns by no means vanished after 1918, when Labour's demand for a capital levy was conceived in terms, not of confiscating but 'reclaiming' communally created wealth and of strengthening rather than wrecking sound public finance.[42] After 1918, however, some rather different strands in Labour's ideas about property gradually moved centre stage. One of these was the argument that large-scale private property was not merely 'unjust' and 'inefficient', but latently antagonistic to parliamentary democracy. The writings of Laski increasingly argued that public ownership was not just an economic but a *political* necessity; it was required, not simply to achieve popular control over the workplace (as envisaged by guild socialists), but in order to purge the state of class bias and protect democracy against subversion by private property.[43] Such subversion, in the face of democratic powerlessness, Laski claimed to have identified in the events of September 1931. And three years later Laski was proclaiming that a revolutionary situation now existed in Britain: 'revolutionary', not because workers were taking to the streets, but because there was a profound structural hiatus between democratic politics and the ownership of property – a hiatus that everywhere in Europe was leading to violent reaction.[44] Ownership and non-ownership in Laski's view necessarily gave rise to class conflict; therefore the only way to attain the solidaristic, harmonious society dreamt of by socialists like Ramsay MacDonald was to transform production into a form of 'public service'. This required utilisation of the 'supreme coercive power of the state' to 're-define' both the actual 'system of ownership' and the logical meaning of the term 'legal right'.[45]

A rather different critique of the moral economy of property came from R. H. Tawney, who questioned not just its distribution and political power, but its moral and spiritual purpose and ever-expanding extent. In Tawney's view there was nothing wrong with private property *per se*, provided that it was generally diffused throughout the population. 'Such property was not a burden on society, but a condition of its health and efficiency, and indeed, of its continued existence'.[46] 'Pure interest', i.e. setting aside part of the fruit of capital for re-investment, was perfectly justified, provided it did not fall into the hands of a specialised rentier class. What was totally *un*justified in Tawney's view, and the fatal source of servility, tyranny and moral corruption, was the separation of property from productive *work* – a separation exemplified in windfall gains, monopolies, mineral royalties and urban ground rents. It was these 'functionless' forms of property that converted it into an entrenched class interest, the great engine of 'inequality', and 'the greatest enemy of legitimate property itself . . . the parasite which kills the organism that produced it'.[47] And Tawney also echoed Ruskin in questioning how far developed societies really *needed* more property than they had already. Was *lack of property* – in the form of 'poverty' – really the 'most terrible of human afflictions' (as conventional perceptions of welfare proclaimed), or was it a mere 'symptom and consequence' of a much deeper social disorder? In Tawney's view what people needed was not more goods but better ones, produced not as a medium of exchange but as a form of 'social service'. 'Is not *less* production of futilities as important as, indeed a condition of, *more* production of things of moment? Would not "Spend less on private luxuries" be as wise a cry as "produce more"?'[48]

Negative and positive liberty

When Winston Churchill in 1909 reputedly declined 'to be locked in a soup-kitchen with Mrs Beatrice Webb', he was voicing the misgiving of many free-born Englishmen that socialism – even gradualist, democratic socialism – was antithetical to personal liberty. A similar suspicion lurked in public perceptions of 'peaceful picketing' – that trade unionists, while claiming 'natural liberty' for themselves, denied it to fellow workers who disagreed with them. Throughout the twentieth century the charge that Labour was the enemy of personal freedom was to prove a potent weapon in the hands of its ideological opponents; and in many classic documents of Labour's political thought there appeared to be some ground for this charge. Admirers of John Ruskin in Labour's ranks were well aware that Ruskin, when writing of liberty and equality, had declared that he 'detested the one and denied the possibility of the other'.[49] Sidney Webb, when expounding his plans for a 'national minimum', had portrayed it as being enforced even-handedly on all institutions and citizens, whether they wanted it or not ('among local authorities as among individuals, the laggards are being increasingly screwed up').[50] Not just the Webbs, but many Edwardian socialists favoured compulsory rehabilitation of industrial incompetents in reformatory training camps (a view shared by many

Liberals, among them Churchill himself).[51] Even the mild and saintly George Lansbury made it clear that his plans for resettling workers in idyllic co-operative communities would leave no room for those private pleasures with which they consoled themselves under *laissez-faire* capitalism ('It is . . . quite certain that in Socialist England there will be no "pubs" as we know them today'[52]). Despite a 'libertarian' fringe among the Fabians, leading members of the Labour Party were actively involved in movements for public enforcement of private morals – in the Temperance movement, the Purity movement, and campaigns against betting and gambling. Most Labour apologists in Edwardian Britain unashamedly equated liberty with decency, self-discipline, social control, and active fostering of private and public virtue: as Sidney Ball (citing Plato) put it, 'Can there be anything better for the interests of the State . . . than that its men and women should be as good as possible?'[53]

Nevertheless, within the early history of Labour there were certain powerful currents in a rather different direction – *against* state control and interference, even for worthy purposes. Not least among these counter-currents were trade-union resistance to legal incorporation, Nonconformist attacks on the established church, and a more widely diffused working-class distaste for all forms of official regulation. Trade-union and co-operative 'mutualist' culture was viewed by many contemporaries as a rich seed-bed of personal independence and Anglo-Saxon liberties. Even in the Fabian Society, supposedly the stronghold of 'mechanical' state compulsion, there were many expressions of the opposite view: that compulsory 'altruism' was worse than pointless, because it led towards 'a tyranny which will be utterly ruthless because you think it scientific'. Instead, the true aim of socialism was personal 'spiritual freedom', which meant *choosing* virtue without any element of external constraint.[54] And from the late 1900s the guild socialist and shop stewards' movements insisted that liberty lay not in protective legislation, but in democratic control of the workplace – a theme taken up not just by shop-floor activists but by younger Labour intellectuals like Tawney and Cole, and later Harold Laski.

Tawney in 1913 began to develop his lifelong critique of the 'mechanical' reformist view that the most pressing social problem was quantitative material poverty. He argued instead that the true evil of industrial society was 'absence of liberty, i.e. of the opportunity for self-direction: and for controlling the material conditions of a man's life . . . To give men the *will* not to be poor, we must first of all give them the control of the material conditions on which their lives depend, that is set them free'.[55] Two decades later Tawney's *Equality* argued that the perceived antithesis between equality and liberty was often false, but that 'liberty is rightly preferred to equality, when the two are in conflict'.[56] Laski's early writings linked 'social-democratic' liberties to the notion of 'positive liberty' developed by T. H. Green – that liberty positively *required* state intervention in order to promote 'the eager maintenance of that atmosphere in which men have the opportunity to be their best selves'.[57] But Laski was later unexpectedly to draw back from 'positive liberty', at least in its classic 'idealist' form. By the late 1920s, concurrently with his first flush of enthusiasm for Soviet Russia, he had reverted to 'negative liberty' as the more fundamental good: it was *private* liberty of the old-fashioned kind, he claimed, that was now at greatest risk from the structural inequalities of capitalism and the bias that private property gave to the common law.[58] The great triumphs of liberty won in the previous century had been forgotten, and 'we must anticipate an epoch in which the attitude to liberty characteristic of . . . the nineteenth century, will be at a discount'. The heirs and successors of the pioneers of liberty were now 'prepared, in the name of the rights of property, to destroy all the advantages of the advance they represent'.[59]

The politics of planning

Differences of emphasis among Labour supporters about political activism, the role of the state, private property, and personal freedom were by no means straightforward conflicts between left and right – as could be seen in the crisis of 1931, which was blamed throughout the party upon the 'Fascist fallacy' of an idealised, non-party perception of the 'national interest', ascribed by his erstwhile followers to Ramsay MacDonald.[60] Nevertheless the years after 1931 saw a sharpening of division not just over policy but about Labour's underlying purpose and political philosophy – a division that was to be clearly spelt out through Labour's involvement in the 1930s' movement for economic and social planning.

Ideas about 'planning' had a long pedigree in socialist thought, dating back to the Saint-Simonian movements of the early nineteenth century; but the immediate spur during the inter-war years came from the lessons of state economic management between 1914 and 1919, particularly the conjunction of high taxation, deficit finance and physical controls over manpower and supply, which socialists saw as having been wilfully thrown away by post-war financial retrenchment. The argument that what had been done in wartime could equally well be done to counteract depression in peacetime became a core theme of a long series of Labour documents both before and after the debacle of 1931. Serious thought about planning first emerged in the ILP's 'Living Wage' proposals of 1926, which advocated the setting-up of a National Industrial Authority to run a high-wage, home-consumption-based, corporatist economy, based on the 'underconsumptionist' analysis of J. A. Hobson (himself now a convert to the ILP). Similar ideas were advanced by Cole, who proposed direction of manpower and 'scientific planning of production' under a National Economic Council; and after 1931 by Cole's New Fabian Research Bureau, which called for a National Investment Board to direct capital spending throughout the economy. These themes were carried much further by the Socialist League (founded within the Labour Party by Cole, Laski, Stafford Cripps and others in 1932), which envisaged that a future Socialist government would inaugurate an 'immediate transition' to a Soviet-style five-year plan, involving 'complete socialisation of industry, and the complete disappearance of existing class-divisions and property claims'. Particular emphasis was laid on control of the banking system, which was seen as crucially responsible for having scotched Labour's democratic mandate in 1931. In the event of a 'run on the banks', a Socialist government should guarantee deposits and authorise the printing of paper money – confident of making the public understand that money on deposit and money in circulation were both totally dependent on 'the credit of the community'.[61] In the event of resistance, wrote Cripps, 'it would probably be better and more conducive to the general peace and welfare of the country' for the government 'to make itself temporarily into a dictatorship until the matter could again be put to the test at the polls'.[62]

Elsewhere in the party, however, ideas about planning evolved along very different lines. Within the trade-union movement 'planning' was largely interpreted to mean job creation through large-scale public works, as introduced by the New Deal in the United States; there was no trade-union enthusiasm for, and much latent criticism of, the centrally planned direction of prices, wages and manpower demanded by the circle of Cripps and Cole.[63] The 'complete socialisation of industry' advocated by the Socialist League was increasingly rivalled by the public corporation model of common ownership put forward by Herbert Morrison, which envisaged that day-to-day management decisions would be taken on orthodox economic lines (though for the benefit of taxpayers rather than private shareholders).[64] Within the New Fabian Research Bureau, initially dominated by Cole, the initiative passed to a group of younger economists, Durbin, Gaitskell, Meade and Jay, who saw a National Investment Board in a much more modest light, as a tool for steering a 'mixed economy'. And among these younger economists there was increasing interest in the regulatory and reflationary ideas of J. M. Keynes – ideas that were explicitly designed to stimulate investment and expand employment *without* the massive political and bureaucratic controls required by a strategy of 'complete socialisation'.

The full range of Labour's planning ideas cannot be recounted here, but some attention must be paid to what they reveal about Labour's underlying social and political thought during this period. In all sectors of the party earlier confidence that the sheer organisational complexity of modern life must inevitably tend towards socialism appeared at least temporarily to be in abeyance; and in all sectors there was a much greater willingness to subordinate political economy to the power of the state than had been seriously contemplated before 1931. There was much disagreement, however, about how far the total displacement of economics by political 'fiat' was either possible or desirable. Planning theory on the left was clearly inspired by romantic rumours of the first Soviet five-year plan; but a more long-term influence was the continuing sway of the Ruskinian view – revived and mediated by Hobson – that economics was not an autonomous science, but was inextricably mingled with ethics, politics, aesthetics, and the whole panoply of 'human life'.[65] Such a view was not without influence in the rest of the party. But among the New Fabians there was a much stronger sense that market forces could not be wholly willed out of existence: that economic factors *did* have a certain inexorable, supra-political potency, and that, even in a socialist economy, markets would have a legitimate role to play both in registering consumer preference and maintaining efficiency.[66] The New Fabians were unanimous in believing that certain key economic functions *should* be wholly removed from private control; but they were also moved by the wider objections of the Hayekian school that holistic planning was not just politically undesirable but (in view of the sheer limitation of human knowledge) logically impossible.[67]

A more intractable difference between the Socialist League and its opponents, however, lay in their conceptions of democracy. The Labour left in the early 1930s frequently wrote as though they believed that parliamentary democracy, at least in its current form, was in terminal decline: under advanced capitalism formal political rights were being irretrievably negated by inequality and the institutional power of private property. The New Fabians largely concurred in denouncing inequality, but persisted in the view that parliamentary democracy was a good in its own right, and one that could not be traded off for any enforced gain in structural equality. This view, somewhat timidly expressed in the early days of opposition to the National government, grew in confidence as more became known of totalitarian experiments on the continent; and key figures such as Clement Attlee, initially an adherent of the Socialist League, increasingly distanced themselves from demands for a Popular Front with the Communists and talk of 'dictatorial' emergency powers.[68] The writings of Tawney, whose passion for 'equality' could scarcely be doubted, but who clearly affirmed the lexical priority of 'liberty', were a major influence in discouraging notions of *ultra vires* shortcuts to economic reconstruction. The centrality of democracy – however flawed, obtuse and inconvenient – was spelt out in a long series of writings by Evan Durbin, culminating in *The Politics of Democratic Socialism* composed in 1938–9. Durbin there defended parliamentary democracy, not just in terms of citizen rights, but as the best way of finding viable solutions to complex intellectual problems, and as an institutional index of collective 'psychological health' and 'absence of neurosis'. In Durbin's view, excessive 'purity' in political doctrine was a sign of unsublimated fear, guilt and social aggression. Compromise and concession, by contrast, indicated not a lack of principle but 'a relatively free and healthy emotional life'.[69] To the Labour left, however, this smacked of mere vacuous sentimentalism: Durbin's 'philosophy of planning', pronounced Laski, was built on 'a theory of the State which all recent history seems to me to disprove'.[70]

Political thought in war and peace

Throughout the 1930s Harold Laski was complaining that the vast majority of the Labour Party did not have the political will to pursue the ends which their ethical principles told them were just and right. On one level Laski's point was correct. Many Labour writings of the period cut deep into the problems of poverty and inequality, but were baffled by how to solve them through democratic channels. Not just the supposed intransigents of the Socialist League but supporters of more limited change like Durbin, Gaitskell and Jay had no clear strategy for putting their proposals into effect. Despite Labour's ambitious nationalisation programme of 1934 (which included land and joint-stock banks as well as key industries) there is no convincing evidence to show how they would have put this into operation; and it seems unlikely that, if Labour had miraculously won the election of the following year, their policies would have differed markedly from those of the much reviled Ramsay MacDonald. And, quite apart from the constitutional issue, the institutions and techniques required for a programme even of modest Keynesianism were almost wholly lacking before 1940 – let alone for the 'complete socialisation' envisaged by the Socialist League.[71] Even the practical Durbin was unclear about how to combine a socialised command economy with Britain's role as an exporter of capital and centre of overseas finance.[72] No Labour theorist, not even Laski himself, seriously addressed the question of how to disentangle Britain's economy from the global structure of international capitalism (other than by hoping that similar shifts towards socialism would happen simultaneously elsewhere). The responses of the trade-union movement to fascism, rearmament and Popular Frontism suggested that there was no possibility of re-directing the bulk of the party towards the socialist internationalism favoured by many on the left. The British empire likewise attracted much moral opprobrium, but little serious discussion of how it could be reformed or dismantled. Thus Labour by the end of the 1930s was a party rich in ideas about what it thought should be done, but with little conception of how to bring it all about.

As it happened, however, the riddle of how to attain radical change by constitutional means was solved by historical events: the great gap in Labour's political thought was to be filled, at least in domestic affairs, by the waging of the Second World War. Between 1939 and 1945 the functional imperatives of total war were to legitimise state power in ways that would have been inconceivable in the 1930s, other than in the realm of revolutionary speculation. Similarly, the economic fact of single-minded concentration on war production circumvented, at least temporarily, the underlying conflict between cosmopolitan capitalism and centralised autarkic planning. Moreover, all this happened with a high degree of popular consent and appeared to be buttressed by an unusual level of cross-class social solidarity. After its victory in 1945 Labour thus became the residuary legatee of a vast range of legal, economic and administrative powers that even its most radical theorists had scarcely dreamt were attainable before 1939.[73]

The war therefore rescued Labour's theorists from their most intractable dilemma – of how to pursue their social goals without violating what was for most of them a prior commitment to constitutional legality. Not overnight, but over a relatively short period of time, wide-ranging controls over incomes, property, supply, manpower and information became not merely possible but morally and practically mandatory. The existence of such powers provided a practical legal framework for the policies of public ownership, redistributive taxation, fiscal and physical planning techniques, and communitarian social services that were favoured in one form or another by all sections of the party. This dramatic change of environment was reflected in Labour's political thought in a variety of ways. For a minority on the left the war was explicitly a 'revolutionary war', in which every opportunity for nationalisation of key resources had to be seized, even when not strictly required for war purposes; and, after Hitler's fortuitous attack on Russia, there was a wave of enthusiasm for reorganising British society on the model of 'the vast practical example of the Soviet Union'.[74] In place of the 'centralising and bureaucratic tendency' of government in Britain, there would in future be 'democratic self-government of neighbours street by street . . . with a constant and real contact between the members of the neighbourhood group and those who represent it upon the larger civic authority'. 'In a sheerly realistic sense', proclaimed Cole, 'the Russian peoples are a great deal more free than we are, or can be until we forsake our atomism, and set out to make a determined pursuit after collective, instead of merely individualistic, values.'[75]

In the party at large, however, there was a widespread sense that dramatic changes were happening anyway, without resort to the precedent of Stalinist Russia. The war was seen as proving what Labour stalwarts had known all along – that 'collective' control of resources was not merely more 'just' but more cost-effective than the muddles of market economics. There was much reference back to the betrayed promises of the previous war, and a determination to forestall any return to an imagined pre-war 'normality'.[76] There was also a marked decline in the language of class conflict. The Beveridge Plan, though written by a progressive Liberal, was interpreted as a practical embodiment of the transition from the 'police state' to the 'social service' state long advocated by Labour.[77] After 1945, parliamentary speeches by Labour ministers who introduced the party's welfare reforms took great pride in the fact that this was in no sense a programme of 'class-legislation'. On the contrary, it involved a universal 'levelling-out' in two different directions: privileges formerly available only to the rich, and remedial services formerly available only to the poor, would henceforth extend to the whole community. It also drew upon the 'communitarian' arguments for public appropriation of communally created wealth (by taxation of 'development-values') that had been part of a cross-class radical rhetoric since the mid-nineteenth century.[78] And even Harold Laski now portrayed the new era of socialist collectivism as a 'natural' evolution stemming from 'early Victorian individualism' as well as from 'the foundation of our own social effort'.[79]

The sense that history was once again powerfully running in a collectivist direction might have been expected to promote a sharper and more coherent definition of Labour's underlying philosophy. But, despite the far-reaching principles implicit in Labour's social legislation, this did not in fact happen. Reasons for this are not perhaps hard to find. The sheer size of the 1945 Labour victory meant that the party was now a more diverse 'coalition' than at any earlier or later period in its history. Between the expulsion of Ramsay MacDonald and the election of Tony Blair, no Labour leader was interested in using 'theory' as a dimension of mass politics; and this was perhaps particularly true of the laconic and low-key leadership of Clement Attlee.[80] Prolonged economic crisis and the Cold War forced Labour ministers, including Attlee himself, into acts of pragmatic *Realpolitik* that they had never contemplated when in opposition. Certain statements of principle that had been clearly spelt out by Labour in wartime (such as the need to subordinate union interests to national planning requirements) proved much more difficult to act upon when in power. Moreover, the fact that Labour for the first time had a secure majority did not in itself resolve the endemic tensions between liberty and equality, and between micro-democracy and macro-planning. Ministers bent on introducing 'universalist' social services could not bring themselves to acquiesce to the demand of many Labour back-benchers that these should be run on democratic lines by self-governing friendly societies (notorious for their unequal benefits and administrative inefficiency) rather than by professional public officials.[81] Despite Labour's strong local government tradition there was little attempt to restore the autonomy enjoyed by pre-war local authorities; and Aneurin Bevan made it quite clear that the main organ of democracy for the new national health service was to be himself as Minister of Health. The 1945 election manifesto had explicitly conjured up the Webbs' vision of a 'Socialist Commonwealth of Great Britain'. But though Labour's victory certainly mobilised the Fabian 'expert', there was little sign of the other side of the Webbian coin – those multiple tiers of active citizen participation from Parliament to village street (much favoured in pro-Labour reconstruction circles *during* the war).[82]

At a more diffuse level the war and its aftermath coincided with a period in which grand political theory of the kind prominent in British intellectual life since the mid-seventeenth century was becoming increasingly marginal in the wider political culture. In all areas of politics, but perhaps most markedly within 'progressive' circles, there was a shift of interest away from core political ideas towards more instrumental problems of social engineering.[83] Many Labour intellectuals greatly overestimated the degree to which the war had irreversibly collectivised both popular attitudes and public institutions, and were inclined to assume that 'public service' and 'equitable distribution' had become conventional wisdom, no longer in need of serious explanation and

Jose Harris

defence. In Labour policy discussions there was a widespread sense that fundamental problems of principle seemed to have solved themselves, and that the party's thinkers and policy-makers should be getting on with what they did best, which was devising schemes for practical reconstruction.[84] This cultural shift was also reflected in Labour's changing 'academic' complexion. In 1945 the holders of two of the country's three major university chairs in political philosophy (Laski and Cole) were senior Labour intellectuals; but the younger generation of 'academic' Labour theorists was largely made up of economists, sociologists, statisticians, and social-policy experts – many of them based at the Oxford Institute of Statistics and the London School of Economics. Moreover, Cole, as Oxford's professor of social and political theory, proved much more interested in empirical 'social studies' (of a kind that would service the new social order) than in analytical theories of the state (which he saw as fatally linked to outworn notions of the 'atomised individual').[85] Sidney Webb would doubtless have approved these practical trends; but there was nevertheless a marked decline of interest in the 'systematic political theory' that Webb had also prescribed as imperative for social democracy a generation earlier.

All this meant that the theoretical objections to planning and state power raised by critics like Hayek and Oakeshott were viewed by many Labour adherents as irritating, unintelligible and scarcely worth refuting.[86] The material shortages of the post-war years seemed to require and legitimate rationing, state regulation, and steeply redistributive taxation no less than the hardships of wartime; and there were certainly some Labour apologists who appeared to welcome continuing scarcity as more conducive to co-operation and commonwealth than affluence and plenty.[87] An essay by Tawney in 1949 rejoiced that, 'judged by the distribution of income', Britain was now a more egalitarian society than either the United States or the Soviet Union. In observing trends around him, Tawney could discern only two causes for possible anxiety. One was that government, in its concern to maintain living standards, was becoming increasingly utilitarian and economistic – leading to a danger that 'the State, as its grasp extends, will make a desert, and call it efficiency'. The other was that social democracy 'may be tempted . . . to pander to popular tastes, instead of instructing them, and to devote an excessive proportion of its annual income to needs pressed on it by a mass demand, to the neglect of less clamorous, but, on a long view, more important requirements'.[88] This latter point echoed a concern voiced with increasing frequency among Labour intellectuals of the period, even those most committed to sovereignty of the people. This was the

30

fear that, despite full employment and secondary education, 'the people' might need time to adapt themselves to the full responsibilities of mature social democracy. In a famous example that was to play fatally into the hands of Labour's critics, Douglas Jay drew a distinction between personal freedom which was 'absolute', and economic freedom which was 'a secondary freedom, often approaching a luxury': in the latter sphere citizens often needed help in knowing how to use their freedom ('the gentleman in Whitehall really does know better what is good for the people than the people know themselves').[89]

Equality and affluence

Early Labour theorists had always rejected the view (often imputed by their critics) that equality was to be crudely equated with mere equalisation of incomes.[90] It was assumed that large-scale *structural* inequality would vanish once jobs, housing, health and education were available to all, but that a modest *personal* 'rent of ability' would remain, after public ownership had eliminated inequalities arising from privilege and monopoly. The market argument, that large-scale inequality was essential for encouraging initiative and creativity, seemed to most Labour apologists absurd – far outweighed by the vast reserves of talent being wasted by structurally determined lack of opportunity.[91] The model of equality traditionally envisaged by Labour had been one in which manual workers would share the material security, educational standards and access to jobs and public offices enjoyed by the professional middle classes (while both would eschew the vulgar display and conspicuous consumption of the very rich). 'The educational system', wrote Cole, 'should be designed to assimilate social habits of speech, dress, and common behaviour to the highest attainable standards, without destroying local or national variations . . . an educated man should be able to marry his cook, and *vice versa*, without the probability of clashes of social behaviour; there should be no difficulty about sending a dock labourer's son to Eton . . . Proletarianism, as well as snobbery, should become out of date.'[92]

This assumption – that the culture and living standards of the educated middle classes were a universal aspiration and birthright – was a commonplace of Labour thought throughout the earlier twentieth century. Tawney, when writing of a national 'common culture', had constantly emphasised the hunger of workers for university education; while working-class organisations themselves had demanded unrestricted access to 'humane learning' and resisted attempts to fob them off with 'technical' and 'vocational' training.[93] The tripartite secondary

schooling sanctioned by the 1944 Education Act had been largely welcomed by Labour as a move towards equal access, with only a few dissident voices urging the alternative of a 'common school'. After the war
there was a confident expectation that public ownership, full employment, social security and the dramatic narrowing of post-tax income
differentials were all combining to produce both 'equality of opportunity' for individuals, and a more egalitarian social structure. T. H.
Marshall's famous Cambridge lectures of 1949 claimed that Labour's
post-war welfare reforms had universalised social rights in much the
same way as struggles over *habeas corpus* had universalised legal rights in
the mid-eighteenth century.[94] Even after Labour's defeat in 1951 there
was an underlying confidence that these trends were irreversible – and
that, in any case, a Labour government would soon be back in office.[95]

The next two decades, however, were to bring some profound changes
in Labour's ideas about equality and its conception of wider social structure. As political theory gave way to a more sociological approach, a
younger generation of Labour theorists began to question the view that
removing material obstacles to education and achievement would automatically lead to dissolution of class barriers. Class analysis became less
a way of explaining political power, more a way of mapping the distribution of 'positional' goods and individual success and failure. Labour
commentators began to question strategies that propelled clever
working-class children out of their own communities; and by the late
1950s there were signs of reaction against the assumption that the
'common culture' was universal, high-brow and uncontested.
Sociologists claimed that social mobility in post-war Britain had been
relatively limited; that widespread poverty had tenaciously survived the
'universalist' welfare state; and that, even among more prosperous
workers, there was much less enthusiasm for 'middle-class' lifestyles
than earlier Labour theorists had hoped and imagined.[96] Forty years
earlier Tawney had conjured up a vision of a 'new race' of workers, who
would 'stand on the threshold with the world at their feet, like barbar-
ians gazing upon the time-worn plains of an ancient civilisation'.[97] But
their descendants of the 1950s and 1960s appeared much more interested in the new culture of affluence, with its expanding opportunities
for leisure, labour saving, and mass consumption: priorities that were
successfully targeted by the Conservative election campaigns of 1951,
1955 and 1959.

Labour commentators of the 1950s adjusted to these new perspectives in a variety of ways. Despite the much publicised conflicts over
nationalisation and nuclear disarmament, ideological allegiances on

right, left and centre were less clearcut than they had been two decades earlier, and often hinged on clashes of personality and sentiment rather than sustained political analysis.[98] The Cold War and Russian occupation of Eastern Europe made it difficult for Labour's *Marxisant* wing any longer to claim a 'vast practical example' in the Soviet Union; indeed many on the Labour left now saw the communist bloc as a major barrier to the further advance of socialism.[99] Among Labour economists of right and left, discussion of fiscal and monetary management displaced broader debate on principles of a 'socialist' commonwealth. No new political thinker of the stature of Webb, Tawney, Laski or Cole emerged in any quarter of the party. Nevertheless, certain key groupings can be identified which tried to shape the party's overall priorities. On the left a series of more or less formal pressure groups (the 'Keep-Left' movement, the Tribune group, the Bevanites) campaigned to keep 'public ownership' as the definitive core of Labour philosophy. Their goal was partly a technocratic one, stemming from the belief that the public sector was inherently more rational and efficient than the private; but, more fundamentally, it stemmed from the view, trenchantly maintained by Bevan, that – quite apart from efficiency – public ownership was the tangible embodiment of real working-class power. In this latter sense Bevan and his adherents were faithful disciples of the doctrine expounded by Laski that the prime arguments for abolition of private ownership were political and structural rather than economic. But the Keep-Lefters were also aware that if nationalised industries were to be successful they needed sustained public investment – hence their support for high levels of taxation, compulsory saving, and 'physical' rather than Keynesian-style models of planning.[100] There was similar nostalgia for the wartime ethos of state control and communal sharing in the writings of the Socialist Union – a body of intellectuals dedicated to advancing Tawney's philosophy of 'fraternity' and 'fellowship', who produced a stream of writings on ethical socialism between 1951 and 1959.[101] But elsewhere in the party there was growing apprehension that the image of austerity, regulation, and doctrinaire nationalisation was fatally damaging Labour's chances at the polls, hence the emergence of increasing interest in 'Keynesian socialism', in state planning without state ownership, and in promotion of equality via education and social welfare rather than through large-scale changes in the structure of private property.[102]

It was within this context that C. A. R. Crosland attempted a fundamental redefinition of Labour's priorities in *The Future of Socialism*, published in 1956. Crosland, whose personal history spanned many bridges between older and newer Labour traditions (he was a secularist with roots in evangelical Nonconformity, a Keynesian with training in philosophy as well as economics), produced a work that came to be regarded as the classic text of British 'revisionist' socialism for the rest of the twentieth century. *The Future of Socialism* was overtly an attack on the Fabian legacy of Sidney and Beatrice Webb, with their emphasis upon 'the solid virtues of hard work, self-discipline, efficiency, research and abstinence', their willingness to 'sacrifice private pleasure to public duty' and their expectation 'that others should do the same'.[103] In framing his argument in these terms Crosland successfully tuned in to the dawning consumerism of the late 1950s and the burgeoning materialism and libertarianism of the following decade. Yet, though it was only too easy to caricature the Webbs as frumpish and out-dated, it seems unlikely that they were Crosland's real target. Indeed, in substantive terms, *The Future of Socialism* – with its emphasis on a mixed economy, its optimism about the irreversible advance of social democracy, and its faith in administrative social engineering – displayed marked underlying affinities with the Webbs in their prime. A much more major target was the whole corpus of doctrines associated with Harold Laski, whom Crosland rarely mentioned by name, and then only in tones of thinly veiled disparagement.[104] The whole thrust of Crosland's argument was to dismiss as obsolete and untenable the central thesis of Laski's mature political philosophy – that democracy, welfare and personal liberty were all fatally undermined by the structural class antagonism inherent in private property and private ownership of capital.

The Future of Socialism argued instead that the relationship between economic and political power had fundamentally altered since the 1930s. 'Classical capitalism', where control over all aspects of economic life had lain in private hands, had been replaced by a process whereby production, distribution, business management and welfare were all regulated by the power of the state acting on behalf of the public interest. The overwhelming fact about modern business enterprise was not whether it was private or public, but the vastness of its organisational scale; most of the social and psychic problems ascribed by Marxists to 'capital' in fact stemmed from lack of personal control over the work environment ('a collective economy, with no private owners, is no less characterised by the alienation of control than a capitalist economy').[105] In the face of large-scale public ownership and fiscal redistribution, the analysis of power structures advanced by both Marxian and non-Marxian Labour theorists of the 1930s had become 'irrelevant' – and this was so even though a non-Labour government was temporarily in power ('counter-revolution' was not in the 'nature of the British Conservative Party', whose leaders were invariably 'cautious, realistic Peelites').[106] Such changes did not mean that poverty, inequality and class difference had vanished. But in Crosland's view these took a quite different form from what earlier Labour analysts had imagined: they stemmed more from 'education, style of life and occupational status' than from inequality of income, and were not to be cured merely by greater doses of universal social security.[107] Instead they were to be tackled through various kinds of institutional social engineering. Poverty should be remedied not by additional cash payments but by 'therapy, casework and preventive treatment'. Tripartite secondary schooling should be replaced by the socially unifying 'comprehensive school', together with some form of egalitarian incorporation of public schools into the state system. State provision of education, rented housing and healthcare should be raised to such a quality that the private market in these sectors would wither away from want of custom.[108] Such policies needed to be accompanied by large-scale structural changes in inherited (as opposed to earned) wealth, but these could just as well be achieved 'in a pluralist as in a wholly State-owned economy, with much better results for social contentment and the fragmentation of power'.[109] Much the same was true of the cherished panacea of 'planning'. Detailed planning of specific industries had been found unworkable without democratically unacceptable direction of labour. The price mechanism had proved to be a perfectly adequate way of distributing 'the great bulk' of consumer and capital goods. The task of planning was simply to enable ministers to find ways of harmonising the goals of 'high investment, exports, and social expenditure without inflation' – which again applied just as much to private as to public enterprise. Beyond that, there was nothing more to be said about planning, except in very general terms which were 'abstract to the point of futility'.[110]

Crosland's analysis initially met with far from universal acclaim within the Labour Party. Many found his implied critique of universalist social services distasteful, and his suggestion that the poor needed therapy and casework positively offensive.[111] Others were horrified by the claim that structural class conflict had been superseded by the managerial revolution and the benign administrative state.[112] The late 1950s and early 1960s saw a resurgence of Labour interest in social security and poverty – indicating that Crosland's position on these issues was out of step with that of many other Labour thinkers.[113] Moreover, the early 1960s brought a revival of Labour commitment to centralised economic planning, stimulated partly by Conservative attempts to harness planning techniques to a private-enterprise economy. A policy document drafted by Richard Crossman, Harold Wilson and Thomas Balogh in 1961 declared – with a powerful echo of the sentiments of Laski – that 'those who identify laisser-faire with freedom are enemies, however unwittingly, of democracy. The enlargement of freedom which we all desire cannot be achieved by opposing State intervention.'[114] Nevertheless, *The Future of Socialism* signalled a sea-change in the undercurrents of Labour's social and political philosophy. It hinted that the future might lie with consumerism and private libertarianism rather than control of production: with the taming of capitalism to social-democratic ends (and of social democrats to capitalism), rather than in large-scale structural transformation.

Apotheosis of Old Labour

None of this was clearly apparent in 1964, when Labour recaptured power after thirteen years in opposition. Technocratic approaches to economic problems appeared to be at their zenith, and the new Prime Minister was an avowed admirer of Soviet planning techniques and of the Russian capacity to 'plan their economic life in a purposeful and rational manner – however much we may detest their political frame-work'.[115] The early years of the Wilson governments were to bring in a series of highly interventionist strategies, aimed at encouraging produc-tivity and labour mobility, and shifting resources *away* from consump-tion towards savings and investment. Lobbies within the party arguing for large-scale housing, education and social security reforms were much more organised and vocal than they had been a decade before. The 1960s was also to see a resurgence of interest in various forms of Marxism, on a scale far more widespread than the elite Marxism of the 1930s; and a powerful backwash of quasi-Marxian sentiment was to sweep through Labour local authorities, constituency parties, and many sections of the trade-union movement. Public spending at the end of the 1960s exceeded 50 per cent of GDP for the first time in peacetime history, whilst income for a four-person household dependent on social security rose to over 74 per cent of average earnings.[116] All of this seemed to herald a shift towards a much *more* centralised, *dirigiste*, socialised economy than had been attained by Labour in the post-war years.

Very little of this was mirrored, however, in Labour political thought, and the earlier aspiration that Labour policy should be rooted in 'the best Political Science of its time' was conspicuous by its absence. Labour apologists of the period studiously avoided the issue of how far large-scale government interventionism was systemically compatible with Britain's inescapable dependence on an international trading economy.

Labour's senior politicians were certainly aware of, but unable to generate any solution to, the endemic structural tension between centralised economic management and trade-union autonomy: a fundamental issue of 'political theory' if ever there was one.[117] Powerful new socioeconomic trends – the emergence of the EEC, the rise of feminism, massive international migration and increasing ethnic pluralism – posed problems that traditional Labour thought (rooted in a powerful, culturally homogeneous, unitary state with a common national history) was largely unprepared for. The 1960s saw the beginnings of an Anglo-American revival in the kind of analytical political philosophy that had fallen into eclipse during the middle decades of the century. But this revival was slow to penetrate into writings by democratic socialists, which with few exceptions remained wedded to the positivism and technocratic perspectives of the 1940s and 50s. The radical insights of neo-liberal political thought (both in its Rawlsian and Hayekian forms) went largely unacknowledged by Labour writers before the mid-1970s.[118] Despite the increasing pervasiveness of radical sentiments among Labour's grass-roots, serious debate on the relevance or otherwise of Marxist thought took place largely outside the boundaries of the Labour Party.

It would of course be absurd to suggest that this lack of systematic theory was the sole key to the ultimate failure of Labour's post-war socialising project. Labour's 1945 vision of an imminent 'Socialist Commonwealth' receded for many other reasons – monetary, international, cultural, generational and electoral – and it was always unlikely that a set of ideas forged during prolonged depression and legitimised by a war of national survival would transplant easily into the wholly different domestic and global conditions of the post-war era. Some degree of haziness and eclecticism in political ideas is arguably a prerequisite for any successful mass party; and, as suggested above, unresolved weaknesses in earlier phases of Labour thought had been overcome less by superior reasoning than by the events of history. Nevertheless, intellectuals in the early Labour Party had viewed systematic theory as playing an important role both in generating coherent policies and in democratic persuasion – tasks that in the 1930s had seemed of crucial importance in resisting the breakdown of civilisation.[119] Labour ultimately lost its post-war political hegemony, not to rival pragmatists in the shape of 'cautious realistic Peelites', but to a party that, temporarily at least, took seriously the analytical and polemical weapons offered by political theory. It seems plausible to infer that negligence and sentimentalism in these areas were of some contributory significance in Old Labour's long-term political demise.

Jose Harris

Lineages of New Labour

Labour in 1995 abandoned its commitment to 'common ownership', enshrined in Clause Four of the 1918 constitution, and replaced it by a quest for 'community' in tandem with a 'dynamic market economy'[120] – two goals that throughout the history of democratic socialism have been seen as inherently incompatible. Whether or not they are so, remains a question for future history – as does the more general significance of the philosophy of 'New Labour'. The question may be posed, however, of how far the intellectual roots of New Labour may be discerned in earlier epochs of Labour history, or whether its emergence was largely a reflex to Thatcherism, the collapse of Soviet communism, and impatience with prolonged exclusion from office. There can be little doubt that, quite apart from the abandonment of Clause Four, many earlier Labour intellectuals would have seen certain aspects of New Labour thought as well-nigh unintelligible – and, where intelligible, profoundly unsympathetic. Harold Laski would have found New Labour views on the *rapprochement* of 'social democracy' with capitalist enterprise as absurd as he found Evan Durbin's in the 1930s; while Durbin himself would have been horrified by New Labour's apparent manipulation and stage-management of mass psychology. G. D. H. Cole would have been amazed to find that social equality no longer meant marrying one's cook or educating dock labourers' sons at public schools. With the exception of Shaw and H. G. Wells, the vast majority of early Labourites would have very much disliked a version of 'personal liberty' that promoted sexual pluralism and de-regulation of pornography, but ignored the issue of autonomy in the workplace. Most Labour feminists down to the 1960s and later believed that 'willing and efficient motherhood' was best induced by adequate state support in the home, rather than by propelling mothers into paid employment.[121] The 'post-modernist' idiom of much of New Labour's political rhetoric would have seemed strangely devious and insubstantial to such strongholds of 'modernist' thought as the Fabian Society, the War Emergency Workers Committee, the Living-Wage Inquiry, and the Socialist League. And a movement whose political imagination was shaped by Anglo-Saxon liberties, the Civil War and Commonwealth, the Industrial Revolution and Chartism, would have been deeply baffled by New Labour's seeming indifference to the epic struggles of centuries of English history.

Such discontinuities can be exaggerated, however, and it is not difficult to discover presages of New Labour thought in earlier strands of Labour's intellectual odyssey. There are clear links between New Labour and the themes of *The Future of Socialism*, particularly in Crosland's suggestion that it was easier to mediate social change through education, culture and consumption than through public ownership (easier to close grammar schools or to ban fox hunting than to control finance capital). At the same time, however, there are also powerful resonances in New Labour thought of the multitudinous, many-faceted and fast-changing concerns of Crosland's *bête noire*, Harold Laski. These echoes can be heard most strongly in Laski's focus on pluralism (religious, social and racial); in his highlighting of 'exclusion' as the clue to civic disaffection; and in his identification of a loosely conceived 'conference of final responsibility' rather than state sovereignty as the ultimate fount of constitutional power.[122] Indeed, nothing more aptly demonstrates the curious duality of New Labour's links to its own past than the shade of Harold Laski. Dismissed as the mouthpiece of a dead Marxism, Laski nevertheless remains tacitly omnipresent in much of Labour's current political discourse – as the prophet of multiculturalism, global migration and federation, and of the step-by-step discrediting and dismantling of the unitary sovereign state.

Similar points may be made about more humdrum themes in the history of Labour ideology. The Edwardian concern with 'duty and citizenship', largely sidelined by the technocratic culture of the midcentury, resonates strongly through many New Labour documents, as do Edwardian ideas about reciprocal relationships between welfare and work, punishment and fraud. Although ideas about what constitutes virtue have changed beyond recognition, early Labourites would certainly have endorsed the New Labour view that policies should be 'ethical' and citizens 'virtuous'. 'Focus groups', in substance if not in name, were a feature of Labour's strategy for 'collectivising' popular opinion in the 1940s (not always with results gratifying to those who promoted them).[123] New Labour's efforts to dissipate power away from London to the periphery would certainly have been approved by early Fabians, who would have objected only that such policies should be more consistently and coherently applied. Above all, there appears to be a deep affinity between early and current Labour views about the overall thrust of long-term historical change. The confidence of Edwardian Labour that social evolution was inexorably unfolding in a labourist direction finds echoes in the mind-set of many New Labour supporters. There can be little doubt that, in this respect if less in others, the young Ramsay MacDonald would have found in New Labour at the end of the twentieth century a congenial spiritual home.

Jose Harris

Notes

1 Sidney Webb, *Socialism: True and False*, Fabian Tract no. 51 (1894).
2 *Labour Party Foundation Conference and Annual Conference Reports*, 1900–5 (London: Hammersmith Bookshop Ltd, 1967), pp. 104, 157, and passim.
3 David Howell, *British Social Democracy. A Study in Development and Decay* (London: Croom Helm, 1976); Ben Pimlott, *Labour and the Left in the 1930s* (Cambridge: Cambridge University Press, 1977).
4 Webb, *Socialism: True and False*, pp. 9–10; *Labour and the New Social Order* (London: Labour Party, 1918), p. 23.
5 Peter Clarke, *Liberals and Social Democrats* (Cambridge: Cambridge University Press, 1978); Eugenio F. Biagini and Alastair J. Reid (eds.), *Currents of Radicalism. Popular Radicalism, Organised Labour and Party Politics in Britain 1850–1914* (Cambridge: Cambridge University Press, 1991).
6 The English *locus classicus*, read by many early Labour intellectuals, was the discussion in J. S. Mill's *A System of Logic: Ratiocinative and Inductive*, especially book VI. *Collected Works of John Stuart Mill*, ed. J. M. Robson, 33 vols. (Toronto: Toronto University Press, 1973), vol. VIII.
7 *Report of the 23rd Annual Conference of the Labour Party* (London: Labour Party, 1923), pp. 178–9.
8 J. Ramsay MacDonald, *The Socialist Movement* (London: Williams and Norgate, 1911), chs. 1 and 2; Bernard Barker (ed.), *Ramsay MacDonald's Political Writings* (London: Allen Lane, 1972), pp. 14–37.
9 Henry Collins, 'The Marxism of the Social Democratic Federation', in Asa Briggs and John Saville (eds.), *Essays in Labour History* (London: Macmillan, 1971), pp. 47–69.
10 *New Statesman*, 31 May 1913.
11 George Bernard Shaw, *Ruskin's Politics* (London: Christophers, 1921), pp. 7–9, 21–2.
12 John Ruskin, *Unto this Last. Four Essays on the First Principles of Political Economy* (London: Smith, Elder and Co., 1862); Jose Harris, 'Ruskin and social reform', in D. Birch (ed.), *Ruskin and the Dawn of the Modern* (Oxford: Oxford University Press, 1999), pp. 27–8.
13 David James, Tony Jowitt and Keith Laybourn (eds.), *The Centennial History of the Independent Labour Party* (Halifax: Ryburn Academic Publishing, 1992); Peter Grosvenor, 'A mediaeval future: the social, economic and aesthetic thought of A. J. Penty', Ph.D. thesis (University of London, 1997).
14 G. D. H. Cole, introduction to Jean-Jacques Rousseau, *The Social Contract and The Discourses* (London: J. M. Dent, Everyman edition, 1913): G. D. H. Cole, *Guild Socialism Re-Stated* (London: Allen and Unwin, 1920); A. W. Wright, *G. D. H. Cole and Socialist Democracy* (Oxford: Clarendon Press, 1979), pp. 50–101.
15 *Labour and the New Social Order* (1918), pp. 5–15, 18–21.

16 S. and B. Webb, *The Decay of Capitalist Civilization* (London: Longmans, 1923), pp. 77, 201–36.

17 Ramsay MacDonald, *Socialism: Critical and Constructive* (London: Cassell, London, 1921), cited in Barker, *Macdonald's Political Writings*, p. 211.

18 George Lansbury, 'Policy of the left wing', in H. B. Lees-Smith (ed.) *Encyclopaedia of the Labour Movement* (hereafter *ELM*), 3 vols. (London: Caxton, 1927), vol. II, pp. 191–4.

19 William Sanders, *Municipalisation by Provinces*, Fabian Tract no. 125 (1905).

20 *Labour Party Foundation Conference and Annual Conference Reports*, p. 21.

21 George Lansbury, *My England*, (London: Selwyn and Blount, 1936), p. 23; H. Finer, 'Monarchy', *ELM*, vol. II, pp. 270–2.

22 Clifford D. Sharp, *The Case Against the Referendum*, Fabian Tract no. 155 (1911); H. Finer, 'Proportional representation', *ELM*, vol. III, pp. 66–71.

23 *Labour Party Foundation Conference and Annual Conference Reports*, p. 96.

24 Lewis Minkin, *The Labour Party Conference. A Study in the Politics of Intra-Party Democracy* (London: Allen Lane, 1978), pp. 3–29, 272–89; Kenneth Harris, *Attlee* (London: Weidenfeld and Nicolson, 1982), pp. 63, 107–8.

25 Barker, *MacDonald's Political Writings*, p. 199; Harold Laski, *A Grammar of Politics* (London: Allen and Unwin, London, 1925), p. 250.

26 John Davis, *Reforming London. The London Government Problem, 1855–1900* (Oxford: Oxford University Press, 1988); and 'Radical clubs and London Politics 1870–1900', in David Feldman and Gareth Stedman Jones (eds.), *Metropolis. London. Histories and Representations since 1800* (London: Routledge, 1989), p. 114.

27 *New Statesman*, 31 May 1913; 'The State and Private Industry', by Harold J. Wilson, 17 May 1950, PREM 8/1183, Public Record Office.

28 Sidney Ball, *The Moral Aspects of Socialism*, Fabian Tract no. 72 (1896), pp. 11 and 12.

29 The Webbs, for example, despite their membership of Labour via the Fabian Society, did not come to regard the party as the main channel of reformist policies until 1912.

30 J. Ramsay MacDonald, *Parliament and Revolution* (London: National Labour Press, 1919), pp. 53–4; MacDonald, *Parliament and Democracy* (London: National Labour Press, 1920), p. 24.

31 B. Kingsley Martin, 'General Strike', *ELM*, vol. II, pp. 24–9.

32 Laski, *Grammar of Politics*, pp. i–xxvii.

33 Ibid., 3rd edn, pp. xii–xiii.

34 Harold Laski, *The State in Theory and Practice* (London: George Allen and Unwin, 1935), pp. 72, 89–90, 213.

35 Aneurin Bevan, *In Place of Fear* (London: Heinemann, 1952), pp. 25–9.

36 S. and B. Webb, *A Constitution for the Socialist Commonwealth of Great Britain* (London: Longmans, Green and Co., 1920), passim, especially pp. 108–31, 203–15.

37 S. and B. Webb, *Decay of Capitalist Civilization*, esp. ch. IV.

38 John Allett, *New Liberalism. The Political Economy of J. A. Hobson* (Toronto: University of Toronto Press, 1981), pp. 70–7.

39 MacDonald, *Socialist Movement*, pp. 125–32.

40 *The Works of John Ruskin*, ed. E. T. Cook and A. Wedderburn, 39 vols. (London: George Allen, 1903–12), vol. VIII, p. 233, and vol. XVI, pp. 23–65; Hastings Rashdall, 'Is the Christian necessarily a socialist?', *Economic Review* 18 (1908), 315–36; Charles Gore (ed.), *Property: its Duties and Rights* (London: Macmillan, 1913), p. 31.

41 MacDonald, *Socialist Movement*, pp. 159–61; Fabian Society, *Capital and Land*, Fabian Tract no. 7 (1908 edn), pp. 8–18.

42 Richard Whiting, 'The Labour Party, capitalism and the national debt', in P. J. Waller (ed.) *Politics and Social Change in Modern Britain. Essays Presented to A. F. Thompson* (Sussex: Harvester Press, 1987), pp. 141–7.

43 Laski, *State in Theory and Practice*, pp. 138–69.

44 Ibid., pp. 117–18, 122–5, 143–4, 290–3.

45 Laski, *Grammar of Politics*, 3rd edn, p. 202; Laski, *State in Theory and Practice*, pp. 199–200.

46 R. H. Tawney, *The Acquisitive Society* (London: G. Bell and Sons, 1921), pp. 60–1.

47 Ibid., pp. 64–95.

48 R. H. Tawney, 'John Ruskin', in *The Radical Tradition: Twelve Essays on Politics, Education and Literature* (London: Allen and Unwin, 1964), pp. 41–2; Tawney, *Acquisitive Society*, p. 42.

49 Edith J. Morley, *John Ruskin and Social Ethics*, Fabian Tract no. 179 (circa 1918), p. 2.

50 Sidney Webb, 'Social movements', in *Cambridge Modern History*, vol. XII: *The Latest Age* (Cambridge: Cambridge University Press, 1910), pp. 751–2.

51 J. Keir Hardie, *The Unemployed Problem with Some Suggestions for Solving It* (ILP, 1904); J. Ramsay MacDonald, *The New Unemployed Bill of the Labour Party* (ILP, 1907).

52 Lansbury, *My England*, p. 237.

53 *Prevention: The Journal of the Purity Movement* (1910–19); Ball, *Moral Aspects of Socialism*, p. 5; MacDonald, *Socialist Movement*, pp. 137–8.

54 A. Clutton Brock, *The Philosophy of Socialism*, Fabian Tract no. 180 (1916), pp. 1–12.

55 *R. H. Tawney's Commonplace Book*, ed. and with an introduction by J. M. Winter and D. M. Joslin (Cambridge: Cambridge University Press, 1972), p. 34.

56 R. H. Tawney, *Equality* (London: Allen and Unwin, 1931; 1964 edn), p. 164.

57 Harold J. Laski, *Authority in the Modern State* (New Haven: Yale University Press, 1919), pp. 37, 54–6; Laski, *Grammar of Politics*, p. 142.

58 Laski, *Grammar of Politics*, preface to 2nd edn (1929).

59 Laski, *State in Theory and Practice*, pp. 322–3.

60 Harris, *Attlee*, pp. 130–1; *House of Commons Debates*, 5th series (1931), vol.

CCLVI, cols. 1659–1738; Stafford Cripps et al., *Problems of a Socialist Government* (London: Gollancz, 1933).

61 E.F. Wise, 'Control of finance and the financiers', in Cripps et al., *Problems of a Socialist Government*, pp. 72–4.

62 Stafford Cripps, 'Can socialism come by constitutional methods?', in ibid., pp. 45–6.

63 Daniel Ritschel, *The Politics of Planning. The Debate on Economic Planning in Britain in the 1930s* (Oxford: Clarendon Press, 1997), pp. 134–5, 212–13.

64 Ritschel, *Politics of Planning*, pp. 109–18.

65 J. A. Hobson, *Work and Wealth: A Human Valuation* (London: Macmillan 1914 and 1918 edns); Amabel Williams-Ellis, *The Tragedy of John Ruskin* (London: Jonathan Cape, 1928).

66 Elizabeth Durbin, *New Jerusalems. The Labour Party and the Economics of Democratic Socialism* (London: Routledge, 1985), pp. 131–2; Ritschel, *Politics of Planning*, pp. 129–30: Douglas Jay, *The Socialist Case* (London: Faber and Faber, 1938), ch. 30.

67 F. A. Hayek (ed.), *Collectivist Economic Planning: Critical Studies on the Possibility of Socialism* (London: Routledge, 1935), ch. 8.

68 Clement Attlee, 'Local government and the socialist plan', in Cripps et al., *Problems of a Socialist Government*, pp. 189–208.

69 Evan Durbin, *The Politics of Democratic Socialism. An Essay on Social Policy* (London: Routledge, 1940), pp. 243–75.

70 Harold J. Laski, 'Choosing the planners', in *Plan for Britain* (London: Fabian Society, 1943), p. 103.

71 Roger Middleton, 'The Treasury in the 1930s: political and administrative constraints to the acceptance of the "new" economics', *Oxford Economic Papers* 34 (1982), 48–77.

72 E. Durbin to Attlee, circa 1941, Attlee MSS, dep. 7, Bodleian Library, Oxford.

73 Bevan, *In Place of Fear*, p. 29.

74 Aneurin Bevan, 'Plan for work', in *Plan for Britain*, pp. 38–9; G. D. H. Cole, 'Plan for living', in ibid., p. 4.

75 Cole, 'Plan for living', in ibid., pp. 4, 11, 27.

76 R. H. Tawney, 'The abolition of economic controls 1918–21', *Economic History Review*, 1st series, 13 (1943).

77 Attlee's notes to a speech at Greenwich, 12 July 1943, Attlee MSS, dep. 9, f. 56, Bodleian Library, Oxford. Cf. Laski, *State in Theory and Practice*, p. 200.

78 *House of Commons Debates*, 5th series (1945–6), 414, cols. 2347–8; (1947–8) 444, cols. 1607–13.

79 H. J. Laski, 'The "working-out" of Victorian ideas', in *Ideas and Beliefs of the Victorians* (London: Sylvan Press, 1948), pp. 417–22.

80 On Attlee's explicit hostility to theory, see C. R. Attlee, *The Labour Party in Perspective* (London: Gollancz, 1937).

81 *House of Commons Debates*, 5th series (1945–6), 417, cols. 1039–50; 418, cols. 1754–8.

82 S. and B. Webb, *A Constitution for the Socialist Commonwealth*, passim; Reports of the Joint Committees of the TUC, the Labour Party and the Co-operative Union on the 'Beveridge Report', 8 and 20 January 1943 (Labour Party Archives, Manchester (hereafter LPA), microfilm, 303); and Standing Joint Committee on Working Women's Organisations, memorandum on 'Design of Dwellings', January 1943 (LPA microfilm, 304).

83 Jose Harris, 'Political thought and the state', in S. J. D. Green and R. C. Whiting (eds.), *The Boundaries of the State in Modern Britain* (Cambridge: Cambridge University Press, 1996), pp. 15–28.

84 *Report of the 42nd Annual Conference of the Labour Party* (London: Labour Party, 1943), especially speeches by Sidney Silverman and Barbara Betts (later Barbara Castle); Donald G. Macrae, 'Domestic record of the Labour government', *Political Quarterly* 20(1) (1949), 1–11.

85 G. D. H. Cole, *Essays in Social Theory* (London: Macmillan, 1950), pp. 15, 31–46.

86 Jay, *Socialist Case* (1948 edn), p. 128; Tawney, *Radical Tradition,* pp. 162–4. Ironically, the rhetoric of Liberty versus Serfdom employed by Hayek had been extensively used by Labour apologists throughout the early 1940s (e.g. the Labour policy statement, *Labour and the War*, January 1940).

87 Nicholas Ellison, *Egalitarian Thought and Labour Politics. Retreating Visions* (London: Routledge and LSE, 1994), p. 41.

88 Tawney, *Radical Tradition*, pp. 138–67.

89 Jay, *Socialist Case* (1948 edn), p. 258.

90 S. and B. Webb, *Problems of Modern Industry* (London: Longmans, 1902), pp. 215–8; MacDonald, *Socialist Movement*, 112–14, 139–41.

91 Laski, *Grammar of Politics*, p. 155.

92 Cole, *Essays in Social Theory*, p. 70.

93 Tawney, *Radical Tradition*, pp. 70–81: *Labour Party Foundation Conference and Annual Conference Reports*, p. 51.

94 T. H. Marshall, *Citizenship and Social Class and Other Essays* (Cambridge: Cambridge University Press, 1950).

95 Tawney, 'British socialism today', in *Radical Tradition*, pp. 172–3.

96 D. V. Glass (ed.), *Social Mobility in Britain* (London: Routledge, 1954); A. H. Halsey, J. Floud and C. Arnold Anderson, *Education, Economy and Society* (London: Collins Macmillan, 1961); John H. Goldthorpe and David Lockwood, 'Affluence and the British class structure', *Sociological Review*, n.s., 11 (1963).

97 Tawney, *Radical Tradition*, p. 81.

98 Ellison, *Egalitarian Thought and Labour Politics*, chs. 2–3; Catherine Torrie, 'Ideas, policy and ideology: the British Labour Party in opposition, 1951–1959', D.Phil. thesis (University of Oxford, 1997).

99 R. H. S. Crossman, 'Towards a philosophy of socialism', in *New Fabian Essays* (London: Fabian Society, 1952, 1970 edn), p. 12.

100 Bevan, *In Place of Fear*, pp. 81–2, 93–4; Ellison, *Egalitarian Thought*, pp. 36–72.

101 Members included Allen Flanders, Rita Hinden, Phyllis and Peter Wilmott, and Michael Young. Its major publications were *Socialism: A New Statement of Principles* (London: Lincolns-Prager, 1952) and *Twentieth Century Socialism: The Economy of Tomorrow* (Harmondsworth: Penguin, 1956).
102 Ellison, *Egalitarian Thought*, pp. 73–104.
103 C. A. R. Crosland, *The Future of Socialism* (London: Jonathan Cape, 1956), pp. 220, 356–7.
104 Ibid., pp. 10, 33, 159n.
105 Ibid., pp. 5–42.
106 Ibid., pp. 27–8.
107 Ibid., pp. 106–11, 123–4.
108 Ibid., pp. 84–7, 96–7, 190–7, 201–7.
109 Ibid., p. 340.
110 Ibid., pp. 341–52.
111 Barbara Wootton, *Social Science and Social Pathology* (London: Allen and Unwin, 1959); Barbara Wootton, 'Daddy knows best', *The Twentieth Century* (October 1959), 248–61.
112 R. H. S. Crossman, *Socialism and the New Despotism*, Fabian Tract no. 298 (1956).
113 P. Townsend, 'Measuring poverty', *Planning* 9 (1954); B. Abel-Smith and P. Townsend, *The Poor and the Poorest* (London: Bell and Son, 1965).
114 Labour Party, *Signposts for the Sixties* (London: Labour Party, 1961).
115 Ben Pimlott, *Harold Wilson* (London: HarperCollins, 1992), p. 276.
116 B. Abel-Smith, 'Public expenditure on the social services', *Social Trends* 1 (1971), 12–19; M. Wright, 'Public expenditure in Britain', *Public Administration*, 55 (1977), 143–69.
117 Richard Crossman, *The Diaries of a Cabinet Minister*, 3 vols. (London: Hamish Hamilton and Jonathan Cape), vol. III (1976), pp. 299–331.
118 And even then somewhat meagrely (e.g. Anthony Crosland, *Socialism Now and Other Essays*, ed. Dick Leonard (London: Jonathan Cape, 1974), p. 15.
119 Laski, *Grammar of Politics*, 3rd edn, p. xxvii: Durbin, *Democratic Socialism*, pp. 22–6.
120 Geoffrey Foote, *The Labour Party's Political Thought*, 3rd edn (London: Macmillan, 1997).
121 'Report of the National Executive Committee', *Report of the 42nd Annual Conference of the Labour Party* (London: Labour Party, 1943).
122 Harold Laski, *The Problem of Sovereignty* (New Haven: Yale University Press, 1917), pp. 283–5: Laski, *Grammar of Politics*, pp. 27, 39–40, 150, 271, 285–6.
123 Standing Joint Committee on Working Women's Organisations, memorandum on 'Design of Dwellings'(LPA microfilm, 304).

2 | Labour and the economy

Jim Tomlinson

A large part of the Labour Party's political energy has always gone into plans for reforming the economy. Indeed, for much of the last century economic policy, broadly defined, has been at the core of what the party has seen as its socialism. This chapter explores the development of Labour's ideas on the economy, and what these ideas have achieved in practice. Two key issues are: how far ideas in this area have been consistent over time; and, second, how far Labour's approach has been affected by other, non-Labour, ideological and political forces. It is argued that, while there have been considerable twists and turns in the specific policies put forward by Labour, there have also been important continuities in the general assumptions embodied in the approach to the economy, often associated with certain essentially ethical or moral notions about how society should function. At the same time, the way in which these underlying assumptions have been deployed in policy-making has been strongly affected by events and ideas in the world outside the party.

In understanding this broader context in which the party's approach to the economy has developed, two frameworks are especially important. First, twentieth-century British economic policy can usefully if not exhaustively be summarised as a process of the rise, consolidation and eventual weakening of national government economic management. Labour has been a major contributor to this process, but it has also interacted with others who have pursued similar aims. Second, the party's approach to the British economy has been fundamentally affected by perceptions of economic decline, and the consequent need for 'modernisation'. Again, this concern has not been limited to Labour, but decline and modernisation have been key terms shaping its approach. These two frameworks structure much of the chronological account which this chapter provides.

Labour and the unmanaged economy before 1914

Britain in 1900 had an unmanaged economy which was extraordinarily open internationally. Government spending was under 10 per cent of GDP, much of it by local authorities. Free trade had encouraged dependence on imports, amounting to 60 per cent of food consumption and similar levels for key raw materials, paid for by British dominance of export markets for manufactured goods. Britain was by far the world's largest exporter of capital. This was largely financed by huge receipts from the export of 'invisibles' such as shipping, insurance and other financial services. Together the gold standard, free trade and a low-spending state underpinned a regime where notions of national governments actively managing their economies – socialism's main economic idea – could find little purchase.[1]

However, by the time the Labour Representation Committee (LRC) was formed in 1900 this liberal and unmanaged system was under challenge. The rise of international competitors, especially the USA and Germany, threatened the overwhelming predominance of British trade, and led to the first stirrings of the debates over alleged British 'decline', which were to recur so frequently over the next century.[2] At the same time, sharp cyclical fluctuations in unemployment coupled to growing concern with the consequences of chronic casual underemployment, made the labour market a much greater political issue.[3] The tariff reform campaign led by Joseph Chamberlain crystallised many of the discontents with the prevailing regime. Its call for protection linked the issues of trade performance and employment to those of tax and the empire in a direct challenge to the liberal orthodoxy.[4] Conflict over free trade threw into relief two political economies: a liberal one emphasising limited government, free markets and international commerce as the basis for consumer prosperity; and a conservative version grounded in a state consciously shaping the economy to maximise national production and power through tariff barriers and 'national' economics.

For the new Labour Party neither version was satisfactory. The immediate advantages of the 'cheap loaf', which continued adherence to free trade promised, were obvious, and drove the overwhelming bulk of Labour supporters into the anti-Chamberlain camp.[5] But the liberal emphasis on the benefits of free markets, and the associated reverence for the interests of the consumer as opposed to the producer, cut across beliefs which were well established among Labour supporters. Many nineteenth-century British radicals and socialists defined their politics in opposition to liberal notions about the beneficence of the free market. They emphasised the instability of the market economy (often accompanied by a belief in a forthcoming 'final collapse' of this type of economy). They stressed the interests of the worker in well-paid and secure employment, rather than the consumer's interest in low prices. Perhaps above all, they attacked the selfish, competitive environment which they saw as the inescapable accompaniment to free market, capitalist society. Here notions of the inherent dignity of labour (and the inherent degradation of wage-labour), and the requirements of a 'moral economy' cut sharply across liberal assumptions about the 'invisible hand' guiding selfish actions into a wealth-maximising public good.[6]

In a position of electoral subordination to the Liberal Party, and in the absence of its own 'big idea', Labour before 1914 did not develop an overarching programme of economic reform. Each of its major elements – ethical socialists, who emphasised the moral shortcomings of capitalism, Marxists and Fabians – brought to bear distinct if overlapping perspectives on economic issues.[7] Ethical socialists, notably in the Independent Labour Party (ILP), argued that protectionism was a last desperate attempt to shore up a doomed capitalism from its crisis of overproduction, with low-wage competition leading to the 'immiseration' of British workers. Some Marxists drew on the same analysis, but also recognised the logical problem of hostility to 'the market' while favouring free trade. Fabians most consistently refused to endorse either free trade or protection. Instead they linked trade issues to their more general critique of the failure of British capitalism to sustain minimum wage standards, with the consequence that international competition was based not on comparative efficiency, but on degradation of the workers' conditions.[8]

On another plane, all strands of Labour's economic thinking shared an evolutionist perspective, which assumed that an immensely powerful movement was in progress towards the creation of industrial 'trusts' (monopolies and cartels) which, while reducing costs of production, extracted 'rents' from the rest of society, thereby impoverishing the many for the advantage of the few. This line of argument was most highly developed in Fabian circles, but it plainly embraced Marxist themes about the potential replacement of a capitalist class which no longer served any useful purpose in the capitalist system. It could also be made to fit with the idea that capitalism, by giving such high incomes to capitalists, and such low ones to the mass of workers, led to inadequate demand for goods – the concept of 'underconsumption' developed most thoroughly by the New Liberal theorist, J. A. Hobson.[9] From this perspective capitalist industry was becoming more and more 'efficient' in the sense of producing technical advances, creating economies of scale, and reducing costs, but was 'inefficient' in degrading the standards of the workers so that their health and skills deteriorated. This approach underpinned the key Labour aim of securing a 'national minimum' for all, by which was meant a level of income which would raise the standards of all to those it hoped could be achieved by the best-organised workers through collective bargaining. This national minimum would eliminate poverty, and at the same time improve the 'efficiency' of workers by improving their education and health – higher wages would be paid for by greater productivity, but would make still greater productivity possible.[10]

In 1904, at the first ever conference of Labour MPs and candidates to discuss policy, a number of economic themes were evident: taxation of the 'unearned increment' (the income paid to capitalists who performed no useful role), opposition to tariffs, nationalisation of the railways, the introduction of a national minimum. Nationalisation, while significant, was not the defining core of the proposals. The central thrust of policy was not the transformation of society by seizure of the 'commanding heights', but the regulation of the trusts, and the elimination of maldistribution of income brought about by monopoly control of key industries.[11] In 1908 the party agreed by a narrow majority to write a socialist objective (a commitment to common ownership of the means of production) into its constitution, but at the same time explicitly refused the idea of treating such common ownership as a programme, rather than a broad aim.[12] This flowed from the rejection of detailed programmes as not only largely irrelevant given the electoral situation, in which any idea of Labour taking office looked wholly implausible, but potentially destructive of the unity of the party.[13]

The most prominent principle at work in Labour's economic arguments in the Edwardian years was 'the Right to Work'. This was Labour's main response to concerns with unemployment which, for different reasons, animated all political forces, inside and outside the party. Labour's approach was threefold. First, it called for restrictions on child labour and a reduction of working hours, in the belief that since technological change was reducing the overall demand for labour, there was a need to spread work around. Second, there was a call for relief works as a *palliative*, not fundamental, measure. Third was the campaign for 'the Right to Work or full maintenance' which was intended to expose the inability of capitalism to provide employment for all, and provide a link to demands for welfare provision for those who lacked work. This campaign was consistent with the general thrust of Labour thinking towards demanding minimum standards for all, an approach which was seen, for example, in the support for 'Trade Boards' which set minimum wages in some 'sweated' industries.[14]

It is very important to stress the difference between this slogan of the 'Right to Work' and later discussions of full employment. The latter was linked to a belief that national governments had the means to deliver jobs for all, but commonly lacked the will to do so. Before 1914 almost no one believed governments had this capacity, and certainly in Britain the openness of the economy to international influences and the small scale of central government meant that any notion of managing the national economy to maximise employment was almost unthinkable. Criticisms of Labour's failure to develop a comprehensive programme of national economic management in this period are rather anachronistic; many things had to change before such notions became plausible. And it is important to note that while Labour was calling for greater state action in this period, especially on unemployment, many Labour figures were worried that extended state action would simultaneously involve state coercion and undermine independent collective action by bodies such as trade unions and friendly societies, hence the opposition to both labour exchanges and national insurance in this period.[15] While some Fabians and others in the party were enthusiasts for an active state, as is evident most obviously in the pressure for minimum wages and standards, many on the left feared what such an interventionist state might do.

War and its aftermath

The First World War not only greatly enhanced Labour's electoral standing, but also emphasised the need to develop a detailed policy programme, not least on the economy. While drawing on much pre-war writing, Labour's first official, detailed programme was *Labour and the New Social Order*, largely written by Sidney Webb, and adopted by the 1918 conference. Labour's New Social Order would be built on four pillars: universal enforcement of the national minimum; democratic control of industry; a revolution in national finance; and surplus wealth for the common good. The national minimum proposal was a direct development of pre-war ideas. Similarly, the sections on national finance and surplus wealth basically adapted pre-war themes to post-war circumstances, demanding that the rich pay for the war, and that in future state revenue be increased by a programme of municipalisation and nationalisation.[16]

In the long run the most important feature of the document was the emphasis given to the gradual elimination of private ownership. Part of the case for this echoed the pre-war theme of using public ownership to redistribute income, with private ownership pilloried as 'a perpetual private mortgage upon the annual product of the nation'. Such views continued to be crucial to important figures like Philip Snowden and Ramsay MacDonald, and the Fabian authorship of *Labour and the New Social Order* should not be allowed to obscure the continuing importance in party thinking of the ethical socialist, ILP tradition. Perhaps the most distinctively Fabian note was struck when the document asserted that:

the Labour Party refuses absolutely to believe that the British people will permanently tolerate any reconstruction or perpetuation of the disorganisa-tion, waste and inefficiency involved in the abandonment of British industry to a jostling around of separate private employers . . .What the Labour Party looks to is a genuinely scientific re-organisation of the nation's industry no longer deflected by individual profiteering, on the basis of Common Ownership of the Means of Production.[17]

In underpinning the case for nationalisation in this way, Webb was reflecting the common opinion across the political spectrum that the Great War had exposed major shortcomings in British industry, and from this time on Labour's arguments have always included assertions about the productive weaknesses of the economy, and the need for Labour's policies to address these weaknesses.

This enhanced enthusiasm for nationalisation was famously embod-ied in Clause Four of the new party constitution, which read as follows:

to secure for the workers by hand or by brain the full fruits of their industry and the most equitable distribution thereof that may be possible on the basis of the common ownership of the means of production, distribution and exchange, and the best obtainable system of popular administration and control of each industry or service.

Two features of this wording were particularly important. First, the ambiguity about the limits to common ownership: the clause could be said to suggest that this should extend to the whole economy, but this was not explicitly stated. Second, the form of this common ownership was not specified, so that the enormous ambition of the clause was not matched by any clear notion of the institutional forms this could involve. Nationalisation as constructed by the Attlee government thirty years later was not set down in Labour's constitution.[18]

While Clause Four talked of 'popular administration and control' it did not pronounce on a key issue for Labour – how far industries in common ownership were to be run by the workers within them. There was a long tradition of co-operatives in Britain, though these flourished much more in distribution than production. Many socialists in the nineteenth century saw co-ops as the prototypes for a future socialist economy, but such ideas came under considerable attack from the 1890s. 'Associations of producers' were seen as inefficient – modern industry required 'the subordination of the individual worker to masses of capital directed by expert intelligence' – and likely to pursue their own interests. They would end up exploiting the consumer.[19]

Despite such frequently reiterated objections, the idea of 'workers' control' gained much new ground in the years from just before to just after the First World War. In particular, guild socialism, with its project of a society built on the re-invention of medieval guilds as the basis for industrial democracy, gained many adherents (most importantly, G. D. H. Cole), in part because of the perceived failings of parliamentary Labour politics. Even the Webbs showed some signs of retreat on this issue, though when the economy collapsed after 1920 it took the nascent guilds with it, and proponents of 'workers' control' were on the defensive, until decisively defeated in discussions about the form of future nationalisation at the Labour Party conferences in the early 1930s.[20]

Whatever its precise form, nationalisation was to be at the core of Labour's economic programme from 1918 until the 1940s, and crucial to its rhetoric until the 1990s. Its importance rested on the diversity of aims that public ownership was believed to achieve; at different times different aims gained prominence, though the picture was always one of considerable diversity and disagreement. Before 1914 the policy was given a primarily redistributive function. From 1918, it was seen as a means to concentrate and rationalise production, in order to enhance efficiency. From the 1930s, it was integral to the idea of economic planning, a prime means of securing government power over the whole economy. Labour shared each of these perspectives with others. Many liberals favoured the nationalisation of monopolies like the railways. Many non-socialists came to see public ownership as a way of promoting industrial efficiency. Enthusiasm for planning underpinned by public ownership was popular in several circles during the 1930s.[21] Yet this is not the whole story; nationalisation *did* have special status for Labour. Above and beyond the kind of specific aims listed above, it was the belief of most people in the party that public ownership would be the defining characteristic of the future socialist society, because it would simultaneously deprive the capitalists of their power and make possible the end of production guided by the search for profits. Profits, it should be emphasised, were not seen as simply an 'economic' category, but as *morally* indefensible, as the fruits of illegitimate ownership rights enjoyed by a parasitic class. In this sense public ownership was not a technical means to socialism, it was intrinsic to socialism; it would bring both a rational and a moral order to society. It thus achieved an ideological and moral status above and beyond whatever pragmatic justifications could be advanced for it.[22]

If public ownership was ensconced at the heart of Labour's economic ideology from 1918, its hostility to markets was to be re-affirmed only after considerable debate in the 1920s. This outcome was linked to a growing disillusion with the operation of markets across the political spectrum, especially because of the failure to deal with the problems of the staple export industries.[23] Public ownership and hostility to markets inherited from the previous period underpinned much of the more detailed policy formulation of the 1930s. But in the immediate circumstances of the 1920s, what mattered most to Labour was unemployment. After a brief post-war boom, a slump brought mass unemployment, and over one million workers remained out of work through the later 1920s. This was an unprecedented and wholly unexpected circumstance which Labour (like other political parties) had great difficulty grappling with. It cut across the evolutionist perspectives of key Labour theorists like Philip Snowden, who had anticipated that as capitalism evolved it would without difficulty generate the revenues from which social reform could be financed. But in the 1920s British capitalism proved both inefficient and unstable, and it was therefore logical to restrict reforms until prosperity returned. The only significant policy put forward to improve efficiency in this period was 'rationalisation'. This was a vague term, which revolved around the belief that by amalgamating firms and concentrating production in larger units, American-style mass production could be achieved. Unfortunately, such a policy clearly implied higher unemployment in the short run, and once the slump began in 1929, previous enthusiasm for this panacea, especially on the part of trade unions, quickly waned.[24]

Caution over policy until the return of prosperity is an important key
to the much-lamented economic orthodoxy of Snowden and others in
the Labour leadership in the 1920s. It led to policies very similar to
those of the Liberals and Conservatives, which aimed, above all, at
restoring pre-war 'normalcy' by stabilising the international economy,
re-establishing the gold standard, and seeking to secure domestic and
international investor confidence in British governments. The most
painful outcome from a Labour point of view was an adherence to a
return to gold at the pre-war parity, which meant an overvalued
exchange rate and the loss of export markets, and a fanatical commitment to the fiscal orthodoxy of low and above all balanced budgets.
Snowden saw this objective in a socialist light: for him, government bor-
rowing and government debt meant transfers from the poor taxpayer to
the rich bondholder.[25] In this respect Snowden's stance was clearly
different in motive from that of Conservatives, who advocated budgetary balance but had no interest in egalitarian tax systems. Nevertheless,
it was hardly either imaginative or adventurous. Yet there were few real
alternatives. For example, proto-Keynesian solutions to Britain's economic problems, most notably those of the Liberals in *We Can Conquer
Unemployment* (1928), did not answer the central British dilemma of
trying to restore the staple export industries by policies which could
only affect the home economy. Any policy aiming to make a serious dent
in the unemployment figures would have had to have done something to
increase demand for exports, but the difficulty was that such demand
was beyond the reach of any direct policy lever wielded by the government.[26] Likewise, though innovative reformist programmes were put
forward by sections of the ILP, they remained underdeveloped as economic strategies, and politically marginal. The party leadership kept a
firm hand on policy formation, and successfully stigmatised their critics
as 'disloyal'.[27]

In Labour's brief period of office in 1924 only two things of note for
economic policy occurred. First, Snowden repealed the McKenna tariff
duties of 1915, thereby emphasising his profound commitment to free
trade. Second, Labour provided some of the spadework for the eventual
nationalisation of electricity distribution under the Central Electricity
Board. Here was a classic case where private enterprise was regarded by
all political parties as unable to achieve a necessary 'rationalisation', and
where therefore a technical, non-political case for public ownership
could have wide appeal.[28]

Much more dramatic, of course, were events under the second
Labour government of 1929–31. This administration was beset by two

powerful conflicting pressures. On the one hand, to sustain the living standards of its working-class constituency in the face of the slump, it had to bail out the unemployment insurance fund from the general national budget. On the other hand, to respond to the downward movement of the pound, it had to borrow from financial bodies which would only lend if budgetary balance was restored by cutting unemployment benefit. There was no easy way out of this position, and eventually MacDonald and Snowden determined that their responsibilities to sustain Labour as a responsible governing party outweighed the need to support the unemployed.[29]

This episode was overlaid with enormous bitterness because for many in the party it could only be understood as a betrayal of all that Labour stood for, whereas MacDonald and Snowden saw the split as evidence of Labour's failure to put reason above sentimental attachment to trade-union self-interest. But the failings of the 1929–31 government went beyond the personal shortcomings of a few individuals. The MacDonald/Snowden strategy of electoral advance through the gaining of respectability was predicated on combining a strong rhetorical commitment to a future inevitable socialism with extremely cautious immediate reform. This strategy hit the rocks of an economic storm which was not 'the final crisis' of capitalism but a combination of worldwide recession and peculiar British problems with the staple export industries. To deal with this successfully required a sharp departure towards national economic management for which Labour was intellectually and even emotionally ill prepared. It was to take the shock of 1931 to open the way to combining the rhetoric of socialism with detailed policy programmes.

The year 1929 was a disastrous time for Labour to come to power, especially as a minority government, and criticism of its performance in office must be tempered by recognition of the extraordinary severity of the economic circumstances it faced. No government anywhere in the world found a ready answer to the slump.

Forward from 1931

For Labour, 1931 represented an ideological as well as an electoral disaster; the party's performance in office seemed to belie its claim that its socialist ideals could provide the key to resolving Britain's economic problems. But subsequently, for the first time, Labour slowly developed detailed economic policy proposals which laid the basis for much that was to be done after 1945. In developing this programme, Labour drew in part on its existing ideas, but was influenced by major changes in the context in which it operated, both institutional and intellectual.

The crisis of 1931 marked a major break in the institutional arrangements of the British economy. Two pillars of the 'unmanaged economy', free trade and the gold standard, disappeared, the first as a deliberate act of policy, the second because of external pressure. Willy-nilly these changes opened the way to much more active economic management by the 'National' and Conservative governments of the 1930s. The world of *laissez-faire* was left well behind. Not only did governments manage foreign trade and the exchange rate, but also, if only indirectly, they intervened in industry to try to rationalise and modernise its structures.[30] Crucially for Labour, the 1930s saw a loss of faith in market mechanisms across the political spectrum, and an enthusiasm for 'planning' which was remarkably widespread, if vague in precise content. This enthusiasm owed something to the Soviet example, which was believed even by many who were vehemently anti-communist to show what economic planning could achieve. It also owed a great deal to the perception that 'the market' had failed to resolve the problems of Britain's staple export industries, or the consequent unemployment.[31]

Intellectually, the figure of Keynes loomed large in the economic policy discussions of the 1930s. Labour intellectuals responded to his ideas, not least because of his emphasis on unemployment as the key issue, but Keynesianism was only one component in the wide-ranging debates on economic policy on the left in this period.[32] Keynes added to the widespread scepticism on the left about the automatic stability of a capitalist economy, and in this way contributed to Labour's proposals for monetary and fiscal measures. On the other hand, Keynes remained convinced that if governments created full employment by appropriate macro-economic policies, the market provided the best way of allocating resources, and, while he was not opposed to public ownership of natural monopolies and basic industries, he followed the traditional liberal belief that private property was essential for freedom. These latter views stood in contrast to those in *For Socialism and Peace*, Labour's key policy pronouncement published in 1934, in which the central theme was the need for 'a policy of full and rapid Socialist economic planning under central direction'.[33] A similar focus may be found in the future Labour Chancellor Hugh Dalton's *Practical Socialism for Britain* of 1935. Other major Labour figures moved closer to Keynes's position, such as Douglas Jay in *The Socialist Case* (1937), but this was considered highly 'revisionist', and the core of Labour's ideas was undoubtedly built on a combination of public ownership (including the financial system) and planning, not Keynesianism.[34]

Another new development was that for the first time Labour began attracting a significant number of academics and intellectuals to its ranks, so that policy discussion became much more sophisticated.[35] This was part of the party's general success in attracting more middle-class support, but it was notably weak in one crucial area. As G. D. H. Cole lamented: 'We have not a few doctors, scientists – even People in the "City"; and of course we have a number of leading Trade Unionists and politicians. But we are, to put the matter plainly, very short indeed of high-up practical businessmen who are engaged in productive industry.'[36] This was to remain an issue until at least the 1990s.

By the end of the 1930s Labour, like the other parties, was clearly developing strategies for national economic management. This outlook was also evident in Labour's approach to public ownership, which in the 1930s took on a more 'technocratic' flavour, as it was increasingly seen as a building block of a planned economy, and a route to greater efficiency, rather than as a means to enhance workers' control. At Labour Party conferences in the early 1930s the role of workers in Labour's planned public corporations was passionately debated, with an eventually resounding victory for those who proposed the 'Morrisonian' pattern, modelled on the London Passenger Transport Board initiated by the 1929–31 Labour government. In this guise, the public corporation was to be run by experts, with no representation of interests, thus excluding any notion of 'workers' control'. However, the politically neutral, 'technocratic' aspect of Labour's policies was not totally dominant. Even an arch 'technocrat' like Morrison continued to see public ownership as a basis for transforming motives and relationships at work, not just as a way of producing more.[37]

Mission accomplished? The Attlee government, 1945–1951

Labour's commitment to planning was reinforced by the experience of the Second World War. The incoming government of 1945 believed that the extensive system of controls over almost all aspects of economic activity brought in after 1940 demonstrated the superiority of a planned economy, and that its key task was to use the same methods to reconstruct the economy on a peacetime basis. From this perspective the nationalisation of 'the commanding heights', such as coal, railways, gas and electricity (but notably not manufacturing industry), was about putting in place the infrastructure of a planned economy. Other motives – greater efficiency, improving workers' conditions, reducing the power

of private capitalists – were also in play in the extension of public ownership, and the nationalisation of coal and the railways especially had
been important in Labour politics since before 1914, but it was the planning aspect which predominated.[38] This was very much the agenda of
the 1930s, though there was one key difference, in that nationalisation of
the financial system never became a serious possibility. Right up to the
1945 election, control of the financial system by public ownership and
the creation of a National Investment Board were regarded as integral to
Labour's plans, both for macro-economic stabilisation and the allocation
of investment funds. In the event, beyond the largely token nationalisation of the Bank of England, nothing happened. Inertia stemmed from a
belief that the other nationalisations and controls would give enough
governmental leverage over economic activity, and from opposition to
any board which would derogate from the 'sovereignty' of Parliament.[39]

Once in office, Labour gradually retreated from this idea of the
planned economy. The nationalisations brought about substantial
improvements in some of the industries affected, but did not provide the
basis for overall national planning, in part because they were not concentrated in the most dynamic sectors of the economy (like engineering),
and in part because ministers had only relatively limited control over the
autonomous boards which ran the new corporations. Morrison lamented
in 1950: 'In some respects . . . the Boards have not fulfilled our hopes,
and there is a good deal of disillusionment even among the supporters of
the principle of socialisation.'[40] The planning ideal was also eroded by
the growing public distaste for the rationing and controls which were its
public face.[41] Introduced in wartime to restrict consumption in the cause
of the war effort, 'austerity' rapidly became irksome when victory had
been gained. The government gradually reduced controls, but
insufficiently to prevent a loss of support amongst some sectors of the
population, notably middle-class women, who particularly disliked the
daily queuing and skimping that widespread rationing produced.[42]

Yet austerity was inescapable if Labour was to pursue its objectives.
These included a maximisation of output in order rapidly to expand
exports, together with import restrictions, as the means to deal with the
disastrous balance-of-payments position inherited from the war.
Alongside this immediate necessity was a desire to improve the
efficiency of British industry, in recognition that 'the audit of war' had
revealed serious deficiencies in many sectors. This attempt at 'modernisation' led to a wide range of initiatives, from the creation of
Development Councils to rationalise fragmented consumer industries,
and the founding of the British Institute of Management, through to the

encouragement of Joint Production Committees aimed at involving workers in production decisions. Also of considerable note was the creation of the Anglo-American Council on Productivity, a reflection of immediate political pressures, but also symbolic of Labour's longstanding if ambivalent interest in American industrial methods.[43]

Some modernisation was achieved, and productivity grew rapidly from the late 1940s.[44] Nevertheless, the various constituent policies faced obstacles. There was an unavoidable tension between maximising current output and investing in modernised capacity for the future.[45] Politically, the problem for the government was that much of the desired modernisation was in the private sector, but business as a whole showed marked reluctance to co-operate with ideas they saw as introducing government (and union) 'interference' into their domain. The situation was made more difficult because, as Harold Wilson noted, the whole question of the private sector was 'a vacuum in socialist thought'.[46]

Tensions also arose over whether resources for investment should be allocated to industry or to the welfare state. This problem did not apply to the new systems for income maintenance (national insurance and national assistance) because these simply transferred money from taxpayers to recipients. But in areas such as schools, hospitals and housing there were choices to be made. Almost always the choice went in favour of industry. School-building only just kept up with expanding pupil numbers, and few of the ambitious plans of the 1944 Education Act, endorsed by Labour, and which involved the use of physical resources such as steel and timber, were realised. A similar story is true of the health services, where none of the envisaged new district general hospitals were begun, and even the low-cost health centres remained very few in number. An ambitious house-building programme started in 1945, but this was reined back sharply from 1947 as the resource constraints became apparent.[47]

In sum, the Attlee government largely fulfilled its promises. Perhaps the most important of these was full employment, where the period saw, instead of the expected unemployment, a shortage of labour, and desperate attempts by the government to increase the supply of workers. Yet this most dramatic reversal of 1930s' economic fortunes probably owed little *directly* to government action, since it stemmed mainly from worldwide demand for exports and a boom in private investment. It was also facilitated by the Bretton Woods agreement of 1944, which ushered in almost thirty years of exchange rate and general financial stability in the world economy, aided by the establishment of the International Monetary Fund, which facilitated international economic co-operation and provided funds to ease countries through balance-of-payments difficulties. Nevertheless, the priority accorded to employment in Labour's rhetoric, and its clear unwillingness to allow a repeat of the post-1918 cycle of boom and slump, affected expectations and helped make full employment a reality. The other key promises were nationalisation of the 'commanding heights' and the creation of a 'national minimum' of income maintenance, education and healthcare. The government also increased investment, expanded output, righted the balance of payments and improved productivity. It reconciled these aims by a severe dose of austerity, holding down both private and collective consumption. It did not, however, create the 'planned economy' envisaged in the 1930s or in the war years. The boundaries of the state had expanded by nationalisation, increased public spending, and widespread regulation of the private sector. But 80 per cent of the economy remained in private hands, and market relationships were restored, albeit slowly, over much of the economy. The combination of full employment and expanded welfare enormously enhanced economic security and reduced poverty (though it was not eradicated), and this above all else vindicated Labour's policy measures. Yet the legacy of Attlee was clearly not a 'planned, socialist economy', and ideologically this 'failure' was a problem to be wrestled with over much of the next fifty years.

Where to now? Revisionism, affluence and a new agenda, 1951–1964

Mass unemployment was the key reason for the political importance of economic management from the 1930s. By the mid-1950s this problem seemed to have gone forever, and increasingly governments across the Western world placed growth rather than employment at the centre of the economic agenda, as they sought to provide their electorates with higher standards of living. The Conservatives after 1951 were slow to accept this notion, but by the late 1950s the political appeal of affluence led the Conservative leadership to put promises about the standard of living centre-stage. In part this was a response to pressure from the Labour Party, which seized on the deflationary period after the 1955 general election to denounce Conservative economic policy. Gradually Labour built up a strategy centred on such criticism, drawing on the extensive statistics and analyses which emerged in this period showing Britain at the bottom of the 'league table' of industrial countries in economic performance. From the Labour leadership's point of view this new emphasis on growth promised at least to paper over the cracks in the party between the right, who wanted to consolidate rather than expand public ownership, and in some cases, such as Crosland dethrone the notion from its place in Labour's agenda; and the left who regarded the 1945–51 period as simply a first instalment on the road to a fully publicly owned economy. The 1950s was a period of confusion and division in Labour ranks, and while some serious rethinking was done, particularly on how to run the nationalised sector, much of the debate was high on rhetoric and low on policy proposals.[48]

But the new strategy faced significant difficulties. Criticism of Conservative failings in delivering 'affluence' fitted uneasily into Labour's traditional focus on the conditions of production, rather than consumption, as central to 'the good life'. Some references had been made to asserting the consumer's interest in the 1940s, and these gained ground in the 1950s, but there were still a large number of Labour people who regarded affluence as a snare and a delusion.[49]

However, the evident difficulties of the Conservatives in responding to allegations that they had presided over Britain's economic 'decline', and the adept clothing of the case for growth in socialist rhetoric, especially by Harold Wilson, brought a major shift in opinion. By the time the key policy document *Signposts for the Sixties* was published in 1961, the presentation of Labour as the party of modernisation was clear, and this was to be the basis of Labour's approach to the election of 1964, with Wilson characteristically calling for a 'socialist inspired scientific and technological revolution releasing energy on an enormous scale . . . for enriching mankind beyond our wildest dreams'. For a while this new approach seemed to sweep all before it, and licensed some important changes in Labour's policies. One very important such case was that of the Common Market (as the EU was then known). In 1962 the leader of the party, Hugh Gaitskell, had come out emotionally against Britain's membership. But under Wilson (leader from 1963) the idea of 'modernisation' was used to argue (with many equivocations) for entry, on the grounds that it would provide a large market for British goods, and a competitive stimulus for producers.[50]

Despite its rhetorical excesses, Labour's talk of modernisation and 'the white heat of technology' was solidly grounded. On the one hand, the need for modernisation had been a key concern in Whitehall since at least the late 1950s, and in many areas Labour's proposals drew heavily on policies discussed, though not implemented, under the Conservatives.[51] Second, as already suggested, the Attlee government had pursued an extensive programme of modernisation, and in part Wilson's strategy was just a revival of those concerns and approaches.

Jim Tomlinson

This continuity fitted with the technocratic, rationalist mode of understanding common amongst Labour's intelligentsia through much of the
post-war period.[52]

Modernisation and its difficulties, 1964–1970

In office, aspects of this inherited modernisation agenda were pursued
with considerable zeal. Reforms to the labour market such as redundancy payments and earnings-related unemployment benefit were introduced to encourage labour mobility, a shift of resources into research
and development in the civilian sector was pushed ahead, and various
productivity initiatives pursued.

What was distinctive under Labour was the linking of this reform
activity to the National Plan, produced as the centrepiece of 'modernisation' in 1965. But 'planning' proved to be little more than tripartite
(government/employer/union) consultation, which had existed in some
form since the war, though in re-invigorated form under the National
Economic Development Council from 1962. Similarly, the creation of
the new Department of Economic Affairs (DEA) in 'creative tension'
with the Treasury was a high-profile policy with rather less substance
behind it. The aim had been to create a powerful body to emphasise the
long-term and productive aspects of the economy, as a counterweight to
what was seen as the short-term and financial concerns of the Treasury.
But the idea that economic policy could be compartmentalised in this
way proved an illusion. The balance-of-payments position, a consequence of the Conservatives' pre-election boom, quickly proved so
serious as to require a strong dose of deflation. When this was implemented in the 'July measures' of 1966, the DEA, and with it the
National Plan, were effectively dead.

However, the demise of the plan did not mean that 'modernisation'
was at an end. Much serious and interesting modernisation work went
on under the aegis of the Ministry of Technology and the Ministry of
Labour (later the Department of Employment and Productivity). Major
reforms of technology policy, of industrial structure, and of the labour
market were carried through.[53]

But the government's drive for modernisation was partly frustrated
by the determined and sustained attempt to prevent the devaluation of
the pound (which was eventually forced in 1967). Labour was responding here to political pressure, including American desires to maintain the
integrity of the Bretton Woods system, and a concern to avoid being
seen as the 'party of devaluation'.[54] This commitment led to deflationary
policies which had previously been denounced. Yet though this deflation

62

did not aid the modernisation programme, nor did it bring it to a close. It continued, not without success, in the late 1960s. The unsuccessful search for policies to avoid the 'devil' of devaluation, and the 'deep blue sea' of deflation, led to a greatly increased weight being given to incomes policy, a measure that promised to combine expansion with low inflation. But this policy hit at the heart of the commitment (in both union and party circles) to the idea of free collective bargaining. Huge political divisions eventually led to the defeat of Wilson and his allies over the proposals for legal restraints on trade unions, as outlined in the ill-named White Paper *In Place of Strife* (1969). The government was unable to achieve the success in this area attained in the Attlee period, when government/union relations had worked well, with union leaderships trading restraint on wage bargaining, and support for the government's productivity agenda, against legislation on welfare and reform of the labour market. However, by the 1960s, both the problem of inflation and the alleged impact of union restrictive practices on growth led to a much more difficult climate. Initially an agreement along the lines of the 1940s' incomes policy appeared viable, but as the government pursued deflation, relationships deteriorated, especially when a compulsory incomes policy was introduced. The battle over *In Place of Strife* soured party/union relations, with long-term consequences. Ideologically, the battle pointed to the difficulty within Labour thinking of combining a 'planned economy' with support for free collective wage bargaining. This combination made it difficult for a Labour government to gain support for any type of incomes policy, because critics could contend that until a 'fully planned' economy was introduced, workers should be allowed to bargain freely with their employers.[55]

The party, the government and the end of the 'golden age'

Recoiling from the perceived failures of the 1964–70 government, and especially the breakdown of the relationship with the trade unions, the Labour Party's economic policy stance moved sharply leftwards in the early 1970s.[56] A key lesson drawn from this alleged 'failure' was that the private sector of the economy was no longer responsive to persuasion and incentives offered by government, and that a major extension of public ownership into the private manufacturing sector was required if a reforming government was to deliver its economic policy objectives. The idea that future public ownership should move away from the monopoly, public corporation form pursued under Attlee had been around in Labour circles since the end of the 1940s.[57] It had originated with

Jim Tomlinson

Douglas Jay on the right of the party, but in the 1960s and 1970s was taken up by the left, partly drawing on the Italian IRI (Institute for Industrial Reconstruction) example of how competitive publicly owned companies could spearhead industrial modernisation.[58] In this way the left combined a traditional attachment to public ownership with a recognition that coal, railways and utilities were no longer (if they had ever been) the 'commanding heights' of the economy, and that any project of modernisation would have to address the role of major manufacturing companies. This approach was made concrete in the proposal for a National Enterprise Board (NEB), a public body which would acquire share holdings in a range of major manufacturing companies and stimulate others in those sectors to improve their performance. The NEB proposal was driven from within the left of the national party, and gained widespread grass-roots support. But the parliamentary leadership, while willing to accept the broad idea of using public ownership to increase investment and galvanise manufacturing, was resistant to the quasi-Marxist form the proposal often took.[59] In Stuart Holland's key text, *The Socialist Challenge*, for example, the problem of the 'meso-economic' multinational company was posed very much in terms of their power to evade government control, and the NEB response, in this framework, was inherently coercive.[60] Most of the leadership of the parliamentary party, however, believed that *co-operation* with the private sector was the only viable strategy. The outcome of this struggle was the creation of an NEB after 1974, which far from spearheading an assault on the citadels of profitable corporate power, acted largely as a home for the 'lame ducks' of British industry, though it did do some useful, less-noticed work in encouraging some high-tech sectors, such as silicon chip manufacturing.[61]

The other key thrust of Labour's policy leading up to the 1974 government was the 'Social Contract'. This was the rather portentous term given to the agreement between the party and the TUC whereby in return for policies congenial to the unions, such as repeal of the Conservatives' Industrial Relations Act, a commitment to full employment and expanding welfare provision, the TUC would support policies of wage restraint. However, the agreement did not amount to acceptance of a statutory incomes policy, which had become anathema to the unions and many in the party after the experiences of the late 1960s. While this agreement was desirable for patching up the quarrels of the previous period of Labour government, it had to be pursued in an economic situation which had deteriorated beyond all expectations by the time Labour came to power.[62]

The golden age of Western capitalism began to recede in the late 1960s in the face of accelerating inflation, rising unemployment and increasing instability in the international economy. In the early 1970s inflation accelerated further, the Bretton Woods system of international financial institutions fell apart, and the quadrupling of oil prices forced by the Organisation of Petroleum Exporting Countries in 1973/4 led to an international economic crisis. As a result, output stagnated or fell, inflation and budget deficits increased, unemployment ratcheted upwards, and a period of 'stagflation', combining high inflation with high unemployment, began. While such trends were common to most industrial countries, Britain did worse than many, especially on inflation. This crisis was accompanied in the last days of the Heath government (1970–74) by major industrial unrest in coal-mining, so that Labour came to power in 1974 faced with an immediate problem of resolving this industrial dispute, but with a much more profound problem of dealing with the new phenomenon of stagflation.

Initially, Labour hoped to deal with the situation by an agreement with other Western European governments that they should not respond to the crisis by deflation, which would cut demand for oil but at the expense of higher unemployment. But these hopes soon foundered on fears of inflation. Price rises continued to accelerate to a peak of 25 per cent in 1974–5. At this stage the trade unions and their members drew back from the abyss of threatened hyper-inflation and economic collapse. The government was able to get agreement to a wage policy which, over the next three years, was to facilitate a fall in inflation to under 10 per cent, while stabilising unemployment, albeit at a level of over one million. The Labour government was also beset by fiscal problems. Public expenditure was on a sharp upwards momentum from the early 1970s, and stagflation greatly widened the fiscal deficit. This deficit could be interpreted as a useful way of injecting demand into the economy – the 'fiscal stabiliser' of Keynesian analysis, and therefore a welcome feature of the situation. But such an approach was vehemently opposed by the financial markets, which regarded the mounting deficit as a sign of financial irresponsibility, and as portending accelerating inflation. There was a panic in financial circles which spread through much of the political class; the 'end of civilisation' was allegedly at hand, with the government as the culprit, despite the existence of similar problems elsewhere, and the clear evidence that relevant palliatives were being introduced. Given its inheritance of 1974, both of domestic inflationary pressures and external shocks, it can be argued that the government's performance was as good as could reasonably be expected.[63]

But whatever the final verdict, the period imposed massive strains on Labour's approach to the economy.

As early as the spring of 1975 Denis Healey was repudiating the 'Keynesian' approach to the crisis, which would have required bigger public deficits to combat unemployment, and giving most attention to defeating inflation. Public expenditure was reduced in successive rounds from 1975 onwards, and was to fall by an unprecedented 6.7 per cent in 1976/7 (a far larger fall than in any of Margaret Thatcher's 'rolling back the state' years). However, despite the clear improvement in the underlying performance of the economy (rising output, falling inflation) evident from late 1975, the panic in financial markets continued. The consequent fall in the value of the pound led to a situation in the summer of 1976 which had echoes of 1931: the government came under pressure from financial markets to cut expenditure against the threat of further falls in the exchange rate. As in 1931 this led to agonised cabinet discussions over the scale of public spending cuts, though ironically those already in the pipeline were larger than those demanded by the International Monetary Fund, which offered a loan to the government conditional on such cuts.[64]

This was not just a political and economic crisis, but also an ideological one. The 'Keynesian consensus' of the golden age, which suggested that governments both should and could maintain full employment without unacceptable fiscal or inflationary problems, broke down. While Keynesianism had never been fully accepted in the Labour Party, it provided the *de facto* basis on which the parliamentary leadership conducted policy. But in the mid-1970s' crisis this approach had to be publicly repudiated to appease financial opinion. Thus, the Prime Minister, Jim Callaghan, told the Labour Party conference of September 1976: 'We used to think that you could spend your way out of recession . . . I tell you now in all candour that that option no longer exists and in so far as it ever did exist, it only worked . . . by injecting a bigger dose of inflation in the economy.'

Yet the government's stance was quite clearly more complex than such avowals suggested. For while public spending was cut sharply in the 1975–7 period, it expanded again once the crisis was over, as the government tried to sustain employment levels. Thus, though public rhetoric moved towards a monetarist focus on the money supply as the key factor in determining the level of inflation, the central instrument actually used by the Labour government to contain inflation was the social contract, a very non-monetarist concept, because of the implication that wage bargaining could affect inflation rates.[65]

In the end, however, it was the trade-union issue which finally led to Labour's demise. The 1979 'winter of discontent' was the consequence of an incomes policy which bore disproportionately on low-paid workers in the public sector, where the government's attempt to enforce a 5 per cent norm when inflation was several points higher was too much for unions and workers who had, at least partially, accepted previous norms as the way out of a crisis, but had never accepted the legitimacy of a permanent pay policy. The discontent of 1978/9 had a much less significant impact on the economy than subsequent accounts would suggest. The number of days lost in strikes, and numbers of workers involved were quite small, but the electoral damage was huge, as the Conservatives were able to present the period as a clear demonstration of union excesses, and of the need for radical union reform. Yet, in truth, the problem was over-reliance of the government on co-operation with trade unions whose main *raison d'être* was collective bargaining, and who were ideologically opposed to national wage norms. Eventually union leaders had to respond to grass-roots pressure when the economy was clearly on the mend, but the benefits were not showing up in wage packets.[66]

For many on the left of the Labour Party the events of the 1970s seemed to illustrate their belief that governments were now too weak to deliver their programmes without a massive extension of public ownership, and enforcement of other controls over economic life. Resistance on the right to such notions was weakened by the evident failure of both 'Keynesian' policies and social-contract-style reliance on agreement with trade unions. This was the genesis of the Alternative Economic Strategy (AES), which dominated Labour Party discussion of the economy in the early 1980s. The AES began from an emphasis on the limits on national economic management brought about by the rapid growth of international trade, the mushrooming of international capital flows, and the role of multinational companies. These together were seen as weakening the ability of any national government to pursue its own objectives, especially where these gave priority to increased public spending and full employment – priorities likely to be rejected by those who controlled many of these international flows. The AES proposed to deal with this problem by 're-nationalising' the economy, by imposing trade controls, and stiffening regulation of capital flows and the operations of multinational companies. It also involved an extension of public ownership broadly on the same track as the NEB proposals of the early 1970s. The aim of the AES was not only to restore full employment without unacceptable trade deficits, but also to revive British manufacturing industry, which was seen as suffering from chronic underinvestment.[67]

The most contentious aspect of the AES was its protectionism. While its more sophisticated proponents could argue that, by allowing the economy to grow faster, but with a lower propensity to import, controls were compatible with an *increase* in total imports, to many protectionism represented a reversion to the bad old days of the closed economies of the 1930s. While post-war Labour had never made support for free trade a central plank of its manifestos, *de facto* it had supported trade liberalisation. This partly reflected the desire to stay in step with America's ambitions for the world economy, but it also followed from the recognition that expanding export markets yielded benefits, and that British consumers were increasingly fond of foreign goods. Thus, opponents could represent the AES as a suggestion for an Eastern-European-style 'siege economy', with connotations of heavy state regulation and absence of consumer choice. However, though the AES gained considerable popular support in the 1980s, in the end it was swamped by other issues in the disastrous 1983 general election campaign.[68]

The later 1980s, and indeed the whole period down to the election of 1997, were years in which the logic of the AES's rejection slowly worked its way through the Labour Party. If national economic management had been rendered impossible by changes in the international environment, what was left of traditional Labour ideas of using government powers to regulate and manage the economy? There was no ready answer, and the consequences of the perceived weakening of government could in fact lead to a variety of conclusions. One possibility was to look to other layers of government in the hope that these might prove more effective: for example, the European Community, or local, metropolitan and regional authorities.

In the 1970s Labour's radicals had overwhelmingly been against the European Community, on the basis that it was grounded in the free market precepts of the Treaty of Rome (1957), which would allegedly prevent a British Labour government pursuing its interventionist policies. This was always a paradoxical view, given the left's enthusiasm for French indicative planning in the 1960s and for Italian public enterprise in the 1970s. Both policies suggested that EC governments were less constrained by the Treaty of Rome than a literal reading of its provisions implied. In the 1980s, the evident weakness of Labour in domestic politics, and the difficulties of national economic management shown again by the failure of the Mitterrand experiment in France led to a widespread positive re-evaluation of the EC, expressed most optimistically in proposals for a 'European-wide reflation', initially an idea from the unorthodox left of the party.[69] But this was always a political chimera, given the commitment of most European governments to tough anti-inflationary policy. Nevertheless, the hold of anti-Europeanism on large parts of the Labour Party weakened decisively in the 1980s, even if the perception of what 'Europe' might offer had a substantial component of wishful thinking.

Less important practically, but ideologically significant, were the local economic strategies which enjoyed a fleeting popularity on the left in the 1980s. These drew on the relative strength of Labour in local government in the Thatcher years, and upon long-existing, but only patchily employed, local powers to raise money for economic purposes. Under left-wing leadership in this decade, a number of Labour authorities, most famously in London, created Enterprise Boards to try to stimulate local investment and employment. These were interesting for bringing together a number of themes in Labour's attitude to economic activity. On the one hand, there was an emphasis on local and worker control of the economic environment, drawing on the decentralising strand in Labour thought. On the other hand, these Boards brought about a practical engagement with issues of employment and enterprise management which was at odds with the traditional left distance, cultural and political, from such concerns. While largely a passing phenomenon, Enterprise Boards bequeathed an interest in the nittty-gritty of industry which had not existed in Labour circles since the 1940s. For the leadership such initiatives seemed to offer more threats than promises, because of their association with the left of the party, and the ease with which they could be pilloried as wasting public money on ideologically driven and uneconomic projects.[70]

Some of the reshaping of Labour policy through the 1980s is evident in the policy review of 1987/8, which was an attempt by the leadership to rethink strategy in the face of the confusion and loss of direction which followed Margaret Thatcher's third election victory. The leadership shared a lack of clarity with the rest of the party, though it initiated the review with the presumption that it would lead to a rejection of much of traditional Labour thinking. The documents bore witness to the increasing focus on 'supply-side' issues, or matters of industrial efficiency, at the expense of macro-economic concerns. If trade controls were rejected, and such proposals were nowhere in evidence in the review, then balance-of-payments issues would have to be dealt with by improved competitiveness. This meant that traditional Labour modernisation proposals – increased state intervention in finance, higher spending on research and development – could be placed in a new context.[71] But both of these proposals involved a degree of intervention in corporate affairs or in 'the market' that was progressively repudiated, so that one particular 'supply-side' measure increasingly predominated – education and training. By 1990 a party document could claim this area of policy as 'the new commanding heights'.[72]

Parallel to this evolution on the supply side was a progressive drawing back from macro-economic policy activism. There was much debate about exchange rate policy in the 1980s. Initially this concerned the traditional Labour desire to avoid an excessively strong pound, a view reinforced by the grotesque overvaluation at the beginning of the decade. But as the pound depreciated in the mid-1980s this approach came into question. The efficacy of devaluation in improving competitiveness came under increasing doubt, and this was coupled to the recognition of the need to reassure international finance of Labour's commitment to anti-inflation policy. The benefits of a stable exchange rate therefore appeared compelling. By the time of the 1992 election, Labour, in line with its new-found pro-Europeanism, had become an advocate of joining the Exchange Rate Mechanism.[73]

Policy changes in the decade after the review involved a repudiation of some of Labour's most cherished beliefs. Most obviously, the role of markets was increasingly accepted, though by the early 1990s this had not as yet evolved beyond the careful statement that these were 'good servants but poor masters'. But such notions were to be displaced by an explicit celebration of the benefits of market forces, and the subordination of government to them in the Blair years. Most strikingly, the new Clause Four of the party constitution of 1995 read 'we work for: a dynamic economy, serving the public interest, in which the enterprise of the market and the rigour of competition are joined with the forces of public ownership and co-operation to produce the wealth the nation needs . . . with a thriving private sector and high quality public services'.[74]

Nothing new under the sun? New Labour, new government

No government has been as insistent upon its novelty as the Blair administration elected in 1997. Thus, for example, in 1999 Stephen Byers, the Industry Minister, claimed, against all the evidence, that 'Old Labour' had been concerned with the *redistribution* of national income rather than expansion of the total produced.[75] Such claims were compounded of a desire to distance the government from the preceding Conservative ministries, plus a perhaps even more fervent wish to distance New Labour from past Labour governments and the ideas that (allegedly) informed them. For the historian, claims of novelty always arouse suspicion and certainly, in the economic field, New Labour appears less of a departure than its rhetoric suggests.

Blair insistently proclaimed New Labour's priority as 'education, education, education', and the policy developments since 1997, both in initiatives for reforming education, and its budgetary priority suggest this was no empty slogan. The focus derived from the belief, above all, that training and skills were the key to improved economic performance. Education has traditionally been highly valued on the left, but New Labour was striking in its insistence that, above all, education was the key to economic improvement. This understanding was in turn grounded in the notion of 'globalisation', which could not be resisted and therefore had to be adapted to.[76] Yet it was far from obvious that globalisation really was such an overwhelming force. While the term became a cliché amongst the chattering classes in the 1990s, the evidence suggests that though economic internationalisation was in some respects advancing, it was both less novel and less dramatic than was commonly imagined. Financial capital did flow readily around the world, but the transfer of productive resources was much less common and volatile than usually suggested. Much internationalisation was a process of 'regionalisation', with Britain's links with other rich European countries remaining overwhelmingly important. In particular, the idea that Britain faced massive low-wage competition from Asia was simply wrong.[77] It follows that the focus on competitiveness in modern economic policy was exaggerated; it was striking that Britain's productivity problems were most evident in the non-tradable sector, such as transport and distribution, where competitiveness was irrelevant.[78] Finally, directly on the issue of education, it was in fact very difficult to demonstrate that Britain's deficiencies in some types of skills accounted for poor economic performance.[79]

Much of what was presented as new by the Blair administration, like Wilson's policies in 1964, was inherited from the Conservatives. The Thatcher/Major governments had broadly accepted the globalisation thesis, had put competitiveness at the centre of their analysis, and pursued educational reform ruthlessly. But there were other continuities with Labour's own past. The focus on 'improving competitiveness' recycled the theme of industrial modernisation in a new guise. The belief in capital mobility as a major constraint on policy was a well-rehearsed theme from the 1970s onwards. The obsession with education was just the latest version of viewing 'labour' as the key to Britain's economic performance.[80] Yet what was arguably new for a Labour Party and government was the combination of the priority given to education with

71

the virtual disappearance of other supply-side measures. Policies for technological improvement were less prominent than at any time since the 1930s; and proposals for reform of the financial system were almost invisible, uniquely in the party's history. One obvious explanation for all this was that education neatly combined concern with industrial efficiency with an absence of intervention in the private sector. Education was a 'supplier' to industry, and educational change involves not so much government intervention in industry, as industrial 'intervention' in government.

At the time of writing it is too early to judge whether there can sensibly be said to be a Blair 'project' involving a fundamental rethinking of economic ideas. For example, on markets, there was in the 1980s a revival of ideas of 'market socialism' in Labour circles and this may be linked to the reform of Clause Four and the undoubted ideological enthusiasm for pro-market reforms evident in policy after 1997.[81] Yet how far this was compatible with notions of 'ethical socialism', which were also revived by New Labour, is unclear. Can the doctrine of the invisible hand, which underlies arguments for markets, and depends on self-interested actions yielding collective benefits, be reconciled with ethical socialism's emphasis on individual moral conduct? Perhaps the electoral success of 1997 served to conceal some of the continuing tensions in Labour's economic thinking.

A winding path?

This survey of Labour's economic policies has necessarily focused on the big picture, avoiding many intriguing sidelines which a fully rounded account would cover. The story has emphasised how much Labour's approach was affected by forces outside itself, especially the rise and decline of national economic management and notions of economic 'decline' and 'modernisation'. But what of distinctly Labour themes? Three may be teased out: first, the focus on public ownership. For most of the century, for most Labour Party members, nationalisation had a status above all others as what defined Labour as different and socialist. This belief was embedded in Labour's programmes from the 1930s, and to a large extent enacted in the 1940s. The Attlee measures could be pragmatically justified as necessary to improve industrial relations, rationalise industry and control monopoly. But the idea that they were the beginning of the road to a new, socialist society was, in retrospect, plainly in error. Yet such assumptions continued to obstruct clear thinking about economic issues in the Labour Party through the late twentieth century.

The obverse of the advocacy of public ownership has been the hostility to market forces. What seems striking here is the absence of a sustained debate in Labour circles, other than amongst a few economists, of the *economic* case for and against reliance on market forces. Instead most discussion took place in a different, moral register, in which the normal view was that any form of competition was seen as antithetical to the good society The common assumption of the majority on the left has been that competition engendered by the market was a determining principle of every facet of society, insidiously undermining all co-operative, fraternal or other-regarding endeavours. Yet this was often to mistake the rhetoric of pro-market ideologues for the substance of how societies work. All capitalist economies in fact have complex mixtures of competitive and co-operative components, and so the moral case against competition and for co-operation in one sphere could logically be coupled with the acceptance of the usefulness of market forces elsewhere.

Finally, there is the issue of work. Labour, as its founders and many of their successors have stressed, was formed to represent the workers. It has sustained an emphasis on the centrality of work through the last century. Much of its early energy went into the 'Right to Work'; much of its mid-century success was based on the promise and delivery of 'work for all'; its defeat in 1979 was, in part, because, as the Conservative slogan of 1979 said, 'Labour isn't working'. Under Blair 'Welfare to Work' may make work as much a duty as a right, but the theme remains. This emphasis has obvious roots. Most of Labour's constituency has depended on paid work for survival. Its finances have come from bodies – trade unions – who exist to improve the conditions of work. More broadly, the emphasis on work stems from ethical socialists' emphasis on self-improvement and effort as key components of moral behaviour. None of these are to be decried. But a party of work and workers has obvious difficulty facing up to issues of consumption, so that paradoxically, while, as this chapter has emphasised, it has spent so much time working for higher living standards, it has not centred attention on how those standards manifest themselves in people's lives. The widespread enjoyment of foreign holidays and an extensive consumption of an ever-widening range of consumer durables have too often been treated as suspect features of 'consumerism', a term which itself suggests a puzzling discomfort felt for the welcome consequences of the higher living standards Labour has fought to achieve for as many of the population as possible.

The focus on work in Labour's thinking derived from a time when the idea was closely associated with the male breadwinner, the archetypal worker. Again, this cannot just be decried; male breadwinners did predominate in the early twentieth century, and were the mainstay of the party (though not to the extent they themselves believed). But this legacy has been an obstacle to Labour adjusting to the changes in work and household patterns of the late twentieth century. The traditional goals of full employment (work available to all who want it) and minimum standards of life for all (including those who cannot work) are still relevant. Incomes from employment (including deferred income in the form of pensions), or the lack of such incomes, are still overwhelmingly important determinants of individuals' and families' standards of life. But Labour's ability to adjust these goals to the new patterns of domestic and work life remains an open question.

Labour and the economy

Notes

1 R. Floud, 'Britain, 1860–1914: a survey', in R. Floud and D. McCloskey (eds.), *The Economic History of Britain since 1700*, vol. II: *1860–1939*, 2nd edn (Cambridge: Cambridge University Press, 1994), pp. 1–28.
2 A. Friedberg, *The Weary Titan: Britain and the Experience of Relative Decline 1895–1905* (Princeton: Princeton University Press, 1988).
3 J. Harris, *Unemployment and Politics* (Oxford: Oxford University Press, 1972).
4 E. H. H. Green, *The Crisis of Conservatism: The Politics, Economics and Ideology of the British Conservative Party, 1880–1914* (London: Macmillan, 1995), pp. 27–56.
5 Noel Thompson, *Political Economy and the Labour Party* (London: UCL Press, 1996); F. Trentmann, 'Wealth versus welfare: the British left between free trade and national political economy before the First World War', *Historical Research* 70 (1997), 70–98.
6 Noel Thompson, *The Market and its Critics: Socialist Political Economy in Nineteenth Century Britain* (London: Routledge, 1988); Duncan Tanner, 'Ideological debate in Edwardian Labour politics: radicalism, revisionism and socialism', in E. F. Biagini and A. J. Reid (eds.), *Currents of Radicalism. Popular Radicalism, Organised Labour and Party Politics in Britain, 1850–1914* (Cambridge: Cambridge University Press, 1991), pp. 271–93.
7 Thompson, *Political Economy*, pp. 1–34.
8 Trentmann, 'Wealth', 77.
9 H. W. Macrosty, *Trusts and the State* (London: Grant Richards, 1901); S. and B. Webb, *Problems of Modern Industry* (London: Longmans, Green, 1902); J. A. Hobson, *The Evolution of Modern Capitalism* (London: Walter Scott, 1894). For an assessment of Fabian thinking, Thompson, *Market and its Critics*, pp. 250–72.
10 S. Webb, *Twentieth Century Politics: A Policy of National Efficiency* (London: Fabian Society, 1901); J. Harris, 'Political values and the debate on state welfare', in H. L. Smith (ed.), *War and Social Change* (Manchester: Manchester University Press, 1986), pp. 250–4.
11 Infancy of the Labour Party, vol. I, 'Conference of Members and Candidates, April 1904', R (Coll) MISC 196, British Library of Political and Economic Science, London School of Economics.
12 *Report of the 3rd Annual Conference of the Labour Party* (London: Labour Party, 1908), pp. 57–9, 64, 76–7.
13 *Report of the Third Annual Conference of the Labour Representation Committee* (London: Labour Representation Committee, 1903), p. 36; D. Tanner, 'The development of British socialism, 1900–1918', in E. H. H. Green (ed.), *An Age of Transition: British Politics 1880–1914* (Edinburgh: Edinburgh University Press, 1997), p. 55.
14 K. D. Brown, *Labour and Unemployment 1900–1914* (Newton Abbott: David and Charles, 1971), p. 117.
15 Pat Thane, 'The working class and state welfare', *Historical Journal* 27 (1984),

Jim Tomlinson

877–900; Duncan Tanner, *Political Change and the Labour Party* (Cambridge: Cambridge University Press, 1990), pp. 51–6.

16 *Labour and the New Social Order* (London: Labour Party, 1918).

17 Ibid., p. 19.

18 *Report of the 13th Annual Conference of the Labour Party* (London: Labour Party, 1918), pp. 44–6.

19 B. Webb, *The Co-operative Movement in Great Britain* (London: Swan Sonnenschein, 1891), p. 120; Jim Tomlinson, *The Unequal Struggle? British Socialism and the Capitalist Enterprise* (London: Methuen, 1982), pp. 47–62.

20 A. W. Wright, *G. D. H. Cole and Socialist Democracy* (Oxford: Clarendon Press, 1979), pp. 72–101; S. and B. Webb, *A Constitution for the Socialist Commonwealth of Great Britain* (Cambridge: Cambridge University Press, 1920), pp. 27–58.

21 Daniel Ritschel, *The Politics of Planning* (Oxford: Clarendon Press, 1997), pp. 20–49.

22 R. Millward, 'The 1940s' nationalizations in Britain', *Economic History Review* 50 (1997), 209–34.

23 N. Thompson, 'Hobson and the Fabians: two roads to socialism in the 1920s', *History of Political Economy* 20 (1994), 203–20; R. H. Tawney, *The Acquisitive Society* (London: G. Bell, 1921), pp. 25–34.

24 Andrew Thorpe, *The British General Election of 1931* (Oxford: Oxford University Press, 1991), p. 13; Andrew Thorpe, 'The industrial meaning of "gradualism": the Labour Party and industry, 1918–1931', *Journal of British Studies* 35 (1996), 84–113.

25 P. Snowden, *Labour and National Finance* (London: Labour Party, 1920); Alan Booth and Melvyn Pack, *Employment, Capital and Economic Policy: Great Britain 1918–31* (Oxford: Blackwell, 1985), pp. 6–34.

26 Robert Skidelsky, *Politicians and the Slump* (Harmondsworth: Penguin, 1967); R. McKibbin, 'The economic policy of the second Labour government', *Past and Present* 68 (1975), 95–123; Booth and Pack, *Employment*, pp. 185–91.

27 Skidelsky, *Politicians*, pp. 190–214: Robert Skidelsky, *Oswald Mosley* (London: Macmillan, 1975), pp. 179–220.

28 Booth and Pack, *Employment*, p. 26; Tanner, *Political Change*, pp. 436–41; R. Lynam, *The First Labour Government, 1924* (London: Chapman and Hall, 1957).

29 Thorpe, *General Election*, pp. 8–29, 219–76; Philip Williamson, *National Crisis and National Government* (Cambridge: Cambridge University Press, 1992), pp. 427–54.

30 Jim Tomlinson, *Public Policy and the Economy since 1900* (Oxford: Oxford University Press, 1990), pp. 98–133; Alan Booth, 'Britain in the 1930s: a managed economy?', *Economic History Review* 40 (1987), 499–522.

31 Ritschel, *Politics*, pp. 97–143. British enthusiasm for planning was paralleled elsewhere in Western Europe; see Donald Sassoon, *One Hundred Years of Socialism: The West European Left in the Twentieth Century* (London: I. B. Taurus, 1996), pp. 60–9.

Labour and the economy

32 D. E. Moggridge, *Maynard Keynes: An Economist's Biography* (London: Routledge, 1992), pp. 446–74; Elizabeth Durbin, *New Jerusalems* (London: Routledge and Kegan Paul, 1985), pp. 147–59.

33 The Labour Party, *For Socialism and Peace* (London: Labour Party, 1934), p. 2.

34 Stephen Brooke, *Labour's War* (Oxford: Oxford University Press, 1992), pp. 12–33; A. J. Oldfield, 'The Labour Party and planning: 1934 or 1918?', *Bulletin of the Society for the Study of Labour History* 25 (1972), 41–55.

35 Durbin, *New Jerusalems*, pp. 280–6; Alan Booth, 'How long are light years in British politics?', *Twentieth Century British History* 7 (1996), 1–26; the only important economist in Labour's ranks in the 1920s was J. A. Hobson, and his ideas were defeated by an alliance of Fabian and ethical socialism: Noel Thompson, 'Hobson and the Fabians: two roads to socialism in the 1920s', *History of Political Economy* 26 (1994), 203–20.

36 G. D. H. Cole, *Letter to an Industrial Manager* (London: Fabian Society, 1937).

37 Tomlinson, *Unequal Struggle?*, pp. 70–9; Martin Francis, *Ideas and Policies under Labour 1945–1951* (Manchester: Manchester University Press, 1997), pp. 65–99.

38 Brooke, *Labour's War*, pp. 253–60, 275–92.

39 Jim Tomlinson, *Democratic Socialism and Economic Policy* (Cambridge: Cambridge University Press, 1997), pp. 147–66.

40 Ibid., pp. 68–93; Stephen Brooke, 'Problems of socialist planning: Evan Durbin and the Labour government of 1945', *Historical Journal* 34 (1991), 678–702.

41 H. Morrison, 'Efficiency and Accountability of Socialised Industries', 13 March 1950, CAB 21/2330, Public Record Office (hereafter PRO).

42 Ina Zweiniger-Bargielowska, 'Rationing, austerity and the Conservative Party revival after 1945', *Historical Journal* 37 (1994), 173–97; but see J. Hinton, 'Militant housewives: the British Housewives' League and the Attlee government', *History Workshop* 38 (1994), 129–56.

43 Nick Tiratsoo and Jim Tomlinson, *Industrial Efficiency and State Intervention* (London: Routledge, 1994), pp. 64–152.

44 Bernard Alford, '1945–51: years of recovery or a stage in economic decline?' in Clive Trebilcock and Peter Clarke (eds.), *Understanding Decline* (Cambridge: Cambridge University Press, 1998), pp. 186–211.

45 Martin Chick, *Industrial Policy in Britain 1945–1951* (Cambridge: Cambridge University Press, 1998), pp. 141–71.

46 H. Wilson, 'The State and Private Industry', 4 May 1950, PREM 8/1183, PRO.

47 Tomlinson, *Democratic Socialism*, pp. 237–62; Jim Tomlinson, 'Why so austere?', *Journal of Social Policy* 27 (1998), 63–77.

48 Jim Tomlinson, 'Inventing "decline": the falling behind of the British economy in the post-war years', *Economic History Review* 49 (1996), 731–57; on Bevanism, John Campbell, *Nye Bevan: A Biography* (London: Hodder and Stoughton, 1994), pp. 279–300, 356–68.

Jim Tomlinson

49 Nick Tiratsoo, 'Popular politics, affluence and Labour politics in the 1950s', in A. Gorst, L. Johnman and S Lucas (eds.), *Contemporary British History 1931–61* (London: Pinter, 1991), pp. 44–61; Norman Dennis and A. H. Halsey, *English Ethical Socialism* (Oxford: Clarendon Press, 1988), pp. 219–20.

50 Cited in Stephen Haseler, *The Gaitskellites: Revisionism in the British Labour Party 1951–1964* (London: Macmillan, 1969), p. 42; D. Butler and A. King, *The British General Election of 1964* (London: Macmillan, 1965), pp. 57–76. On the Common Market, Philip Ziegler, *Wilson: The Authorised Life* (London: HarperCollins, 1995), pp. 130–3, 240–2.

51 Samuel Brittan, *The Treasury under the Tories* (Harmondsworth: Penguin, 1971), pp. 204–45; Jim Tomlinson, 'Conservative modernisation 1960–64: too little, too late?', *Contemporary British History* 11 (1997), 18–38.

52 David Edgerton, *England and the Aeroplane* (London: Macmillan, 1991), pp. 39–47.

53 David Edgerton, 'The "White Heat" revisited: the British government and technology in the 1960s', *Twentieth Century British History* 7 (1996), 53–82; Richard Coopey, 'Industrial policy in the white heat of the scientific revolution', in R. Coopey, S. Fielding and N. Tiratsoo (eds.), *The Wilson Years* (London: Pinter, 1993), pp. 102–22.

54 Alec Cairncross, *The British Economy since 1945* (Oxford: Blackwell, 1992), pp. 150–71.

55 Derek Robinson, 'Labour market policies', in W. Beckerman (ed.), *The Labour Government's Economic Record 1964–70* (London: Duckworth, 1972), pp. 300–34.

56 Michael Hatfield, *The House the Left Built: Inside Labour Policy-Making, 1970–75* (London: Gollancz, 1978).

57 Douglas Jay, 'Future Nationalisation Policy', Research Department Report 161 (1948), Labour Party Archive, Manchester.

58 Michael Posner and Richard Pryke, *New Public Enterprise* (London: Fabian Society, 1965); Stuart Holland (ed.), *The State as Entrepreneur* (London: Wiedenfeld and Nicolson, 1972).

59 Hatfield, *The House*, pp. 230–51.

60 Stuart Holland, *The Socialist Challenge* (London: Quartet, 1975), pp. 44–73.

61 Malcolm Sawyer, 'Industrial policy', in Michael Artis and David Cobham (eds.), *Labour's Economic Policies, 1974–79* (Manchester: Manchester University Press, 1992), pp. 158–75.

62 William Brown, 'Industrial Relations', in ibid., pp. 213–28.

63 Leo Pliatzky, *Getting and Spending* (Oxford: Blackwell, 1982), pp. 117–70.

64 Kathy Burk and Alec Cairncross, *Good-bye Great Britain: The 1976 IMF Crisis* (New Haven: Yale University Press, 1992), pp. 179–228.

65 Cited in Thompson, 'Hobson and the Fabians', pp. 206–7; David Cobham, 'Monetary policy', in Artis and Cobham (eds.), *Labour's Economic Policies*, pp. 38–55.

66 Brown, 'Industrial relations', pp. 225–6.

67 Sam Aaronovitch, *The Road from Thatcherism* (London: Lawrence and Wishart, 1981), pp. 5–12.

68 Mark Wickham-Jones, *Economic Strategy and the Labour Party* (London: Macmillan, 1996), p. 190.

69 Stuart Holland, *Out of Crisis: A Programme for European Recovery* (Nottingham: Spokesman, 1983), pp. 57–66.

70 Paul Hirst and Jonathan Zeitlin (eds.), *Reversing Industrial Decline* (Oxford: Berg, 1989), pp. 1–16.

71 The Labour Party, *Social Justice and Economic Efficiency* (London: Labour Party, 1988), pp. 3–7.

72 The Labour Party, *Looking to the Future* (London: Labour Party, 1990).

73 Richard Hill, 'Social democracy and economic strategy: the Labour Party in opposition 1979–1992', Ph.D. thesis (Brunel University, 1998).

74 Quoted in Steven Fielding, *The Labour Party* (Manchester: Manchester University Press, 1997), pp. 148–9.

75 Stephen Byers, *Independent*, 2 February 1999.

76 Colin Hay, *The Political Economy of New Labour* (Manchester: Manchester University Press, 1999), pp. 145–80.

77 Paul Hirst and Grahame Thompson, *Globalization in Question* (Cambridge: Polity Press, 1996), pp. 99–120.

78 M. O'Mahoney, N. Oulton and J. Vass, *Productivity in Market Services: International Comparisons* (London: National Institute of Economic and Social Research, 1996).

79 Peter Robinson, 'The British disease overcome? Living standards, productivity and educational attainment', Centre for Economic Performance, London School of Economics (1995).

80 A. Cutler, 'Vocational training and British economic performance', *Work, Employment and Society* 6 (1992), 161–83.

81 Raymond Plant, *Equality, Market and the State* (London: Fabian Society, 1984); Ian Forbes (ed.), *Market Socialism: Whose Choice?* (London: Fabian Society, 1986).

3 | Labour and welfare
Pat Thane

In 1907, James Ramsay Macdonald, secretary of the parliamentary Labour Party and its most effective and prolific propagandist wrote:

> We are never without the unemployed now . . . The State has a duty to these people. That duty is to tax the wealth which they have created (but which has gone to enrich other people) so that they may be rescued from deterioration and helped during the most trying times of their poverty-stricken lives, e.g. when they are underfed children at school, unemployed adult men and women, aged workers . . . [But] . . . if this help is given as a mere palliative or as charity, the real conditions are only perpetuated . . . Unemployment schemes must therefore be educational; they must be in the form of training.[1]

This summarised the approach of the early Labour Party to the welfare role of the state. It was most clearly embodied in the succession of Right to Work Bills which the new party, with general support from its ranks, repeatedly put before Parliament under the slogan 'The Right to Work or Full Maintenance'. The wording signified Labour's order of priorities. These were embedded within a code of rights and responsibilities which Labour thought appropriate for what was not yet called a 'welfare state'. As MacDonald explained:

The Right to Work clause recognizes the right of the unemployed workman to demand an opportunity to work . . . We want to keep him from losing his self-respect . . . We hope that only under very special circumstances would the maintenance grant be given . . . This Clause is a Right to Work clause not a Right to Doles clause . . . Some men are born loafers, more still are made loafers by evil social conditions; but whatever may be his origin, the loafer exists and must be dealt with. He must not be allowed to damage the claims of the deserving temporarily unemployed . . . He too must be educated.[2]

But 'loafing' was not a failing only of the poor. MacDonald regretted that compulsory work training 'cannot as yet be applied to men who loaf about preying upon society like slugs on cabbages, but who find themselves well-supplied with the world's goods. That may come some day.'[3]

Meanwhile, he argued that 'our educational institutions should be revolutionized',[4] to 'provide equality of opportunity'. Complete equality of outcome was not expected, given the variability of human capacities. As MacDonald put it, 'all that Socialism and a Socialist system of distribution can claim to do is to destroy social parasites and secure that everyone who gives service to Society shall receive from Society an ample measure of opportunities to live and enjoy living'.[5] Criticisms of 'loafers' by working-class leaders are too readily interpreted as expressions of contempt or ignorance of the struggling poor by the secure elite of workers. More often in Labour rhetoric it expressed criticism of the conditions and structures which robbed individuals of human dignity. This was George Lansbury's meaning when as leader of the Labour group on the Board of Poor Law Guardians in Poplar, East London, in the 1890s he insisted that poor relief should be adequate for respectable survival, but also that it should be conditional upon strict controls against 'malingering'. The right to relief must be balanced by the obligation to the 'community' (a key word in Labour's language at this time) to take work when it was available. The community in turn was obliged to ensure that suitable work or training was available and to provide relief when it was not.[6]

Labour statements routinely assumed that social reform was secondary to economic reform which alone could deliver lasting 'welfare'. Work and adequate wages were the best defences against poverty. Publicly funded welfare was for those who could not be supported either by their own efforts or by their families. It should be constructive and where possible preventive. MacDonald argued:

You can take your children, feed them, clothe them and house them at public expense, but that does not help you. That is simply patching up the old tin kettle. It does not help you to recreate society so that these poor things will disappear altogether . . . We must do better than that. What do we want?

Pat Thane

Increased incomes from labour – not doles in aid of low wages. We want wages boards applied to every [low-paid] industry . . . [these] . . . will immediately lift up the wages and then you will supply that reservoir of possession and economic power which is the source of working class liberty[7] . . . Under Socialism, family income will be equal to family requirements.[8]

MacDonald saw the family as the ideal fundamental social unit for which there was no obvious alternative and which the socialist state should both encourage and support. Work and wages would improve only if the economy was transformed. This required optimal use for the public good and under public ownership of underused resources such as the land and of essential services, firstly at municipal, then at national level, 'from water to trains and from light to milk', together with punitive taxation of unearned income.[9]

Labour's election programmes up to the First World War embodied all of these assumptions. They were underpinned by the belief that the state could act in the interests of the 'masses of the ordinary people'.[10] As Keir Hardie put it: 'The State . . . is what its people make it . . . As the political education of the working class progresses, and they begin to realise what are the true functions of the State, their power will be exerted in an increasing degree in the direction of transforming the State from a property-preserving to a life-preserving institution',[11] though it was not assumed naively that it would necessarily or unconditionally do so, especially in its current undemocratic form.[12] 'Socialism', wrote MacDonald, 'can discriminate between mistaken and fruitful methods of state action' and did not assume that 'self-help and state activity are opposed to each other . . . they are naturally interdependent'.[13] Hardie vigorously endorsed this package of social and economic reform as desirable in itself and consistent with the programmes of socialist parties in other countries. He rejected a strand of opposition which Labour's welfare programmes were to encounter for long after: 'By this school of thinkers reforms for the amelioration of the lot of the people were anathematized as the wiles of the enemy to withdraw their attentions from Socialism and make them contented with their lot as wage slaves'. He pointed out that 'the Socialist leaders in every constitutionally governed country' had abandoned such tactics. In both Germany and France social reforms enacted by the state had benefited the working class but this had not prevented the advance of the socialist parties.[14]

Before the Labour Party

Hardie, MacDonald, Lansbury and other Labour leaders expressed and systematised views long held in important sectors of Labour's support, particularly the trade unions and friendly societies. By the end of the nineteenth century these provided protection against poverty due to sickness, old age and (in the case of the unions) unemployment, through non-profit, mutual funds managed by members. Both operated strict safeguards against 'malingerers'. Overwhelmingly their members were the minority of working-class men in better-paid, more stable employment, who could afford regular contributions and prided themselves on their independence. For the remainder, including their own wives and children, the only resort was the stigmatising Poor Law or the uncertainties of charity. By the end of the nineteenth century the Poor Law was under assault, in particular as increasing numbers of women and working men became eligible for election to the local Boards of Guardians which administered it. Labour-led resistance was most open in Poplar where a substantial group of Labour Guardians included Lansbury and Will Crooks.[15] At the same time there were campaigns, most of them supported by the labour movement, for state old-age pensions, unemployment relief, improved housing, and more humane state support for those in need through no fault of their own.

Friendly societies and trade unions recognised the existence of very needy groups who could not afford to join them and did not deserve the degradation of pauperism, in particular the large numbers of women who were very poor, but too badly or irregularly paid to help themselves.[16] Working men had good reason to support state aid for women, since few families could afford more than one contribution to a friendly society and neither societies nor unions paid widows' pensions. It was highly likely that their own wives would outlive them in severe poverty. In the 1890s, as in the 1990s, the most miserable poverty was concentrated among older women. But while supporting a stronger, less punitive, state safety net for the poorest, they insisted that, ultimately, such poverty was best prevented by work and wages adequate to secure the needs of all family members.

Campaigns around social welfare were an important source of support for Labour. From the 1880s growing numbers of local elective bodies had powers in key areas of social policy and Labour representatives were increasingly active in them, pressing in particular for provision for needs which people could not fulfil for themselves: improved water supplies and sanitation, better housing, free school meals, fair employment contracts for council employees and anti-unemployment measures. They were spurred on by local trades councils, branches of the Women's Co-operative Guild (WCG) and the Women's Labour League (WLL), campaigning for improved services accountable to local

Pat Thane

voters. Female ratepayers, not all of them middle-class, had the local vote from 1869 and could stand for a number of local authorities.[17] Labour slowly but steadily gained seats in local government despite the disadvantage of an electorate weighted against them by franchise restrictions. Woolwich was the first Labour-controlled council in 1898–9.

To an important extent, Labour's early strength was built upon practical everyday engagement with social conditions affecting life in the home as well as with workplace issues, though by 1914 it was still unclear whether Labour or the Liberals would be the long-term beneficiary of the electoral appeal of reforming politics.[18]

New Liberalism

The Liberal government which gained a large majority in 1906 was conscious of the growing threat from Labour. The programme of the Labour Representation Committee (LRC) for the 1906 election incorporated the welfare issues raised in the previous twenty-five years by its leaders and supporters.[19] The Liberals responded by introducing wide-ranging and innovative social welfare measures designed to convince working-class voters that a Liberal government could work to their advantage. But the Liberals were constrained by fear of alienating their middle-class support (not least by raising taxes) and by the opposition of the Lords. They were responsible for decisive new moves by the state into the sphere of social welfare and for establishing important and lasting principles, but their legislation was cautious and inexpensive and not significantly redistributive. The most important measure, national insurance, was funded partly by workers' own contributions. Others such as old-age pensions were tax-funded, but the workers at whom they were targeted contributed as much to national revenue at this time, through indirect taxes on such items as beer and tobacco, as did the better-off through direct taxes. [20]

The earliest Liberal measures, the introduction of free school meals for the poorest schoolchildren in 1906 and compulsory medical inspection in state schools in 1907, originated in bills introduced by Labour back-benchers. The former had been the subject of campaigns by the WCG and other socialists for many years. Workmen's compensation, first introduced in 1897, was also extended in 1906, more radically than originally intended as a result of Labour amendments. Among others, Keir Hardie persuaded Parliament to allow 'illegitimate' children to qualify as dependants for receipt of compensation.

The Old Age Pensions Act of 1908 also dealt with a topic which had long been a focus of labour campaigns. It represented a decisive shift away from the Poor Law for the largest single group of impoverished people. They received the first state-funded cash benefit outside the Poor Law.

Pensions were non-contributory, minimal, stringently means-tested and paid only at seventy, by which age many had died in penury. They were also subject to character tests intended to exclude those with records of criminality, drunkenness and 'habitual failure to work'. Women, as intended, were a majority of the first pensioners since they were a majority of the destitute aged. Labour opposed the exclusions. How, asked Will Crooks, from his long experience of Poor Law administration, were such tests to be applied? 'What particular degree of drunkenness was to disqualify for a pension? – half stewed, half drunk, steadily drunk, talkatively drunk, quarrelsome drunk, maudlin drunk, dead drunk?' Drunkenness, he pointed out, was not unknown in the Houses of Parliament.[21]

Labour criticised the timidity of Lloyd George's controversial budget of 1909, announcing its support for a steeply graduated income tax (in place of the existing flat-rate tax of sixpence in the pound), a supertax, greatly increased estate duties, a monopoly tax and a more swingeing land tax than Lloyd George had risked. The Trade Boards Act of 1909, which effectively introduced minimum wages into a number of very low-paid, mainly female, trades was the outcome of campaigns by women, especially in the Fabian Women's Group and the Women's Trade Union League. The next equally innovative measures, the introduction of labour exchanges in 1909 and of national health and unemployment insurance in 1911, were more controversial within the Labour Party. The Liberals adopted these measures in preference to the principles of Labour's Right to Work Bill, which was introduced into the Commons annually from 1907. MacDonald criticised the Liberals' failure to combine economic policy and unemployment policy in a single department of state. The principle of national insurance was opposed by Beatrice and Sidney Webb, who feared that payment of benefits in return for contributions would grant a right to benefits, which they believed should be conditional on good behaviour. MacDonald, characteristically less authoritarian than the Webbs towards poor people, recognised that adequate safeguards against malingering could be built into national insurance as they were into contributory trade-union and friendly society schemes, and that the establishment of a right to benefit rather than further extension of 'doles' was a desirable acknowledgement of workers' dignity. He believed, as he did of other Liberal schemes, that for all its imperfections national insurance provided better for real need than any previous system and, given the limits of revenue and a decidedly limited political commitment to redistribution, it was the best any non-Labour government was likely to give. Also in return for giving Labour's support to national insurance, he extracted from the Liberals the reversal of the Osborne judgement, which restricted trade-union contributions to Labour Party funds, and the introduction of salaries for MPs – both no small gains for Labour. Others, such as Philip Snowden, objected to making workers pay for their own welfare, arguing for redistributive non-contributory benefits, financed by progressive taxation. They pointed out, correctly, that the poorest, including most female workers, would be excluded from national insurance because they were too badly paid and irregularly employed to afford the weekly contributions. Snowden and Lansbury argued: 'The husband in the case of the working classes at any rate does not support his wife. The wife supports herself and is contributing by her labour to the economic upkeep of the home.' Hence care for the health of wives working at home was as vital to the economy as that of men in paid work, for 'she takes charge of [the workman's home]. She works just as hard as he and she is just as much a wage-earner as he is'.[22] Hardie, MacDonald and Lansbury tried unsuccessfully to extend maternity benefit to unmarried mothers (as the mothers of both Hardie and MacDonald had been).

Lansbury used his position as editor of the newly founded (1912) newspaper the *Daily Herald* to oppose labour exchanges and national insurance, which the paper represented as designed to register and control unemployed workers rather than to help them – the first steps to what the libertarian Liberal, Hilaire Belloc, Lansbury's associate in this campaign, called the 'servile state'. This view was not widely shared in the labour movement. There was some trade-union opposition to national insurance, but it did not outlast the implementation of the scheme and was largely defused by the incorporation of trade unions and friendly societies into the administration. They administered benefits under the title of 'approved societies'. The involvement of working people in administration (of pensions and labour exchanges as well as national insurance) was a significant theme of the Liberal legislation. It was conveniently inexpensive and seductive to Labour as a gesture towards democratic control.[23]

This first substantial band of Labour MPs, who entered Parliament between 1906 and 1914, had all been born in the working class. Most had known poverty at some point in their lives and most had been manual workers. They spoke from experience in debates on 'welfare', as when the Lib–Lab MP Fred Maddison described the 'nasty class feeling' experienced by his daughter when she won a scholarship to a fee-paying secondary school. They reacted fiercely to criticisms of working-class life casually and routinely uttered on the other benches, as when Keir Hardie responded to opponents of free school meals. He:

did not think that the honourable gentlemen who had spoken so often that afternoon knew what it meant to them to sit there and listen to their wives being described as slatterns and themselves as spendthrifts . . . the insinuation that under this bill there would be an indiscriminate feeding of children of drunken and thriftless parents was to caricature the Bill and totally to misrepresent the ideas of those who supported it. They had heard a great deal about home life. What proposals had the honourable members to make who wanted them to brighten home life? Would they support a bill for a minimum wage? That would be socialism.[24]

They believed that most legislators had little idea of the real lives of poor people. They expressed themselves as speaking for the whole working class, whom they represented as aspiring to independence, respectability and hard work, but often frustrated by circumstances outside their control. They often spoke most urgently for the poorest women and men who were not unionised and whom they did not directly represent because they were not qualified to vote. George Barnes of the elite Amalgamated Society of Engineers, not known as a man of the left, commented in the pensions debate:

it was one of the saddest features, perhaps, of our present industrial and social system that the heaviest of life's burdens fell upon the weakest among them and in that category, of course, must be placed the womenfolk. Their wages were smaller and they therefore had less chance of making any provision for their old age compared with men and they were more entitled to consideration and help.[25]

A recurrent theme was that trade unionists could hope and should be expected to achieve a degree of economic and social independence with only limited support from the state; it was the remainder of the working class who needed state welfare because they had no other source of protection. Charles Duncan, an ex-shipyard worker, and MP for Barrow-in-Furness, told the House in the national insurance debate: 'I am a skilled worker and I would be prepared to say, so far as the skilled worker is concerned, keep him out of it and let him stand his corner; but there are hundreds of thousands of [labourers] who cannot afford to be in any union at all.'[26] It was of course to the advantage of trade unionists to limit the possible challenge to their own security from the low-paid and desperate industrial 'reserve army'. They were also well aware that this

Pat Thane

might include their own wives and children, or one day, with ill luck, themselves.

The First World War

One reason for the Labour Party's growing strength during the First World War was its prominent role in a series of campaigns for improved social welfare, building on pre-war agitations. It was active from early in the war in successful campaigns for controls of prices and supplies, improved old-age pensions and benefits for the families of servicemen, including unmarried partners and children, for rent controls and improved housing. The WLL and WCG campaigned actively and successfully for maternity and child welfare. Some of these activities were co-ordinated by the War Emergency Workers' National Committee (WEWNC), which was established at the beginning of the war to maintain Labour unity and activism and to defend workers' living standards.[27]

The beneficial experience of state control of the economy during the war probably increased general acceptance of social and economic action by the state. MacDonald, however, drew the different conclusion that 'the war has revealed to us dangers of state authority which have hitherto appeared to be only fanciful', in particular the suppression of minority views, such as his own opposition to the war.[28] He proposed in 1918 a programme for *Socialism After the War* which suggested that Labour's thinking had also developed during these years. This programme advocated a 'large conscription of wealth'. MacDonald and others argued that working people's expectations had been raised by the improved civilian living standards of the war period.[29] Income tax should remain at the high wartime levels and death duties increased. Fortunes made during the war should be enquired into and forfeited. National standards of wages should be fixed and enforced. There should be 'a vast scheme of re-housing' and urgent action to reduce infant mortality, unemployment and poverty in old age, while 'women must enter a new world of political and economic freedom'. But greatest prominence went to education. He wrote that the watchword should be 'educate' – 'the right education, the education that makes independent minds, not servile and imitative ones' – and explained:

if we were compelled to assign to one cause all our national shortcomings we should choose our bad education. The reform of this should begin with our training colleges . . . the age of pupils must be raised . . . secondary education must be amplified into a national system and the universities remodelled, lock, stock and barrel on democratic grounds.[30]

88

MacDonald also reiterated his belief in the centrality of the family to welfare as to all aspects of society. But the campaign for social policies remained secondary to the campaign to improve wages, because 'the share of labour is not enough to keep it in a state of self-sufficiency from its cradle to its grave'.[31]

Between the wars

Labour fought the first post-war election in December 1918 on a new programme, *Labour and the New Social Order. A Report on Reconstruction*. Its drafting is attributed to Sidney Webb and it was certainly written in more dispassionate language than that of, for example, MacDonald. But the principles it expressed were recognisably those of the pre-war party. The war brought the Webbs into greater prominence in the party, though their influence on social policy was less than is often claimed. They had decided to support Labour in 1912 after the failure of their campaign to persuade the Liberals to 'break up' the Poor Law on the model they had advocated in the Minority Report of the Royal Commission on the Poor Laws of 1909. Other influences on Labour's approach to social policy, such as those of the Independent Labour Party (ILP), were longer established and stronger, though the ILP and the Fabians could agree on many things, such as the principle of the 'national minimum'.

The new programme proclaimed that: 'The first principle of the Labour Party . . . is the securing to every member of the community, in good times and bad alike . . . of all the requisites of healthy life and worthy citizenship.' It aimed to secure 'to every worker, by hand or by brain, at least the prescribed Minimum of Health, Education, Leisure and Subsistence'; to push for the improvement of all legislation affecting working conditions and wages, including a minimum wage and 'Equal Pay for Equal Work wherever both sexes are employed'; and 'to urge trade unions to admit women to membership in all trades in which they have actually secured employment and to insist, in such cases, that the women shall receive the trade union rates'.

Still central to Labour's vision of how 'welfare' was to be secured was the duty of government to provide 'productive work at Standard Rates', fundamentally by economic restructuring through nationalisation of the land and of key industries and by the 'conscription of wealth'. Unemployment was to be reduced initially by scheduling public works, raising the school-leaving age to sixteen, providing bursaries for further and higher education and shortening the working week. Where these measures failed to eliminate unemployment, adequate maintenance should be provided, together with 'such useful training as may be practicable, according to age, health and previous occupation'. Equally important was the democratisation of the constitution and of industry and the decentralisation of government, with social policies as far as possible administered by local government, which was in closer touch with local needs. The Poor Law should be abolished, local health services reorganised and a house-building programme was urgently needed. But what was described as 'the first step to social reconstruction' would later be called 'lifelong learning': 'a genuine nationalization of education, which shall get rid of all class distinctions and privileges, and bring effectively within the reach not only of every boy and girl, but also of every adult citizen, all the training, physical, mental and moral, literary, technical and artistic of which he is capable'.

Labour's commitment to welfare played an important role in extending and consolidating its support through the inter-war years. It was active on the most salient issues of inter-war social policy: housing and unemployment. After the war, for the first time successive governments put substantial resources into these two key areas of working-class 'welfare'.

The first Labour government

Labour came closer to putting its ideas into practice when MacDonald was for the first time Prime Minister in a Labour government from January to October 1924. As a minority government, easily outvoted by the other parties, in a period of economic dislocation, the chances of this being a major reforming government were slight. The key social policy cabinet post, the Minister of Health (which included responsibility for housing, the Poor Law and local government) went to a left-winger, the Clydesider John Wheatley. Glasgow was notoriously one of the worst housed cities in Europe and it had long been a focus of housing campaigns, most notably in the wartime rent strikes.[32] Wheatley's Housing Act was the one undisputed success of this government. It increased subsidies for council house-building, abolished the previous stipulation that local authority building could only fill gaps in the private market, and stipulated higher building standards than before. This was to remain a keynote of Labour housing policy. Equally important, and in keeping with Labour's commitment to linking social and employment policy, Wheatley negotiated with the building unions to increase the building labour force by providing more apprenticeships and shortening their duration. It was the most determined attempt to date to expand working-class housing of a high standard, though it remained difficult to keep rents at levels many working people could afford. Legislation was also introduced to protect tenants from unfair eviction.

The mass, regionally concentrated unemployment of the inter-war years was so different from anything foreseeable when the 'Right to Work' strategy had been devised that Labour, and indeed everyone else, had difficulty in developing an alternative. Snowden cut taxes in the sincere belief that in the short run this was the only means to keep industry afloat. Despite such actions by Snowden and his successors, a striking feature of the period, compared with the slump of the late twentieth century, was that it saw a significant *expansion* of government welfare activity and expenditure compared with admittedly low previous levels. Total local and central government expenditure on social services rose from 4.1 per cent of GNP in 1913 to 11.3 per cent in 1938.[33] Conservative-controlled governments were in office for eighteen of the twenty-one years between the wars but it is hard to believe that this pattern of expenditure owed nothing to pressure from the increasingly strong electoral presence of Labour. For all the inadequacies of unemployment benefit and the degrading methods of administration, for the first time in history the great majority of unemployed people received a regular cash benefit which was enough for survival. For many families its regularity, compared with the uncertainty of earnings when in work, was a gain in security and even preferable to the irregular, low-paid work they had experienced. As one unemployed man put it: 'I'll take the job tomorrow if they'll guarantee me constant work and a steady wage. But I'm for no more of this in and out business with a different pay every week. It's just hopeless for a married man with a family of youngsters.'[34]

But Labour's primary aim that families should receive at least one adequate and regular wage was notably hard to achieve in 1924. Instead the government raised unemployment benefits and, despite opposition from employers, removed the hated household means test for the long-term unemployed. But, in keeping with their traditional resistance to malingerers, Labour tightened the obligation that the claimant must be 'genuinely seeking work'. This was especially discriminatory against women, for it was all too easy to argue that married women had work enough in the home and so could not 'genuinely' be seeking work outside it, or that any women who refused work as a domestic servant (which was available everywhere but for many women was the last resort) was not 'genuinely' in need.

Labour appointed a Royal Commission to investigate the national health insurance system which faced increasing criticism for the unevenness of its coverage and the variable competence of approved societies, and for the exclusion from it of most women and all children. It reported in 1926. Labour's 1924 budget earmarked £36m for the lowering of the pensionable age to sixty-five (both to counter real need among older people and to cut unemployment) and the introduction of widows' pensions. Labour lost office before this could be done, but Snowden did immediately extend eligibility for the existing pension so that it covered 70 per cent of all over-seventies. Lone-parenthood caused by widowhood ranked with old age (also primarily a female condition) as a major cause of poverty. Widows' pensions were a priority of the very active women's movement of the inter-war years and were seen as a desirable first step to their other goal of family allowances. Child poverty and malnutrition were repeatedly revealed as major problems in the inter-war years, but the Labour leadership was unpersuaded by the arguments of many Labour women that family allowances were the solution.[35]

Labour also increased expenditure on education and established the Hadow Committee to advise on the way forward for secondary education, which in 1926 produced the report that gave birth to the selective tripartite secondary school system. In a short and vulnerable period of government Labour made a start in all major areas of social policy.

Local government

Local government in the inter-war years had wide discretion in the administration of social policies. At this level, at least as notably as at national level, Labour administrations promoted 'welfare' with increasing effectiveness as they had increasing electoral success. This was first evident over poor relief. The Poor Law was still administered locally by separately elected Boards of Guardians, the first level of government at which Labour was notably successful. Throughout the 1920s Labour-controlled Boards of Guardians in areas of industrial strife (as in the General Strike) or high unemployment (most dramatically in Poplar in 1921[36]) paid higher rates of relief than recommended by central government. They were censured and some Boards were dismissed and replaced by Conservative governments. The outburst of Labour-led resistance hastened the demise of the Poor Law. Neville Chamberlain's Local Government Act of 1929 abolished the Guardians, transferring their responsibilities for the unemployed to local Public Assistance Committees under stricter central control.

The assertion of central over local government control was a general trend from the 1920s, but it did not move fast enough to prevent a growing number of Labour-controlled councils using their newly acquired powers. In 1919 Labour made substantial gains, taking control of three counties – Durham, Glamorgan and Monmouthshire – all coal-mining areas. In London in the same year it increased its representation on borough councils from 46 to 572.[37] The first major city to come under Labour control was Sheffield in 1926. The new council embarked rapidly upon a programme of providing housing, schools, baths and other public services. Thereafter, despite high unemployment, the local death rate fell markedly. It is hard to believe that these processes were unconnected. By 1935 Labour controlled most big city councils, including Glasgow and the London County Council (LCC) and it was an important influence in others, such as Manchester, which was controlled by progressive Liberals, while Labour held 35 per cent of seats. Labour's welfare activities at local level, building new housing and clearing old 'slums', subsidising rents, improving working-class education, increasing expenditure on healthcare and improving local transport, helped to build hopes of what it might achieve nationally.[38] Significantly, in the year following the disastrous general election of 1931, there was a swing to Labour in the local elections.

Women and welfare

An important source of pressure on the party at central and local level to increase the salience and the range of welfare issues on its agenda was the growing numbers and activism of women in the party.[39] Increasing numbers of women became local councillors: of the 729 Labour borough councillors in London in 1934, 150 were women, many of them working-class women in working-class districts: fifteen in Bermondsey, fifteen in Hackney, eight in Poplar, sixteen in Southwark, twelve in Stepney.[40] In these and other districts women campaigned for the building of more and better houses – the workplace of most women – just as they advocated better conditions of paid work for women. They not only promoted national legislation but put pressure on local authorities to use the powers they already had under housing, maternity and child welfare, education and health legislation. The campaigns of the women's sections (WS) of the Labour Party built directly on the experience of their working-class members. At various times in the 1920s, WS members were deputed to investigate housing conditions, the implementation of rent controls, levels of nutrition and conditions in maternity hospitals. The findings were embodied in reports which formed the basis of policy recommendations which were repeatedly pressed upon the party leadership. Where (all too rarely) it has been studied, it is clear that women's activism made a difference to Labour's electoral fortunes and to levels of welfare expenditure.[41] The women complemented the party's traditional

Pat Thane

emphasis on male work and wages as the key to better 'welfare' by prioritising the kinds of institutional change – as in delivery of healthcare – that would not flow automatically from increased household income. They also insisted on the need to give mothers real choice between work in or outside the home and support, both of family allowances and services, for those who chose to work at home. There could be conflict between women and the male leaders of the party, as over family allowances and birth control,[42] but women did much to set Labour's welfare agenda in the inter-war years and in particular to ensure that the needs of women and children were well represented on it.

The second Labour government

Labour's period out of office between 1924 and 1929 was more notable for developments in social policy at local level than for new thinking at national level. Labour fought the election of 1929 on a programme, *Labour and the Nation* in which R. H. Tawney had an influential hand. Wheatley, among others, criticised it, with good reason, for containing too many statements of principle and long-term policies when what was needed was a tough choice of policies to be implemented in a five-year term.[43]

Nevertheless Labour emerged from the election with the largest number of seats in the Commons, though fewer than the Conservatives and Liberals together. The election was shortly followed by the worldwide slump and soaring unemployment. Once more, Labour was in government in a situation which made decisive action peculiarly difficult.[44] Unemployment benefit was kept at reasonably generous levels compared with past times. An Unemployment Insurance Act in 1930 extended eligibility for benefit, which could now be refused only if the claimant refused suitable employment. As before, this benefited many men but disadvantaged married women, alienating many of them from the party. Labour again followed an active housing policy designed both to improve social conditions and to provide employment. By 1929 the most tractable end of the housing problem, the poor accommodation of many skilled workers, had largely been solved by a combination of local authority housing and building for sale. The serious remaining problem was overcrowded, often insanitary and bug-ridden, privately rented 'slum' housing in town and country, inhabited by the very poorest. Labour focused on 'slum clearance' and rebuilding. The Housing Act of 1930 subsidised local authorities on the basis of the number of families rehoused and the cost of rehousing. Each local authority was instructed to survey their housing stock and to produce a five-year plan for clearance.

94

Despite cuts by the National government in 1931–3, between 1935 and 1939 house-building reached its highest ever level, much of it by Labour-controlled local authorities. Labour proposed to raise the school-leaving age to fifteen but was defeated by an alliance of the churches and the Lords. This, and Labour's inability to amend the constraints upon trade unions introduced after the General Strike, suggests the limits to its freedom of manoeuvre.

The government lasted only twenty-six months and broke over the issue of unemployment benefits, when a majority of the cabinet rejected MacDonald's and Snowden's proposal to cut benefits as part of the package to reduce the budget deficit amid the worsening economic crisis.[45] The National government, with the massive majority gained in the election which followed, instituted severe, though mostly temporary, cuts in most areas of social policy.

The thirties

Social combined with economic policy moved still closer to the heart of Labour politics for the remainder of the 1930s. There was growing support, as in other countries, for economic and social 'planning' as the answer to the long-term economic crisis, though much disagreement and uncertainty about its practical implications. There were growing demands for more state intervention in healthcare, as medicine became capable of curing a wider range of conditions and in consequence become more expensive, and as evidence accumulated of continuing high levels of ill health, in particular among women and children. Competing proposals for a socialised system of healthcare multiplied. Such a move had long been a focus of Labour Party discussion and the party was committed, in general terms, to a free health service available to all, but it was never salient. This was partly because the details were contentious. On the one hand were the advocates of a salaried, locally based service, such as the Socialist Medical Association and Herbert Morrison, the champion of local government. On the other hand, the British Medical Association (BMA) was hostile to any government control. Also Labour leaders were inclined to believe that much ill health could be prevented by full employment, better pay and living standards, improved housing and environmental conditions, which should take priority.

In 1937 the new leader, Clement Attlee, published his vision for Labour.[46] Attlee had observed poverty as a resident at Toynbee Hall in East London and as Poor Law Guardian and mayor of Stepney, though unlike previous Labour leaders he had not experienced it. Attlee's writing

Pat Thane

differed from MacDonald's (and Hardie's and Lansbury's) in its dispassionate style and total lack of reference to women, except as 'housewives' and dependants of men, but there were only minor differences in his other concerns. Secure (male) employment was essential:

A Socialist State cannot afford to allow men to remain idle. As soon, therefore as there ceases to be a demand for a man's labour in one direction, he will be given some other kind of work to do. He will be certain as long as he is capable of making a contribution to the national wealth he can be sure of a job and of sufficient money to keep himself and his family at a reasonable standard of living.[47]

The next Labour government would follow a 'general plan'. First, it would set about planning the economy to maximise production, efficiency and employment and would nationalise the Bank of England and key industries. It would raise the school-leaving age immediately to fifteen and as soon as possible to sixteen 'with adequate maintenance allowances, and extend considerably the present facilities for secondary education up to eighteen'. There would also be 'adequate pensions on condition of retirement' for older people; shorter working hours; and a 'bold programme of works of public development . . . the building of new housing estates, schools, hospitals . . . a programme of electrification . . . a vigorous programme of agricultural development'.[48]

Attlee believed that British society was becoming more equal, but that it had further to go, though, like MacDonald, he thought that unequal human capabilities made equality of outcome an unrealistic goal.[49] He also shared MacDonald's concern about the dangers of overcentralisation, and favoured regional devolution and encouragement of active participation in voluntary organisations.[50] Also the state should promote leisure, culture and 'beauty'; for, he wrote, 'one of the heaviest indictments against the capitalist system is that it is destructive of beauty. The widespread ugliness of Britain is the result of putting profits first.' He gave greater prominence to the quality of life than previous Labour leaders, in keeping with the increased expectations of many working people, especially of the relatively prosperous workers in new and expanding industries: 'The aim of socialism will be to see that every family in the country has a house with electric light and power for cooking, central heating, refrigerator and plenty of floor space, one in fact that is well-furnished with everything that a modern housewife needs'.[51] This had been an unthinkable ambition in 1900.

Attlee was conscious that Labour could not predict the circumstances in which it would next come to power – as well he might, given its unfortunate experience so far – and argued that it would have to satisfy short- as well as long-term needs:

It will come in backed by the demands of its supporters for immediate relief from the economic evils from which they suffer. It cannot concentrate on major measures of Socialisation alone, the result of which will not be apparent for some time; it must satisfy the immediate needs of those who suffer from unemployment, low wages, long hours, bad housing, malnutrition and many other evil things which are concomitants of capitalism.[52]

The Second World War

This was the programme with which Labour went into the Second World War and which it substantially implemented after it. The circumstances of war favoured its long-term electoral chances and its economic and welfare proposals. Labour members were as prominent in the wartime coalition as Conservatives and were considerably more so in the key domestic ministries. As deputy Prime Minister, Attlee was effectively in charge of domestic affairs, whilst Churchill directed the war, with occasional dramatic eruptions into home affairs. Bevin was a highly successful Minister of Labour, while Morrison held the Home Office equally effectively. The 'White Paper trail' of proposals for post-war reconstruction from 1942 proved highly popular and were closer to the aspirations of Labour than of Conservatives, notably the Beveridge Report, and the White Papers on Town and Country Planning, Employment Policy and Health Policy. The co-ordination of health services under state control for wartime purposes increased pressure for permanent co-ordination and nationalisation. More generally, as in the previous war, effective central direction made the continuation of controls after the war more appealing to electors. Education was reformed in the Act of 1944, on the tripartite model, and generally in line with Labour aspirations. At this time the expert opinion of educational psychologists that testing at age eleven could be a socially neutral means of delivering equality of opportunity was widely accepted and support for what were later called comprehensive schools was limited. Family allowances for all but the first child in every family were also introduced before the end of the war.[53]

The Attlee governments

Churchill's evident lack of enthusiasm for extensive social reform, and a widespread desire not to return to the insecurities of the 1930s, must be a major part of the explanation for Labour at last obtaining a decisive majority in the election of 1945. Overwhelmingly, the primary task was seen as the reconstruction of the economy and the achievement of full male employment, and the perceived needs of the economy were consistently given priority over welfare expenditure.[54] To an extent, of course, improved 'welfare' was complementary to economic growth. Improved housing, health and education could improve the quality of what was later described as 'human capital'. But the government made little of such arguments. It was as concerned about 'burdening' the economy with excessive welfare costs as any of its subsequent critics.[55]

Expenditure of real resources, capital and materials for welfare purposes were strictly controlled throughout the Attlee years. The needs of industry came first. In consequence, though the school-leaving age was at last raised to fifteen, little was spent on school buildings. The third strand of secondary education promised in 1944, technical schools, hardly materialised due in part to the costs of building and equipping them. Not until 1950 did education expenditure exceed that pre-war, and then by only 4 per cent. The promised 'housing drive' to solve the housing problem, which had been worsened by the war, was severely constrained and only in 1948 did Labour meet the promised target of 240,000 new houses per year. In the economic crisis of 1947, only 189,000 were completed in the United Kingdom. A total of 1,192,000 had been added to the stock by 1951. The level of investment in housing was no higher than in 1925–37. The number of council house completions was held back by the insistence of Aneurin Bevan, Minister of Health, that building should be to a high standard, but more important were the strict expenditure controls imposed by the Treasury. The health service was reorganised and nationalised, but little was spent on hospitals or health centres. No new hospital was built until the late 1950s. Expenditure on nursery schools was sanctioned only in areas 'where exporting industries need the services of working mothers'. Total government expenditure on social services rose only from 10 per cent to 14 per cent of GDP between 1945 and 1950, whilst total government expenditure fell by over 20 per cent, mainly due to defence cuts. The steeply progressive wartime income tax structure was retained. By 1949–50 the income tax and surtax structure was more progressive than in 1938. Basic rates of income tax had been cut and the exemption level raised, but surtax increased until incomes over £20,000 were liable for 19s 6d in the pound. Death duties were increased. By 1951 Labour was considering a capital gains tax.

Against this background the outcome was a remarkable transformation. Full employment for men was achieved, though to what extent as a direct result of government policy is debatable. As Labour had always predicted, this did far more than welfare measures to improve living standards. More married women were officially recorded as being in paid work after the war and those who were not mothers of young children were encouraged to work as the labour shortage became apparent. But women were treated as optional extras to a male workforce and there were no official attempts to improve their opportunities. It was assumed that the mothers of young children would stay at home. Labour refused to implement equal pay following the report of a Royal Commission on the issue in 1946, arguing that it would harm exporting industries which were seen as the key to British economic success. Even the rhetoric of gender equality was scarcely visible.

The two major, and outstandingly important, welfare measures were the National Insurance Act and the National Health Services Act, both passed in 1946 and implemented from 1948. The National Insurance Act was based, loosely, upon Beveridge's Report of 1942. This document, written by a life-long Liberal, recommended integration of the existing health, pensions and unemployment insurance schemes and their extension to cover the whole population. Wives of male workers who were not themselves in paid employment should be covered by their husbands' contributions. Benefits and contributions were to be uniform for the whole population. Benefits were to be adequate to live on, but no more, following a twenty-year period in which contributions would mature. Beveridge had long favoured universality over the means-tested benefits which had characterised pre-war welfare. He believed means tests to be stigmatising, socially divisive and inefficient at targeting need, a view that was widely shared within the labour movement. Beveridge was also convinced that to obtain a higher than minimum income individuals should provide for themselves, ideally through non-profit, mutual aid institutions such as trade unions and friendly societies. He was aware of the problems posed by a national insurance system for divorced and separated wives and for unmarried women who remained at home to care for elderly relatives, but his attempts to resolve these issues were either dismissed by the Treasury on grounds of cost or could not be fitted into the relatively inflexible insurance framework. After the war Labour did not pursue these issues.

Importantly, Beveridge believed that his proposals could be effective in eliminating 'want' only if supported by a range of other measures including a national health service, a minimum wage, subsistence-level family allowances, rationalisation of the labour market, industrial training, strict price controls, statutory limitation of free collective bargaining, public ownership of the land and essential services and, if necessary,

the phasing out of private ownership of most of the means of production, some of which aroused more enthusiasm in the Labour Party than
others. He aimed to introduce an effective 'national minimum of civilized life'.[56]

The Labour government incorporated certain principles of the
Beveridge Report in the 1946 legislation. Old-age pensions were paid at
a rate slightly above the level recommended by Beveridge and the
government appears to have believed that they were set at the current
subsistence level. It rejected the insurance principle which required that
benefits should mature as the insurance fund built up, because it was
believed that voters could not wait for higher pensions. Hence the
British social security system became effectively tax-based despite the
notional insurance principle, unlike those of many other European
countries. Unfortunately, living costs had been measured incorrectly
and at the time the scheme came into effect in 1948 benefit rates were
significantly below the level adequate for subsistence. In view of their
flat-rate character, it would have been costly to raise them. The desire of
the Minister of Pensions and National Insurance, James Griffiths, to
link benefits to an index of prices or wages was rejected. In consequence,
means testing was not abolished: the poorest still required a means-
tested supplement to pensions and other benefits. The National
Assistance Act of 1948 replaced public assistance with a theoretically
less stigmatising system of means-tested benefits. In its first year,
495,000 old-age and widowed pensioners required a means-tested
national assistance supplement. The post-war British social security
system was closer to the spirit and practice of its deeply rooted Poor
Law tradition than commentators then and now have always recognised.[57] Friendly societies and trade unions lost their roles in the administration of national insurance, which was taken over by government
officials. In consequence these traditional working-class savings institutions were weakened and were unable to play the role envisaged by
Beveridge of providing a supplementary system of pensions and other
benefits. Labour, influenced by criticisms of their inefficiency as
'approved societies', did nothing to encourage their survival.

There was criticism in the Labour Party of the low level of benefits,
but surprisingly little of the limited and inflexible character of the
system as a whole, or of the regressive character of the flat-rate contributions, which took relatively more from the pay packets of the poor
than of the rich. The scheme was widely believed to be redistributive,
which it was only to a very small degree. The level of benefit quickly
slipped behind those of other European countries. It was widely

believed in the 1990s that the post-war 'Beveridge' system provided well for the needs of the 1940s but had become out-dated due to economic and social change. In truth it was never adequate.

No serious consideration was given to more flexible, income-related, social insurance systems such as had long operated in Germany and which were to be introduced by social-democratic governments elsewhere in Europe. Labour was wedded, more firmly than its supporters always realised, to a minimal conception of public welfare supplemented by private effort. Increasingly, at least among male workers, this took the form of occupational pensions, which spread rapidly, especially in the nationalised industries. The government rather disapproved of this development but did nothing to prevent a dual system of pensioning emerging for the worse and for the better paid in what was proclaimed as a new universal 'welfare state'.

The national health service legislation was the work of Aneurin Bevan. Bevan, like Wheatley in 1924, was associated with the left and was a surprising appointment given his previous lack of experience of health administration, though his early life in South Wales had given him plenty of experience of ill health in working-class communities, and of the efforts of the miners' unions to protect their members from it. He was also an unlikely minister to overthrow the policy on which Labour had been elected. But instead of the integrated, wholly nationalised system staffed by salaried personnel, excluding private practice, which Labour had proposed, the NHS was tripartite in structure, divided between local authority, GP and hospital services. Doctors were paid on a per capita fee basis and they retained their rights to private practice. These were almost certainly the only terms on which the medical profession would have accepted an NHS, much though many of them needed it for survival, given the growing costs of medical care. Bevan was shrewd and flexible enough to recognise that clinging too piously to party dogma would destroy the possibility of achieving the improvement in medical care for everyone which he passionately, and rightly, believed was essential in a civilised society. Perhaps only a left-winger could have got away with such compromises without a scourging from the left.

The outcome was a transformation in medical care, especially for women and children, within a highly cost-efficient system. Unlike the new social security system, though universal, it was not intended to be minimal in its level of provision. Under Labour the costs were kept to a minimum. Partly in consequence, regional inequalities long survived. Despite publicly expressed fears of the crushing costs of public demand for a bonanza of free teeth and spectacles – the real need for which had been seriously underestimated – up to the early 1950s the rise in costs of the health service only just kept pace with the rise in the birth-rate.

Bevan delivered a 'national' health service rather than one organised around the well-established local authority services, which Herbert Morrison – who criticised Bevan's 'left-wing speeches and right-wing policy' – among others, advocated. Probably no other structure would have been acceptable to senior doctors, but the choice was symptomatic of the Labour government's general preference for central over local administration, in line with the long-run trend of government, but out of line with its pre-war statements about welfare. This aroused criticism at the time and Attlee confessed in 1950 that 'we have taken too much away from local government'.[58]

Labour also introduced a range of innovative services ranging from legal aid and funeral benefit to improved childcare. These were also confined within strict budgetary limits. Tomlinson has commented, rightly, that, far from recklessly diverting funds which could have rescued the economy, as some suggest,[59] 'the "welfare state" of the 1940s was an austerity product of an age of austerity'.[60] Nevertheless, it provided as never before a secure basis for the lives of the mass of people who could not provide for all their own needs – at last a 'national minimum' – whilst carrying out a major task of economic reconstruction – a considerable achievement. It was hardly at all redistributive, but it provided a real safety-net which prevented the poorest falling too far behind the rising standards of the remainder, at least until the 1980s. Among its beneficiaries were middle-class people whose children stayed longest in education and who lived longer. Later commentators were to interpret this as an unintended consequence of a welfare state designed primarily to eliminate poverty. But rather it was the conscious *intention* of a government aware that it could not be re-elected on the votes of the poor alone, and equally conscious that many lower middle-class people could not afford to pay for their own pensions, health and children's education and had much to gain from a welfare state.[61] For this same reason the Conservative governments of the 1950s could not dismantle what Labour put in place. Only in the 1980s did they come to believe that the middle classes could afford their own welfare and that it was safe to try to roll back the welfare state.

Labour and its supporters were perhaps too complacent about what had been achieved in the post-war 'welfare state'. In the circumstances it was magnificent but the impression was too readily conveyed that what had been erected was a more or less complete edifice, a coherent structure operating on uniform principles, rather than a ramshackle one which combined means-tested and universal, minimal and high-quality, redistributive and regressive principles – a closure rather than a highly praiseworthy beginning which would need revision and development. The very term 'welfare state' implied a coherence which was misleading.

Thirteen wasted years

If Labour was complacent about the 'welfare state' by 1951, it was partly because it could congratulate itself on having implemented most of the promises in its 1945 manifesto. Introducing the 1949 policy statement, *Labour Believes in Britain,* which formed the basis of the 1950 election manifesto, Herbert Morrison pointed out that since 1945 Labour had delivered 'items of policy with which we were familiar and behind it all there was forty years of thought and propaganda'. Labour now had the task of deciding where to go next. Though many of the leaders of the party were ageing and weary, a young generation of intellectuals was close to the leadership and developing new ideas: Gaitskell, Michael Young, C. A. R. Crosland, Roy Jenkins, Evan Durbin and, to the left of the others, R. H. S. Crossman. They were encouraged especially by Hugh Dalton and Herbert Morrison.[62] As became clear from their writings during the 1950s, they shared Labour's traditional values but felt that their practical concomitants were changing as social and economic circumstances changed. But they were only one sector of a party which too often seemed to waste more of its thirteen years of opposition in internal strife than in constructive re-thinking.[63] However, few disowned what had been achieved or disavowed past Labour principles. There is as little sign of 'consensus' in *Labour Believes in Britain* as there was in the clear preference of the Conservatives in the 1950s for private over publicly funded welfare.[64] If there was little open dissension between the parties over social welfare it was because the Conservatives were constrained by the electorate from dismantling the welfare state as energetically as many of them wished.

A section of Labour was satisfied with what it believed the Attlee governments had achieved in terms of the abolition of poverty and redistribution, and questioned whether serious developments of policy were required. But by the mid-1950s social research was demonstrating that although poverty had indeed diminished from the horrific levels of the 1930s, it survived among groups who had not benefited directly from full employment, most visibly old people; that the system of theoretically impartial selection by ability of schoolchildren at age eleven

Pat Thane

favoured middle- over working-class children; and that new out-of-town housing did not necessarily improve the quality of life of the re-housed. In particular Richard Titmuss, Professor of Social Administration at the LSE trenchantly criticised the confusions and inadequacies of the health and social security aspects of 'the welfare state' (his inverted commas).[65]

Underlying much of the criticism was the belief that essential though full employment and economic growth were to 'welfare', they could not solve the technical problems of delivery of enhanced services; and that, although pockets of absolute poverty remained, state action was also required to improve the quality of life for many above that level. There was growing awareness of 'relative poverty', the exclusion from opportunities available to most of the population of many who were not absolutely destitute. Crosland's *The Future of Socialism* (1956) was characteristic of influential thinking at the time in its optimism that 'the worst economic abuses and inefficiencies of modern society have been corrected'. Like many of his contemporaries Crosland was strongly aware that 'it is in the backward nations that the real poverty exists; and the inequality between those nations and Great Britain is far more glaring than the inequality between the rich and poor in Britain'. But his main concern was with Britain, including the extension of the British welfare state, 'to make our state schools and hospitals and all the services which go with them, the equal in quality of the best which private wealth can buy'. Crosland believed that this could be achieved with sustained economic growth, which he regarded as more or less inevitable. His somewhat flabby analysis was influenced more by the growing fields of sociology and social psychology than by economics, emphasising that certain problems, such as the presumed 'decline of the family' would 'not be cured simply by doubling the standard of living in twenty-five years', though he offered no clear solutions. For Crosland, the school system, 'the most divisive, unjust and wasteful of all the aspects of social inequality', was the key to social change. He advocated removing private school privilege by the extension of free places and became the foremost advocate of comprehensive schooling.

Famously, though not for the first time among Labour leaders, he stressed the importance of enhanced quality of life:

as our traditional objectives are gradually fulfilled and society becomes more social democratic with the passing of the old injustices, we shall turn our attention increasingly to other, and in the long-run more important, spheres – of personal freedom, happiness and cultural endeavour: the cultivation of leisure, beauty, grace, gaiety, excitement and of all the proper pursuits, whether elevated, vulgar and eccentric, which contribute to the varied fabric of a full private and family life.[66]

Roy Jenkins, describing himself as a 'liberal socialist',[67] shared many of Crosland's objectives but was less enraptured by contemporary sociology and was a more incisive analyst with a clearer grasp of historical change. He recognised that social and economic conditions had improved but that 'there is still a great deal of very harsh poverty which could be considerably alleviated by government action'. He challenged those who believed change had gone far enough: 'the fact that conditions are generally fairly tolerable does not mean that they could not be much better . . . we still have only one bathroom for every two households . . . holidays away from home for only half the population; and an average wage of £13 a week, which at present prices certainly offers no material paradise'.[68]

Jenkins recognised that it was not now enough simply to alleviate the grimmest poverty, which in the past, reasonably, had been Labour's aim. Labour had to come to terms with the reality which had given such resonance to Harold Macmillan's 1957 soundbite: 'Let us be frank about it, most of our people have never had it so good.' Jenkins countered: 'What is necessary is to attempt both tasks at once: to destroy the islands of acute poverty which still disfigure our society and at the same time to offer a continuing improvement to those who have already attained average prosperity.'[69]

Economic growth was at the centre of his proposals for such change and he did not believe that it would come without 'planning', 'partly for ourselves and partly to reduce poverty in other parts of the world' and to prevent Britain falling behind other nations. Next came reform of education on the lines advocated by Crosland: 'Equality of opportunity is not in itself enough either as a social or an educational aim. It needs to be supplemented by respect for the unsuccessful and by a scepticism towards the values and rights of elites, but it is a great deal better than inequality of opportunity.'[70] Contemplating the costs of this and other desirable reforms, Jenkins assaulted, quite accurately, 'the conventional wisdom . . . that this country is staggering under the burden of top-heavy and extravagant social services . . . [which] . . . it is suggested, apart from mollycoddling huge sections of the population, prevent most people from spending their money as they wish, and impairs our competitive position in the world by imposing penal rates of taxation upon British industry and enterprise'.[71] Insofar as Britain had relatively high tax rates, the reason, he believed, was relatively high rates of defence rather than social service expenditure. He continued:

Nor is the evidence of our eyes any more conducive to the view that extravagance with over-lavish services are the order of the day. Look at the condition of our hospitals . . . and of many of our schools. Compare them with the vast prestige buildings, often of hideous design, which are currently being erected by many large private firms. They all make a claim on national resources . . . Our social services are not particularly generous and most of the benefits accruing to the lowest income groups are paid for, not by redistributive taxation, but by these groups themselves.[72]

But he did not favour financing improved social services from further increases in income tax. There must be economic growth combined with a changed structure of taxation, to tax capital gains, business expenses and higher incomes. Progressive reduction of the tax threshold and increased taxes at lower levels, drawing poorer people into the tax system were increasing the electoral perils of increasing direct taxes.

Jenkins, like Crosland, was convinced of the need for reform 'to make this country a more civilized place to live'. He advocated encouragement of the arts, improvement of town and countryside, abolition of capital punishment and theatre censorship, homosexual law reform, reform of the betting, licensing and divorce laws and of the administration of the immigration laws, legalisation of abortion and decriminalisation of suicide. He stressed the major divergences, the absence of consensus, between the parties on these issues (though there cannot have been said to be consensus within his own party on most of them), but he believed 'in the long run these things will be more important than even the most perfect of economic policies'. Strikingly absent among the pleas of both Crosland and Jenkins for a more civilised society was any reference to gender equality.

For the time being, however, economic policies played a more prominent role in Labour election manifestos, together with social policies such as comprehensivisation, which first appeared in 1959, and a major reform of state pensions, drafted in 1957 by a committee chaired by Crossman and advised by Richard Titmuss and Brian Abel-Smith of the LSE. The largest cluster of visible poverty was among old people, very many of whom refused to seek the means-tested alleviation of national assistance. The cumbersome flat-rate pension system could not meet the needs of the poorest except by raising all pensions at great expense. Titmuss and his colleagues proposed a system of contributions and pensions linked to incomes which was potentially more flexible and redistributive. This scheme, known as national superannuation, was promoted in the 1959 and 1964 manifestos, despite opposition from sections of the party who believed that the flat-rate principle was egalitarian and socialist, despite its failure to help the poorest, and despite its Liberal heritage.

The Wilson governments, 1964–1970

When Labour at last scraped an election success in 1964 it campaigned primarily on the need to modernise the economy and, once in government, economic policy took primacy over social policy, though the two were recognised to be closely related. The Wilson government saw itself as carrying forward the agenda of the Attlee governments. Economic growth and full employment were, once more, represented as the prerequisite of reform and social progress. But the government immediately faced two problems: the unforeseen economic crisis which immediately engulfed it and the slimness of its majority which necessitated strategies to win a quick election.

Largely for electoral reasons NHS prescription charges were immediately abolished and pensions raised to the highest level in their history, about 21 per cent of average male industrial earnings. This was popular but wrecked any possibility that the national superannuation scheme could be afforded and the pension system reconstructed; and still many pensioners could not survive without a means-tested supplement. To help them, national assistance was overhauled and renamed supplementary benefit. The detailed personal investigation of 'means', reminiscent of the dole and deterrent to respectable older people, was replaced with a statement of income. Benefit rates for pensioners, the great majority of claimants, were increased, granting them a real gain in income.

Also before the further election which followed in 1966, the widow's pension was increased from 10s (50p) to 30s (£1.50). Redundancy payments and earnings-related supplements were introduced for short-term sickness and unemployment benefits. The purpose of these and of the higher short-term unemployment benefits was to promote not only 'welfare', but flexibility in the labour market. Within two years the government had markedly expanded social security benefits and fulfilled its election pledges.

Crossman, to his surprise, had been appointed Minister of Housing, about which he knew nothing, rather than placed in charge of social security, to which he had devoted much time and thought. Wilson persuaded him that housing was a more important issue with voters, as it was. Crossman immediately joined the game of setting huge annual house-building targets – this time 400,000, 150,000 of them in the public sector. This target was not achieved until 1966, but by this time Crossman had raised the target to 500,000. Crossman also introduced rent controls in the private sector and protection of tenants following the scandals of Rachmanism.

Within six months of Labour's taking office in 1964, Crosland, as Minister of Education and Science, issued circular 10/65 requesting that local education authorities submit plans for the reorganisation of secondary education on comprehensive lines. A Public Schools Commission was established to enquire into the independent sector, but it reached no satisfactory conclusion. As in its previous period of office, Labour, though convinced that independent schools crucially reinforced social inequality, could decide neither to abolish them nor to flood them with state-funded pupils, so did nothing. More positively, planning began for a project much favoured by Wilson: a University of the Air, later named the Open University. Courageously, given the atmosphere of the time, and the fact that a Labour front-bencher, Patrick Gordon Walker, had been defeated on the race issue at the previous election, a Race Relations Act was introduced before the election. Labour did not, however, repeal the immigration restrictions which they had criticised while in opposition.

Labour went into the 1966 election with a creditable record in which social policy was prominent. It won a decisive majority. Almost immediately it faced a new economic crisis, leading to devaluation in 1967. In consequence the raising of the school-leaving age to sixteen was postponed once more. The housing targets were again not met. Nevertheless, more new houses were built between 1964 and 1970 than in the last six years of Conservative rule. Labour placed much faith in town planning as in other forms of planning, introducing conservation areas and a new generation of New Towns, notably Milton Keynes. It also switched from encouraging the cheap, high-density and often high-rise council house-building, which had enabled the Conservatives to push up the housing figures, with consequences which were becoming worrying obvious, and symbolised by the collapse in 1968 of a tower block in east London, Ronan Point. Labour instead subsidised the renovation of old houses, rather than destruction and replacement, and encouraged owner-occupation with low-cost mortgages by retaining the much criticised, regressive, mortgage tax relief. One aim was to encourage better-off workers to vacate council housing to free them for those unable to buy, thus unintentionally making council estates even more socially divisive. By the time Labour left office in 1970, for the first time more than 50 per cent of households were owner-occupiers.[73]

Another response to the economic crisis was the reimposition of prescription charges in 1968. This was chosen as an alternative to cutting the hospital building programme which had, at last, begun under the Conservatives. Labour's Minister of Health, Kenneth Robinson, consoled himself that those most in need (old-age pensioners, children, the long-term sick and supplementary benefits claimants) were exempt from charges. The numbers of the latter were rising and becoming more diverse because of the rise in unemployment and in divorce and separation, which increased the numbers of lone parents. It was increasingly evident that old people were not the only group in poverty. The researches of Abel-Smith and Townsend, both close to leading members of the government, revealed the extent of poverty in working families, especially those with several children. These findings led to the formation of the Child Poverty Action Group (CPAG), one of a number of high-profile single-issue organisations which emerged to hound the government in the later 1960s. Shelter, the Disablement Income Group and Gingerbread, among others, embracing modern technology as fervently as Wilson himself, made innovative use of the willing mass media to expose appalling housing, shocking conditions in residential homes for old people and for the mentally ill, and other horrors. Single-issue groups were not new in British politics but these methods were. Together with other critics in a growing number of left-wing, often Marxist or *Marxisant*, groupings, they put the Wilson governments under pressure to improve social policies to which the Attlee governments had not been exposed.

The CPAG, directed by Frank Field, posed an especial challenge. The cabinet was divided between supporters of universal or selective benefits for working families. In 1968 Labour went for the expensive option of raising the universal family allowance for the first time in a decade. This was inadequate and unpopular, the more so because it was partially financed by reducing child tax allowances. It was to some degree redistributive, from richer to poorer and from mainly male taxpayers to mothers who received family allowances, a tentative move towards what Roy Jenkins called 'civilized selectivity'. Despite pressure from the CPAG the government went no further in providing cash benefit for poor families.[74] A committee was established to investigate the growing number of lone parents and their needs but it did not report until 1974. Crossman, from October 1968 Minister of Health and Social Security at last, started to prepare legislation to reconstruct the pension system on the basis of national superannuation, but it did not go through before Labour lost the 1970 election.

Despite the economic difficulties and despite (and to some degree in response to) the criticisms of its own supporters, between 1964 and 1970

Pat Thane

Labour presided over a notable expansion of state welfare, and, for good or ill, less obviously subordinated it to economic priorities than its predecessors in the 1940s. Education expenditure grew by 6–7 per cent. There was a net increase of 1.3m houses. In no other five-year period since 1918 were so many new homes built as from 1965 to 1969. Britain, like most other developed countries, devoted in the 1960s exceptional levels of capital spending to such public institutions as schools, universities and hospitals.[75]

In other less costly respects the Wilson governments were both innovative in their impact on British culture and part of an international wave of change, often against the will of many of their own supporters.[76] The government initiated or supported a remarkable succession of reforms concerning personal life, of the kind advocated by Jenkins and Crosland in the 1950s, many of them implemented while Jenkins was Home Secretary from 1965 to 1967. In 1964 the first Minister for the Arts, Jennie Lee, was appointed and support for the arts increased. In 1965 (again courageously, given its unpopularity before the election) capital punishment was abolished, temporarily at first, and then in 1969 permanently. In 1967 local authorities were empowered to provide family planning advice to anyone who requested it and to provide supplies free of charge; amid tabloid shrieks of 'sex on the rates', initially few did so. Also in 1967 Labour enabled a Liberal Bill legalising abortion to pass and homosexual acts between consenting males over twenty-one were decriminalised. In 1968 the Lord Chamberlain lost his power to censor the theatre. 'No fault' divorce was introduced in 1969 and a Matrimonial Property Act gave partners an equal share of household assets following divorce. The Race Relations Act was extended in 1968, the year in which Enoch Powell's notorious 'Rivers of Blood' speech indicated the seriousness of racism in Britain, but in the same year immigration was further restricted. In 1970 Barbara Castle, as Minister of Labour, rushed an Equal Pay Act through the Commons before the election, responding to another powerful new pressure group of the 1960s, a renewed women's movement.

The Labour governments of 1974–1979

Labour lost the election of 1970. It returned in 1974, once more as a minority government in a growing economic crisis, on a decidedly more left-wing programme than before, promising a wealth tax, price controls and further nationalisation, as well as increases in pensions and other benefits. The manifesto outlined plans for a 'fundamental and irreversible shift in the balance of power and wealth in favour of working people and their families'.[77] The government was anxious to go for a quick election to gain a decisive majority. In consequence, in March 1974 an extra two billion pounds were announced for benefits, housing and food subsidies, including a record 25 per cent rise in the pension. Council house rents were frozen. In the absence of significant economic growth this had to be financed by tax rises, which increasingly affected the low- as well as the high-paid. In the election of October 1974 Labour gained a small but temporary majority which was soon eroded by by-election losses.

Thereafter the economy worsened as the oil crisis hit, but Labour proceeded with longer-term attempts to restructure the welfare system. Richard Crossman had died, but Barbara Castle, advised by Brian Abel-Smith, guided through the long-awaited reform of pensions in the Social Security Pensions Act of 1975. This introduced a state earnings related pension scheme (SERPS). A new pension, inflation-proofed and linked to earnings was added to the basic pension which was also to rise in line with earnings for the first time. Workers could contract out into approved occupational schemes. Women were assisted by the linking of pensions to the 'twenty best years' of earnings, and those who worked at home caring for children or others were counted as contributors. The aim was to introduce a flexible pension suited to the needs both of the very poor and of the better paid. It had taken Labour twenty years to implement national superannuation and it had come too late. By the time Labour left office in 1979 insufficient pension rights had been built up to establish resistance against the erosion of the scheme by their Conservative successors. Because the state pension had always been inadequate, the cuts in its real value which followed caused little public outcry.[78]

Prompted by the disability lobby Labour also introduced for the first time a mobility allowance and invalid care allowance, together with a non-contributory invalidity pension for those unable to contribute through national insurance, amongst other measures to assist disabled people. The government was similarly responsive to continuing pressure from the CPAG. Barbara Castle introduced the Child Benefit Act of 1975, countering the means-tested family income supplement for working families introduced by the Conservatives. The 1975 Act at last gave the benefit to all children, financing it by removing the child tax allowance. Before it could be implemented, the oil crisis hit with full force and Wilson resigned and was replaced by James Callaghan, who was a supporter neither of the new legislation nor of Castle. The government attempted to avoid implementation, introducing instead a new lone-parent benefit which targeted some of the poorest families, though it was also paid to the less poor. It was a minimal response to the Finer Report on one-parent families which appeared in 1974. In the end, a vigorous campaign by Castle and the CPAG shamed the government into introducing child benefit in full.[79]

Another campaign which had grown in the 1960s was against violence (generally towards women) in households. Following the recommendations of the Law Commission, which Labour had established in 1965 as a permanent body to review and update aspects of the law, the Domestic Violence and Matrimonial Proceedings Act gave victims some legal protection. This was strengthened somewhat by the 1978 Domestic Proceedings and Magistrates Court Act. The 1977 Housing (Homeless Persons) Act enabled local authorities to provide accommodation for mothers escaping violence. The Sex Discrimination Act of 1975 took further the gender equality legislation rushed through in 1970, giving women the right in principle to equal access to jobs and equal treatment at work with men. Also in 1975 the Employment Protection Act introduced statutory maternity leave.

There had been a real extension of the range of state 'welfare' action and serious attempts at redistribution, through a mixture of universality and targeting at a time of serious world economic crisis and minimal economic growth. But successive accretions to a 'welfare state' which had been incoherent from its inception and had been subjected to no co-ordinated review since the war was creating an increasingly complex structure which was failing to deliver support efficiently to many in need. This was most starkly exposed by the 'poverty trap', which prevented increasing numbers of households from raising their incomes by moving from welfare into paid work. Too often those who tried to make this move found that the combined impact of loss of benefits with low pay and taxation meant an actual reduction in their already inadequate incomes. Even some who desperately wanted to work could not afford to do so.[80]

In the 1960s and still more in the 1970s, the close relationship of social with economic policy within a framework of a vision for long-run social change, on which Labour had insisted since its foundation, was broken. Rather, social policy was often made primarily in response to short-term electoral and/or party pressures. Labour lost the election of 1979 and spent the 1980s defending the welfare state against Conservative attempts to erode it, amid evidence of widening disparities of income and of a growing cultural as well as material gulf between those who were included in and excluded from the taken-for-granted opportunities of the dominant culture.

Social justice and New Labour

When John Smith became leader in 1992 he set Labour to serious, long-term thinking about aspects of policy. Smith believed that fifty years after the Beveridge Report a co-ordinated review of social policy was required. He established the Social Justice Commission for this purpose, but did not live to see its report in 1994.

The commission 'was established independently of the Labour party . . . but the Shadow Secretary of State for Social Security, Donald Dewar, provided encouragement throughout the 18 months of our deliberations'. The secretary of the commission was to become a close adviser of the Blair leadership and it included one future New Labour minister. Its recommendations read like a blueprint for the actions of New Labour and, to a greater degree than its authors may have realised, as a restatement of very old Labour values and policies, with some adjustment for a century of change and translated into the soundbites of 1990s New Labourspeak. They rested on four propositions:

- We must transform the welfare state from a safety net in times of trouble to a springboard for economic opportunity. Paid work for a fair wage is the most secure and sustainable way out of poverty.
- We must radically improve access to education and training, and invest in the talent of all our people.
- We must promote real choices across the life-cycle for men and women in the balance of employment, family, education, leisure and retirement.
- We must reconstruct the social wealth of our country. Social institutions, from the family to local government, must be nurtured to provide a dependable social environment in which people can lead their lives.[81]

The commission advocated what it called 'Investors' Britain' which would 'combine the ethics of community with the dynamics of a market economy' as distinct from the 'Deregulators' Britain' of the Conservatives or the 'Levellers' Britain' of sections of the Labour Party in the recent past, who 'argue that economic renewal should not be the concern of a Commission on Social Justice . . . They believe that we should try to achieve social justice primarily through the tax and benefits system.'

'Investors' Britain' assumed that 'Paid or unpaid, work is central to our lives', so 'government must commit itself to a modern form of full employment', suited to what was recognised as a two-sex labour force in what was assumed to be a less stable, more flexible, labour market than that of the 1940s. It was taken for granted, as it had not previously been in British social policy, that women, like men, might be independent household breadwinners and should be treated accordingly. The first essential was 'a high and sustainable growth rate' and a more competitive economy. Also prioritised were education ('lifelong learning'), help with childcare and other measures to reintegrate the long-term unemployed, including mothers of young children, into the economy, a minimum wage, rights at work, and an integrated tax and benefit system to eliminate the 'poverty trap' and provide incentives, not disincentives, for employment. The new welfare state should be preventive and redistributive, with 'a Minimum Income Standard . . . set as a benchmark for employment and social security policy'. It should promote a more equal and open society in all respects, including racial and gender equality. It 'must offer a hand up, not just a hand-out'.[82] It could 'promote personal independence and produce significant savings to the Exchequer . . . conscious that low and middle income families are now facing higher taxes than before'.

The soundbites of New Labour in office after 1997 carried the same message, as one minister announced: 'By running the economy well you can do more for those in need.'[83] But there was every sign that there was substance behind the soundbites, above all in the Treasury-led drive for 'Welfare to Work'. For all the (justified) New Labour protests that unemployment and lack of income were not the only causes of the visible, multiple symptoms of large-scale deprivation, there is no doubt that Gordon Brown, as Chancellor, believed as firmly as Ramsay MacDonald and trade unionists in 1900 that work provided the fastest track to welfare. However, an important change from the past was the central and positive role of the Treasury in New Labour welfare policies, above all in the formulation of the working families tax credit, which integrated rates and benefits for families on low earnings.

Conclusion

The continuities between New Labour welfare policies and deep-rooted Labour traditions are clear, and the actions of New Labour suggested greater awareness of this than their rhetoric betrayed. An important new departure, clearly informed by a study of Labour's history,[84] was that Labour came into government in 1997, as it proceeded thereafter, promising less than it hoped to deliver rather than more, and seeking to avoid the pressures born of inflated expectations that had driven the Wilson and Callaghan governments into sometimes unwise courses. New Labour avoided language that triggered expectations – such as redistribution of wealth and income – even while planning and delivering redistribution, as Brown's first two budgets did. Though, in reality, the caution of the Labour Party of Blair and Brown scarcely outdid that of Attlee's party; nor did their desire to deliver both to the poorest and to the wider nation.

A more decisive apparent break with the past was a late twentieth-century unease about mothers who preferred to make childcare their primary work, which sits oddly with a commitment to the family as the ultimate guarantor of personal security as strong as at any time in Labour's history. More familiar in New Labour rhetoric are the hints of the old Labour finger-wagging tendency, echoes of Douglas Jay's notorious comment of the Attlee years that 'the gentleman from Whitehall really does know better what is good for the people than the people know themselves'.[85] But Labour has always displayed a tension between puritanism and a highly restrained libertarianism.

Labour entered the twentieth century behind the slogan 'The Right to Work or Full Maintenance'. It ended the century offering 'Welfare to Work'. There had been a shift from a conception of work as a right to work as an obligation. This shift was propelled by profound social, economic and cultural changes, of which one outcome was that by the end of the century the poorest section of the population was no longer routinely described as the working class, because many had lost any hope of paid work. In giving priority to ending an often despairing, destructive culture of non-work, New Labour could seem insensitive to those unable to work for such reasons as disability or old age. They could appear to forget that there was still severe poverty to be cured as well as a need to provide equal opportunities and prevent future poverty, and to overlook another of its slogans, which more obviously shared the values of Labour when it was really new, in 1900: 'Work for those who can, welfare for those who can't.'

But nor was this aspiration hidden from sight, and by the end of its first century Labour's new welfare policies were still in the making and were necessarily unfinished after less than three years in office. A clear lesson from twentieth-century history was that fundamental change takes time. Throughout the century no Labour government had experienced more than five years with a secure majority in which to devise and implement new policies and to guide them to fruition. New Labour is entering the new millennium determined to break this pattern. The outcome remains to be seen.

Notes

1 J. Ramsay MacDonald, *The New Unemployed Bill of the Labour Party* (London: ILP Publications, 1907), pp. 3–4.
2 Ibid., pp. 6, 10–11.
3 Ibid., p. 14.
4 J. Ramsay MacDonald, *The Socialist Movement* (London: Williams and Norgate, 1911), p. 173.
5 J. Ramsay MacDonald, *Socialism and Society*, 2nd edn (London: ILP Publications, 1905), pp. 177–8.
6 P. A. Ryan, '"Poplarism", 1894–1930', in Pat Thane (ed.), *The Origins of British Social Policy* (London: Croom Helm, 1978), pp. 56–83.
7 J. Ramsay MacDonald, *Labour Party's Policy*. Speech delivered in Halifax, 24 November 1912 (London: ILP Publications, 1912), p. 11.
8 MacDonald, *The Socialist Movement*, pp. 155–6.
9 Ibid., pp. 179–2. Also MacDonald, *Labour Party's Policy*, p. 12; *The Socialist Movement*, pp. 157, 166–8. J. Keir Hardie, *From Serfdom to Socialism* (London: George Allen, 1905), p. 9.
10 MacDonald, *Socialism and Society*, p. 133.
11 Hardie, *Serfdom to Socialism*, pp. 23–4.
12 Ibid., p. 12
13 MacDonald, *Socialism and Society*, p. 134 fn.
14 Hardie, *Serfdom to Socialism*, pp. 25–6.
15 Ryan, 'Poplarism'.
16 Bentley B. Gilbert, *The Evolution of National Insurance in Great Britain* (London: Michael Joseph, 1966) argues strongly, and wrongly, that friendly societies and trade unions opposed state pensions for self-interested reasons, pp. 159–232.
17 Patricia Hollis, *Ladies Elect. Women in English Local Government, 1865–1914* (Oxford: Oxford University Press, 1987).
18 Pat Thane, 'Labour and local politics: radicalism, democracy and social reform, 1880–1914', in Eugenio. F. Biagini and Alastair J. Reid (eds.), *Currents of Radicalism* (Cambridge: Cambridge University Press, 1991), pp. 244–70.
19 Pat Thane, 'The Labour Party and state "welfare"', in K. D. Brown (ed.), *The First Labour Party* (London: Croom Helm, 1985), pp. 184–5.
20 Ibid.
21 Ibid., p. 195.
22 Ibid., pp. 190–1.
23 Pat Thane, 'The working class and state "welfare" in Britain, 1880–1914', *Historical Journal* 27 (1984), 877–900.
24 Thane, 'The Labour Party', p. 192.
25 Ibid., pp. 201–2.
26 Ibid., p. 191.
27 Royden Harrison, 'The War Emergency Workers' National Committee,

1914–1920', in Asa Briggs and John Saville (eds.), *Essays in Labour History, 1886–1923* (London: Macmillan, 1971), pp. 211–59.

28 J. Ramsay MacDonald, *Socialism After the War* (Manchester and London: ILP Publications, 1918).

29 J. M. Winter, *The Great War and the British People* (London: Macmillan, 1985).

30 MacDonald, *After the War*, pp. 79–80; J. Ramsay MacDonald, *Parliament and Democracy* (London: National Labour Press, 1920), p. 66.

31 J. Ramsay MacDonald, *Socialism, Critical and Constructive* (London: Cassell, 1921), p. 203.

32 Joseph Melling, *Rent Strikes: Peoples' Struggle for Housing in West Scotland, 1890–1916* (Edinburgh: Polygon, 1983).

33 A. T. Peacock and J. Wiseman, *The Growth of Public Expenditure in the UK* (Princeton: Princeton University Press, 1961), p. 204.

34 John Stevenson, *Social Conditions in Britain Between the Wars* (Harmondsworth: Penguin, 1970), pp. 278–9.

35 See ch. 6 by Martin Francis in this volume.

36 Ryan, 'Poplarism'.

37 Andrew Thorpe, *A History of the British Labour Party* (London: Macmillan, 1997), p. 53.

38 M. Powell, 'Did politics matter? Municipal health expenditure in the 1930s', *Urban History* 22 (1995), 384–403; Andrew Saint (ed.), *Politics and the People of London. The London County Council, 1889–1965* (London: Hambledon Press, 1989).

39 See ch. 6 of this volume.

40 Kim Yoonok Sternberg, 'Working class women in London local politics, 1894–1914', *Twentieth Century British History* 9 (1998), 331 n. 28.

41 Pat Thane, 'Women in the British Labour Party and the construction of state welfare, 1906–1939', in S. Koven and S. Michel (eds.), *Mothers of a New World. Maternalist Politics and the Origins of Welfare States* (London: Routledge, 1993), pp. 343–77.

42 See ch. 6 of this volume.

43 Thorpe, *Labour Party*, p. 65.

44 See ch. 2 by Jim Tomlinson in this volume for a detailed discussion of the economic background.

45 Ibid.

46 C. R. Attlee, *The Labour Party in Perspective* (London: Gollancz, 1937).

47 Ibid., p. 145.

48 Ibid., p. 194.

49 Ibid., p. 147.

50 Ibid., p. 153.

51 Ibid., p. 163.

52 Ibid., p. 166.

53 Stephen Brooke, *Labour's War. The Labour Party during the Second World War* (Oxford: Oxford University Press, 1992).

54 See ch. 2 of this volume.

55 Corelli Barnett, *The Audit of War* (London: Macmillan, 1986).
56 Jose Harris, *William Beveridge, a Biography*, 2nd edn (Oxford: Oxford University Press, 1997), pp. 411–12.
57 Ibid., pp. 182–4.
58 Martin Francis, 'Economics and ethics: the nature of Labour's socialism, 1945–51', *Twentieth Century British History* 6 (1995), 220–43.
59 Barnett, *Audit of War.*
60 Jim Tomlinson, 'Welfare and the economy: the economic impact of the welfare state, 1945–1951', *Twentieth Century British History* 6 (1995), 219–20.
61 Peter Baldwin, *The Politics of Social Solidarity: Class Bases of the European Welfare State, 1875–1975* (Cambridge: Cambridge University Press, 1990), pp. 131–3.
62 Francis, 'Economics and ethics', 222.
63 Catherine Torrie, 'Ideas, policy and ideology: the British Labour Party in opposition, 1951–1959', D.Phil. thesis (University of Oxford, 1997).
64 Harriet Jones, 'The Conservative Party and the welfare state, 1942–1955', Ph.D. thesis (University of London, 1992).
65 Collected in R. M. Titmuss, *Essays on 'the Welfare State'* (London: Allen and Unwin, 1958).
66 C. A. R. Crosland, *The Future of Socialism* (London: Jonathan Cape, 1956).
67 Roy Jenkins, *The Labour Case* (Harmondsworth: Penguin, 1959).
68 Ibid., p 54.
69 Ibid., pp. 56–7.
70 Ibid., p. 87.
71 Ibid., p. 118.
72 Ibid., p. 119.
73 Howard Glennerster, *British Social Policy since 1945* (Oxford: Blackwell. 1995), pp. 141–5.
74 Ibid., pp. 115–120; Nicolas Timmins, *The Five Giants. A Biography of the Welfare State* (London: Fontana, 1995), pp. 255–8.
75 Glennerster, *British Social Policy,* pp. 120–1.
76 P. Thompson, 'Labour's "Gannex conscience"? Politics and popular attitudes in the "permissive" society', in R. Coopey, S. Fielding and N. Tiratsoo (eds.), *The Wilson Governments, 1964–1970* (Pinter: London, 1993), pp. 136–50.
77 Timmins, *Five Giants*, p. 316.
78 Glennerster, *British Social Policy*, pp. 113–14.
79 Ibid., pp. 119–20; Timmins, *Five Giants,* pp. 345–7.
80 Glennerster, *British Social Policy*, pp. 227–33.
81 *Social Justice. Strategies for National Renewal. The Report of the Commission on Social Justice* (London: Vintage, 1994), pp. 1–2.
82 Ibid., pp. 7–8.
83 Alistair Darling MP, quoted in the *New Statesman*, 10 August 1999.
84 As Tony Blair has admitted, interview the *Guardian*, 25 September 1999.
85 Douglas Jay, *The Socialist Case*, 2nd edn (London: Faber, 1948), p. 258.

4 | Labour and international affairs

Stephen Howe

It is arguable that the British Labour Party has never had a distinctive foreign policy. At least it cannot be said to have had an original, coherent 'package' of views on Britain's place in the world, traceable right across the party's history and shaped by underlying principles peculiar to socialist or social-democratic thought, in the way that (at least until the 1990s) it had in such spheres as welfarism, egalitarianism or economic management.[1] None of the varied strands of socialist thought influencing the party, from Marxism to Fabianism, offered a distinct, coherent approach to international affairs: all were essentially theories about social and economic organisation *within* particular states. British Labour's form of socialism thus had few tools of its own for handling the peculiarities of 'its' state. The British state was both multinational and imperial, uneasily poised in ever-shifting balances between globalism and insularity, between Atlanticism and Europeanism, between a formal colonial empire which was in evident decline well before Labour ever held real power and a wider 'informal empire' of trade and finance, military strength and diplomatic influence which, though also steadily diminishing, shaped British state strategies throughout Labour's century.

Rather than a distinctive socialist or labourist philosophy of foreign affairs, Labour politicians – especially on the party's left wing – tended toward a set of ethical stances, fairly directly inherited from Victorian radical liberalism. Most of the party's debates and disputes on international and imperial affairs were shaped by the tensions between this ethical appeal and the demands of *Realpolitik*. This was already evident very early in the party's evolution, with the bitter schisms within the Fabian Society over the second Anglo-Boer War, and then within the Independent Labour Party at the outbreak of the First World War. Labour's debates over appeasement and rearmament in the 1930s, over imperial reform and then decolonisation from the 1930s to the 1960s, and over nuclearism in the 1950s and again the 1980s, revealed the same broad patterns.

Principles

The basic premise of this ethical stance was internationalism, both as a value in itself and, for some, one reinforced by an idea which was of mostly Marxist lineage, that 'the workers have no country'. In 1914 Labour and the Independent Labour Party (ILP) found themselves so deeply split over attitudes to European war, as did most of their Second International sister parties, that many have seen this as the early death knell of Labour's ethical faith. In fact Labour recovered its cohesion and sense of purpose very quickly after 1914. Since then, 'workers' internationalism' has had a very chequered career. On the positive side, although the primary impulse toward internationalism was inherited from earlier liberal ideologies, European socialists gave it far stronger institutional expression than nineteenth-century liberals had ever done: most obviously through the Second International, but also via a myriad of initiatives from workers' travel associations to enthusiasm for Esperanto.[2] Arguably, the internationalism of socialists and social democrats was – or became, gradually if unevenly – far more inclusive than that of their liberal precursors, in terms of class, gender and race.

Yet socialist internationalism often seemed to involve an abstract or utopian posturing, as with the notion especially strongly associated with orthodox Marxists in the 1930s, or with the 1980s' 'entrist' group the Militant Tendency, that all national or ethnic conflicts were soluble by the working classes on both sides uniting. At worst, it sometimes meant uncritical support for any movement or regime calling itself 'socialist'. Some left-wing critics, especially in the 1930s, resorted to an almost vulgar Marxist interpretation of foreign policy, as did even so brilliant and so unorthodox an intellect as Stafford Cripps. No pacifist or orthodox communist, and a passionate anti-fascist, Cripps nonetheless felt that the essential motivation of British international behaviour 'is, and must be, the urgent necessities of the capitalist economic system itself'.[3] Both fascism and Marxism were direct and inevitable outgrowths of imperialism, as imperialism was of capitalism: therefore Britain must first become socialist before it could be truly anti-fascist. Such stances were, however, always minority ones, and most efforts to find a major force in world politics around which they could rally have been disappointed.

A second core value has been the aspiration to settle international disputes peacefully: an aspiration which, as we shall see, has had many different variants. This has also derived from several different roots, including again the radical–liberal inheritance, and the mostly Marxist-inspired idea that international conflict was usually (or even solely and inevitably) a result of capitalist rivalries. Sometimes the belief proceeded from or moved into fullblown pacifism, though this of course was never either specifically socialist or a majority creed within the Labour Party. More influential in Labour's ranks, especially in the late 1950s and again the early 1980s, was 'nuclear pacifism', mainly expressed in demands that Britain unilaterally renounce its own nuclear weaponry, as mobilised by the Campaign for Nuclear Disarmament (CND). For much of the party's history, advocacy of free trade – sometimes seen as an almost miraculous solvent of international antagonisms – was thought to be a key part of conflict resolution or prevention. Support for international regulatory or peace-making bodies – especially the League of Nations, then the United Nations – was also a cause with which Labour was often suggested to have a special affinity.

A third very widely shared belief was anti-imperialism or anti-colonialism. Its implications appeared relatively simple when directed against formal, juridical colonial rule. However, not all socialists, even on the 'far left', were proponents of general decolonisation, especially where parts of the British empire were concerned. Some felt support for nationalist movements, even where these proclaimed themselves anti-colonial or anti-imperialist, sat uneasily with a generalised internationalism. Such dilemmas emerged at the party's very birth, as with the Fabian Society's divisions over the Boer War, and recently over conflicts in the former Yugoslavia. Some asked whether nationalism could ever be supported in principle by socialists. The standard contrast between 'good' nationalisms of the oppressed and 'bad' nationalisms of the powerful, was obviously too simple. The one has too often turned into the other.

Since the general end of formal colonialism, such problems have been messier still. Arguments by parts of the left, for instance, that the

Falklands, Northern Ireland or Gulf conflicts were straight 'colonial' disputes received only minority support within Labour's ranks. The word 'imperialism' itself became fairly unfashionable, even on the left. In cases like the Gulf War, those who used the term faced arguments that even if this was a case of 'Western imperialism' at work, socialists should view this imperialism as a lesser evil than Iraqi 'fascism'. Similar dilemmas emerged with Britain's leading participation in the NATO war against Serbia in 1999.

A fourth and most general principle, underpinning all the others, was the belief that universalist standards, such as the advancement of human rights and the elimination of exploitation, should guide and be pre-eminent in the conduct of foreign policy. Thus, perhaps the main trait that distinguished almost all currents of Labour thinking on international affairs from a powerful strain in their partisan opponents' thought was quite simply the belief that there *should* be principles in foreign policy – as opposed to the 'realist' stance that national interest was all. The main enemy was the idea of national interest in itself as the yardstick for foreign-policy decisions. Yet politicians contending for state power could never wholly, and certainly not openly, reject appeals to the conception of national interest. At best, they might seek to redefine it in ways more consistent with their other values. This naturally carried different implications at different times. For many in the 1990s, it meant support for any transfer of power away from the United Kingdom state, whether 'upwards' to the European Union or United Nations, or 'downwards' through Scottish and Welsh devolution.

In the party's first decades, opposition to war and to aggressive imperialism was the core of this value, but its active expression was unsurprisingly ambiguous. For most early socialists, 'imperialism' meant the conquest, exploitation or occupation of subject races; or (more usually, in the earlier usages) the attitudes and ambitions which encouraged these, and which were also felt to be inimical to democracy and social progress within Britain. Dislike of such practices or attitudes did not, however, necessarily, or for early Labour thinkers and politicians even usually, imply support for decolonisation. Where eventual self-government for 'non-white' subject peoples was envisaged – as it increasingly was for India – it was usually placed in the distant future. Even then, it would be within a framework of association keeping them closely tied to Britain, for which the title 'Commonwealth' began to be used. Widespread belief in 'racial' hierarchies of development, if not of innate capacity, made it as hard for socialists as for their contemporaries to imagine most colonies becoming rapidly or fully self-governing. When calls for wholesale decolonisation were made, they were mainly based on 'Little England' arguments invoking metropolitan self-interest, not on universalist principles or on the rights or political claims of the colonised.

Internationalism has thus long been central to Labour self-perceptions; but it has sometimes seemed largely describable as a 'Eurocentric', or (especially in the party's very first years) a 'white imperial', or British-diasporic form of internationalism.[4] It has also sometimes been argued that the 'international faith' was largely a concern of Labour leaders and party intellectuals, with the rank and file being characteristically far more parochial in their preoccupations, although this may have changed in recent years.[5] Patrick Seyd and Paul Whiteley's study of *Labour's Grass Roots* (1992) did not find interest in international questions – unless one counts British nuclear disarmament in this category – to feature at all among respondents' stated reasons for joining or being active in the party. However, significant numbers of those polled were also members of other, evidently internationalist organisations like the Anti-Apartheid Movement (11.8 per cent of the sample), Oxfam (7 per cent) or Amnesty International (6.8 per cent).[6]

However widespread strong *feelings* about international questions may have been within Labour's ranks, extended *thought* about them often seemed to operate in some isolation from the rest of the party's intellectual life. The great programmatic statements of Labour philosophy, including the successive volumes of Fabian essays, Anthony Crosland's *The Future of Socialism*, or Nye Bevan's *In Place of Fear*, up to Roy Hattersley's *Choose Freedom* or the late 1990s' outpouring of writing on the 'Third Way', were all notable for their lack of attention to international relations.

It continued to be assumed, until perhaps the late 1980s, that British Labour could in effect 'go it alone' in economic and social reform: though this was hardly a uniquely British socialist failure, as the experience of the first Mitterrand years in France indicated. Embrace of Euro-federalism from the late 1980s appeared to represent, among other things, acceptance that neither 'informal empire' nor 'social democracy in one country' was now viable.

People

Alongside the influence of ideas and principles was, naturally, always that of personnel and of particular personalities. The conduct of Labour's international policy, perhaps more than that of other major

123

spheres, bore the stamp of a small number of powerful individuals. In the first decades, Ramsay MacDonald and the less colourful figure of Arthur Henderson bestrode the party's international policy scene. In the 1930s and especially the 1940s the dominant figure was of course Ernest Bevin, the British Labour politician with the best claim to world-historical significance as an international statesman. One must note, too, the importance, perhaps unusually great in this sphere, of party officials and 'backroom boys' (including a few women). In the inter-war era William Gillies as head of the International Department, and Leonard Woolf as secretary of the party's Committees on International and on Imperial Questions,[7] played crucial roles. Later, little less essential were such figures as the Fabian organiser and colonial expert Rita Hinden, the party's long-serving Commonwealth Officer John Hatch, and International Secretary Denis Healey.

One major problem for Labour across much of the party's history was that in relation to foreign affairs its ranks included comparatively few professionals and formally accredited experts. Many highly qualified professional experts in domestic social and economic policy, at least since the 1940s, have been sympathetic to Labour's agenda and many have been official or unofficial advisers to the party. In international relations, this was far less often the case. The networks of serving or retired diplomats and other practitioners were overwhelmingly Conservative in orientation. Only a dissident minority were close to Labour, or gave the party the benefit of their expertise, especially in opposition. Its resources of expertise on imperial questions were more slender still. There were former colonial officials involved in the party's policy-making and advisory circles, but they were few and on the whole had not occupied senior positions in colonial administration. In the early period the most prominent exception was Sydney Olivier, a veteran Fabian and former colonial governor. But when Olivier became involved in Labour policy circles he was already an elderly man. So far as military affairs were concerned, the situation was little different: few senior military men were natural Labour sympathisers. Although many Labour ministers had seen active service – for instance, both Clement Attlee and Hugh Dalton had courageous First World War records, and Denis Healey among others served with distinction in 1939–45 – this was mainly at junior levels, and was no substitute for the kinds of expertise on which the Tories could draw.

Thus, in the inter-war years, Labour was left heavily reliant for foreign-policy advice on the so-called 'Foreign Legion', a coterie of veterans from the pre-1914 ranks of radical liberalism. The most important body in such circles was the Union of Democratic Control (UDC), in which not only many of these veterans, and most of the ILP's foreign-policy experts, but such figures as Ramsay MacDonald, were long active. Campaigning during the First World War for a negotiated settlement, and courting deep unpopularity by its conviction that Britain and the other Western allies were as much to blame for the war as was Germany, the UDC after 1918 advocated a wide range of internationalist causes, supporting peaceful resolution of international disputes, campaigning against the arms trade, and increasingly demanding colonial indepen-dence. After 1945, though of diminished influence, the UDC lobbied actively on African affairs.

The party's main internal critics on international policy also tended to be drawn from relatively restricted circles, with the same figures appearing as familiar gadflies across numerous issues and over many years. An emblematic figure was the Indian-born missionaries' son Fenner Brockway who, in a political lifetime that spanned Labour's entire century, also covered the spectrum of left-wing dissent on inter-national affairs. This embraced conscientious objection to the First World War and pacifist activism thereafter. It included championing Indian independence and founding numerous anti-colonial pressure groups, culminating in the Movement for Colonial Freedom in 1954. It continued with still vigorous involvement in anti-nuclear campaigning into his nineties. Indeed there was hardly a left-wing internationalist cause in Labour's entire history in which Brockway was not prominent.

It is arguable that Labour did not make best use of the resources of expertise which it did possess. The 'Foreign Legion' specialists and their successors almost invariably felt that their advice was not adequately taken by party leaders; and it is striking how rarely Labour governments have given responsibility for foreign affairs to those most obviously suited to such a role. In 1945–51, Hugh Dalton was the obvious choice for the post; and although Bevin was a brilliant success, it is hard to imagine any less suitable successor to him than Herbert Morrison, whose knowledge of the world beyond Lambeth was notably restricted. In the 1960s, Michael Stewart's whole career had prepared him to be a great reforming Education Minister, not a Foreign Secretary; nor was George Brown suited to the job by anything other than his own stubborn desire to do it. In 1997, Robin Cook was placed in the least appropriate of the great offices of state for his particular talents. Meanwhile, people who clearly aspired to the Foreign Secretaryship and were eminently suited to it by experience and specialist knowledge – most obviously, in the 1960s and 1970s, Denis Healey – never held the post.

Stephen Howe

The other major post of international responsibility, the Colonial Secretaryship, was no better treated. It was taken in 1924 by Jimmy Thomas, whose great influence within the early labour movement has mystified most later commentators, being unmatched by any apparent great imagination, intellect, or administrative or debating skills (or, as it turned out, by any great personal honesty). He was certainly not an active or innovative Colonial Secretary. Nor was the almost equally uninspiring George Hall, the ex-miner who was given the post in 1945. Arguably the only Labour Colonial Secretary with significant experience or expertise in the field was Arthur Creech Jones (1946–50), but even his qualities were outweighed by his perceived weakness in cabinet, in the House and as an administrator. The awarding of cabinet posts had little to do with expertise, experience and interest. This is an endemic problem of twentieth-century British government, not one peculiar to Labour or to foreign affairs. But it may have had especially damaging consequences in that sphere.

Policy-making on international questions was also highly dispersed. Thus, when Clement Attlee became Prime Minister, it was the direct responsibility of no fewer than eight members of cabinet: the Foreign, Colonial, Dominions, India and Burma, Defence, Admiralty, Air, and War Ministers or Secretaries. There was reorganisation and rationalisation. The India Office disappeared with the Raj itself; the Admiralty, Air and War posts were removed from the cabinet in October 1946 as military matters were concentrated in the Ministry of Defence. Much later the Foreign Office swallowed up the Colonial and Dominions Offices. Yet divided or overlapping responsibilities in the foreign-policy field – and the close personal interest taken by all Prime Ministers – increased the potential for conflict with their Foreign Secretaries. The watchful eye (and, its victims always felt, the tight fist) of the Treasury affected every Labour government at least as much as those of other parties.

The fate of the Fabian Society's forays into international policy is both significant and symptomatic. The Society almost entirely ignored international questions in its earliest years, until effectively forced into a debate on the 1899 Anglo-Boer War. The majority view was supportive of the war and of the 'imperial mission'. Reasons of domestic political calculation were important. However, efficiency was also proclaimed as the pre-eminent socialist virtue, and small states like the Boer Republics were thought inherently less efficient than a global British empire.[8]

Thereafter there was very little active Fabian involvement in foreign affairs until the Second World War, during which the Society established an International Bureau for the first time. This was modelled on the very influential Fabian Colonial Bureau; but whereas the latter played a key role in forming post-war colonial policy, the International Bureau had little success. Although it brought together many of the European socialists who were exiled in Britain during wartime, such links did not persist after 1945. Attempts to produce a volume of 'Fabian International Essays' foundered, for the sad and telling reason that it was not possible to achieve enough common ground among potential contributors to produce a cohesive volume. Renewed attempts to publish such a book, after long delays, disputes and changes of editor, bore rather disappointing fruit in 1957 with a volume which again had neither coherence of perspective nor discernible influence.[9]

Meanwhile, the part of the Labour coalition which played consistently the least active role in foreign policy was always the trade-union movement. There were, of course, notable exceptions to trade-union insularity, like Walter Citrine who, as General Secretary of the TUC from 1926 to 1946, sponsored greatly increased British union involvement in international and especially colonial affairs. Citrine served on the crucial Royal Commission investigating the future of the West Indies in 1938, visited the Soviet Union many times without denting his firm if cautiously expressed anti-communism, played a key role in the establishment of the World Federation of Trade Unions, and encouraged British trade unionists to extend direct aid and advice to their counterparts in developing countries and especially in British colonies. To hostile eyes, this was tying the labour movement to British colonialism and Cold War policies. Nonetheless it was a departure from the parochialism of earlier years, even if the British TUC never played as powerful a role in fostering colonial unionism as the CGT did in French colonies.[10] There were other individual union leaders who exerted an influence on international matters – Bevin on appeasement and rearmament in the 1930s, several left-wingers in the nuclear battles of the 1950s and 1980s – but the usual role of the unions in Labour's internal foreign-policy debates, even more than on other issues, was to provide support for the leadership against tendencies to dissidence in the constituency parties.[11]

Policies to 1945

In the party's early years, international affairs rarely featured in its debates, policy-making or ethos. The two successive party leaders, Keir Hardie and Ramsay MacDonald, were the main and often the only regular contributors to foreign-policy debates. Hardie's and, more particularly, MacDonald's approaches set the party's tone: indeed the main

planks of Labour's foreign policy after 1918 echoed closely the principles worked out by MacDonald and the small group of friends who had
founded the UDC. There should be general adherence to the principle
of self-determination: no territory could be ruled by another, or transferred from one to another, without the agreement of its inhabitants
(though for Labour leaders at this time, as for Woodrow Wilson and the
Versailles treaty-makers, this appeared to apply only within Europe, and
not to the colonial empires or to League of Nations Mandates). Foreign
affairs must be subject to democratic control, with no secret diplomacy
or any treaties or agreements, let alone acts of belligerence, which were
not agreed by Parliament. Instead of pursuing a balance of power,
Britain should support collective security through a strong international
regulatory body. And the UK should press for sweeping global agreements on great-power disarmament, plus the nationalisation of armaments industries to prevent private profiteers fomenting conflict.[12]

There could be little doubt about the sincerity or moral intensity of
leading Labour figures' commitment to such ideals, nor (as Stefan Berger
stresses in chapter 10 of this volume) about the importance of their role in
rebuilding the Socialist International after 1918. Although few Labour
politicians were widely travelled, and even fewer were able to communi-
cate in any language other than English, MacDonald's and Henderson's
stature in the wider socialist movement was high in these years, their range
of contacts wide. While such contacts were still mainly confined to Europe
and to the British imperial diaspora (especially the Australian and New
Zealand Labour parties), an increasing range of links with Indian nationalist politicians was also forged, especially by Labour left-wingers.[13]

Yet set against this wide-ranging (indeed in critics' eyes utopian) programme for the transformation of Britain's international relations was
MacDonald's desire to achieve a degree of cross-party consensus on
foreign and colonial affairs. He, like a majority of the Parliamentary
Labour Party (PLP), hoped this would secure Labour's aspiration to be
accepted as a responsible party of government. Thus, on colonial affairs,
Labour's leaders were in the main 'constructive imperialists'. They
believed in the doctrines of trusteeship and the 'Dual Mandate': that
Britain should exercise a moral responsibility towards the colonised
peoples and the international community. There would be progress
towards self-government, including extended political rights for 'native'
peoples, but this would be very gradual, especially in Africa, and would
remain self-government *within* the empire.[14]

As historian Henry Winkler suggests, in the years after the First
World War Labour gradually moved from possessing merely a set of

attitudes to international questions – attitudes characteristic of a small and essentially powerless propaganda group – to the advocacy of a fairly coherent foreign policy.[15] Its main characteristic was support for international or collective security and resolution of disputes. Yet this broad consensus concealed sharp divisions. The main dispute was between MacDonald, who believed that international organisations could resolve conflict by agreement and without recourse to arms, and Arthur Henderson, who by contrast felt that the backing of force would in the last resort always be necessary. Despite these differences, in Winkler's view Labour's stance would have been coherent and viable but for the rise of fascism, which destroyed all the old assumptions.

Henderson was one of the few Labour figures with ministerial experience in the 1920s: he had been in Asquith's and Lloyd George's wartime coalition cabinets. He was a crucial and retrospectively underrated influence on Labour's international thinking.[16] His trade-union background, his organisational role within the party, his passionate Christian beliefs, his unusually early and firm hostility to the Bolsheviks, and his presidency of the Geneva Disarmament Conference in 1932, testify to the breadth of his interests and influence. In 1934 he received the Nobel Peace Prize – one of only two British Labour politicians to have received this honour.[17]

Henderson's approach dominated Labour thinking from the mid-1930s onwards. The Labour politicians who, from 1935, repudiated George Lansbury's pacifism, and played so crucial a role in the wartime coalition government, were Henderson's heirs. The more idealistic and pacific strands of subsequent Labour foreign-policy thinking, meanwhile, owed much to the legacy of MacDonald. To the sad end of his career, he continued to regard 'the militarists' as the greatest enemy that he, Labour, Britain and the world had. This was ironic, given MacDonald's unenviable position in Labour collective memory and folklore as the Great Betrayer.[18]

MacDonald's and Henderson's last years, and the whole of Labour international thinking from the mid-1930s, were dominated by the rise of Nazism and the gradual descent to war. Yet war, when it came, appeared to some as an opportunity. Many on the left agreed that the conflagration could or should usher in a social revolution – or indeed that the war could not or should not be won unless there was such a revolution. It would be a war for democracy and for socialism. Socialism would come in and through the war. The strongest version of such beliefs was naturally held by Marxists, a few of whom continued to oppose the British war effort as 'imperialist'. A milder version of this association of the war effort with social, indeed socialist, transformation was held by many Labour left-wingers. Bevan continued to believe that the Tories did not really want to fight fascism effectively. Thus the war against the Nazis and the war against the Tories were two inseparable parts of the same fight.[19]

Most Labour politicians adopted a yet more modest conception of the relationship between prosecution of the war and social transformation. Their rose-tinted version became part of Labour mythology, extending far beyond Labour's own ranks. For many, this was a people's war, imbued with an unprecedented democratic and egalitarian spirit of Britain. The comradeship of the Blitz, the imposed equality of rationing, the newly politicised and undeferential armed forces, among other manifestations of this spirit, supposedly made possible both victory in war and Labour's own 1945 electoral success.

The Attlee governments and after

Foreign policy after 1945, far more than between the wars, was substantially shaped by the tradition or ethos of bipartisanship, even if this notion was at all times honoured almost as much in the breach as in the observance.[20] Certainly in the years after 1945 bipartisanship was far more evident than had seemed likely at the time of the 1945 election. Labour campaigning had emphasised the distinctiveness of the party's foreign policy, at least with regard to the superpowers if not to colonial affairs. The 1945 Labour manifesto had said, in relation to the Soviet Union, that 'left can speak to left', and would continue to do so.

Very soon thereafter the idea of such a partnership came to appear implausible. Attlee's ministers became by and large enthusiastic Cold Warriors. The symbolic moment of transition came when a secret cabinet committee, meeting on 8 January 1947, decided that Britain would proceed to develop its own nuclear weapons programme. The dominant figure on that committee, and in international affairs generally after 1945, was Ernest Bevin. Bevin was an extraordinary figure. Often crude and brutal in personal manner, cantankerous and flatulent, plagued by ill health which during his years as Foreign Secretary included numerous heart attacks, only semi-literate, he none the less commanded at least the grudging respect and often the awed devotion of all who worked with him, including his permanent officials. To the famously patrician senior staff of the Foreign Office, with products of the major public schools and of Oxbridge so heavily represented amongst them, ministers of self-consciously working-class background and manner could be figures of fun, even of contempt – as Jimmy

Thomas was at the Colonial Office – or class antagonism could imbue personal relations with constant strain, as was to be the case with George Brown. There is hardly a hint of this with Bevin. His officials' reminiscences breathe an air of almost unanimous admiration.[21]

Bevin presided over a foreign policy that was still truly global and imperial. His was also an 'imperial' Foreign Office in relation to other departments, in that he intervened, often decisively, in many areas beyond the strict or conventionally defined remit of his office. His impact can hardly be overestimated: the creation of the North Atlantic Treaty Organisation, of the Marshall Plan, and indeed even of the European Union, all owed a very great deal to his initiatives, despite Britain's insistence on remaining outside the infant framework of the EU. Indeed Bevin may with the perspective of time be seen as the most important architect of the whole structure of the Western Alliance, in its military, economic and political manifestations. As his biographer Alan Bullock comments: 'What is remarkable is that, in carrying out a policy which throughout depended on American resources and willingness to accept the British as partners, Bevin managed to combine an independence that frequently exasperated the Americans to the point of angry protest, with retaining their confidence as the man on whom they could rely amongst their allies.'[22]

After Bevin, Hugh Dalton was the party's most influential figure on foreign affairs during and after the Second World War. Many people disliked Dalton, and some were afraid of him. Tall, patrician, loud voiced, a gossip and a bully, he was also one of the most formidable intellects ever to engage in foreign policy for Labour. It was Dalton, more than anyone else except Bevin, who argued Labour out of its pacifist and isolationist position in the 1930s, persuading it to support rearmament and face the reality that war against Germany was coming. After 1945, by contrast, Dalton was among those who fought most fiercely for his government to cut military spending and global commitments. In this he was far less successful, though arguably the passage of time has proved that he was right here too.[23]

Attlee himself, meanwhile, also had decided and distinctive views on international questions. It has been suggested (most forcefully by John Saville) that these were considerably more realistic in their acceptance of a diminished post-imperial role for Britain than the attitudes of Bevin or most other statesmen.[24] Thus, oddly, the Prime Minister was the only significant senior critic of British foreign policy, the only person even partly to break from the consensus that Britain should and would remain a truly global power. His failed attempt to introduce a new, more modest,

Stephen Howe

precociously post-imperial vision of Britain's role in the Middle East exemplifies the point. The question of whether Attlee's government, in encouraging moves toward European integration whilst remaining largely a sympathetic bystander, thereby missed one of the great opportunities of modern British history, has been debated ever since. Most commentators today would concur that it proved in the long run damaging for Britain not to be truly at the heart of Europe from the start of post-war reconstruction. It must be asked, however, whether under the circumstances and with the assumptions of the time it could have been otherwise. Britain remained an imperial power, and it can hardly be overstated how strongly almost all parts of the political spectrum in the 1940s, and indeed the greater part of the 1950s, continued to believe in the centrality of a global imperial role for Britain in the foreseeable future. Ernest Bevin had been talking of a United States of Europe, at least on the level of economic integration, back in the 1920s. He repeated similar sentiments as late as 1945, whilst Hugh Dalton too, on behalf of Labour's National Executive, warmly endorsed the idea of a 'united socialist states of Europe'. These, though, were rhetorical flourishes. Neither Bevin nor Dalton was really a European at heart. Meanwhile broad swathes of the party held attitudes closer to those expressed in the supposed words of Herbert Morrison on European integration: 'the Durham miners won't wear it'.[25]

Even as policy-makers adjusted to or even initiated the dismantling of formal colonial empire, it was quite generally assumed that it was to be replaced by a no less extensive network of informal influence, shading into control. A genuine 'informal empire' would be created through strategic agreements, economic and cultural ties, military aid, shared ideology and interest including anti-communism, and organised through the institutions of the Commonwealth. This was expected to be both a more powerful and tightly knit and a far more thoroughly British-dominated institution than it subsequently proved to be.

Alan Bullock argues that much subsequent criticism of Bevin's pursuit of continuing great power status depends on false assumptions. It is supposed that, because it came to be recognised after the 1950s that Britain could no longer be a global power, it must follow that an earlier scaling down of ambitions and commitments would have been better. Bullock suggests there are good reasons for doubting whether this was necessarily the case. Above all, a world in which Britain had played a less active role between 1945 and 1950 might have been a far more unstable one.[26] And it may be added that Bevin broke decisively from the most important of all earlier, longstanding traditions in British foreign policy – the tradition well summed up in Lord Palmerston's supposed dictum that Britain had no permanent friends or enemies, only permanent interests. Bevin decided that there were to be permanent friends, the democracies of North America and Western Europe, and thus permanent commitments to those friends. That decision, that commitment, has never subsequently been altered – for good or ill.

American assistance and involvement in Europe was appealed to not only in order to guard against the supposed threat of Soviet invasion, but also to sustain Britain's global role. It was, perhaps, accepted that the British–American partnership would be an unequal one, with the United States as the senior player. However, it would be a partnership – one in which Britain would retain a powerful independent voice, not simply assuming the role of client or subordinate. Its role was to sustain, not to replace or wind down, Britain's global, imperial and world power position.

The crucial moment when it became apparent that the relationship with the USA would and could not be an equal one came in July 1947. Attlee's government implemented the agreement to make sterling fully convertible, a condition of the desperately needed post-war American loan. The result was a disastrous draining away of British gold and dollar reserves. Although the government suspended convertibility and implemented sweeping austerity measures, the consequences were lasting. Not only was the Attlee administration never to recover the reforming zeal of its first years, but the true underlying weakness of the British economy, its dependence on the USA, was starkly revealed, even if British politicians still took a very long time to learn the lessons. British foreign policy could never again be as independent as politicians had long believed it was. The Suez crisis of 1956 was in this sense merely the last nail in the coffin.

The views of the dominant ministers on Britain's international position were, then, in many ways highly traditional and imperial ones. Bevin is reported frequently to have posed to his officials the (real or rhetorical) question: 'What would Lord Curzon do if he were in my shoes?'[27] Such attitudes were reflected in a myriad of particular decisions, like the determination to sustain British power in places as far apart as Malaya and Iran – and indeed to strengthen it by building up a vast new imperial centre in the Middle East, the eastern Mediterranean and central-east Africa to replace the partly lost former centre of gravity in India – but perhaps above all in financial commitments. Thus, military and other overseas expenditure, in both formal and informal empires as well as the far-flung flashpoints of the new Cold War, were sustained at a level which, with hindsight, were simply unsustainable to an impoverished post-war Britain. Over a million servicemen remained under arms across the globe, maintenance of the Royal Navy and Air Force as striking forces with a global reach was taken for granted, as in 1950 was a major rearmament programme and deep commitment to the Korean War, despite the costs to a domestic social welfare and reform programme already facing financial squeeze.[28] Famously, this involved Chancellor Hugh Gaitskell demanding welfare cuts, whose combination of symbolism and near masochism seemed to others – especially left-wing critics – incomprehensible, and led to the resignations of Nye Bevan and other ministers.

Perhaps most striking of all was Britain's commitment to the nuclear weapons programme. This, it seems, was motivated overwhelmingly neither by perception of Soviet threat as such, nor by any American demand that the burden of the West's nuclear defence be shared, but by desire to uphold the United Kingdom's superpower status. When Stafford Cripps and Hugh Dalton protested that the nuclear programme was unaffordable, Ernest Bevin apparently retorted: 'We've got to have this thing over here, whatever its costs . . . We've got to have a bloody Union Jack flying on top of it.'[29]

Many, including Attlee himself, regarded the granting of independence to Britain's South Asian colonies in 1947–8 – India, Pakistan, Sri Lanka, and Burma – as Labour's greatest international achievement. The disengagement was peaceful, so far as British direct involvement was concerned (though not, of course, for the victims of the widespread ethnic cleansing that accompanied Partition). Moreover, British withdrawal was accompanied by important defence and strategic agreements with the newly independent states. Of more lasting importance, both India and Pakistan remained within the Commonwealth. This was seen as a crucial transition from a Commonwealth composed of states of white settlement to a much broader and more multiracial entity.

There were notable failures to set alongside this success. In the Middle East, British withdrawal from the Palestine mandate came to appear an undignified and unethical washing of hands, leaving bad feeling and accusations of bad faith against Britain from both Jewish and Arab quarters. More broadly, the Labour government's plans not only to sustain British influence in the Middle East, but to make the region the new centrepiece of British global power, were gradually but completely revealed as hollow. The aim of replacing direct colonial rule or the sponsorship of tame local autocrats with a new, less obviously manipulative partnership with Arab and other regional regimes foundered on the rise of radical Arab nationalism, and Britain's own ever-diminishing capacity to exert power.[30]

Elsewhere, the major thrust of Labour's colonial rethinking was directed toward economic development, which was seen as a precondition for any viable political advance. Retrospectively, the Attlee government's colonial reform programme, especially in Africa, was claimed to have opened the way for the rapid decolonisation which followed after 1957. In some respects it did, but this was clearly not the intention at the time.[31] Indeed, Labour plans to sponsor economic modernisation in the colonies were substantially negated by Britain's desperate need for dollars: colonial reserves and export earnings were raided to meet this need. Despite ministers' undoubted good intentions, the relationship between Britain and her colonial empire was perhaps more financially exploitative under Attlee than at any other time before or since.

Nor should one overstate the smoothness of Britain's decolonisation: there were significant military conflicts in Palestine, Malaya, Kenya, Cyprus, Aden and Borneo.[32] They were mostly small wars – at least on Britain's side. Britain's commitments of manpower and British loss of life were modest by comparison with France's wars of decolonisation in Indochina and Algeria, or Portugal's in Angola and Mozambique. But if losses among British servicemen were small (little over a thousand fatalities in all the country's post-Korean embroilments), death tolls among Britain's adversaries and among civilians were vastly greater. And there is no serious doubt that in all of these conflicts the British forces were responsible for widespread atrocities including murders of civilians and of prisoners, with excesses probably most widespread during the Kenyan 'Mau Mau' rebellion. If 'pleas in mitigation' can reasonably be entered, they would be that in most cases the worst incidents were the responsibility of police or auxiliary forces rather than British regulars or conscripts; and that torture never seems to have become as routine as it was for the French in Algeria.

There was, then, considerable potential for Labour to experience sharp divisions over these 'little wars' of decolonisation, several of which either began under Attlee, or were still live issues when Wilson took office, and whose conduct appeared so inconsistent with Labour's ideals. Yet such dissension was surprisingly minimal. Between 1945 and 1965, Labour Party conference debated resolutions even *referring* to Britain's wars of decolonisation just seven times: it never had a debate *specifically* on any of them. Labour (or its leaders) perceived the eruption of violence in British colonies essentially as intrusions into a narrative of progress.

Stephen Howe

The narrative itself changed with time: from civilising mission, to trusteeship, to colonial development and welfare, to that of 'empire into Commonwealth'. At each stage, though, it was colonial revolt which disrupted what would otherwise have been a smooth transition. Even if the ultimate causes might be traceable to the misdeeds of the colonisers of an earlier imperialist phase, from which Labour dissociated itself – of Malayan rubber companies' exploitation or Kenyan settlers' land-grabbing – there was no doubt in most Labour minds that the immediate culpability lay with those who launched guerrilla war. The dominant impulses among Labour leaders were surely the preservation of perceived British interests in the regions concerned; and more immediately an unwillingness to court domestic unpopularity by wholesale condemnation of British forces' actions. In the one post-war case where Labour – after much internal turmoil and misgiving – *did* clearly oppose British military intervention, the Suez crisis, public opinion was pretty decisively against the party.[33]

Thus colonial military conflict did not (with Suez as a very partial exception) seriously shake a general picture whereby, in British domestic politics, decolonisation was an astonishingly marginal issue. Not one British general election after 1945 featured the empire as a major campaign issue or one significantly influencing voting behaviour. The major disagreements ran within rather than between the parties; but no party split on colonial questions either, and Labour experienced only a few rather minor back-bench or constituency revolts on colonial questions.

Critics: Marxists, unilateralists and anti-colonialists

If colonial affairs rarely ever threatened to cause profound schisms within Labour's ranks, how far and in what ways did international affairs more generally become a battleground for the party's contending ideological currents?

It was in relation to communism and anti-communism that foreign policy most deeply and pervasively impacted on domestic affairs, with Labour's stances and disputes on a huge range of questions being fought out and characterised in terms of attitudes for or against the Soviet Union. A handful of pro-communist fellow travellers, sympathetic to or even more or less secretly affiliated with the Communist Party, were elected as Labour MPs between the wars. Several entered Parliament in the 1945 landslide. Always marginal in their influence, and with their views on international questions generally scorned, most were soon expelled and lost their seats in 1950. But a far broader current of sympathy for the Soviet Union continued to exist in Labour's ranks, compounded of a vague, often sentimental feeling that there should be no enemies on the left, of admiration for the USSR's supposed achievements in economic planning, and for its anti-fascist credentials. Though much diminished after the advent of the Cold War, and especially after Khrushchev's 1956 revelations of Stalinist crimes, such vague sympathy for communist states or the ideals of the communist movement retained a certain presence in Labour's ranks until very recently, well symbolised in the 1980s and 1990s by the charismatic miners' leader Arthur Scargill.

More widely supported were what became known in the 1940s and 1950s as 'third force' advocates. They mostly had no special sympathy for Soviet-style systems – indeed many people in such circles were staunch advocates of human rights and democratic freedoms in the communist world – but held that the United States was at least as repugnant a force in world affairs, and perhaps as deplorable a social system internally, as was the Soviet Union. They tended to believe that a middle way could be found between the two superpower blocks and the two social systems. For some, this middle way was to be sought via a federal Western Europe. Others, especially in the 1950s and 1960s, looked to newly emerging post-colonial states for the 'third force'.[34] The notion that a powerful non-aligned movement, or even new, more innovatory and humane models of socialism, could emerge in the new states of Asia and Africa, was quite widely held. In some cases, an idealised vision and intense attachment to particular Third World states took the place that for others had been occupied by images of the Soviet Union: Cuba, Tanzania, India, Nicaragua, Yugoslavia, communist China, even North Korea all had their fans.

The left therefore called repeatedly for a 'socialist foreign policy', as expressed in such publications as the famous pamphlet *Keep Left* of 1947. Yet there were few clear formulations, and certainly no agreement, about what this might imply. The question was: was the world divided between two ideologies or three? If the Soviet Union embodied one ideology and led one power bloc, the United States another, could Britain and Europe (or Britain at the head of a post-colonial Third World) offer a third alternative? Was Britain part of a Western or Atlantic bloc, a Free World locked in mortal combat with Soviet unfreedom? Or could and should there be a third way in which Britain – again perhaps at the head of Europe, or of the Commonwealth – combined political democracy with a fully socialist economic system?

An indirect successor to such aspirations was the movement for British nuclear disarmament, many of whose proponents – like 'third

Stephen Howe

force' advocates, and indeed like UDC supporters in the 1920s –
believed that Britain could give a practical or at least moral lead towards
a more peaceful world by herself disarming. Arguably, this aspiration
required unilateralism to be embedded in a comprehensive alternative
vision of the international order, and of Britain's place in it. Few if any
of its proponents actually made that case in any detail, either in the late
1950s' first wave of CND or in its 1980s' renaissance.[35]

And equally few leading Labour figures, even on the party's left,
appeared willing or able to articulate such a vision. Nye Bevan, like
Ernest Bevin, took it for granted that Britain would remain a global great
power. If the Labour left – the handful of active pro-communists aside –
had been in charge of the party's foreign policy after 1945, that policy
might not have been dramatically different. There would have been a
more publicly ostentatious effort to retain friendship with the Soviet
Union: but this would have been more a difference of rhetoric than of
practice. There would also, no doubt, have been more vocal support for
democratic socialists in both Western and Eastern Europe, and for
nationalist aspirations in the colonial world. British support for the
reimposition of French and Dutch colonial control in Indochina and
Indonesia at the war's end might not have been so readily forthcoming.
But it is doubtful whether policy in regard to Britain's own colonies
would have been very different. The sharpest differences that Bevan
expressed with the Attlee government's foreign policy related to the
Middle East, where he, and other left-wingers like Richard Crossman,
were far more wholeheartedly pro-Zionist than was government policy.[36]

For some on Labour's left, enthusiasm for various Third World revolutionary movements became the dominating emotion in relation to foreign
affairs. Such enthusiasm sometimes accompanied or derived from communist views, or, more often from the 1970s onwards, Trotskyist ones.
Frequently, though, it was a somewhat free-floating emotional attitude.
Labour's wilderness years of the 1980s were the high-water mark of such
feelings within the party. Often generous in inspiration, and certainly evi-
dencing a wider and more passionate internationalism than the Labour
mainstream, it still also contributed to the atmosphere of extremism and
unreliability that Labour possessed in the media and many public eyes
during this period. It was reflected in rank-and-file support for revolutionaries in southern Africa, Latin America and the Caribbean, and most
controversially for Irish Republicanism. This last did not extend, so far as
most even on the party's far left were concerned, to endorsement of the
IRA campaign of violence. It did, though, mean that for some time
Labour's official policy leaned strongly towards the nationalist side in the

Northern Irish conflict. During the 1990s, the party shifted away from many of these positions, adopting a more middle-ground stance on the Israeli–Palestinian conflict and on Northern Ireland. These two issues, Ireland and the Middle East, were among those where there were well-organised and vociferous lobbies within the party from the 1960s onwards, pressing often sharply conflicting policy preferences on the party leadership. Adherence to such groups was certainly not confined to particular ethnic or national lobbies, but the multi-ethnic character of late twentieth-century Britain meant that an ever wider range of people felt strong links to particular foreign-policy causes. Since the ethnic minorities concerned were mainly Labour voters, and were concentrated in inner-city areas represented by Labour councils and MPs, they tended to concentrate on lobbying Labour. By comparison with some other democratic polities, such as Canada, Australia and above all the United States, this had not become a significant phenomenon in British politics by the end of the 1990s. Still, on such issues as Caribbean development, Indian–Pakistani rivalry or Sikh separatism in South Asia, the variety of voices that had to be heard by the makers of foreign policy was greatly expanded.

From Gaitskell to Callaghan

Hugh Gaitskell, Labour leader from the end of 1955, had spent a politically formative period in 1930s' Vienna. He had developed close friendships with, and a sympathetic understanding of, Austrian Socialists. Later, his relations with European and American politicians were often warm, and his understanding of their national circumstances close. Yet Gaitskell too could oscillate between Little Englandism and imperial nostalgia.[37] Never was this more apparent than in his passionate and much praised party conference speech of 1962, opposing British entry into the European Community. The notion that European integration, bringing peace and harmony to a continent so long and bloodily divided, could be a moral project no less noble than those of Commonwealth co-operation or a worldwide Pax Britannica, was as alien to him as to most British politicians of his generation.

His successor and Labour's longest-serving Prime Minister, Harold Wilson, has attracted even more divided political and historical judgements than did Gaitskell. The middle ground of these sharply contrasting views, however, holds that his perspectives were – perhaps unavoidably – always dominated by crisis management rather than long-term strategic thought. Nowhere was this more true than in his governments' handling of foreign affairs.

Stephen Howe

Three issues dominated Labour's foreign policy in the 1960s. First, and overshadowing all else, was the relationship with the United States. In many respects, notably over attitudes to the American war effort in Vietnam, the Wilson governments appeared to Labour critics as almost slavishly responsive to American priorities. In so far as this was the case, it owed a great deal to the plight of the British economy in these years. The prospects and stability of sterling, in particular, seemed to be dependent on American goodwill. Conversely it was evident that, despite Wilson's hopes and protestations to the contrary, Britain had little influence over American policy in Vietnam or elsewhere.[38] Yet the symbols of British strategic independence and global might remained important even as the substance dwindled. Thus it was with the decision to proceed with the Polaris programme, despite Wilson's previously proclaimed scepticism on its value. Neither perception of Soviet threat nor American pressure appears to have been decisive here. Indeed the United States had apparently wished Britain to subsume its nuclear weapons capacity into a unified NATO system. More crucial seems to have been the simple fact that the nuclear deterrent was the most important symbol of Britain's great-power status still available.

The second overarching issue was the effort to negotiate terms for British entry into the European Community. Opinion within the Labour Party, and indeed within the cabinet, was of course intensely divided on the question. Harold Wilson himself often appeared ambivalent, or in critics' eyes devious, over how vigorously Britain should pursue attempts at entry. In any case, throughout his governments' lifetimes, French President de Gaulle continued to veto British applications. For many in the cabinet, including Wilson himself, de Gaulle's stance was a source of private relief, letting their divided party off the hook.[39]

The third crucial general question in international affairs was the continuing legacy of empire, and its complex diplomatic and strategic aftermath. Most obviously, Labour undertook in 1968 the long-delayed withdrawal from British military commitments east of Suez. Again this involved delicate negotiations with the United States, as well as with such friendly Commonwealth leaders as Lee Kuan Yew of Singapore, since both the Americans and various Asian governments disliked the prospect of Britain abandoning longstanding commitments to military defence in the region. Such feelings were echoed within the cabinet. Wilson had said in Parliament in December 1965: 'Whatever we may do in the field of cost effectiveness we cannot afford to relinquish our world role . . . Our East of Suez role.'[40] Yet the Wilson governments were constantly haunted by balance-of-payments problems, which were at the heart of their problems and divisions throughout. The biggest single cause of the difficulties was public spending abroad, which was almost entirely on the military. This ran at well over £400 million per year. Britain continued to spend a higher proportion of GNP on defence-related expenditure than any other Western European country. Many critics have associated this defence-related 'overstretch' with the country's generally poor post-war economic performance. After devaluation was finally found unavoidable in November 1967, it might have been thought natural that the military role east of Suez must and could be dismantled. Apart from anything else, the quid pro quo that had previously operated (by which the Americans supported sterling in return for continued British defence commitments in Asia) no longer applied. Yet the cabinet decision in January 1968 was reached only with deep reluctance and amidst some bitterness.

Otherwise the political legacy of colonialism seemed by comparison relatively easily dealt with, as many of the remaining British colonies gained self-government with little controversy and without bloodshed.[41] There were two notable exceptions to this picture of consensual decolonisation. One was in South Arabia where a small but vicious guerrilla war in Aden persisted for much of the Wilson government's life. Even after formal decolonisation there, continued British commitments to support local rulers against left-wing and nationalist attempts to overthrow them meant the more or less open involvement of British troops well into the 1970s.[42] Far more troubling and controversial, however, were developments in southern Africa. In Rhodesia, the white minority regime of Ian Smith unilaterally declared independence in 1965. Wilson's government, committed to instigating democratic non-racial successors to British rule in Africa, faced a profound dilemma. Was it politically or militarily possible to overthrow the Smith regime by armed force? The answer, it was quite rapidly decided, was no. Could the breakaway regime be brought to heel by economic sanctions? Again the answer appeared to be no, though much was made of Britain's efforts to do this. Could a negotiated settlement between the Smith government and its opponents be tried? Here the efforts of Wilson's 1960s' administrations were also unsuccessful, but so were those of their successors until 1979.[43] Meanwhile policy towards South Africa itself remained difficult and intensely contentious. Opposition to apartheid arguably aroused more passion and more generalised commitment among Labour activists and back-benchers than any other international issue from the 1960s to the 1990s, and this was at least potentially at odds with the economic and strategic interests which successive British governments felt they must safeguard in the region. It was perhaps fortunate, at least for Labour's image of unified opposition to racism, that the party was in opposition almost throughout the 1980s and 1990s, during the bitter struggle and eventual transfer of power in South Africa. Already in the 1960s there had been sharp differences in the cabinet and the parliamentary party over the sale of arms to South Africa.[44]

Under Wilson, the most influential figures in the conduct of Labour's foreign policy were George Brown and Denis Healey. Brown, who took over as Foreign Secretary in August 1966, was among the most colourful, but also, it must be said, among the least successful, politicians ever to hold the office. Notoriously erratic, unpredictable, often inebriated, the man for whom the phrase 'tired and emotional' was coined, Brown squandered considerable political gifts. In critics' eyes, he also weakened the pro-European cause, for which he was the cabinet's strongest senior enthusiast, by his personal behaviour and by the deep rivalry, indeed enmity, that existed between him and Wilson.[45]

Denis Healey was never Foreign Secretary, but he dominated Labour's approach to international affairs for longer than almost anyone who occupied that post.[46] In the perpetually embattled Wilson–Callaghan governments of 1974–79, a succession of Foreign and Defence Secretaries came and went. Healey appeared as the real intellectual powerhouse in the field. In opposition, after Labour's electoral defeat in 1979, Healey remained the crucial figure in international policy for almost another decade. He was sharply at odds with the strongly left-wing orientation of party activists during these years. In particular, his commitment to Britain's nuclear deterrent clashed with the rank-and-file desire for unilateral nuclear disarmament, which was also official party policy for most of this time. He made little secret of his lack of time for the majority party view, but played a substantial role in steering the new leader Neil Kinnock back in the foreign-policy directions which he regarded as more realistic.

After the Cold War: New Labour, new Britain, new world role?

David Marquand says of Labour's post-1945 attitudes to foreign affairs:

Even those who were not conventionally patriotic were more often 'Little England' radicals in the nineteenth-century sense than socialist internationalists. They could, and frequently did, protest violently against what they saw as the abuse of British power, but they took it for granted that Britain had power to abuse. As strongly as Charles James Fox or Richard Cobden or John Bright, they believed that Britain should give a moral lead to the rest of the world: as unshakeably as Fox or Cobden or Bright, they assumed that when Britain spoke, the rest of the world would listen. Now that assumption too was beginning to crumble at the edges.[47]

Certainly a number of the characteristic preoccupations of post-war left-wing international policy might be thought to echo 'Little England' themes. Opposition to British engagement in Cold War politics was sometimes strictly neutralist, sometimes reflected pro-communism or anti-Americanism, but sometimes simply reproduced the time-honoured radical slogan of 'no foreign adventures'. Similarly, the Campaign for Nuclear Disarmament drew on many different impulses, but prominent among these was a Little England concern lest this country become victim of an international conflagration in which, so it was thought, it had no proper involvement.

Hostility to British entanglement in such episodes as the 1991 Gulf War, the renewed assaults on Iraq at the end of 1998, or perhaps more obviously still, the Falklands War of 1981 and the onslaught against Serbia in 1999, might again stem from many sources, but these certainly included straightforward isolationism. Perhaps most obviously of all, opposition to European integration on the left frequently gave overt expression to a very traditional sort of insularity. One might say that if anti-Europeanism on the Conservative right reflected nostalgia for an imperial greater Britain, that of the left echoed something older still: the Never Never Land of Merrie England. A succinct and rather moving statement of Labour Little Englandism was expressed in Douglas Jay's memoirs, *Change and Fortune*, the credo of one of the most passionate of all Labour's anti-Europeans, who supposedly so distrusted all things foreign that he always carried sandwiches with him on ministerial trips abroad rather than risk having to eat non-British food:

What other country, after all, has preserved an unbroken record of constitutional government for nearly 300 years, and fought right through the two Great Wars, without attacking anyone else or being first attacked, to eventual victory? In a morass of transient controversies, let us not forget that. It is one reason why I can conceive of no better fortune when the time comes to cultivate private rather than public aspirations, than to live, love, garden and die, deep in the English country.[48]

Labour ideas of radical patriotism thus frequently seemed not to involve a different conception of the United Kingdom's international role, but rather a denial or willed amnesia that there was such a role. This enabled parochialism to slip almost unnoticed into globalism, or vice versa.[49] So inter-war UDC thinkers or later unilateralist anti-nuclearism could readily drift into what James Hinton has called 'imperialist pacifism'.[50]

Such prominent left-wing Labour politicians as Nye Bevan and Michael Foot donned the mantle of patriotism not by asserting an alternative foreign policy, but by a simple proclamation of superior concern for domestic economic well-being. An alternative view focused on the Commonwealth, or in slightly later versions on nuclear disarmament and non-alignment, as vehicles via which a Labour Britain could pursue a new, still global, but more morally acceptable and politically feasible global role.

If the dismantling of overseas empire proved not to mount a profound challenge to such views (though it remains possible to argue that such a challenge is still quietly being worked through), then it may yet be that a 'break-up of Britain' in the early twenty-first century will do so. Donald Sassoon urges that the key to understanding Europe's various socialisms is that all have passionately identified themselves with, and taken on the colouring of, 'their' national states.[51] One consequence has been the remarkable conservatism about reforming the state's central institutions which has marked most left-wing parties.

The Labour government elected in 1997 seemed to break substantially from that legacy of conservatism, sponsoring far-reaching change in the UK's governing arrangements including internal self-government for Scotland and, to a lesser extent, Wales, and espousing a far more enthusiastic Europeanism than its predecessors. The nature of the state itself was in a process of almost unprecedentedly rapid change. For those who thought that British foreign policy was and must be an expression of beliefs not only about national interest but also national identity, new questions were raised. In the wake not only of globalisation and Europeanisation, but of dramatic change in the positions of Scotland, Wales and Northern Ireland, could a singular 'British' interest and identity any longer exist?[52] Certainly if it did, it bore little resemblance to the largely unspoken assumptions about national uniqueness and long continuity on which the making of foreign policy had been based. The implications for Britain's international role were profound, and as yet little grasped.

Yet even if almost every aspect of the context, whether global or insular, was being transformed almost beyond recognition, still important continuities could be perceived, not least in the underlying values which Labour proclaimed in its international policies. The centrepiece of the Blair government's international policy was said to be the notion of an 'ethical foreign policy', focused on regard for human rights. As Robin Cook, newly appointed Foreign Secretary, stated:

The Government does not accept that political values can be left behind when we check in our passports to travel on diplomatic business. Our foreign policy must have an ethical dimension and must support the demands of other peoples for the democratic rights on which we insist for ourselves. We will put human rights at the heart of our foreign policy.[53]

And Neil Kinnock, addressing Labour's 1994 conference debate on 'Britain in a New World' – not long after he had himself stepped down as party leader – suggested that in a new 1990s era of globalisation and post-Cold War realignments:

There are few one-nation answers to any of the economic, political and environmental challenges confronting humanity.

And since that is now an irreversible fact of life, it is clear that the only practical instrument for the management of the common destiny of nations is co-operation.

It has always been a decent instinct. It has always been a fine purpose.

Now it must be recognised as the most practical tool for achieving global economic and political security.

What Cook and Kinnock proclaimed as new had in reality been, as we have seen, a mainstay of Labour thinking throughout the party's history. The ideal might be vague, and crosscut or compromised by different, perhaps narrower conceptions of national interest. But the ideas of co-operation, with its main practical corollary that of collective security, and of moral universalism, with *its* main corollary an agenda of democratisation and human rights, were always the heart of Labour's international aspirations. On that level Kinnock was perhaps closer to the truth when he concluded that: 'It is the *scale* of the challenge that has changed, not its nature.'[54]

Stephen Howe

Notes

1 There is no modern, book-length study of this subject embracing the party's whole history. The following survey cannot and does not pretend to fill that gap, particularly when it tries to embrace not only foreign policy as narrowly defined, but also the often distinct subjects – with their own, huge, separate specialist literatures – of defence and colonial policies. I am fully aware that some themes, such as international economic relations, have had to be neglected here. Labour's European policies are also given only brief mention, since they are more fully discussed in Stefan Berger's contribution to this volume. Among the relevant works, particular mention should be made of M. R. Gordon, *Conflict and Consensus in Labour's Foreign Policy, 1914–1965* (Stanford: Stanford University Press, 1969); and Partha Sarathi Gupta, *Imperialism and the British Labour Movement, 1914–1964* (London: Macmillan, 1975).
2 Christine Collette, *The International Faith: Labour's Attitudes to European Socialism, 1918–39* (Aldershot: Ashgate, 1998), discusses British Labour members' and supporters' involvement in a wide variety of such social and cultural expressions of internationalism.
3 Quoted in David Marquand, *The Progressive Dilemma. From Lloyd George to Kinnock* (London: Heinemann, 1991), p. 95.
4 For the strength of the party's links and interactions with continental European, and especially German, Social Democrats, see Stefan Berger 'Labour in comparative perspective' (ch. 10 of this volume) and his *The British Labour Party and the German Social Democrats 1900–1931. A Comparative Study* (Oxford: Oxford University Press, 1994). John N. Horne, *Labour at War: France and Britain, 1914–1918* (Oxford: Oxford University Press, 1991), indicates the strength of bilateral socialist and trade-union links during the First World War. On British imperial or diasporic 'white labourism', Alastair Bonnett, 'How the British working class became white: the symbolic (re)formation of racialised capitalism', *Journal of Historical Sociology* 11 (1998), 316–40.
5 So, for instance, Collette, *International Faith*, argues for the strength of a widespread 'grass-roots' Labour internationalism between the wars; while Tom Buchanan's study of a particular – and particularly contested – episode, *The Spanish Civil War and the British Labour Movement* (Cambridge: Cambridge University Press, 1991), suggests how broadly diffused, though also how divided, was engagement with the Spanish tragedy. My own *Anticolonialism in British Politics: The Left and the End of Empire 1918–1964* (Oxford: Oxford University Press, 1993), however, finds that close concern with colonial and imperial questions was almost always the preserve of small minorities even among Labour activists.
6 Patrick Seyd and Paul Whiteley, *Labour's Grass Roots: The Politics of Party Membership* (Oxford: Oxford University Press, 1992), p. 92.
7 Woolf held the former post from 1918 to 1940, the latter from 1924 to 1946.
8 George Bernard Shaw (ed.), *Fabianism and the Empire. A Manifesto of the*

Fabian Society (London: Fabian Society, 1900); and see the discussions in
Bernard Porter, *Critics of Empire* (London: Macmillan, 1968), Patricia Pugh,
Educate, Agitate, Organise: 100 Years of Fabian Socialism (London: Methuen,
1984), and Howe, *Anticolonialism.*
9 Pugh, *Educate, Agitate, Organise,* pp. 130–1, 195–9, 236–7, 241–4, 259–60.
10 Marjorie Nicholson, *The TUC Overseas: The Roots of Policy* (London: Allen
and Unwin, 1986) is a detailed but somewhat uncritical account, centred on
British unions' Commonwealth and 'Third World' links. A far more negative
view of British trade-union foreign policy, focused on East–West relations
during the early years of the Cold War, is Peter Weiler, *British Labour and the
Cold War* (Stanford: Stanford University Press, 1988).
11 Lewis Minkin, *The Labour Party Conference* (Manchester: Manchester
University Press, 1978); Minkin, *The Contentious Alliance: Trade Unions and
the Labour Party* (Edinburgh: Edinburgh University Press, 1991).
12 See Marvin Swartz, *The Union of Democratic Control in British Politics during
the First World War* (Oxford: Oxford University Press, 1971); Martin Ceadel,
Pacifism in Great Britain, 1914–1945: The Defining of a Faith (Cambridge:
Cambridge University Press, 1980); J. M. Winter, *Socialism and the Challenge
of War: Ideas and Politics in Britain, 1914–18* (London: Routledge, 1974) and,
for the subsequent development of such ideas by MacDonald and his colleagues, David Marquand, *Ramsay MacDonald* (London: Jonathan Cape,
1977), chs. 10–15.
13 Significant contacts and interchanges with emerging political leaders elsewhere in the empire and the non-European world were more restricted until
much later, but became increasingly important after 1945: see the discussions
of some such links in Howe, *Anticolonialism,* and Hakim Adi, *West Africans in
Britain, 1900–1960* (London: Lawrence and Wishart, 1998).
14 See, for instance, J. Ramsay MacDonald, *Labour and the Empire* (London:
George Allen, 1907); and for parts of the intellectual background, Peter Cain,
'The economic philosophy of constructive imperialism', in Cornelia Navari
(ed.), *British Politics and the Spirit of the Age* (Keele: Keele University Press,
1996); Michael Cowen and Robert Shenton, 'The origin and course of Fabian
colonialism in Africa', *Journal of Historical Sociology* 4 (1991), 143–74.
15 Henry R. Winkler, *Paths Not Taken: British Labour and International Policy
in the 1920s* (Chapel Hill: University of North Carolina Press, 1994). See also
David Carlton, *MacDonald versus Henderson: The Foreign Policy of the Second
Labour Government* (London: Macmillan, 1970).
16 There were several rather hagiographic early biographies, and modern studies
by F. M. Leventhal, *Arthur Henderson* (Manchester: Manchester University
Press, 1989) and Chris Wrigley, *Arthur Henderson* (Cardiff: GPC, 1990).
17 The other was Philip Noel-Baker, who received the prize in 1959.
18 MacDonald, diary entry for 13 March 1934, quoted in Marquand,
MacDonald, p. 757.
19 See the assessment in John Campbell, *Nye Bevan and the Mirage of British
Socialism* (London: Weidenfeld and Nicolson, 1987), esp. pp. 91–7, 111–24.

20 The best succinct discussion, placing the emergence of such a consensus in European comparative perspective, is in Donald Sassoon, *One Hundred Years of Socialism: The West European Left in the Twentieth Century* (London: I. B. Tauris, 1996) chs. 7 and 12.

21 See, for instance, Sir Frank Roberts's reminiscences, 'Ernest Bevin as Foreign Secretary' in Ritchie Ovendale (ed.), *The Foreign Policy of the British Labour Governments, 1945–1951* (Leicester: Leicester University Press, 1984).

22 Alan Bullock, *Ernest Bevin. Foreign Secretary* (London: Heinemann, 1983), p. 841.

23 Ben Pimlott, *Hugh Dalton* (London: Jonathan Cape, 1985), chs. 13–29 passim.

24 John Saville, *The Politics of Continuity: British Foreign Policy and the Labour Government 1945–46* (London: Verso, 1993), esp. ch. 3.

25 As reported by his junior minister, Kenneth Younger, interviewed in Bernard Donoughue and G. W. Jones, *Herbert Morrison: Portrait of a Politician* (London: Weidenfeld and Nicolson, 1973), p. 481.

26 Bullock, *Bevin*, esp. 'Epilogue: Bevin's place in British history'.

27 Bullock, *Bevin*, pp. 88–9.

28 General assessments of the pattern of post-1945 overseas military commitments include Philip Darby, *British Defence Policy East of Suez, 1947–1968* (Oxford: Oxford University Press, 1973) and Michael Dockrill, *British Defence since 1945* (Oxford: Blackwell, 1988).

29 Sir Michael Perrin's reminiscence, quoted in Peter Hennessy, *Never Again. Britain 1945–1951* (London: Jonathan Cape, 1993), p. 268. The most detailed history of nuclear policy-making is still Margaret Gowing, *Independence and Deterrence: Britain and Atomic Energy, 1945–1952*, vol. I: *Policy Making* (London: Macmillan, 1982).

30 The fullest account remains William Roger Louis, *The British Empire in the Middle East* (Oxford: Oxford University Press, 1984). For an indication of how important the region remained in British strategic thinking, see Michael J. Cohen, *Fighting World War Three in the Middle East: Allied Contingency Plans, 1945–1954* (London: Frank Cass, 1997).

31 Amidst a vast literature, see, for instance, R. E. Robinson, 'Andrew Cohen and the transfer of power in tropical Africa, 1940–1951', in W. H. Morris-Jones and Georges Fischer (eds.), *Decolonisation and After* (London: Frank Cass, 1980), and the historiographical overview in John Darwin, *The End of the British Empire: The Historical Debate* (Oxford: Blackwell, 1991).

32 There is no satisfactory general survey of Britain's wars of decolonisation; though see Frank Furedi, *Colonial Wars and the Politics of Third World Nationalism* (London: I. B. Tauris, 1994) and several of the contributions to Robert Holland (ed.), *Emergencies and Disorder in the European Empires after 1945* (London: Frank Cass, 1994).

33 See, especially, Keith Kyle, *Suez* (New York: St Martin's Press, 1991); William Roger Louis and Roger Owen (eds.), *Suez 1956: The Crisis and its Consequences* (Oxford: Oxford University Press, 1989).

34 Jonathan Schneer, *Labour's Conscience. The Labour Left 1945–51* (London: Unwin Hyman, 1988), esp. chs. 2–3; Eugene J. Meehan, *The British Left Wing and Foreign Policy: A Study of the Influence of Ideology* (New Brunswick: Rutgers University Press, 1960).

35 The most detailed study of 'first wave' CND is Richard Taylor, *Against the Bomb: The British Peace Movement, 1958–1965* (Oxford: Oxford University Press, 1988). More wide-ranging and polemical is James Hinton, *Protests and Visions: Peace Politics in 20th Century Britain* (London: Hutchinson Radius, 1989).

36 Joseph Gorny, *The British Labour Movement and Zionism 1917–1948* (London: Frank Cass, 1983).

37 The major, and strongly sympathetic, biographical study is still P. M. Williams, *Hugh Gaitskell* (London: Jonathan Cape, 1979).

38 For the retrospective view of the minister who was, with Wilson himself, most deeply and durably involved in the Atlantic relationship, see Michael Stewart, *Life and Labour: An Autobiography* (London: Sidgwick and Jackson, 1980) esp. chs. 7 and 9.

39 On Labour and European integration under Wilson, see (among a vast selection of relevant works) L. J. Robins, *The Reluctant Party: Labour and the EEC, 1961–75* (Ormskirk: Hesketh, 1979), and for comparative perspective Kevin Featherstone, *Socialist Parties and European Integration* (Manchester: Manchester University Press, 1988).

40 Quoted in Ben Pimlott, *Harold Wilson* (London: HarperCollins, 1992), p. 385.

41 The most comprehensive overview of the physical remnants of empire, in the form of remaining British overseas dependencies, is now Robert Aldrich and John Connell, *The Last Colonies* (Cambridge: Cambridge University Press, 1998).

42 Unsurprisingly, no published account based on wide primary research has yet proved possible. For British servicemen's memories, see Charles Allen, *The Savage Wars of Peace: Soldiers' Voices, 1945–1989* (London: Futura, 1990), esp. chs. 10–11; for the earlier stages of disengagement, Glen Balfour-Paul, *The End of Empire in the Middle East: Britain's Relinquishment of Power in her Last Three Arab Dependencies* (Cambridge: Cambridge University Press, 1991).

43 No fully documented historical study of British diplomacy over Rhodesia has yet appeared, but Michael Charlton, *The Last Colony in Africa: Diplomacy and the Independence of Rhodesia* (Oxford: Blackwell, 1990), is based on extensive interviews with participants.

44 Before October 1964, Labour had been pledged to end arms sales to the Pretoria regime, but within weeks of taking office had contracted to sell aircraft to the South African navy. The about-turn is traced in detail by John W. Young, 'The Wilson Government and the debate over arms to South Africa in 1964', *Contemporary British History* 12 (1998), 62–86.

45 Peter Patterson, *Tired and Emotional: The Life of Lord George Brown* (London: Chatto and Windus, 1993).

46 There is as yet no full-scale biography of Healey: at the time of writing Edward Pearce is at work on one. In the meantime, Healey's memoirs are among the liveliest and most revealing by any modern British politician: *The Time of My Life* (London: Michael Joseph, 1989).

47 Marquand, *Progressive Dilemma*, pp. 128–9.

48 Douglas Jay, *Change and Fortune. A Political Record* (London: Hutchinson, 1980), p. 505.

49 I here abbreviate yet further an argument briefly sketched in my 'Labour patriotism 1939–83', in Raphael Samuel (ed.), *Patriotism. The Making and Unmaking of British National Identity*, vol. I: *History and Politics* (London: Routledge, 1989).

50 Hinton, *Protests and Visions*, pp. viii–ix.

51 Sassoon, *Hundred Years*, passim.

52 Such wide-ranging reflections were pursued, for instance, by William Wallace in his 'Foreign policy and national identity in the United Kingdom', *International Affairs* 67 (1991), 65–80, and 'British foreign policy after the Cold War', *International Affairs* 68 (1992), 423–42.

53 Robin Cook, speech to an invited audience at the Foreign and Commonwealth Office, 12 May 1997 (FCO press release).

54 Neil Kinnock, reply on behalf of the NEC to the debate 'Britain in a New World', Labour Party Conference, Blackpool, 5 October 1994 (Labour Party news release).

5 | Labour and the constitution

Miles Taylor

As the Labour Party celebrates its centenary, Tony Blair's government is engaged upon the most fundamental reform of the British constitution this century, and possibly since 1828–32. Separate assemblies have been granted to Scotland and Wales, with ramifications for further regional devolution in England. The hereditary element in the House of Lords has gone, with a new-style second chamber to be created in its place. Major reforms to the first-past-the-post voting system have been suggested by the Jenkins Commission, and partially introduced in the case of Scotland, Wales and elections to the European Parliament. After some delay a Freedom of Information Bill has been brought before Parliament, and the European Charter on Human Rights has begun to be incorporated into British law. Additionally, a range of other changes relating to party finance and Commons procedure have been introduced, less noticed, but just as significant.[1] New Labour's remaking of the British constitution has provoked all manner of reactions – from upbeat optimism, to wary scepticism, to diehard hostility[2] – but most commentators share one assumption in common – that the Labour Party has taken a long time to become interested in the agenda of constitutional reform.[3] Such an assumption, this chapter argues, is wrong. The life, times and

151

destiny of the Labour Party in the twentieth century cannot be understood without a proper appreciation of the constitutional factor in its history. Not only have major constitutional developments such as the 1918 Representation of the People Act and the refinement of cabinet government during the Second World War helped transform Labour from minor party status into a governing power, but also many of the key writers on constitutional affairs this century have been Labour politicians of one sort or another – G. D. H. Cole, Harold Laski and Ivor Jennings in the inter-war years, Richard Crossman and John Mackintosh in the 1960s. Moreover, at certain critical moments in its history – over syndicalism in the early 1920s, fascism and communism in the 1930s, and since the 1960s in the face of Celtic nationalism and the assumption of greater powers by European institutions – the Labour Party has been forced to confront the British constitution and openly declare the reason for its allegiance. Yet despite all this, historians and party propagandists alike have tended to ignore Labour's constitutional concerns. What follows is an attempt to remedy this oversight.

Radicals, socialists and the Edwardian constitution

Labour's agenda for constitutional reform before the First World War seems, on the face of it, to have been fairly straightforward – further reform of Parliament. In 1892 James Ramsay MacDonald called for a 'new Charter' for just this purpose. In its 1900 manifesto the Labour Representation Committee (LRC) called for shorter parliaments, adult suffrage and registration reform as well as the payment of MPs. In 1908 and again in 1913 the party organised special conferences on registration and electoral reform, and the call for adult suffrage was made without fail at every party conference from 1906 onwards.[4] Looked at more closely, however, it becomes clear that the Labour Party and the labour movement more generally did not have a particularly coherent approach to constitutional reform.

Each of the component parts of the early Labour Party took a distinct view of the problems created by the Edwardian constitution. The Independent Labour Party (ILP) looked to radical reform of Parliament in order to circumvent party government. ILP writers argued that party politicians at Westminster had become too distant from ordinary voters, and too preoccupied with preserving their hold on office through patronage inside and outside Parliament. As a result legislation was often passed at the behest of vested interests, or because of short-term deals in the division lobbies. The ILP called for greater use of the popular referendum, for the establishment of permanent ministerial positions above party patronage, and the creation of non-partisan committees to initiate legislation in Parliament.[5] During the course of Herbert Asquith's first administration (1908–10), the ILP focused on two complaints about the Edwardian constitution in particular. The first was the role of the House of Lords, which it criticised for being obstructionist, an institution of 'decoy ducks' behind which various wealthy interest groups – company directors, Scottish landowners, employers' associations – could frustrate working-class legislative interests.[6] In 1911 MacDonald and Philip Snowden, prominent members of the ILP, led the Labour Party's criticism of the Parliament Bill, particularly its preamble, which committed Parliament to a two-chamber legislature.[7] Second, the ILP became increasingly vocal in its denunciation of the Labour MPs' support for the Liberal government. Leonard Hall, Victor Grayson and Fred Jowett all called for Labour MPs to uphold agreed party policy in Parliament, even if this meant voting against the Liberal Party on occasion.[8] The ILP therefore, committed like the rest of the labour movement to suffrage reform, was principally concerned with ridding Parliament of the Edwardian version of old corruption, and with enhancing the role of independent MPs.

In contrast, the parliamentary party and the annual conference concentrated on further suffrage reform with a view to increasing Labour representation in the Commons. By 1910 the party had adopted a six-point package of electoral reform, calling for adult suffrage, shortening of the residence requirement, state payment of the fees due to returning officers, single-day polling and the end of plural voting, the strengthening of the law governing corrupt practices, and 'the prevention of election of Members by a minority of votes'.[9] The first and the last of these six points became a source of deep disagreement within the party. Adult suffrage raised a tactical dilemma for the Edwardian Labour Party: should it support any move, however small, towards removing women's political disabilities, or should it hold out for universal adult suffrage? Proposals for limited suffrage reform, namely lifting the sexual disqualification in the parliamentary franchise, were rejected at the party conferences of 1904 and 1908, on the grounds that they would benefit the propertied classes and make an unfair system worse. But the problem reappeared in a new form in 1910 when the Liberal government promised to introduce a suffrage bill reducing the residence requirement without any mention of extension of the franchise to women. At Labour's Newport conference, Margaret Bondfield, of the Women's Labour League, insisted that the labour movement oppose the 'whole bill' of the Liberals, but Arthur Henderson, the party chairman, pointed out that this would leave Labour MPs little room for manoeuvre and lessen the chance of inserting an amendment providing for women's suffrage.[10] Henderson won that particular battle, but the stage was set for further controversy when the Franchise and Registration Bill eventually came before Parliament in 1912.

Electoral reform, in the shape of different voting methods, was also a subject of contention, with some voices in the party believing that proportional representation would better equip Labour to fight three-cornered election contests without relying on pacts with the Liberals. In 1913 a special sub-committee was established to explore the merits and demerits of proportional representation and the alternative vote, and this sub-committee's report was discussed at the party's Glasgow conference the following year.[11] The alternative vote was rejected by the sub-committee on the grounds that electors' second vote would be given to another 'capitalist' party rather than to Labour, and that it would encourage people to vote for personalities rather than parties. But proportional representation found more support. Although concerned by the prospect of higher election costs, many speakers saw proportional representation as the means whereby Labour MPs in the Commons would be truly representative of labour constituencies, and less inclined to follow the Liberal Party whip. In other words, the debate over reforming the voting system quickly reverted to considerations relating to the independence of the Labour Party.

The arguments against proportional representation before the war were led by Ramsay MacDonald, the party chairman from 1911 to 1914, whose influential opposition saw off the challenge. MacDonald argued that proportional representation would not make any difference to Labour's position at Westminster, for as well as being expensive, and having had little effect on the fortunes of socialist parties in Belgium and Germany, proportional representation would also be a recipe for coalitions and slender majorities, not unlike the situation the party faced already. Indeed, throughout these Edwardian debates over which electoral reform would best further Labour aims, MacDonald took something of an iconoclastic line, arguing: 'Do not let us tinker with political machinery. It is a mere waste of time. Mechanical changes in taking ballots will bring no qualitative changes in legislation.'[12] MacDonald's irreverent attitude towards radical electoral reform – 'will-o'-the-wisps leading into bogs those who foolishly follow', as he put it in *Socialism and Government* – has often been misunderstood, taken as a sign of the Labour leadership's weakness and moderation over fundamental constitutional change.[13] But MacDonald was no slouch when it came to remaking the British constitution. Read in full, *Socialism and Government* is a wide-ranging assault on the British political system and it pointed out the direction that party debates on constitutional reform were to take after the First World War. MacDonald took for granted radical parliamentary reform. Although an opponent of the referendum and of proportional representation, he advocated all the other points on Labour's agenda – and more. Cheap elections, shorter parliaments, municipal payment of MPs, tighter control of expenditure at elections and state payment of election officials would, in MacDonald's view, prove the maxim that 'the wider the gates are thrown open, the more enlightened, stable and efficient will be the state'. In other respects MacDonald went further. He thought adult suffrage at twenty-one years was a little high, and he called for 'Home Rule all round'.[14] However, MacDonald's principal concern was with overhauling the legislative machinery of Parliament. He called for fewer MPs (half the present Commons would suffice), for a longer parliamentary year (beginning in October) and a more conventional working day (starting and finishing earlier). Much of the drawn-out procedure for reading bills required reform, and MacDonald, although he rejected the ILP idea of government by committee, did believe that small groups of MPs should draft all legislation once Parliament as a whole had determined the main principles. He also suggested replacing the House of Lords with a small 'Revision Committee' constituted by Law Lords.[15] MacDonald was thus concerned with the ends of parliamentary reform and not simply the means. More bills and more businesslike MPs would deliver the socialist state in a way which the traditional package of electoral reforms could not.

MacDonald clearly wished to push the Edwardian Labour Party into discussing the practical considerations of government, rather than sheltering in the refuge of electoral reform and support for popular sovereignty – 'Rousseauism' as he disparagingly called it. But in the years immediately preceding the First World War many in the Labour Party saw the two as intimately connected. Electoral reform became a test of Labour's mettle in relation to the Liberal government. What brought matters to a head was the party's position on the Liberals' Franchise and Registration Bill of 1912. In June George Lansbury, the MP for Bow and Bromley, broke rank with the parliamentary Labour Party and attacked the Liberal government's treatment of the imprisoned suffragettes. He also called for the Labour Party to insist on adult suffrage, including the enfranchisement of women, rather than chance

Miles Taylor

their luck with an amendment when the bill was discussed in committee. Overwhelmed by letters of support from the women's suffrage movement (and from dissentient Liberal MPs), Lansbury initially considered leaving the Labour Party, but in November he decided to resign his seat and use the by-election to focus attention not only on women's suffrage, but also, just weeks before the party's annual conference, on the quiescent stance that the parliamentary Labour Party had taken on this and other issues.[16] In a similar manner, the parliamentary Labour Party's failure to press the Liberal government into unemployment legislation during 1911 and 1912 fuelled criticism of the party's ineffectual tactics in the Commons. As a result the British Socialist Party was formed, promising direct strike action and 'Parliaments of Industry' to replace 'partisan "Punch and Judy" politics'.[17]

The First World War probably saved Labour from a messy election campaign in which its most prominent and well-known leaders – MacDonald, Henderson, Keir Hardie (who resigned from the party executive over Lansbury's treatment) and Philip Snowden (who opposed MacDonald over proportional representation at the 1914 conference) – would have lined up on different sides on the question of electoral reform and parliamentary tactics. By the close of the war the constitutional scenario was wholly different. The electoral system had been reformed, cabinet government (including Henderson until 1917) had come into its own, and the Labour Party's new constitution of 1918 included much stricter guidelines on the relationship between MPs, the conference and executive, and the party whip. As MacDonald bluntly observed in 1920, the old battles for electoral reform were over and the new question was whether Parliament was suitable for modern social conditions.[18]

Planning for Parliament in the inter-war years

The Labour Party began the inter-war years with a radical constitutional agenda, but twice in office during the period failed to deliver. At its conference in Manchester in June 1918, the party adopted *Labour and the New Social Order* as its manifesto. Among other things the document committed the party to abolition of the House of Lords, separate assemblies for Scotland, Wales and 'even England', and a huge transfer of responsibility for retailing, public utilities and house-building from central to local government. By 1931, none of this had been enacted. From insisting on the abolition of the Lords in 1918, the party retreated by the mid-1920s into learning to live with the upper House. Despite pressure from the ILP and Scottish MPs in particular, Labour made no

devolutionary moves. Indeed by 1928 disgruntled ILP members such as
Roland Muirhead had left to form the National Party of Scotland. And
although the Labour Party leadership paid lip-service to extending the
functions of local government, their experience of headstrong, spendthrift local councillors in the London borough of Poplar made them
reluctant to put decentralisation into practice. Not surprisingly, many
historians look no further than the 1920s for evidence of Labour's reputation as under-achievers in matters of constitutional reform.[19]

Such a verdict is unfair. As a minority government in 1924 and again
between 1929 and 1931, it was perhaps inevitable that Labour's heady
promises of major constitutional reform, along with its commitment to
more radical economic policies such as the capital levy, would be still-
born. Further reform of the franchise (including the abolition of plural
voting and a measure of proportional representation) was in the offing
when the Labour cabinet resigned in 1931. Moreover, Labour pressure
in Parliament did help to secure the lowering of the voting age for
women to twenty-one in 1928 (the party brought in women's suffrage
bills every year from 1920 through to 1926), and it was a Labour MP,
H. H. Slesser, whose initiative clarified the law relating to the right of
women to sit in Parliament. Labour may not have cut any new cloth, but
it did tidy up some of the loose threads. However, where the party was
more innovative was in the consideration it gave to the reform of central
government – the cabinet system and the civil service – and to matters of
parliamentary procedure. The 1920s saw a resumption of the debate
begun before the war by works such as MacDonald's *Socialism and
Government*. Both MacDonald and Henderson, concerned to see off the
threat posed by advocates of 'direct action', looked to 'rehabilitate
Parliament in the eyes of the people'.[20]

In many respects Labour's post-war agenda for the reform of
central government was even more wide-ranging than their promises
on the Lords and on devolution. The Webbs, characteristically, started
from scratch. In 1918 Sidney Webb, as a member of the Ministry of
Reconstruction's sub-committee on the 'machinery of government',
had proposed the organisation of government departments by function
and called for a separate Prime Minister's department to oversee all.
Devolution to separate units of administration (co-operatives, municipal authorities and producers' organisations) was added to this blueprint in 1920.[21] Beatrice Webb was also one of the members of
Labour's own advisory committee, set up in 1918, to look at the
'machinery of government'. By January 1920, the committee, now
including Harold Laski, had produced substantial reports on two areas,

the civil service and 'parliamentary control', and a third followed in June on administrative devolution.[22] All three reports were preoccupied with improving the legislative efficiency of Parliament. Better systems of recruitment and promotion were suggested for the civil service so that a more businesslike and innovative ethos might develop amongst officials.[23] More devolved power was advocated for local authorities so that central government would have 'time to do its proper work'. And an overhaul of parliamentary procedure was recommended not only to check the subordination of the Commons to the cabinet and to the party whips, but also to timetable and streamline the legislative programme more effectively.

Improvement of the 'machinery of government' was thus the test to which the post-war Labour Party submitted considerations of constitutional reform. This is clear in the case of the proposals to reform the House of Lords. Abolition of the upper chamber did not remain agreed policy for very long. By 1922 it had gone from the party's election manifesto, and even before then, key voices could be heard making the case for transforming the Lords into an effective revising chamber, rather than calling for its abolition. In 1917 Sidney Webb suggested a second chamber elected by the existing House of Commons in a proportional voting system – his model was the Norwegian 'lagsthing'[24] – and this became the unofficial but widely supported stance of the party effectively until the Second World War. In 1920, Jimmy Thomas, the TUC president, backed this idea. Hastings Lees-Smith, the party's in-house constitutional expert between the wars, endorsed the scheme in 1923, and even the Fabian Society's Harold Laski, who preferred single-chamber government in principle, supported the Norwegian model in 1925.[25] Lees-Smith in particular saw a reformed second chamber as a useful check on the increasing trend of ministers to delegate, via standing orders or Privy Council procedures, more and more legislation which in previous times had come before Parliament. In an age of expanding legislative activity, the proper sphere of the second chamber lay in restoring such watchdog powers, so that the people were not misrepresented.[26] Reform of the House of Lords, in other words, was not desired for its own sake, but was seen as inseparable from the whole package of expansion and streamlining of Parliament and government.

Labour's approach to devolution and local government in the 1920s also makes more sense if looked at within the wider context of improving the machinery of central government. The party's post-war architects intended that local authorities, including those in Wales and Scotland, should only be given responsibility for those areas of administration with which Westminster and Whitehall were being over-burdened and which could be deemed as residual to the concerns of central government. Home rule or self-government for Wales and Scotland were not treated separately from the problem of decentralisation of power. Indeed, by the mid-1920s the party had lapsed into equating devolution with the reform of local government. As the party's assistant secretary, James Middleton, told a Scottish nationalist in 1924: 'I do not think that . . . all the large measures in which the Scottish, English and Welsh peoples are interested necessarily depend upon self-government for their success.'[27] The party also proved reluctant to give local authorities greater scope to raise their own finances, not only on the grounds that it would open the door to Poplar-style irresponsibility, but also because it would advantage some areas of the country over others. Labour was particularly critical of the Conservatives' Local Government Bill of 1929 because its derating clauses gave a new form of subsidy to some industries, whilst removing from local authority management other aspects of municipal local administration. National problems required nationwide solutions.

Out of office after the crisis of 1931, Labour's constitutional radicalism raged once more, particularly on the left where planners and populists vied for pole position as the new Jacobins. Ramsay MacDonald's handling of the expenditure cuts in the summer of 1931 – heeding the Treasury and the Bank of England, but overriding his Labour cabinet, as well as capitulating to the formation of a national coalition, partly engineered by King George V – all fired up distrust of the constitution. Sidney Webb drafted a 'new reform bill' in which a single-chamber imperial-style Parliament shared power with separate regional legislative assemblies which in turn elected committees to administer all domestic policy. Stafford Cripps went further, calling for a Labour government, if elected, to use the Emergency Powers Act (1920) to override the royal prerogative and the Lords' veto. G. D. H. Cole and Laski, in different ways, pointed to more professional expertise in the civil service, greater cabinet co-ordination, and less reliance on Parliament, as among the ways forward to a socialist Britain.[28] By the time of the party's conference at Southport in October 1934, the mood of root-and-branch reform was dominant, and, urged on by Cripps and the Socialist League, and to the alarm of trade-union leaders such as Walter Citrine, the party adopted the manifesto *For Socialism and for Peace*, committing it to the overhaul of parliamentary procedure (especially financial procedure), delegated legislation, Lords reform and possible use of Emergency Powers.[29] Compared to the small beer of constitutional reform in the 1920s, Labour's new revisionism after 1931 thus appears to mark a dramatic change of approach in which radicals and socialists, albeit temporarily, outvoiced the moderates. However, what is striking about so much of the party's discussion of constitutional reform in the 1930s is how similar the conclusions reached were to the proposals put forward in the aftermath of the First World War. The focal point of reform remained improving the machinery of government.

Labour's new-found commitment to constitutional radicalism after 1931 was not simply the result of pressure from without. As in 1920, the party set up its own advisory panels, including one on 'constitutional problems',[30] and, moreover, Labour moderates – Attlee, Hugh Dalton and Emmanuel Shinwell – took just as much interest in restructuring the machinery of government as did their noisier radical counterparts. Reformers such as Cripps adopted a rather blunderbuss approach, calling for extensive changes to the electoral system (compulsory voting, tighter laws on election spending), alongside turning over parliamentary business to departmental committees and abolishing the House of Lords.[31] The scope of changes envisioned by the party itself was just as wide, but rather more focused. Key Labour politicians put their weight behind the reform of cabinet organisation and parliamentary procedure. G. D. H. Cole played an important part here, initiating the involvement of Attlee, Dalton and Christopher Addison, among others, in his 'Friday Group' during October 1932. Aided by the findings of the New Fabian Research Bureau (NFRB), Cole and his colleagues came up with a raft of suggestions for reform. Attlee proposed a cabinet split into two, the smaller part being charged with the 'higher directive' of policy, whilst Dalton set out plans for overhauling the Commons' timetable by speed-ing up money bills and reducing unnecessary parliamentary debate, though limiting question time, and giving ministers more powers to leg-islate through Orders in Council. Addison called for departmental com-mittees to review ministerial work.[32] The ideas of Attlee and Dalton – cabinet co-ordination and streamlining the financial procedures of the Commons – became central to the party's constitutional agenda during the 1930s. In 1934 the National Executive Committee (NEC) presented its report on 'Parliamentary problems and procedure' to the Southport conference, and although Cripps claimed this as a green light for the radical programme of the Socialist League, looked at more closely, the document can be seen as an endorsement of the ideas supported by Dalton and Attlee. The report pledged the Labour Party to reform par-liamentary procedure 'to enable a much larger volume of legislation to be passed'. This would be achieved by creating a permanent Commons committee which would determine a timetable for all legislation, abolishing the second reading and report stages of financial bills (with the exception of the budget), delegating more legislation to government departments, and abolishing the legislative functions of the House of Lords. Cripps got his way insofar as the NEC committed the party to using the Emergency Powers Act if circumstances arose, but the document made it clear that this would only be done in extraordinary, not ordinary conditions, as had occurred in 1914, 1926 and 1931.

So the constitutional reform agenda after 1931 was increasingly set by the moderates and not the radicals within the party. During 1935 the NEC's constitutional committee put further flesh on the skeletal framework for reform agreed to at Southport. Laski, now a member of this committee, suggested that Labour fill all the non-departmental cabinet posts – the Lord President of the Council, the Privy Seal and the Chancellor of the Duchy of Lancaster – with men of the highest standing in the party. Free from departmental burdens, they would draw up plans for the implementation of Labour's policies. A permanent Commons committee would allocate parliamentary time and debate on financial procedure would be axed. The Lords proved more controversial. The NEC rejected the constitutional committee's suggestion of the Norwegian model and the short-term expediency of a reduction of the Lords' delay from two years to one or six months.[33] For the most part, however, from 1935 onwards, Labour began to speak with one voice on matters of constitutional reform. There would be greater cabinet control (amounting to a 'temporary dictatorship', suggested the young Richard Crossman), a shake-up of parliamentary business, and abolition of the Lords.[34] The war, and Herbert Morrison, turned these plans for Parliament into something of a reality.

Herbert's House: the Morrisonian revolution, 1945–1951

In 1953 Herbert Morrison looked back at the Attlee administration and praised its record on parliamentary reform. For the first time in nearly forty years, the House of Lords' delaying powers had been trimmed, the last remnants of plural voting had been removed with the abolition of the business vote and university seats, MPs' salaries had been increased by two-thirds, and changes in procedure had transformed the Commons from a 'talking shop' to a 'workshop'.[35] As Lord President of the Council and Leader of the House of Commons during Labour's finest hours from 1945 to 1951, Morrison himself was largely responsible for implementing these constitutional innovations, but it is an achievement which has gone largely unnoticed. Derided at the time for gagging Parliament and steam-rollering through legislation, Morrison has sub-

Miles Taylor

sequently been viewed as a latter-day Whig, whose oft-stated preference
for Burke and Bagehot, monarchy and moderation, sat awkwardly with
the post-war party's socialist rhetoric.[36] Yet it was Morrison, riding the
momentum for change created by Churchill's wartime coalition, who
managed to deliver most of the shopping list of constitutional reform
which the party had set out in *For Socialism and Peace* in 1934, as well as
honouring Labour's commitment to reform of the franchise which had
stalled in 1931.

Integral to the Labour Party's well-known plans for post-war social
and economic reconstruction was the issue of constitutional reform. A
large section of the party's key statement on post-war policy – *The Old
World and the New Society* – produced in February 1942, was devoted to
cabinet and parliamentary reform.[37] And reformers and experts within
the party – for example, the Fabians – continued to press for greater use
of parliamentary committees for the scrutiny of bills and for devolving
legislation to local authorities.[38] Morrison, as a member of various NEC
policy committees and (from November 1942) as Home Secretary in the
Churchill coalition, played an important dual role in this process. His
NEC memorandum of January 1942 on 'Parliament and post-war
reconstruction' elaborated how the immediate post-war situation would
indeed constitute an emergency of the sort envisaged by Cripps ten
years earlier, in which a Labour government would need to reserve to
itself, through Orders in Council, 'additional or external powers'.[39]
Morrison's day-to-day activity in the Churchill cabinet proved even
more significant in accelerating Labour's constitutional reform agenda.
On behalf of the government Morrison was responsible for subordinat-
ing Parliament to the extraordinary needs of the war. Private members'
privileges were suspended, all timetabling of legislation was given over
to the government, ministers' powers to handle secondary legislation
were expanded, and, much to the disquiet of many activists and Labour
MPs, an electoral truce was agreed between the two coalition partners.[40]

This continuity between the Churchill and Attlee administrations as
far as the machinery of government is concerned can be seen in two
main areas: parliamentary procedure and the organisation of the
cabinet. In 1944 the cabinet agreed to push for a parliamentary select
committee on Commons' procedure. Although this committee, chaired
by Sir Robert Young, reported in peacetime, its terms of reference were
clearly framed within the context of the ongoing war. The committee
recommended referring all bills after their first reading, except financial
bills and substantial constitutional measures, to standing committees of
which there should be many more, as well as bringing in limits to the

162

time allowed to standing committees to discuss bills.[41] After 1945 Morrison also continued the wartime precedent of the government taking virtually all initiative in the parliamentary timetable. Until January 1949, the Labour government took up all the time of the Commons, allowing no time for private members' bills. Cabinet reform of the sort brought in by the Attlee administration was also a child of wartime necessity: a small cabinet, divided up when necessary into functional and not departmental committees, with non-portfolio ministers such as Morrison as Lord President of the Council used to co-ordinate and timetable the legislative programme, and 'under-minister' secretaries of state used to shoulder much of the everyday administrative burden.

However, the road to 1945 did not begin and end with the creation of the coalition in May 1940. There was much more to Labour's overhaul of the constitution than a fortuitous convergence between the radical pipe-dreams of the 1930s and the sober pragmatism of the war effort. The party entered the war years with a range of unfinished business, especially in two areas: local government reform and the further democratisation of the franchise and the machinery of elections. These issues had died with the collapse of the MacDonald administration in 1931, but during the war new life was breathed into both by NEC discussions and also by the Speaker's Conference on Electoral Reform in 1944. Here too, Morrison's involvement was significant. It was Morrison's successor as leader of the London County Council, Charles Latham, who, as chair of the wartime NEC sub-committee on the machinery of local government, pushed the party into the kind of coherence on municipal reform which it had lacked since the early 1920s. Within the space of two years Latham drafted and gained approval for what became Labour's postwar manifesto for local government, managing not only to recruit the talents of planners such as G. D. H. Cole, who joined the NEC sub-committee, but also to assuage the doubts and fears of councillors and aldermen up and down the country, including in Scotland and Wales.[42] Latham's scheme committed Labour to replacing the untidy patchwork of existing local government units, split unequally between town and country, with two-tier government, comprising around forty 'regional' authorities, responsible for countrywide services and utilities, combined with 300 or so smaller secondary or 'area' authorities, charged with providing purely local services. The plan also envisaged an overhaul of local government finance by making the regional authority both the recipient of any government grants as well as the unit of rates assessment, so enabling some redistribution of wealth between poorer and richer areas.[43]

Miles Taylor

Perhaps surprisingly, Morrison's was the one dissenting voice opposed to Labour's plans for post-war local government reform.[44] Alarmed at the 'apathy' increasingly evident in local government elections, Morrison instead concentrated on reforming the local franchise, by sweeping away the old Victorian ratepaying requirement and putting the local government vote on the same 'broad basis of citizenship' as the parliamentary vote.[45] This was the principal feature of the Representation of the People Act of 1945 which, building on the recommendations of the Speaker's Conference of 1944, also provided for the resumption of the parliamentary electoral register, regular reports by the Boundary Commissioners and postal voting for overseas servicemen.

In the face of competing legislative demands, other constitutional reforms after 1945 only surfaced as Labour neared the end of its five-year term. Of these the most controversial proved to be House of Lords reform. In *Let Us Face the Future* the party had given 'clear notice that we will not tolerate obstruction of the people's will by the House of Lords' – rather a non-committal threat perhaps, but one which proved sensible in light of the co-operative response given by the upper House to Labour's programme of reconstruction in 1945–7. Labour ranks in the Lords swelled after 1945[46] and in 1946 Morrison could speak approvingly to American journalists of 'the remarkable and characteris-tically British spectacle of a Chamber with a large right-wing majority passing one nationalisation Bill after another'.[47] In November 1946, the cabinet decided to postpone plans drawn up by William Jowitt, the Lord Chancellor, for reducing the Lords' power of delay to one year.[48] However, as public support for nationalisation waned during 1947, with the onset of the fuel crisis and the weakening of sterling, the prospect of the Conservative majority in the Lords remaining a benign force dimmed. By May 1947 Morrison was being warned that the remainder of Labour's domestic policy in the current Parliament might be jeopar-dised by the obstruction of the Lords, and by September he himself was convinced that reform of the Lords would prove a consequence of the government's intention to nationalise the iron and steel industry.[49] Even then, plans for reform moved slowly. Early drafts of the government's legislative programme for 1947–8 did not include Lords reform. It was only when securing iron and steel nationalisation at all costs became the top priority that Jowitt's proposals of 1946 were dusted down and included in the King's speech in October 1947, much to the consterna-tion of the cabinet secretariat, one of whom noted that part of the pro-posed bill 'exposed with almost indecent precision the Government's intention to secure that all the major measures of the present Parliament should be passed into law before the next General Election, whatever the attitude of the House of Lords'.[50] This proved an acute observation. In February 1948, prompted by Christopher Addison, the Lord Privy Seal, Labour agreed to an all-party conference on Lords reform. The conference considered the adoption of life peerages (including women) and the creation of salaried 'Lords of Parliament' (i.e. only certain categories of hereditary peers were to retain voting rights). But when the Conservative members of the conference attempted to hold the Lords' delaying powers at twelve months from the third reading (effectively eighteen months or more), Attlee stepped in decisively and brought the emerging consensus on reform of the composition of the Lords to an abrupt end.[51] Thereafter, Labour's Parliament Bill was forced to go the longer route, subject to the two-year delay allowed for by the 1911 Parliament Act, eventually passing into statute in December 1949, shortly after the iron and steel industries were nationalised. Morrison denied that one was consequent on the other, but Labour newspapers saw it as a battle between the peerage and public ownership.[52]

Ironically, Labour's small advance forward over Lords reform was countered by what proved to be a step back over electoral reform. With the Representation of the People Act of 1948 Labour did remain true to its radical traditions and passed legislation based on 'one man, one vote', finally eliminating the plural voter (i.e. the university seats and the business vote) from the parliamentary franchise. However, the accompanying redistribution of seats and the introduction of postal voting from overseas slightly advantaged the Conservatives, as was apparent in the general elections of 1950 and 1951. Electoral reform was to a certain extent inevitable, and the session of 1947–8 was probably the last feasible opportunity to change the system in time for the next election. The remaining recommendations of the Speaker's Conference of 1944, together with the first of the Boundary Commissioners' reports, required consideration and implementation. To its credit Labour did not sacrifice principle to expediency on this occasion. Morrison, Attlee and James Chuter Ede (the Home Secretary) ignored the moderate suggestions of the Speaker's Conference, by which they did not feel bound, and focused their attention on the inequality of the university seats and the relatively small business vote in the City of London.[53] Much of the subsequent discussion in the House of Commons revolved around the government's radical departure from the party compromise on electoral reform which had emerged in 1944. Winston Churchill accused Labour of dishonesty and of gerrymandering a new constituency of the City of

London merged with Finsbury and Shoreditch on behalf of Attlee, whose Limehouse seat was set to disappear.[54] This rather diverted Labour from the wider issue of the redistribution of seats, about which there had been remarkably little cabinet discussion. Only Hugh Dalton noted that the blitzed inner cities, many of which were Labour heartlands, bore the brunt of redistribution. Wise after the event, Attlee later admitted that 'one man, one vote' cost Labour dear in the ensuing general election of 1950.[55]

The Attlee cabinet's haste over Lords reform and lack of foresight over the redistribution of seats point to the Labour Party's priorities on constitutional change after 1945. Those reforms which were required to expedite the delivery of social and economic reconstruction – mainly in parliamentary procedure, cabinet organisation and, latterly, the Lords – took top billing, whilst those which represented the unfinished business of the first two Labour administrations – electoral reform and the overhaul of local government – whilst closer to the party's heart, did not get special treatment. This practical approach bore Morrison's imprint. The test of legislative efficiency was the ultimate consideration in constitutional reform. Of course there remained some constitutional changes which were desirable in principle as well as being practical necessities. Pressure for devolution reared its head again, with the establishment of the Scottish Convention in 1949 and the call in 1953, supported by a handful of Welsh Labour MPs, for a Welsh Parliament. Labour's response was cautious. The party's insistence on the economic integrity of the UK made it supportive of some administrative devolution and greater regional consultation, but left it ruling out any form of national assembly.[56] The activities of the Scottish Grand Committee of MPs were broadened after 1945 as part of Morrison's expansion of parliamentary standing committees, and a Council for Wales was established in 1949. In 1954, under pressure from its own Welsh MPs and the Welsh National Union of Miners, the party finally committed itself to creating a Ministry for Welsh Affairs.[57] But in Wales as in Scotland (further underlined in the 1958 Scottish programme, *Fair Shares of Prosperity*) Labour's Celtic policy remained one of regional economic modernisation. In the 1950s, enjoying an average of 47 per cent of the vote in Scotland and 58 per cent in Wales, Labour could afford to play the economic unity card. By 1974 the situation was altogether different.

The modern Bagehot: Crossman and the constitution

Interviewed by the BBC correspondent William Hardcastle in November 1967, Richard Crossman confessed to keeping a political diary. Its purpose, he explained, was to help him write 'a real analysis of how politics works, to show what Herbert Morrison wrote . . . how wrong it is and how right I am'.[58] With the arrogance of an Oxford don, to which he readily admitted, Crossman not only thought Morrison had got British politics wrong, but so too had Walter Bagehot, whose *English Constitution* Crossman edited for publication in 1963. Both had incorrectly identified cabinet government – Bagehot's 'efficient secret' and Morrison's 'committee of parliament' – as the cornerstone of British parliamentary life. Crossman, influenced by the work of John Mackintosh, argued in his introduction to Bagehot that 'prime-ministerial' government had superseded the old style of cabinet rule at the time of the Second World War, with the diffusion of cabinet energies into various committees, a larger number of key decisions being taken solely by the Prime Minister, and at least one-third of the parliamentary party dependent on the personal patronage of the Prime Minister for promotion.[59] Given such views, putting Crossman in charge of the Labour government's programme of parliamentary reform, as Harold Wilson did by making him Lord President of the Council in August 1966, was bound to produce some interesting results.

Crossman took over Morrison's old post in a Wilson cabinet which had already begun to scorch the institutions of British government with the white heat of modernisation. Within months of taking office in 1964 a parliamentary Select Committee was convened to look at Commons' procedure.[60] In 1965 the Law Commission, a non-political body within the Lord Chancellor's department, was established to review statute. The following February, having been urged on initially by Thomas Balogh and then by Anthony Crosland and Shirley Williams, Wilson appointed a committee under the chairmanship of Lord Fulton to look into the civil service, and in particular its recruitment structure.[61] And Crossman himself was instrumental in setting up a Royal Commission in May 1966, under the chairmanship of Sir John Redcliffe-Maud, to carry out a fundamental review of local government. To this agenda Crossman then added his own particular stamp – a blend of the older Bevanite idea of party mandate with his understanding of 'prime ministerial' government. Overcoming initial reluctance to leave the Ministry of Housing and Local Government, Crossman's first task was to implement the recommendations of the Select Committee on Procedure which reported in March 1966. These included speeding up the handling of financial bills, establishing specialist committees to monitor government, improved timetabling of legislation, and morning sittings. Ted Heath and William Whitelaw gave the opposition's approval to the specialist committees on agriculture and science and technology (though not to timetabling and morning sittings) in October, and in December Crossman unveiled the changes to the Commons' standing orders which the reforms entailed.[62] Crossman's proposals were remarkable, not so much for their content as for the breathtaking candour with which he introduced them. 'Procedurally', he informed the Commons, 'we still behave as though we were a sovereign body which really shared with the Government in real control not only of finance, but of the administration of the Departments.' This was mistaken, Crossman suggested, for like the Lords, the Commons had 'surrendered most of its effective powers to the Executive', and become a 'passive forum' run by the main parties. '[I]t must be the party machines that run most of our business', he declared, and the creation of specialist committees in particular was designed to discipline along party lines parliamentary scrutiny of the government. Crossman's procedural changes were only partially successful – the experiment of morning sittings was soon dropped, and the new specialist committee on agriculture lapsed into inactivity – but he saw the streamlining of Commons business along party lines as the road to be taken. He clearly delighted in sweeping away what he often called the 'mumbo-jumbo' of 'antediluvian' institutions,[63] but there was more than irreverence to his changes. He also desired to reform Parliament in line with the demands of prime ministerial authority. This can be seen most clearly in the two major constitutional changes he attempted to steer through Parliament in the 1968–9 session: the Representation of the People Bill and the reform of the House of Lords.

Further reform of the franchise had been contemplated by the Conservatives in 1964 and coming into office the Labour Party set up a Speaker's Conference on electoral reform which began to draft its report in February 1968. The Speaker's Conference devoted much of its attention to the law relating to broadcasting during elections and also to the question of lowering the age of voting. Labour supported voting at eighteen, and although the conference recommended twenty, the lowering of the age of majority to eighteen, and, to a lesser extent, the student unrest of the previous year, firmed up the cabinet's determination to insist on the younger option.[64] But Labour completely departed from the recommendations of the conference over the issue of party labelling, that is including on voting papers the name of the party for which the candidate was standing. The Speaker's Conference rejected party labelling, and Wilson himself was advised that British parliamentary democracy 'is still rooted in a degree of personal identification between the voter and the candidate, which derives from a conviction that the country is governed by men, not by machines'. Wilson and Crossman, however, would have none of this Victorian nostalgia and insisted on labelling, even contemplating patenting party labels, the distribution of which would then be controlled by the central party organisation.[65] People voted for parties not candidates, as Crossman spelled out clearly in a Harvard lecture two years later: 'they want the party, the battering-ram, the mandate, not me. They are voting for the political machine which will carry out the changes they've been promised'.[66] The Representation of the People Bill, which became law in 1969, included a clause introducing party labels, although registering of names was ruled out by James Callaghan, the Home Secretary, thus doing wonders for Monster Raving Loonies, Literal Democrats and other assorted exotica up and down the country.

Crossman had less success in reforming the House of Lords according to the dictates of prime ministerial government. Like its Attlee predecessor, the Wilson government moved fairly slowly on tackling possible obstruction from the Lords. At the end of June 1966 the cabinet decided to introduce legislation in the following session to abolish the Lords' remaining delaying powers, but, as in 1948, to leave alone the question of composition.[67] Although he inherited this decision, Crossman regarded it as a classic piece of fudge. As a back-bencher in opposition, influenced by Anthony Wedgwood Benn's campaign against his own and all hereditary titles, Crossman had supported both life peerages and withdrawing the automatic right of hereditary peers to vote. He criticised as 'logical but rather reactionary' the position to which Labour had adhered since MacDonald and Snowden voiced their opposition to the preamble of the 1911 Act – 'that an indefensible anachronism is preferable to a second Chamber with any real authority'.[68] So once in government he became the first Labour minister to confront both the power of the Lords and its composition, a task made somewhat easier by the relatively modernising instincts of Peter Carrington, the Conservative leader in the Lords. Throughout the first half of 1968 an inter-party conference debated options for reform, revealing considerable agreement on curbing the rights of hereditary peers and on further limiting the power to delay.[69] A consensus over Lords reform seemed to be emerging, but then in the middle of June the House of Lords narrowly voted against applying economic sanctions to Southern Rhodesia. Inter-party talks on Lords reform ground to a halt and Wilson came under considerable back-bench pressure to take a severe line. This he did, promising 'radical and comprehensive legislation for reform',[70] and when Crossman (now Secretary of State for Health and Social Security) introduced the Parliament Bill to the

Commons the following November he was obliged to place a heavily partisan spin on an issue where there had been broad cross-party agreement six
months earlier.[71] Essentially, the bill provided for three changes: a two-tier
peerage (life peers with voting rights, hereditary peers with the right only
to speak); the reduction of delay to six months; and the end of the power to
obstruct secondary legislation (such as the Rhodesian sanctions). To give
the reformed second chamber effective but not rival authority, the bill
provided that the government of the day should have a working majority in the Lords. Incautiously, Crossman revealed that this would
require Wilson to 'man up' the life peerage almost immediately by eighty
new nominations. This form of prime ministerial intervention, which
Crossman regarded as almost incidental and uncontroversial, was attacked
as a 'constitutional monstrosity' by another Bagehot-watcher (Norman St
John Stevas), and as creating a 'House of Lackeys' (Dingle Foot), and
Labour MPs including Peter Jackson, Michael Foot, David Marquand
and Ian Mikardo joined the opposition vote which defeated the bill the following evening. Once again Labour found the Lords an immovable object.

Although Crossman failed with reform of the Lords, his two years as
Lord President of the Council completed the process of Commons modernisation begun by Morrison. Where Morrison had reshaped the procedures of Parliament in line with the needs of the cabinet, Crossman had
tailored Commons business to the demands of party government. Both
men, in other words, had tamed Parliament and made it a less hostile creature to Labour governments. What MacDonald had aspired to in 1909 –
an efficient legislative machine – had been delivered. But whilst Morrison
and Crossman successfully conquered much of the centre of the British
constitution, the periphery remained beyond their grasp, and in the late
1960s and early 1970s it proved to be the perennial issues of local government and devolution which caused the Labour Party most trouble.

In the years which intervened between the two Lord Presidents,
Labour had kept Scottish and Welsh separatism at bay, but had seen the
Conservative administrations make significant reforms to local government. In 1966 the Labour government referred local government reform
to the Redcliffe-Maud Commission, and two years later when the cabinet
considered devolution (partly in response to a by-election loss to the
SNP), Crossman suggested that they wait until Redcliffe-Maud had
finished his deliberations and in the meantime called for further administrative decentralisation especially to Wales. However, James Callaghan,
the Home Secretary, insisted on a 'complementary commission' on the
constitution, and this was agreed to and set up under Norman Crowther-
Hunt.[72] Ending the decade with the two commissions on the constitution

boded well for Labour's prospects of finally resolving the question of regional devolution. However, two problems arose after 1970: Labour lost office and the separatist nationalist parties began to make sizeable inroads on the Labour vote.

The Redcliffe-Maud Commission finally reported in 1969. Its recommendation of large unitary authorities undertaking statutory responsibilities alongside local councils was strikingly similar to the Charles Latham blueprint of the 1940s. In 1970 the Wilson government commenced legislation to put the Redcliffe-Maud recommendations into effect,[73] only to lose office later that year and see the Conservatives steal another march with the 1972 Local Government Act which reasserted a patchwork of county and district authorities whilst hiving off more utilities to separate authorities. In response Anthony Crosland (the shadow Local Government spokesman) and Wilson hit upon the idea of elected regional or provincial authorities to provide planning and to bridge the gap between local communities and the statutory services.[74] But in 1974 Labour's new commitment to regional government in England met with an unstoppable force coming from the opposite direction. The February election confirmed Labour's dwindling strength in Wales and Scotland – between 1966 and 1974 Labour's share of the Celtic vote fell by nearly 14 per cent – and with a parliamentary majority of only three, Labour became crucially dependent on the nine nationalist MPs in the Commons. In Scotland, in particular, the swing towards separatism could not be written off as short-term economic protest, for North Sea oil shattered the myth of Scottish dependency. Moreover, Labour's own polling revealed that the swing to the SNP was most evident amongst the young and the working class – Labour's core vote.[75] Having taken several decades to come round to the idea of regional government in England, Labour was now accelerated in a matter of months into support for directly elected assemblies in not only Scotland, as recommended by the Kilbrandon (Crowther-Hunt's successor) Commission in 1973, but Wales as well. In September 1974 the Labour cabinet set out its proposals for separate Welsh and Scottish assemblies and promised further consultation on regional government in England. Crossman, who died the same year, would not have approved. The Labour Party had secured the centre of the British constitution only to find it coming apart at the edges.

Breaking up Britain: Labour and constitutional change since the 1970s

Labour's headlong rush into devolution in 1974 heralded the start of five dramatic years during which the question of British sovereignty

171

dominated the party's constitutional concerns. To Celtic separatism was added the problem of Europe – first, membership of the EEC, on which the Wilson government held a national referendum in 1975, and then in the following year, over direct elections to the European Parliament. However, these years were more notable for disagreement over who controlled the party than for discussion of the constitutional issues themselves. In the 1975 referendum, collective cabinet responsibility unravelled, as pro- and anti-EEC ministers were allowed to make their own case in public. In 1976 the NEC pushed on with its plans for referenda on Scottish and Welsh assemblies, ignoring the cries of many backbenchers and ordinary party members. In that year, too, James Callaghan moved ahead with British support for direct elections to the European Parliament, despite the opposition of the NEC.[76] The break-up of Britain was breaking up the Labour Party. Callaghan's Labour government tumbled out of office in May 1979, having 'lost' the referenda on devolution in the previous March, but the battle over the chain of command in the party had only just begun.

In the 1980s Labour's constitutional agenda gathered cobwebs. What reforms were proposed in the Thatcher years smacked of a marginalised party shut out from the corridors of power. Calls for statutory control of the security services, a Freedom of Information Act and state financial aid for political parties (as recommended by the 1976 Houghton Committee) surfaced at conferences and in election manifestos. But beyond this anti-executive posture Labour had little new to say – until, that is, the policy review conducted in the wake of the party's 1987 election defeat. *Meet the Challenge, Make the Change* committed the party to a 'modern democracy', comprised of a bill of rights, an elected second chamber (with special duties to oversee human rights legislation), a Freedom of Information Act, devolution to a Scottish assembly, the creation of a multipurpose authority in Wales, and regional authorities in England itself.[77] On the face of it, 1989 looked like an important turning-point in the Labour Party's conversion to constitutional innovation. In that year leading Scottish Labour MPs joined Liberal Democrats and Scottish Nationalists in the Scottish Constitutional Convention which met to consider the options for devolution. A Labour Party *Charter of Rights* was published in 1990, and in the same year the NEC commissioned a series of reports on alternative electoral systems, Lords reform, and a Scottish Parliament from a group chaired by Raymond Plant.[78] But it would be wrong to exaggerate the novelty of Labour's new agenda after 1989. Devolution to Scotland and Lords reform had been manifesto commitments since at least 1979. At the time of the policy review, pronouncements by the party hierarchy remained limited to the 1980s' agenda of human rights legislation, and since 1994 Tony Blair has proceeded cautiously – ticking off the hereditary peerage, mistaking Scottish devolution for decentralisation, but giving away little else.[79] There is more continuity than is often supposed between New Labour's constitutional designs and the policies it inherited from the 1970s and 1980s.

Indeed, looked at in the longer term, the Labour Party has proved itself a friend of constitutional reform. Although it has been and remains fashionable to see it as constitutionally conservative, its record on parliamentary reform speaks for itself. It has been the Labour Party, both in office and by pressure from without, which has done the most to reform the electoral system in the twentieth century – abolishing the plural vote, ending residence requirements, equalising the local government and parliamentary franchise, improving access to polling stations, lowering the age of voting, and modernising the format of the ballot paper to include party names. Two Labour Lord Presidents – Morrison and Crossman – probably did more to overhaul the ordinary procedure of the Commons than any politician since Gladstone. And slowly but surely, it has been the Labour goal of an upper chamber limited to revision and scrutiny, with a built-in working government majority, towards which Lords reform has edged in fits and starts since the 1940s. Labour's record on local government reform and on devolution has been less impressive, and in other areas, such as civil service reorganisation, blueprints and bright ideas have far outnumbered policy achievements. But although Tony Blair's government may not recognise it, the constitution they seek to reform is very much a system of the Labour Party's own making.

Miles Taylor

Notes

1 Robert Hazell and David Sinclair, 'The British constitution in 1997–8: Labour's constitutional revolution', *Parliamentary Affairs* 52 (1999), 161–78; Robert Blackburn and Raymond Plant, *Constitutional Reform: The Labour Government's Constitutional Reform Agenda* (London: Longman, 1999).

2 For optimism: Rodney Brazier, *Constitutional Reform*, 2nd edn (Oxford: Clarendon Press, 1998), pp. 52–5; Anthony Barnett, *This Time: Our Constitutional Revolution* (London: Vintage, 1998); Robert Hazell, 'The shape of things to come: what will the UK constitution look like in the early 21st century?' in Robert Hazell (ed.), *Constitutional Futures: A History of the Next Ten Years* (Oxford: Clarendon Press, 1999), pp. 7–20. For scepticism: Stephen Driver and Luke Martell, *New Labour: Politics after Thatcherism* (Cambridge: Polity, 1998), p. 157; Peter Riddell, *Parliament Under Pressure* (London: Victor Gollancz, 1998), pp. 106–8. For hostility: John Redwood, *The Death of Britain* (London: Macmillan, 1999).

3 'Labour has been at least as constitutionally conservative as its political opponents and often more so': Vernon Bogdanor, 'Labour and the constitution. Part 1: the record', in Brian Brivati and Tim Bale (eds.), *New Labour in Power: Precedents and Prospects* (London: Routledge, 1997), p. 112; cf. Michael Foley, *The Politics of the British Constitution* (Manchester: Manchester University Press, 1999), p. 192 and Anthony Wright, 'British socialists and the British constitution', *Parliamentary Affairs* 43 (1990), 322–40; Barry Jones and Michael Keating, *Labour and the British State* (Clarendon Press, Oxford, 1985), p. 193; Kevin Theakston, *The Labour Party and Whitehall* (London: Routledge, 1992).

4 J. R. MacDonald, *The New Charter: A Programme of Working Class Politics* (Dover: J. B. Jones, 1892), p. 2; *Manifesto of the Labour Representation Committee* (London: LRC, 1900); Arthur Henderson, *Papers on Elections, Registration, etc, Read at a Special Conference at Hull* (London: Labour Party, 1908); J. R. MacDonald, G. H. Roberts and W. C. Anderson, *The Labour Party and Electoral Reform: Proportional Representation and the Alternative Vote* (London: Labour Party, 1913).

5 H. Russell Smart, *Lords, Commons and the People* (Manchester: National Labour Press, 1910), pp. 13–14; F. Jowett, *What is the Use of Parliament?* (London: Clarion Press, 1909), pp. 7–12, 30. The Social Democratic Federation (SDF) also supported the use of the referendum: *Programme and Rules of the SDF* (London: SDF, 1893), p. 1. In general, see: Logie Barrow and Ian Bullock, *Democratic Ideas and the British Labour Movement, 1880–1914* (Cambridge: Cambridge University Press, 1996), chs. 8–10.

6 H. R. Stockman, *Labour and the Lords: An Indictment* (Salford: ILP, 1909); Russell Smart, *Lords, Commons and People*, p. 5.

7 J. R. MacDonald, *Hansard*, vol. XXI (21 February 1911), cols. 1765–73; Snowden, *Hansard*, vol. XXII (1 March 1911), cols. 450–6; Snowden, 'The Labour Party and the second chamber', *New Statesman*, 7 February 1914.

8 Victor Grayson, *The Problem of Parliament: A Criticism and a Remedy* (London: New Age Press, 1909), pp. 67–73; Leonard Hall et al., *Let us Reform the Labour Party* (Manchester: Fellowship Press, 1910); *Report of the 20th Annual Conference of the ILP* (London: ILP, 1912), pp. 77–8.

9 *Report of the 10th Annual Conference of the Labour Party* (London: Labour Party, 1910), p. 74; *Report of the 11th Annual Conference of the Labour Party* (London: Labour Party, 1911), p. 102.

10 *Report of the 10th Conference*, pp. 75–7.

11 MacDonald, Roberts and Anderson, *Labour Party and Electoral Reform*; *Report of the 14th Annual Conference of the Labour Party* (London: Labour Party, 1914), pp. 104–13; J. Hart, *Proportional Representation: Critics of the British Electoral System, 1820–1945* (Oxford: Clarendon Press, 1992), pp. 164–6.

12 *Report of the 15th Annual Conference of the ILP* (Derby: ILP, 1907), p. 34; cf. J. R. MacDonald, *Socialism and Government*, 2 vols. (London: ILP, 1909), vol. I, pp. xxvii–xxviii.

13 Wright, 'British socialists', pp. 324–5; A. H. Hanson, 'The Labour Party and House of Commons reform – I', *Parliamentary Affairs* 10 (1957), 459–60; James Meadowcroft, *Conceptualising the State: Innovation and Dispute in British Political Thought, 1880–1914* (Oxford: Clarendon Press, 1995), pp. 194–210. MacDonald's much cited 'will-o'-the-wisp' quote actually referred to the obstructionist tactics of Irish nationalist MPs.

14 MacDonald, *Socialism and Government*, vol. I, pp. 48–9, 63n, 120, vol. II, p. 21.

15 Ibid., vol. I, pp. 110–16, 117, 121, 125–6, vol. II, p. 73. On the Lords as a revision chamber see also his comments in *Hansard*, vol. I (22 February 1909), cols. 473–4.

16 Mrs Frederick Hansen to Lansbury, 3 November 1912, Lansbury papers, I/6, fol. 163, British Library of Political and Economic Science, London School of Economics (hereafter BLPES).

17 Leonard Hall, *Industrial Unionism* (London: BSP, 1912), p. 3; cf. *Report of the 1st Annual Conference of the British Socialist Party* (Manchester: BSP, 1912), p. 8.

18 J. R. MacDonald, *Parliament and Democracy* (London: Leonard Parsons, 1920), pp. vi–vii.

19 Hanson, 'Labour Party and House of Commons reform'; Philip Williamson, 'The Labour Party and the House of Lords, 1918–31', *Parliamentary History* 10 (1991), 317–41; Ian S. Wood, 'Hopes deferred: Labour in Scotland in the 1920s', in I. Donnachie et al. (eds.), *Forward!: Labour Politics in Scotland, 1888–1988* (Edinburgh: Polygon, 1989), pp. 36–7; J. S. Rowett, 'The Labour Party and local government: theory and practice in the inter-war years', D.Phil. thesis (University of Oxford, 1979). For an excellent account which dissents from this negative verdict, see P. R. Thomas, 'The attitude of the Labour Party to reform of Parliament, with particular reference to the House of Commons, 1919–51', Ph.D. thesis (University of Keele, 1974).

20 Henderson, *The Aims of Labour* (London: Headley Brothers, 1917), pp. 61–2; J. R. MacDonald, *A Policy for the Labour Party* (London: Leonard Parsons,

Miles Taylor

1920), pp. 75–6, 166–7; J. R. Macdonald, *Parliament and Revolution* (Manchester: National Labour Press, 1919), ch. 8. On 'direct action', see: S. R. Graubard, *British Labor and the Russian Revolution, 1917–24* (Cambridge, Mass.: Harvard University Press, 1956), ch. 4.

21 Ministry of Reconstruction, paper 18, Passfield papers, 4/11, BLPES; cf. Sidney and Beatrice Webb, *A Constitution for the Socialist Commonwealth of Great Britain* (London: Longmans, Green and Co., 1920).

22 National Executive minutes (hereafter NEC), 29 January 1920, p. 4, 22 June 1920, p. 194, Labour Party Archive, Manchester (hereafter LPA); 'Report on Methods of adapting the Civil Service', 'Draft Report . . . on Parliamentary Control' and 'Report on Devolution', JSM/MG/18i–ii, JSM/MG/42, LPA.

23 Cf. H. Laski's 'The civil service and Parliament', in *The Development of the Civil Service: Lectures Delivered before the Society of Civil Servants, 1920–1* (London: P. S. King and Sons, 1922), pp. 27–32.

24 Sidney Webb, *The Reform of the House of Lords* (London: Fabian Society, 1917), p. 12.

25 J. Thomas, *When Labour Rules* (London: William Collins, 1920), pp. 48–9; H. Lees-Smith, *Second Chambers in Theory and Practice* (London: George Allen and Unwin, 1923), pp. 246–9; Harold Laski, *The Problem of a Second Chamber* (London: Fabian Society, 1925), pp. 13–14.

26 Lees-Smith, *Second Chambers*, pp. 27–31, 44–5.

27 Middleton to Roland Muirhead, 17 October 1924, Muirhead papers, box 47, file 129, National Library of Scotland, Edinburgh; R. J. Finlay, *Independent and Free: Scottish Politics and the Origin of the Scottish National Party, 1918–45* (Edinburgh: John Donald, 1994), ch. 1.

28 Sidney Webb, *A New Reform Bill* (London: Fabian Society, 1931); Stafford Cripps, 'Can socialism come by constitutional methods?', in C. Addison et al., *Problems of a Socialist Government* (London: Victor Gollancz, 1933), pp. 43–53; Stafford Cripps, 'Parliamentary institutions in the transition to social-ism', in *Where Stands Socialism Today?* (Fabian Society Lectures, London: Rich and Cowan, 1933), pp. 32–43; G. D. H. Cole, *Economic Tracts for the Times* (London: Macmillan, 1932), pp. 319–20; Harold Laski, *The Crisis and the Constitution: 1931 and After* (London: Hogarth Press, 1932); Harold Laski, *Democracy in Crisis* (London: George Allen and Unwin, 1933), pp. 81–2, 87.

29 *Report of the 34th Annual Conference of the Labour Party* (London: Labour Party, 1934), appdx VIII. For criticism of Cripps and the Socialist League by Citrine, the general secretary of the TUC, see Walter Citrine, *Men and Work: An Autobiography* (London: Hutchinson, 1964), pp. 295–301; Thomas, 'The attitude of the Labour Party', pp. 319–20, 339, 349–53.

30 NEC minutes, 25 January 1932, p. 31, LPA.

31 Cripps, 'Parliamentary institutions'; Stafford Cripps, *Democracy Up to Date: Some Practical Suggestions for the Reorganisation of the Political and Parliamentary System* (London: George Allen and Unwin, 1939), pp. 54–64, 68, 75–9, 92–3, 99–103.

32 Christopher Addison, 'The use of private members of the House of Commons' (7 June 1932), Fabian Society papers, J13/1/27, BLPES; Hugh Dalton, 'A note on the reform of parliamentary procedure' (8 June 1932), Fabian Society papers, J13/1/36–7, BLPES; Clement Attlee, 'Cabinet reconstruction' (12 October 1932), Fabian Society papers, J13/1/44–7, BLPES. These papers built on discussions held under the auspices of the Socialist Society for Inquiry and Propaganda at Easton Lodge in March 1931. For the involvement of the NFRB: NEC minutes, 30 November 1933, p. 457, LPA; Ivor Jennings, *Parliamentary Reform* (London: Victor Gollancz, 1934), esp. ch. 9.

33 Harold Laski, 'The Cabinet and the machinery of government' (June 1935), JSM/CON/3i–iii, LPA; 'Parliamentary procedure' (June 1935), JSM/CON/2i–vii, LPA; H. Lees-Smith, 'The House of Lords' (May 1935), JSM/CON/1, LPA. For the NEC discussion of these: NEC minutes, 26 June 1935, p. 397, LPA.

34 Richard Crossman, *How Britain is Governed* (London: Labour Book Service, 1939), pp. 29–30; cf. Hugh Dalton, *Practical Socialism* (London: George Routledge, 1935), esp. pt. II; Clement Attlee, *The Labour Party in Perspective* (London: Victor Gollancz, 1937), pp. 169–75; Attlee, *Labour's Aims* (London: Labour Party, 1937), p. 8; Michael Stewart, *The British Approach to Politics* (London: George Allen and Unwin, 1938), pp. 202–3; G. D. H. Cole, *Plan for Democratic Britain* (London: Labour Book Service, 1939), ch. 21.

35 Herbert Morrison, *Our Parliament and How It Works* (London: Labour Party, 1953), pp. 10–12, 27–8.

36 For Morrison's defence of his reforms, see his *Britain's Parliament at Work* (London: Labour Party, 1948); 'British parliamentary democracy', in *Parliamentary Government in Britain: A Symposium* (London: Hansard Society, 1949), pp. 1–11; *Government and Parliament: A Survey From the Inside* (Oxford: Clarendon Press, 1959); and *British Parliamentary Democracy* (London: Asia Publishing House, 1962). For the background, see: Bernard Donoughue and G. W. Jones, *Herbert Morrison: Portrait of a Politician* (London: Weidenfeld and Nicholson, 1973), chs. 25–32. For negative verdicts on Morrison, see Hanson, 'Labour Party and House of Commons reform', pp. 455–6; Wright, 'British socialists', p. 325.

37 NEC minutes, 4 February 1942, p. 288, LPA; cf. Emmanuel Shinwell (chairman of the NEC Central Committee on Reconstruction), *The Britain I Want* (London: Macdonald and Co., 1943), ch. 15.

38 W. I. Jennings, *Parliament Must be Reformed: A Programme for Democratic Government* (London: Kegan Paul, Trench and Trübner, 1941), p. 46; R. W. S. Pollard, *How To Reform Parliament* (London: Forum Press, 1944), pp. 9–11, 19, 25–6, 33.

39 Research Department Report 52 (January 1942), LPA; NEC minutes, Machinery of Government Sub-Committee, 11 February 1942, LPA.

40 J. Eaves, *Emergency Powers and the Parliamentary Watchdog: Parliament and the Executive in Great Britain, 1939–51* (London: Hansard Society, 1957), pp. 107–13; Thomas, 'The attitude of the Labour Party', pp. 397–8. For party

concern over the electoral truce: *Report of the 42nd Annual Conference of the Labour Party* (London: Labour Party, 1943), pp. 171–3.

41 War cabinet minutes, 1 August 1944, CAB 66/53, Public Record Office (hereafter PRO).

42 'Local government', Research Department Report 12 (October 1941), LPA; 'Local government in the post-war world', Research Department Report 93 (May 1942), LPA; 'Draft Report', Research Department Report 190 (February, 1943, LPA); *The Future of Local Government: The Labour Party's Post-War Policy* (London: Labour Party, 1943). For Cole's ideas, see his 'The future of local government', *Political Quarterly* 12 (1941), 405–18; Cole, *Local and Regional Government* (London: Cassell and Co., 1947). The importance of local government reform for Labour is brought out well in A. L. Beach, 'The Labour Party and the idea of citizenship, *c.* 1931–51', Ph.D. thesis (University of London, 1996), ch. 4, esp. pp. 153–61.

43 Latham initially backed extensive financial enabling powers for both regional and area authorities, but after the war this idea was again dropped: see 'Some notes upon . . . financial aspects of a reorganised local government structure', Research Department Report 103 (June 1942), LPA; *Local Government Reform in England and Wales* (London: Labour Party, 1946), pp. 4–7.

44 NEC minutes, 19–20 December 1942, p. 33, LPA.

45 Morrison, *Hansard*, vol. CDVI (19 November 1944), cols. 1646–8, vol. CDVII (17 January 1945), cols. 204–5; D. E. Butler, *The Electoral System in Britain, 1918–51* (Oxford: Clarendon Press, 1953), pp. 98–9.

46 Between 1944 and 1951, forty-four Labour Party supporters were ennobled: Philip Bromhead, *The House of Lords and Contemporary Politics, 1911–57* (London: Routledge and Kegan Paul, 1958), p. 27.

47 Morrison, 'Speech to the Association of American Correspondents', 7 November 1946, Morrison papers, 1/6, BLPES.

48 Cabinet minutes, 24 November 1946, CAB 128/6, PRO.

49 Patrick Gordon Walker, 'House of Lords' [memorandum], May 1947, Morrison papers, 1/5, BLPES; Morrison to Attlee, 19 September 1947, Morrison papers, 8/3, BLPES.

50 Norman Brook to A. Johnston, 28 October 1947, CAB 124/305, fol. 20, PRO; cabinet minutes, 14 October 1947, CAB 128/10, PRO; 'Notes for the PM on Bills referred to in the King's Speech on the Opening of Parliament', 17 October 1947, Attlee papers, MSS Attlee, dep. 62, fols. 110–15, Bodleian Library, Oxford.

51 Initially Attlee suggested a compromise of nine months from the third reading: 'Parliament Bill: Memorandum by the Prime Minister' (9 March 1948), cabinet papers, CAB 129/25, PRO; cabinet minutes, 29 April 1948, CAB 128/12, PRO. For the inter-party conference: *Parliamentary Papers* (1947–8), vol. XXII.

52 *Hansard*, vol. CDLXIX (31 October 1948), col. 161; *Tribune*, 17 September 1948.

53 Chuter Ede, 'Electoral legislation', cabinet papers, 3 July 1947, 12 December 1947, CAB 129/22, PRO; Attlee to Morrison, 17 February 1948, Morrison papers, 1/6, BLPES; Butler, *Electoral System*, ch. 5.

54 *Hansard*, vol. CDXLVII (16 February 1948), cols. 864–70.

55 Francis Williams, *A Prime Minister Remembers: The War and Post-War Memoirs of the Right. Hon. Earl Attlee . . . Based on his Private Papers, and on a Series of Recorded Conversations* (London: Heinemann, 1961), pp. 228–9. For misgivings at the time, see Dalton, *Hansard*, vol. CDXLVII (16 February 1948), col. 939.

56 On the cabinet response to the Convention, see Ian Levitt (ed.), *The Scottish Office: Depression and Reconstruction, 1919–59* (Edinburgh: Scottish History Society, 1992), pp. 19–23. The Fabian Society did suggest a nominated legislative assembly for Scotland: William H. Marwick, *Scottish Devolution* (London: Fabian Society, 1950), pp. 24–6.

57 For concern at possible NUM pressure: Cliff Prothero (Welsh Regional Council) to Morgan Phillips, 27 October 1953, GS/WAL/63, LPA; 'Labour's policy for Wales', *Report of the 53rd Annual Conference of the Labour Party* (London: Labour Party, 1954), appdx 1; J. Graham Jones, 'The Parliament for Wales campaign, 1950–6', *Welsh History Review* 16 (1992), 207–36.

58 'Transcript of an interview', 6 November 1967, Crossman papers, MS 154/3/LPO/19, fols. 24–5, Modern Records Centre, University of Warwick (hereafter MRC).

59 Walter Bagehot, *The English Constitution* (London: Collins, 1963). For Crossman's favourable response to Mackintosh, see his 'Left of centre' column in the *Guardian*, 6 April 1962.

60 For its reports, see: *Parliamentary Papers* (1964–5), vol. VIII; (1965–6), vol. III; (1966–7), vol. XVI. For influential statements of the case for parliamentary reform at the start of the Wilson years, see Bernard Crick, *The Reform of Parliament* (London: Weidenfeld and Nicholson, 1964), esp. ch. 9 and 'Three dozen parliamentary reforms by one dozen parliamentary socialists', *Socialist Commentary* (Supplement), July 1964.

61 Geoffrey K. Fry, *Reforming the Civil Service: The Fulton Committee on the British Home Civil Service of 1966–68* (Edinburgh: Edinburgh University Press, 1993); Richard Wilding, 'The Fulton report in retrospect', *Contemporary Record* 9 (1995), 394–408.

62 'Note of a meeting', 17 October 1966, PREM 13/1053, PRO; *Hansard*, vol. DCCXXXVIII (14 December 1966), cols. 471–80; Richard Crossman, *The Diaries of a Cabinet Minister*, vol. II: *Lord President of the Council and Leader of the Commons, 1966–8* (London: Hamish Hamilton, 1976), pp. 74–5, 165.

63 Crossman to Peter Meyer, 10 January 1967, Crossman papers, MSS 154/3/LPO/9, fol. 28, MRC; 'Transcript of the *Week in Westminster*', 13 April 1968, Crossman papers, MSS 154/3/LPO/19, fols. 4–7, MRC.

64 For the Speaker's Conference, see *Parliamentary Papers* (1967–8), vol. XIX. For the cabinet deliberations: 'Electoral reform: Note by the Secretary of State for the Home Dept.' (23 May 1968), pp. 1–2, CAB 129/135, PRO; Burke

Miles Taylor

Trend to Wilson, 29 May 1968, PREM 13/2076, PRO; cabinet minutes, 30 May 1968, CAB 128/43, PRO.

65 Burke Trend to Wilson, 8 May 1968, PREM 13/2076, PRO; D. H. Andrews to B. C. Cubbon, 9 December 1968, and Norman Warner to D. H. Andrews, 10 December 1968, PREM 13/2074, PRO.

66 Richard Crossman, *Inside View: Three Lectures on Prime Ministerial Government* (London: Jonathan Cape, 1972), p. 94.

67 Cabinet minutes, 28 June 1966, CAB 126/46, PRO.

68 Crossman, *Guardian*, 8 February 1963; cf. his 'Crossman Says' column, *Daily Mirror*, 10 July 1956. For Tony Benn's ideas for a reformed second chamber, see his *The Privy Council as a Second Chamber* (London: Fabian Society, 1957), pp. 16–19. For the background, see Janet Morgan, *The House of Lords and the Labour Government, 1964–70* (Oxford: Clarendon Press, 1975), chs. 7–8.

69 For the inter-party conference, see *Parliamentary Papers* (1968–9), vol. LIII. On Carrington's role, see Peter Carrington, *Reflect on Things Past: The Memoirs of Lord Carrington* (London: William Collins, 1988), pp. 206–7.

70 'Note of a meeting', 19 June 1968, PREM 13/2295, PRO.

71 *Hansard*, vol. DCCLXXIII (19 November 1968), cols. 1125–31.

72 'Minutes of Meetings of the Cabinet Committee on Devolution', 18 July, 23 July and 28 October 1968, CAB 130/390, PRO.

73 For the Redcliffe-Maud Report, see *Parliamentary Papers* (1968–9), vol. XXXVIII. For Anthony Crosland's speech of 18 February 1970 introducing Labour's plans, see Anthony Crosland, *Socialism Now* (London: Jonathan Cape, 1974), ch. 15.

74 *Guardian*, 27 November 1972; Harold Wilson, *Democracy in Local Affairs* (London: Labour Party, 1973). See also the NEC's 'Local Government in the Future' (1973), R.D. 521, LPA.

75 NEC Home Policy Committee, 'Implications of devolution within the UK' (June 1974), pp. 2–4, LPA.

76 Neil Kinnock warned that separate assemblies 'could be an obituary notice for this movement': *Report of the 75th Annual Conference of the Labour Party* (London: Labour Party, 1976), p. 200. For the NEC's position on direct elections, see: ibid., appdx 2.

77 *Meet the Challenge, Make the Change: A New Agenda for Britain. Final Report on Labour's Policy Review for the 1990s* (London: Labour Party, 1989), pp. 55–65.

78 *Towards a Scottish Parliament* (Edinburgh: Scottish Constitutional Convention, 1989); *Scotland's Parliament. Scotland's Right* (Edinburgh: Scottish Constitutional Convention, 1995); *The Charter of Rights* (London: Labour Party, 1990). The three Plant reports were on 'Democracy, Representation and Elections' (1991), 'A Scottish Parliament' (1992) and 'Electoral Systems' (1993).

79 *Guardian*, 8 January 1990; John Smith, *A Citizen's Democracy* (London: Labour Party, 1993); *Guardian*, 8 February 1996.

Fig. I 'Labour inside the gate': campaigning cartoon, 1906

Fig. 2 *Labour respectability: the Lanarkshire Women's Advisory Council in the early 1920s (Mitchell Library)*

Fig. 3 *The first Labour cabinet, 1924. Front: W. Adamson, Lord Parmoor,*
P. Snowden, Lord Haldane, Ramsay MacDonald, J. R. Clynes, J. H. Thomas,
A. Henderson; Centre: C. P. Trevelyan, Stephen Walsh, Lord Thomson, Lord
Chelmsford, Lord Olivier, Noel Buxton, J. C. Wedgwood, Vernon Hartshorn,
T. Shaw; Back: Sidney Webb, J. Wheatley, Fred W. Jowett

Fig. 4 *Labour modernity: Marion Phillips MP in the 1929 Parliament,
wearing her self-designed 'really convenient House of Commons
uniform' – 'a well-cut overall of thick crêpe-de-chine, lined with
bright silk which buttons over her dress'*

Fig. 5 *On the stump (i): Clement Attlee meets the voters of tomorrow while campaigning during the 1950 election*

Fig. 6 *On the stump (ii): Clement Attlee addresses a mass rally at Southampton docks, October 1951*

Fig. 7 *Hard work behind the scenes: staff at Labour headquarters in London dispatch literature to the constituencies, January 1950*

Fig. 8 *The rank and file (i): delegates at the 1940 conference*

Fig. 9 *The rank and file (ii): delegates at the 1983 conference*

Fig. 10 *Labour's internationalism: Prime Minister Harold Wilson shares a joke with Golda Meir and Willy Brandt at the 1969 Labour Party conference*

6 | Labour and gender

Martin Francis

The relationship of the Labour Party to issues of gender has been complex and ambiguous. Labour was always more than a party of the organised male working class. It was also the vehicle for a broader project of emancipation which emphasised human dignity for all, irrespective not only of class, but also of sex. The Labour Party was committed to a broad-based humanitarianism which did not conceive of socialism and feminism as incompatible. As the party's Chief Woman Officer put it in 1980, 'Women's rights are fundamental to the fight for socialism.'[1] However, a significant sector of party opinion believed that the Labour Party had been founded primarily not to advance feminism, nor socialism for that matter, but to defend the interests of male manual workers, and at some times more than others, Labour has been indifferent to the specific needs of women, defined in both traditional and feminist terms. These two traditions have coexisted throughout this century, generating conflicts which have rarely been resolved. This chapter charts these tensions, suggesting that women made a vital contribution to shaping the character and programmes of the party (especially in regard to welfare) but found progress in some areas (such as equal pay) unsatisfactorily slow. Structural impediments to the advance of women's issues in the Labour Party are acknowledged,

191

Martin Francis

but this account argues that much more important were ambiguities in Labour's discourses of gender, in particular those relating to feminist ideas, consumption, sexuality and the dominant representations of masculinity and femininity.

Labour women: achievement and frustration

Women's activism in the Labour Party was first given institutional recognition with the creation of the Women's Labour League (WLL) in 1906. The WLL's membership remained at around 5,000 until 1918, when the League was disbanded, to be replaced by women's sections affiliated to local parties. This formal integration into the party structure, and the extension of the parliamentary franchise to most women over thirty later that year, immediately promoted a massive surge in Labour's female membership. By 1922, 100,000 women had joined the women's sections, and the average female party membership during the inter-war period was over a quarter of a million, which accounted for at least half of Labour's individual members at this time. These new women activists came from a variety of social backgrounds and occupations: housewives, manual workers, professionals, nurses and social service workers. While the standard accounts of inter-war Labour women have concentrated on those working-class women who made up the majority of female members, it should not be forgotten that the party's attraction in the 1920s was not just confined to the underprivileged.[2] In the inter-war years the parliamentary party possessed more university-educated women than the Conservatives, not just working-class scholarship beneficiaries like Ellen Wilkinson and Jennie Lee, but a figure like Susan Lawrence, born into a wealthy legal family and educated at Cambridge. For such privileged women, Labour activism was another stage in the long tradition of middle-class female philanthropy. Other middle-class women came to the party through the Fabian Society, 43 per cent of whose members were female in 1912. There were even aristocratic women in Labour's ranks in the 1920s, in the colourful forms of the Countess of Warwick and Cynthia Mosley.[3]

Given such a variety of backgrounds, it is not surprising that Labour women in the middle decades of the twentieth century were committed to pursuing a range of progressive causes. The party's annual reports in the 1920s show women's sections campaigning on issues relating to women's workplace rights, female unemployment, education, social services, the minimum wage, family allowances, birth control and disarmament. A similar spread of interests is evident in the specialist briefs adopted by the handful of inter-war Labour MPs, embracing as they did industry and finance (Jennie Lee, Ellen Wilkinson and Mary Agnes Hamilton), infant mortality (Marion Phillips), industrial relations and employment (Susan Lawrence and Margaret Bondfield), horticulture (Lucy Noel-Buxton) and ecclesiastical affairs (Edith Picton-Turbervill). The next generation of Labour women MPs, entering Parliament in 1945, tackled issues as disparate as the dangers of boxing (Edith Summerskill), children in care (Jean Mann), widows' rights (Eirene White), and transport and energy (Barbara Castle). Whether as members of women's sections or as MPs, Labour women frequently ranged beyond the traditional 'housewife's brief' of education and social services and pursued issues usually considered male terrain, notably foreign policy. Lena Jeger was advised by Herbert Morrison to 'stick to women's issues' in her maiden speech in 1953. When he subsequently rebuked her for choosing to speak on the Foreign Ministers' conference in Berlin, she retorted 'Isn't peace a woman's issue?'[4] Indeed Margaret MacDonald had launched the WLL in 1906 with an insistence that 'if it is to be anything the Labour Women's Movement must be international'. In the 1920s Labour women had been in the forefront of the party's support for disarmament and anti-militarism. In the 1930s Ellen Wilkinson, Lucy Cox (later Middleton) and Leah Manning were prominent in campaigns to support the republican cause during the Spanish Civil War and, in the immediate aftermath of the Second World War, Alice Bacon helped establish the International Council of Social Democratic Women.[5] Women had particular significance in the development of Labour's colonial policy. Not merely did MPs such as Barbara Castle and Judith Hart take a sustained interest in the subject, but the émigré South African and Fabian Rita Hinden played a critical role in transforming the party's emotional anti-imperialism into a series of detailed and coherent programmes for colonial development and eventual self-government during the 1940s.[6]

The activities of Labour women were therefore characterised by vitality and variety. Moreover, they also contributed to fundamentally shaping the party's character and programmes, as can be seen by reference to Labour's attitude to the poor, to welfare and to community politics. At a national level, in the Edwardian era the Fabian Women's Group and key individuals such as Margaret MacDonald, Margaret Macmillan and Mary Macarthur had a considerable impact on the development of the party's policies in relation to education, children and social services. Recent research has shown this influence was reproduced at the local level. In Edwardian Wolverhampton, leading Labour activists had shown little stomach for campaigning among the slum dwellers of the city's 'east end', regarding them as intellectually stunted and morally degraded. However, the local WLL and Co-operative Women's Guild in 1913–14 demanded the introduction of free baby clinics and free school meals in the poorest districts of the city, and urged the party hierarchy to be more sensitive towards, and less judgmental about, the least fortunate stratum of the working class. In so doing they redefined Labour politics so as to be less exclusory, based on a broader conception of the 'working class' than the archetype of the 'respectable' artisan which the party had inherited from nineteenth-century radicalism.[7] In the 1920s Labour women contested Labour men's preference for issues relating to paid labour, and promoted an agenda concerned with social deprivation and welfare. Through pressure from Labour women, inter-war local authorities expanded the provision of health visitors, home helps, mother and baby clinics and public baths. Labour women contributed to the work of city housing authorities, seeking to ensure housewives could expect conditions in the newly built council houses equal to those enjoyed by paid labour in the workplace.[8] Such extensions of local welfare services undoubtedly improved the lives of working-class women.

This pressure from Labour women widened Labour's welfare agenda. Comparisons of male and female activists who joined the Labour Party between the wars reveal that most of the men had, through their workplace experience, seen how organised labour could bring improvements in wages and conditions. The women, by contrast, had little evidence that the poverty they saw in their neighbourhoods and homes could be alleviated by trade-union action alone. Higher wages for husbands would be a help, but never a total solution. Public welfare provision, from both local and central government, was a necessary complement.[9] One local study has claimed that, through the efforts of Labour women, the party became less sectional and exclusive in terms of both personnel and policy, and this brought electoral dividends. In the years immediately after 1918 the Labour Party in Preston resisted appeals to broaden public welfare provision, remaining reliant on the local voluntary hospital, which satisfied the needs of wage earners through a contributory insurance scheme, but offered little for their dependants or those not in regular employment. Such indifference to welfare was accompanied by hostility to Labour women's activism, and women's sections were not initiated until 1924. However, in the late 1920s, the party began to rely less on the trade unions, and more on women activists, with their neighbourhood and welfare agenda. Healthcare provision, education and nurseries became central to

Labour's campaign strategies after 1925 and helped generate unprecedented levels of electoral support, culminating in the party's impressive performance in Preston in the 1929 election.[10] Such success stories were not, of course, universal, and Labour's national growth in the 1920s and 1930s was distinctly uneven. Nevertheless, the Preston experience suggested that Labour women had done a great deal to broaden the party's appeal in the inter-war years.

However, while Labour women had an effect on party policy and identity with regard to welfare issues in the 1920s, in other areas their presence appears to have barely registered. Equal pay for equal work first became an election pledge of the Labour Party in 1918, but it was not until 1969 that a Labour government was willing to introduce legislation on this matter. It is true that during the 1945–51 Labour government, the party's women's sections were largely supportive of the administration's claims that the precarious economic situation made the immediate implementation of 'the rate for the job' impossible. However, the women's sections had demanded equal pay for work of equal value in the 1920s and 1930s, and frustration with the party leadership's inattention to the issue was a marked feature of the annual women's conferences in the 1950s and 1960s. At over half of the conferences between 1953 and 1969 resolutions were passed insisting that future or present governments implement equal pay, and the patience of many women's sections was clearly wearing thin. The party hierarchy's response ranged from indolence to hostility, and in 1967 the NEC took the extraordinary step of forbidding discussion of equal pay at the party conference for three years. When the Wilson government finally got round to honouring the party's pledge in 1969, it did so only halfheartedly, and action was prompted more by electoral considerations than by a sensitivity to the party's women's sections.[11] How then can one explain the peculiar unevenness of women's contribution to the shaping of Labour policy? Why did they succeed in making progress in some areas (such as welfare policy), while they were marginalised or completely ignored in others (such as equal pay)? Why did grass-roots pressure from Labour women sometimes find strong resonances higher up the party, but on other occasions receive only platitudes or icy indifference?

Labour women and the Labour Party

Structural factors certainly had a part to play in the precarious status of women's activism in the Labour Party, and they have therefore featured regularly in critical accounts of the party's record on women's issues. The 1918 party constitution treated women as a distinct interest group,

Martin Francis

recognising their desire for their own local sections and annual confer- ence. However, these institutions were marginalised from the party's real centres of power, the annual party conference and the National Executive Committee (NEC). While women continued to make up a substantial proportion of the party's individual membership (just over 50 per cent in the inter-war years, around 40 per cent in the 1950s and 1960s), women were under-represented at the party conference: as late as the 1970s, only 11 per cent of the party delegates were women. One problem was the overwhelming male dominance of the affiliated trade unions. Even after the dramatic increase in the number of female trade unionists in the 1940s, in 1950 there were still only 1,670,000 women compared to 7,565,000 men in the unions represented at the party conference. While there were four (increased to five in 1929) reserved seats on the NEC for women, these members were not elected by the women's sections, but by the male-dominated party conference, and they consequently did not regard themselves as representatives of women party members only. The NEC's Women's Advisory Committee (whose membership was chosen by individual industrial and political organisations of working women with a membership of over 1,000) was not granted any opportunity to initiate policy, the constitution limiting its functions to the provision of information and the offering of recommendations. The Chief Woman Officer was responsible to the NEC and the party agent, not to the women's sections. Resolutions passed at women's conferences were never binding and the low status of the conferences was reflected in the fact that their proceedings were neither officially minuted nor reported in the Labour press.[12] The women's sections did find ways of compensating for their lack of institutional leverage, forging intermittent alliances with constituency parties (notably, although unsuccessfully, in 1929, during the party conference debate on revising the party constitution), who were also dissatisfied with the dominance of the union block vote over party policy. In 1926 Labour women were able to convince the NEC to lift its ban on the discussion of birth control at the party conference, after forming an alliance with the Miners' Federation, some (although – con- trary to common stereotypes – not all) of whose delegates were not entirely convinced of the value of family limitation, but who were keen to reciprocate the support given by Labour women to the miners during the General Strike.[13] However, such alliances were infrequent, and, as one appraisal neatly puts it, 'women could only rejoice in the security of their place within the Labour Party, not in the influence they wielded'.[14]

Women's lack of influence in the party structure was paralleled by their under-representation in elected office. Precise figures are not available (since Labour did not break down election statistics by gender in this period), but in the inter-war years hundreds of Labour women were elected to local councils and Boards of Guardians. While parliamentary electors often remained wedded to the belief that the national economy and foreign affairs required masculine expertise, at a local level it was recognised that women's household experience made them eminently qualified for local government, which was increasingly concerning itself with the care of housing, health, children (inside and outside the classroom), the aged and the poor. Herbert Morrison was keen to promote women on the London County Council (LCC), and a quarter of the newly elected Labour councillors who took their seats on the LCC in 1934 were women. In 1939 Eveline Lowe became its first female chair.[15] However, such high-profile successes should not be allowed to obscure the broader pattern. In Scotland women were rarely chosen to contest the more prestigious and politically important council elections.[16] Moreover, very little progress was made in women's local government representation after 1945, and in some areas there was a falling back. In 1964 (a good electoral year for Labour) Bristol returned only five women Labour councillors, compared with six in 1937. The party's own study group on discrimination, reporting in 1972, pointed out that women were hardly ever elected to key municipal posts such as Chair of Finance, Planning or General Purposes. It was also alarmed that the local government reforms then pending would make matters even worse, the longer distances involved in getting to meetings (caused by larger local government units) being a major blow to women who were 'less likely to have their own cars' and whose family responsibilities made it difficult to accommodate the extra travelling time involved.[17]

Even if women were relatively well represented on city and county councils, this had to be offset against the post-war decline in the status and responsibility of local government, which had been an unfortunate by-product of Labour's nationalisation and welfare policies in the 1940s. This development made increased female representation at Westminster even more pertinent, but, while the number of women Labour MPs was always greater than that of the other parties, the figures remained paltry, even in years of electoral success: nine in 1929, twenty-one in 1945, nineteen in 1966 and eighteen in October 1974. These meagre figures are not surprising given the low numbers of women selected as parliamentary candidates. There were the same number of Labour women standing for Parliament in 1964 as there had been in 1935 (thirty-three), and that figure had risen only to fifty by October 1974. Moreover, women tended to be selected for marginal seats and therefore were unable to sustain the uninterrupted parliamentary careers usually required for ministerial office. Labour got off to a promising start, Ramsay MacDonald making Margaret Bondfield the first woman cabinet minister in 1929, but Ellen Wilkinson was the only female face around Attlee's cabinet table in 1945. Harold Wilson, while no feminist, admired determined women, and three – Barbara Castle, Judith Hart and Shirley Williams – served in his cabinets in 1964–70 and 1974–76. He also appointed women to a significant number of junior ministerial posts, including Jennie Lee as the first Minister for the Arts.[18] However, women were clearly marginalised from the centres of power in the party, both in opposition and in government, whether on the platform and floor of the party conference or on the front and back benches of the Commons.

It was not until the 1980s that Labour women began to mount a serious challenge to entrenched male privilege. While the NEC was already expressing concern about how few women were coming forward to contest elections on Labour's behalf in the early 1970s, it felt the remedy lay in exhortation directed at local parties. Indeed a party document produced in 1974 exonerated the party structure, placing the blame (with some justification) on 'the organisation and traditions of society at large'.[19] However, in the early 1980s the use of quotas by the Social Democratic Party had led to considerable success in recruiting and mobilising women, and Labour began to shift its emphasis. Even then, the modest proposal that there should be a woman on every parliamentary shortlist was carried at the 1988 party conference against the express wishes of the NEC. Women activists were helped by the changing outlook of trade unions such as the National Union of Public Employees (NUPE), the Confederation of Health Service Employees (COHSE), the General and Municipal Workers (GMB) and Manufacturing, Science and Finance (MSF), who, keen to attract female members to compensate for a decline in male membership, had been introducing reserved seats for women on their executive bodies since the mid-1970s. In 1989 quotas were introduced for the constituency and trade-union sections of the NEC, and for the shadow cabinet. However, affirmative action remained controversial, and was strongly resisted in some local parties. The resolution to create all-women shortlists in half of the 'winnable' seats which became vacant at the next election was carried after a hard-fought debate in 1993, and only after personal intervention by the party leader, John Smith. The NEC was forced to coerce some constituencies into accepting all-women shortlists and the wife of a prominent South Wales MP set up an anti-quota campaign group.

Quotas proved to be much less controversial in party culture in the late 1990s than they had been even five years earlier. While Labour failed to appeal against the 1996 Leeds Industrial Tribunal judgement that all-women shortlists contravened the Sex Discrimination Act (from which political parties are partially exempted), the 'pairing' expedient adopted for the Welsh Assembly elections of 1999 demonstrated an increased commitment to the principle of full and fair representation of women in party and Parliament.[20]

The party's structure might therefore go a long way to explaining the precarious status of women's interests in the history of the Labour Party. However, a full explanation is inevitably more complex and multi-dimensional. At times the institutional marginalisation of Labour women reflected, and indeed contributed to, indifference on the part of the party towards the needs and expectations of women, defined in both traditional and feminist terms. However, if such indifference (or indeed outright misogyny) was not uncommon, it was never universal. The major weakness of an emphasis on structure is that it implies a binary opposition: between 'Labour women' and 'the (male-dominated) Labour Party'. The result is a partial picture, emphasising opposition and alienation at the expense of co-operation and integration. Moreover, it ignores the fact that sexual difference in the discourses (both hegemonic and subordinate) of the Labour Party was rarely disentangled from a larger matrix of identities, derived from religion, region, age, and (most critically) social class. Debates in the party over feminism, consumption and sexuality show that gender played a central role in the shaping of Labour's identity and programmes, yet it is also evident that this process was persistently characterised by diversity and ambiguity.

The Labour Party and feminism

The status of feminist ideas within the Labour Party has, as in the wider society, always been problematic, if not perilous. While in 1911 Margaret Cole remarked that, in becoming a socialist, she 'naturally became at the same time a feminist',[21] for others the identification between socialism and feminism came less easily. Indeed many studies have presented a picture of mutual antagonism and incomprehension between Labour and feminism. Such accounts stress that many prominent feminists in the twentieth century were highly critical of Labour and chose to conduct their activities outside the party. The National Union of Societies for Equal Citizenship (NUSEC), the major feminist pressure group in the 1920s, did give some financial support to Labour parliamentary candidates, but it had much closer relations with the

Liberal Party than it ever did with Labour. While feminists were pleased to see Labour in the 1920s condemn the exclusion of women from the franchise (if under thirty) and the professions, they were concerned that the party appeared less troubled by the exclusion of women from the labour market, through the Restoration of Pre-War Practices Act.[22] According to the standard account of inter-war Labour women this alienation between feminism and the Labour Party deepened as the 1920s went on, and in the 1930s gender issues were further peripheralised as the party's attention became monopolised by the issues of unemployment and the rise of fascism. In an age in which the paradigmatic experiences for the left were Guernica and Jarrow, class solidarity tended to supersede gender identity.[23] This gloomy pattern of feminist failure continued, or so it has frequently been assumed, until the late 1960s. Despite the extensive social and cultural transformations in women's lives which took place during the Second World War, feminist issues continued to be sacrificed to other goals, and this hiatus was only ended by the re-emergence of an organised feminist movement after 1968. Feminism and socialism, prised apart in the late 1920s, had finally come together again, in an uncomfortable, but ultimately productive, coupling which spawned the 1970 Equal Pay Act, the 1970 Matrimonial Proceedings and Property Act, the 1975 Employment Protection Act and the 1975 Sex Discrimination Act.

The problems with this narrative are that it implies another simplistic binary opposition, this time between 'socialism' and 'feminism', and fails to recognise the fact that both 'socialism' and 'feminism' themselves are fluid and multifarious concepts. There was no unanimity among feminists about whether their purposes were best served by working through political parties or through extra-parliamentary agitation and education. Those women who decided on the former stance were themselves divided as to whether common action with men was preferable to separatist initiatives based in women-only political units. In the aftermath of gaining the vote in 1918, the women's movement encompassed an extensive range of opinions and perspectives, and the simplistic division (adopted in many standard textbooks) of women activists into 'equal rights feminists' or 'new feminists' fails to do justice to the complexity of feminist discourse in the 1920s.[24] To complicate matters further, before the 1970s few Labour women, with the major exception of Edith Summerskill, were willing to adopt the appellation of 'feminist'.[25] Shirley Williams, despite being the daughter of one of the leading inter-war women's rights activists, deliberately eschewed the label 'feminist' when she began her political career in 1960.[26] Barbara

Castle was another prominent figure who was averse to being cast in a feminist role. After speaking at a rally to commemorate the fiftieth anniversary of the women's vote, her diary entry testified to her contempt for the 'elderly or earnest women' who had attended, and declared that 'I really think it's time we stopped thinking in this women v. men terms'.[27] However, while Castle resisted being identified with her sex, she sponsored the Equal Pay Act of 1970 and fought for a number of other issues which accorded with the demands of the women's movement. By 1974 she was demanding that the Labour Party put defence of the social wage ('a feminine need') before supporting wage increases ('a masculine syndrome') and two years later even expressed her 'thrill' over Margaret Thatcher's achievement in becoming the first female leader of a major British political party.[28] Castle's career highlights the difficulty of mapping feminism in an age when women's issues lacked the definitional clarity and forcefulness which only came when the academic discourse of patriarchy was established in the 1970s. Most female Labour MPs between the 1920s and the 1960s (Jennie Lee being the major exception), while they denied they were feminists, did give considerable attention to the specific needs of women, even if it was usually as part of a broader agenda of reform.[29] Moreover, an appraisal of key moments in the party's ongoing relationship with feminism – the Edwardian suffrage campaign, debates over family allowances in the 1920s, the revival of the women's movement after 1968 – demonstrates the value of adopting a more nuanced approach than that offered by the 'triumph of class over sex' model. Feminist issues rarely registered in isolation in the Labour Party, and were enmeshed in a rich and complex web of interlocking dialogues about the nature of the party and its relationship to the British state.

The nascent Labour Party and the women's suffrage movement had a certain affinity, in that both emerged from cultural formations which at the turn of the century were under-represented in the world of parliamentary politics and government. Indeed the Labour Party was the only major party unequivocally to support women's enfranchisement before 1914, and in 1912 this received official recognition through the decision of the National Union of Women's Suffrage Societies (NUWSS) to support Labour Party candidates in elections. However, the relationship between Labour and female suffrage was fraught with ambiguity and conflict. Debates about female suffrage in the Labour Party paralleled their response to the state welfare programmes initiated by Edwardian Liberals: both could be construed as progressive, but since they could be (and were likely to be) secured under capitalism, how did they relate to the party's commitment to a more radical (if not necessarily immediate) transformation of society along socialist lines? Edward Pease, reflecting on the disruptive impact of pro-suffragists such as H. G. Wells on the Edwardian Fabian Society, asserted that women's suffrage was 'a question of Democracy rather than Socialism'. He explained: 'no one would contend that approval of women's suffrage was acceptance of a part of the creed of Socialism. It was a belief compatible with the most thoroughgoing individualism.'[30] What troubled many in the Labour Party was that the suffragists' demand for an equal franchise would duplicate the class biases which afflicted the existing male electorate, although most supporters of the equal franchise protested that they saw it merely as a first step towards the ultimate achievement of a universal franchise for both men and women. The dispute between equal and universal franchise proposals caused considerable friction in the Women's Labour League, setting Selina Cooper against Margaret Bondfield, and, in Ramsay MacDonald's opinion, contributing to the premature death of his wife, Margaret.[31] Even where the suffrage issue was less divisive, support for women's enfranchisement did not necessarily imply sympathy for a broader feminist agenda. Leading Labour pro-suffragists like Snowden and Hardie saw the vote as a reward for women's essentially domestic attributes, and in Preston the local party's robust support for votes for women did not preclude them from trying to exclude women from paid employment.[32] Nor should it be forgotten that George Lansbury's highly personal campaign on behalf of women's suffrage cannot be entirely separated from his broader frustration with the cautious leadership of the parliamentary party.[33] The tensions between Labour and the suffrage campaign were exacerbated by the fact that many NUWSS leaders were Liberals who were unsympathetic to Labour. Not surprisingly the 'pact' between the NUWSS and the Labour Party of 1912 was always referred to by Millicent Fawcett as a tactical alliance – 'a whip to beat the Liberal Government with' – rather than as an ideological convergence.[34]

Indeed the long-term consequences of the suffrage campaign were to make Labour deeply hostile to issues which might encourage what it termed 'sex antagonism', a term which became a commonplace in the party's rhetoric in the years immediately after 1918. Arthur Henderson, writing in a volume which was intended to attract newly enfranchised women to the party, firmly declared:

The Labour Party has always advocated the claims of women on the ground of sex-equality; and the women of our movement have consistently opposed every development of the feminist agitation which tended to emphasise the

Labour and gender

unhappy sex-antagonisms produced by the long and bitter struggle for the
franchise . . . the organised working class movement which includes both
men and women, has evolved a policy intended to promote the common
interests of both sexes, and we believe that when this policy is understood by
the bulk of enfranchised women they will recognise that separate sex organisations are fundamentally undemocratic and wholly reactionary.[35]

Another contributor, the party's new Chief Woman Officer, Marion
Phillips, insisted that there were subjects (particularly relating to motherhood and the home) where women's particular expertise was necessary, but that essentially 'the interests of men and women are one and
indivisible'.[36] In 1943 Herbert Morrison condemned the toil and drudgery which characterised the lives of working-class housewives. He
applauded their fortitude, but added that perhaps the working-class
housewife had been 'almost too patient. Had she agitated against her
economic oppression *as some of her more fortunate sisters* used to agitate
for the vote . . . the economic and social emancipation of women in our
island would not have lagged so deplorably behind their political emancipation.'[37] It was frequently asserted that Labour would benefit little
from collaboration with middle-class women, whose 'leisured' status
made them ignorant of the real needs of the poor. Jennie Lee was reprising a popular caricature in Labour discourse when she alleged that feminist groups always seemed to end up talking about the problem of
finding, or keeping, domestic servants.[38] However, this was only partially
a case of class solidarity being placed before gender identity. The party's
hostility to the 'sex antagonism' of the Edwardian era might be better
interpreted as part of a broader desire to restabilise society after the
upheavals of the First World War. 'Making peace' subsequent to 1918
required the purging of 'masculine fantasy' and militarism from public
life, but it also necessitated the ending of female militancy too. In the
new, domesticated political landscape of the inter-war years, 'sex war'
and 'world war' stood equally condemned – not merely by male politicians, but also by Labour women (and by feminists as different as
Eleanor Rathbone and Sylvia Pankhurst) as symbols of a primitive and
brutal past.[39]

Given Labour's hostility to sex antagonism and the trade unions'
desire to protect male privilege in paid employment, it was perhaps
inevitable that Labour women in the early 1920s would have been drawn
to some of the principles of 'new feminism', espoused by the
Independent MP Eleanor Rathbone. Rathbone believed that sexual
equality was perfectly compatible with very different roles for men and
women, and she assumed that most women would remain wives and

203

mothers. Her intention was to support these women and their children through providing them with an independent income, in the form of what she initially termed 'family endowment', later repackaged as 'family allowances'. Such policies obviously accorded with Labour's welfarist agenda and its desire to support motherhood. The problem, as Susan Pedersen's research has shown, was that Labour was also wedded to the notion of the 'family wage', under which women and children would be supported by male wage earners. In 1922 a joint Labour Party–TUC committee rejected universal endowments and declared its preference for services over cash payments. Cash benefits should be given to women and children only in the event of the father's unemployment, illness or desertion. Labour men presented family allowances as a reward for male workers who had maintained their families through their labour, and who thereby felt entitled to know this maintenance would be continued in the event of accident or death. The male breadwinner, not the citizen mother, was at the centre of Labour's conception of family endowment in the 1920s.[40] By 1945 Labour had come round to supporting universal family allowances, although even then it took the intervention of Labour women to ensure that the money was paid directly to the mothers rather than, as originally intended, to their husbands. In Sweden, the notion of 'social motherhood' was used by the Social Democrats in the 1930s to enhance women's rights, including married women's right to paid employment. In Britain, by contrast, Labour's conception of family allowances was much more limited, and it merely served to entrench traditionally orientated configurations of maternalism.[41]

However, once again, it is important not to caricature Labour's attitudes here, which were also inscribed with other contingent concerns in the inter-war years. Labour policy-makers felt that, given the limited public funds available, expenditure on social services such as housing and healthcare was more likely to be implemented, and was more likely to improve the lives of working-class women (especially the very poor) than the payment of allowances. In a period of economic recession, it looked unlikely that the state would be able to afford universal allowances, paid irrespective of the husband's situation. Indeed Rathbone seemed to endorse this realistic assessment of government finances, when she discussed the possibility of allowances being provided by employers. For Labour this raised the spectre of increased employer control of workers. Evidence from France, where employers operated such a scheme, suggested that allowances were often withdrawn during strikes to force the men back to work. Rathbone also implied that it might be necessary for unmarried males to accept reduced wages, to allow the economy to find the additional money necessary to fund family allowances. In a decade which saw the General Strike and widespread attempts by firms to cut wages, it is perhaps not surprising that Labour was suspicious of such proposals.[42] The battles over family allowances did indeed mark a 'failure of feminism', but it would be simplistic to see the victor as simply the masculinist fantasy of the male breadwinner paradigm. Labour was genuinely concerned that family allowances might be achieved at the cost of greater state interference in the labour market, or of increasing the potential for employers to coerce and control their workforces. Labour's scepticism about family allowances was as much about defending equilibrium in the labour market as it was about preserving male privilege in the household.

Labour's cautious attitude to equal pay similarly owed as much to the defence of free collective bargaining as it did to the maintenance of specifically male prerogatives. An NEC spokesman, defending the leadership's tardiness on the issue in 1947, warned that the implementation of equal pay would allow the state to displace 'the ordinary negotiating machinery between the members of the trade unions and the employers under whom they serve'.[43] Even those who demanded that the party fulfil its commitment to equal pay, chose to borrow the vocabulary of labourism rather than the language of feminism. As long as women were paid less than men, they might be employed instead of their more expensive male equivalents, and 'women should cease to be forced into the position of being potential blacklegs'.[44] Family allowances and equal pay, while critical sites for assessing the status of feminism within the Labour Party, were never therefore understood or discussed in terms of gender difference alone.

The emergence of the 'second wave' of British feminism at the end of the 1960s initially seemed to raise the prospect of reprising the tensions between middle-class feminists and Labour women which had marked the 1920s. Post-1968 feminists were highly sensitive to the issue of class, and many adopted the label of 'socialist-feminists'. However, under the influence of American-derived conceptions of consciousness-raising, second-wave feminism all too often promoted a politics of personal liberation which only middle-class women had the time and resources to espouse.[45] There were also generational conflicts between established Labour women activists and the young educated feminists who entered the party in the 1970s and 1980s. In 1986 Hilary Wainwright recorded the complaints of older working-class women from the Gateshead women's section who bemoaned the 'takeover' of 'their' national

Martin Francis

women's conference by 'outsiders'. They were particularly upset that the tradition of a rally addressed by the party leader on the final Saturday of the conference had been ended, one woman lamenting 'That was the high point for me.'[46] However, Labour knew that the revival of feminism could not be simply construed, and thereby rejected, as the voice of leisured middle-class women. Female party activists had already been discussing issues of equal pay and equal opportunities in the late 1950s and early 1960s. Moreover, many of the new generation of female activists came from working-class Labour families, and had gained their college education through Labour's expansion of the university sector in the mid-1960s. The first major women's liberation conference was held in February 1970 at Ruskin, the 'workers' college' at Oxford. Many of the key events in the emergence of 'second-wave' feminism were not the work of gilded youth, but of underprivileged working-class women: Lil Bilocca leading the Hull fishermen's wives in a campaign for greater safety at sea, Rose Boland initiating the Dagenham sewing machinists' strike for equal pay, the London bus conductresses who demanded the right to become drivers.[47] Once again, simple binary polarities between sex and class seem to have limited resonance here. Such a judgement could also apply to the 1984–5 miners' strike. As in the 1926 General Strike, women played an important role in fund-raising, picketing and mobilising support groups. At first there seemed little scope for feminism here, the women using the language of traditional coalfield class solidarity, proclaiming that 'we're behind our men'. However, while the strike sought the restoration of masculine self-respect to men emasculated by unemployment, it was also a movement to defend the pit communities and to chide the state for ignoring its proper role as a guarantor of employment and social services. This broader agenda created space for extensive activism by miners' wives, who formed unlikely alliances with gay rights and peace campaigners, and enlarged the scope for women's political autonomy in a branch of the labour movement which had been frequently condemned by feminists for its cultural conservatism.[48] It is a further testimony to the complexity of gender issues in the Labour Party that feminist impulses have often been nurtured in the most unpromising of environments.

Gender, consumption and sexuality

While the Labour Party has never been a mere producers' party (and it has already been stressed that Labour women in the 1910s and 1920s successfully ensured that it never retreated into a narrowly economistic philosophy), there have been times this century when the party has

206

appeared uncomfortable with the by-products of individual (as opposed to collective) consumption. In the late 1940s this unease was frequently gendered, as Labour lionised the Stakhanovite productivity of the male manual worker (and the expertise of the technician and manager) while appearing unsympathetic to the expectations of female consumers. Under the Attlee government, the maintenance of fair shares was secured by the continuation of wartime controls and rationing, and personal consumption was suppressed. Much of the Conservative Party's success in exploiting public discontent with continued austerity can be attributed to their targeting of housewives, whose everyday experience of queues, shortages and ration books made the critique of controls immediate and pertinent. Labour frequently responded with impatience, if not hostility, towards those women who dared to complain about the burdens of austerity. Such indifference contributed to a gender gap in male and female voting patterns between 1950 and 1966, the most substantial margin being in 1955, when Labour's vote among women was thirteen points behind the Conservatives.[49] As the young Anthony Wedgwood Benn confided to his diary, 'The housewives are our weakest spot, and I am sure that with men alone voting we would win easily.'[50]

However, while there is much truth in this model of post-war voting behaviour, an element of qualification is required. Opinion poll data for the 1950s and before is, by later standards, unsophisticated, and so the extent of the gender gap in that period, while probable, cannot be definitively proven. Moreover, the austerity debate reflected how generational and class cleavages complicated the status of gender in Labour discourse. The party's condemnation of 'selfish' housewives was usually articulated in class terms, expressing particular distaste for middle-class women who put the accumulation of luxury goods before the securing of a national minimum standard of living for all. The suburban membership (and Conservative Party associations) of the Housewives' League seemed to confirm Labour's belief that opposition to austerity represented the frustrations of the middle classes, who yearned for a return to the free market of the 1930s.[51] Labour was also concerned about the frivolous teenage 'good time girls', whose apparent promiscuity, frivolity and fondness for fashion, drink, cigarettes, movies and cheap novelettes seemed to threaten the social discipline and unselfishness needed to build the post-war New Jerusalem.[52] However, there were similar anxieties about the good time girl's male companion, the anti-social 'spiv' or (from the early 1950s) the hedonistic 'teddy boy'. In other words, Labour's attitude to the post-war consumption debate was less anti-female *per se* than

Martin Francis

it was hostile towards the values and expectations of particular categories (both social and generational) of women, and it is important to appreciate that this criticism also extended to their male peer group equivalents. Most critically of all, even if Labour was insensitive to women's needs as consumers, they were highly attentive to their needs as beneficiaries of welfare, and the creation of a free health service and the implementation of other social service reforms in the Attlee years brought tremendous benefits to women.

Nor did Labour women allow a simple gender binarism between workplace and home, producer and consumer to go uncontested. In the first three decades of the century they attempted to destabilise the producer/consumer dichotomy by insisting that the home too was a place of (albeit unpaid) work. The WLL claimed that the housewife was as much a worker as the miner or docker. Drawing on the language of nineteenth-century radicalism, in particular its critique of the 'leisured classes', Margaret MacDonald asserted: 'We glory in the name "Labour". To us it means that every able-bodied woman shall do useful work for the community, whether as housewife or as worker for wages.'[53] There were obviously radical implications to such language. If housework was similar to factory work, then it deserved financial remuneration and better conditions (i.e. improved housing, electricity and labour-saving machinery), and there was no reason why much of it could not be organised collectively rather than carried out at the level of the individual household. Labour women did discuss schemes for municipal laundries, home helps and the collective provision of meals, but usually without enthusiasm, for such plans conflicted with a working-class culture which was becoming increasingly privatised. The Fabian Women's Group found a preference among working-class women for detached houses with gardens over flats with collective facilities, and for washing in their own homes rather than communal laundries.[54] A forgotten footnote to the history of the Attlee government was its abortive attempt to create a social-democratic variety of domestic service through the National Institute of Houseworkers which would extend domestic support down the social scale into the working class. This failed, however, in the face of opposition to using taxpayers' money to 'train maids' (once again demonstrating how the tropes of class ceaselessly intruded on gender issues), and by the 1950s the early interest in the communal provision of domestic service had been replaced by the individualist alternative of technological innovation in the home.[55] Another example of how Labour women's activism could transcend the distinction between workplace and home was the WLL's campaign to force mineowners to introduce

pit head baths. They argued that wherever an industry was responsible
for soiling the person or clothing of a worker, the employers should
provide ample means for their cleansing, rather than leaving it to
the already overburdened housewife.[56] Katherine Glasier declared 'the
grime and grease, the flue and dust, that is incurred by workers in the
factories, machine sheds, mills and mines, ought not to be allowed to
enter . . . the homes of the people'.[57] The desire to alleviate domestic
burdens and ensure environmental standards in the home therefore
necessitated female participation in debates over conditions in the workplace, thereby trespassing on the traditional prerogatives of male trade-
unionists.

Even if they did not represent a simple gender bias, Labour's attitudes to austerity in the late 1940s (and to the affluence which succeeded
it in the late 1950s) did suggest a conservative response to issues of the
personal, which had important implications for women. Labour's
agenda was never narrowly materialist, but its bureaucratic and economic focus in the middle decades of the century left little space for the
realisation of psychological and imaginative yearnings. Carolyn
Steedman's mother was not alone in discovering that her dreams of
Hollywood-style glamour and escapism in the Attlee years found no
echo in the serious and self-disciplined strictures of post-war Labour.[58]
In particular Labour's pursuit of a planned, rational and equitable
society was deeply unsympathetic towards expressions of sexuality,
which were regarded as dangerous, self-indulgent and destabilising.
While issues of sexual behaviour were rarely foregrounded in Labour
discourse, there was an implicit tension between the collective long-term
social planning with which the party was identified, and the instant self-
gratification offered by sexual incontinence. This friction had social
implications, representing as it did another episode in Labour's sometimes fraught relationship with working-class popular culture, a dialogue which in the early years of the century had crystallised around
issues such as leisure pursuits, drink and gambling.[59] However, Labour's
awkwardness towards questions of sexual behaviour was also to impact
on gender relations, particularly in regard to birth control and abortion.

While some late Victorian and Edwardian intellectuals (notably
Edward Carpenter and Havelock Ellis) had attempted to yoke socialism
to the findings of modern sexologists, the Labour Party's attitude was,
from the beginning, dominated by traditions of working-class moralism
and Fabian puritanism.[60] The party rejected the sexual utopianism of
the 'fellowship of new life', Labour's 'Grundyism' being bolstered by
the need to compete with a Conservative Party, which, while it had once

presented itself as the defender of the robust and full-blooded pleasures of the working man, was by the 1920s reinventing itself as the protector of the home and family.[61] Unlike the Social Democrats in Germany (or indeed the Women's Co-operative League at home), most men in the Labour Party remained inert on the issue of birth control during much of the inter-war era. This inattention has often been seen as a symptom of female party activists' shift from gender to class issues at the end of the 1920s.[62] However, this is an unconvincing explanation, since it fails to recognise the continued interest among Labour women in birth control issues during the 1930s and ignores the tendency for female activists who proposed both birth control and abortion law reform to argue in terms of social, as much as sexual, justice, making available to working-class women services already widely used by the rich. While the major pressure group concerned with abortion law reform, the Abortion Law Reform Association, had a predominantly middle-class membership, its submission to the Birkett Committee in 1937 concentrated on the impact of unwanted children on working-class families, and one member told Birkett 'the working woman needs this relief more than her sisters'.[63] Given this emphasis among reformers, how can Labour's failure to champion birth control and abortion at the highest level be explained? Fear of a backlash among Catholic voters was certainly a factor, for support for local authority provision of family planning advice contributed to Dorothy Jewson losing her Norwich seat in 1924, and cost Edith Summerskill the nomination at Bury in 1935.[64] Equally significant was an identification of birth control with Malthusian and other reactionary movements, Mosley's advocacy of birth control in the mid-1930s to 'improve the race' creating unfortunate associations in Labour's eyes between family planning and fascism.[65] There was possibly also a widespread belief in the 1930s that birth control was being made available to those who needed it. In 1930 the Labour Minister of Health, Arthur Greenwood, sent a discreet memorandum to local health authorities, permitting the provision of birth control information to women in cases of 'medical necessity'. While this was a limited measure, recent research on Wales has suggested it was flexibly interpreted in many Labour-controlled health authorities. However, the fate of these inter-war campaigns also reveals that Labour defined the 'public' for much of this century in a way which precluded the discussion of such lifestyle issues at the highest level. The party's women's conferences frequently urged the party to make birth control a national issue, but the national conference insisted that such subjects were a 'private' rather than a 'public' matter. The party's Chief Woman Officer, defending the

National Executive's stance to women activists, insisted that 'Sex should not be dragged into politics.'[66]

In the 1940s the apparent disappearance of poverty weakened abortion reformers' hands even further, since family limitation could no longer be presented as a means to maintain, or raise, working-class living standards. Indeed some Labour leaders, notably Morrison, became deeply troubled about the falling birth-rate, and hoped families with five or six children would not be unusual in future. The onset of the welfare state also made Labour less sympathetic to female prostitutes, who once might have been pitied as the victims of poverty and hunger, but were now represented as guilty of 'fundamental laziness, which makes regular work anathema to them', and as a menace to be cleared from the streets.[67] A younger generation of Labour leaders in the late 1950s and early 1960s (especially Roy Jenkins and Anthony Crosland) adopted a more libertarian stance, and it was a Labour government in the 1960s which presided over a battery of measures – 'civilised' to some, 'permissive' to others – which legalised abortion, decriminalised homosexuality and made divorce easier. However, most of these were the result of private members' bills, and at local and national levels Labour was divided about the new sexual freedom.[68] Labour's caution on the issue of sexuality frequently accorded with the temper of the times. Judging from the reminiscences of Richard Hoggart and Robert Roberts, in the inter-war years working-class men were reticent publicly to discuss sex-related subjects.[69] James Callaghan's biographer has made a convincing case for placing the Home Secretary's desire to draw a line under the libertarian legislation of the mid-1960s in the context of extensive unease about the new moral climate among Labour's core constituents.[70] Labour's ambivalent stance on issues of personal behaviour has continued into the 1990s. The Blair administration's equivocation over the repeal of Section 28 (forbidding local authorities and schools to 'promote' homosexuality) reflects the puritan ethos of the Prime Minister and the Home Secretary, Jack Straw. However, the party has been largely supportive of prominent figures, notably ministers Chris Smith, Nick Brown and Angela Eagle, who have gone public about their sexual orientation. As the twentieth century draws to a close the party continues to oscillate between a liberal instinct and an ongoing commitment to the (sometimes authoritarian) codes of moral traditionalism and respectability it has inherited from its nineteenth-century forebears.

Representations of masculinity and femininity

The complex and ambiguous status of gender within Labour discourse is also evident at the level of representation. The constructions of masculinity and femininity embedded in the party's culture are decidedly polyphonic. In 1967 a veteran of the party's women's sections claimed that Labour 'was the most masculine dominated and masculine orientated movement she had ever encountered'.[71] This was not merely a partial view, but also one which raises a further question: what type of masculinity (or masculinities) did Labour represent? For while masculinism (the ideology which legitimises and naturalises male dominance) remains fairly constant, masculinity (its representational expression) takes divergent, competing and changing forms. Not surprisingly, a party created by the trade unions celebrated the quiet dignity and physical strength of the male manual worker. In the third quarter of the nineteenth century, working-class manliness had been expressed in terms of the 'independent artisan', whose moral worth was projected by his ability to support his family and by his honest toil. Labour blended this tradition with radical tropes of masculinity in which working for one's living or belonging to a union were praised, and the idle world of the aristocrat and millionaire was derided and condemned.[72] In the 1890s there was less emphasis on respectability and more on physical strength (interestingly paralleling a shift from morality to physical fitness in the codes of manliness developed in elite private schools at this time), the illustrations of Leon Caryll portraying Labour as a muscular and bearded man, reminiscent of an Anglo-Saxon warrior.[73] This emphasis on the physicality of working men was a common motif in Labour discourse in the twentieth century. Workers were strong, stoical and dependable, especially if, like the miners, their work was elemental, unmediated by machinery.[74]

The problem, however, was that, even among the working class, only a minority of workers were involved in this 'heroic' type of manual labour. Equally significantly, Labour always sought to be a genuinely 'national' party and that meant an eagerness to recruit from the middle classes. Eulogies to the dignity of manual male labour were supplemented by respect for the expertise embodied in the disinterested professional manager or technician, and the 1918 party constitution sought to restore the fruits of their labour to workers of both hand *and* brain. During the post-Second World War reconstruction and productivity drives, and again in Wilson's 'white heat' of the 1960s, Labour placed a high value on the technocratic expert, a signifier of the party's commitment to modernity and meritocracy. Both worker and technocrat were counterpoised with various others: the effete (not to say effeminate) and languid patrician Conservative, the gaudy and bloated plutocrat and the anti-social (and 'flashily' dressed) 'spiv'. However, while Labour's desire for inclusivity seemed to legitimise a number of masculine archetypes, some of the more plebeian elements in the party clearly accorded a greater sense of authenticity to labouring conceptions of manliness. In the post-war decades, Jim Griffiths (a former South Wales miner and deputy leader of the party) lamented the eclipse of the proletarian Labour Party, with its 'old "cloth-cap" MPs . . . those horny-handed sons of toil'. He was distressed that 'the "cloth cap" is giving way . . . to the "cap and gown". The [post-war] Labour benches . . . are rich in academic talent, but those of the thirties were richer in the character moulded in life's struggles.'[75] Yearnings for masculine authenticity were not confined to working-class socialists. Tony Benn, the classic modern technocrat in the 1960s (and one of the first Labour MPs to obtain a photocopier and answerphone) still filled his office at the Ministry of Technology with miners' helmets and other symbols of heroic manual labour.[76] If Labour was a 'man's party', then the types of manliness it endorsed were varied and, to a certain extent, contradictory.

Moreover, the Labour Party often vested the strength and hope of the working class in the female rather than the male. In the 1920s, despite the ambivalence about issues such as family allowances, the party's campaign posters frequently deployed visual images of the working-class mother. However, Labour's representations were complex, simultaneously suggesting both female empowerment and a limited definition of women's roles. Women could be presented as workers, albeit in subtly different terms from their male equivalents. In 1893 Leon Caryll presented a design for a banner to the Independent Labour Party, featuring two of the large, muscular workers of the type described previously. When a party member protested about the absence of female figures from the banner, the design was amended, two women being added, both wearing work clothes, one with rolled-up sleeves. Nevertheless, they lacked the physical presence of the two men, being smaller in stature and presented sitting rather than standing. So while the ILP banner acknowledged female labour, it suggests it has less significance than that of men.[77] Indeed, in the Edwardian era working women were often represented, not as independent and assertive, but as the downtrodden victims of an exploitative system. The dominant image of working women became that of sweated labour, and many socialists declared that the presence of women in the workplace reflected the shame of capitalism.[78] Labour leaders who supported women's suffrage saw women not as independent political agents but as the agents of family moralisation. Hardie lauded women for their 'motherly sympathies' while Snowden condemned capitalism for 'the unsexing and condemning to slavery of what should have

213

Martin Francis

been pure and cultured womanhood'. Ramsay MacDonald's memoir of his wife Margaret, an activist and WLL pioneer, chose to discuss her largely in terms of her maternal qualities. To Margaret 'motherhood contained everything that was redemptive . . . she believed that only by doing that work could woman fulfil her destiny and attain to her maximum liberty, and she never budged from that anchorage in considering what political and social programmes she would support'.[79]

The working-class 'Mam' was a popular figure in Labour's imagination. She was located largely in the domestic context, but this did not imply marginalisation or insignificance. Indeed the 'Mam' was a key signifier of Labour's commitment to a working-class community, and a sense of solidarity, which extended beyond the workplace. It was for this reason that figures on the left in the 1950s such as Richard Hoggart lamented her passing, perceiving the inter-war generation of working-class mothers as a reminder of an older, more cohesive working class, uncompromised by consumer affluence.[80] Certainly working-class women who joined the Labour Party in the 1920s testified to how their mothers offered an inspirational model of social conscience, sacrificing their health for the sake of their husbands and children.[81] Despite her predominantly domestic location, the 'Mam' could be mobilised to confer legitimacy and authenticity on the public careers of her offspring. George Thomas's mother, Emma, became a regular escort for her son on state occasions after his election to Parliament in 1945, offering reassurance that his penchant for the trappings of ceremonial office did not imply an abandonment of the social and religious values he had learnt as a boy in the South Wales valleys.[82] However while the 'Mam' could be idealised, younger women were on occasion presented as a disruptive or dangerous presence in Labour's landscape of gender. In the 1930s they were identified by Orwell and Priestley with affluence, Americanisation and unregulated and threatening sexuality, a cluster of motifs which were refurbished in the 1950s. 'Good old Mam' could be respected because, in Hoggart's hideous phrase, she was 'shapeless', her active sexual life already passed.[83] Younger women, however, sought sexual gratification and material self-improvement in the private sphere, an instinct which appeared to threaten working-class solidarity. Moreover, from the 1970s, Labour often appeared bewildered by the increasing number of young single mothers, whose brand of maternalism fitted uncomfortably into the party's traditional and patriarchal conceptions of domesticity.[84] So while the importance of the 'Mam' demonstrated that Labour was willing to see its essential values represented in feminine as well as masculine terms, the party's conception of acceptable womanhood ultimately proved to be relatively narrow, especially when compared to the various genres of manliness permitted to men.

Conclusion

Gender therefore has had a problematic status within the history of the Labour Party. Labour women have achieved a great deal, both within the party and in national politics. It was partly as a result of female activism that Labour became the party of social welfare. If women in the party have not always attained their goals (or if their goals have lacked a radical edge) this failure cannot simply be ascribed to structural impediments or the indifference of a male-dominated party. The uneven pattern of rejection and receptivity towards women's issues reflects the fact that gender is part of the complex matrix of identities, rooted in generational and social, as well as sexual, difference which characterised the party. Labour is continuing to wrestle with this tangled and enigmatic legacy at the century's end. The 1997 general election saw an unprecedented influx of female Labour MPs, and the coming to power of a government pledged to be more 'woman friendly'. However, there has already been criticism of the glibness of the document *Delivering for Women: Progress So Far*, frustration at the marginalisation of the Cabinet Office's women's unit, and concern (especially after the Mandelson resignation) that Labour leaders have fallen back on to what a former female minister has termed 'militaristic, macho, hierarchical language and behaviour'.[85] Gender looks likely to remain (as in other political parties, and in British society as a whole) a site of both resistance and opportunity for Labour, a locus in which the diverse and competing identities of the 'People's Party' will continue to be played out, without the likelihood of immediate (or indeed ultimate) reconciliation.

Martin Francis

Notes

1 Joyce Gould, foreword to Labour Party, *Women, Sexism and Socialism* (London: Labour Party, 1980), p. 3.

2 Pamela M. Graves, *Labour Women: Women in British Working-Class Politics, 1918–1939* (Cambridge: Cambridge University Press, 1994), pp. 5–79.

3 Brian Harrison, *Prudent Revolutionaries: Portraits of British Feminists Between the Wars* (Oxford: Oxford University Press, 1987), pp. 131–3.

4 Elizabeth Vallance, *Women in the House: A Study of Women Members of Parliament* (London: Athlone, 1979), passim and p. 85.

5 Mary Walker, 'Labour women and internationalism', in Lucy Middleton (ed.), *Women in the Labour Movement* (London: Croom Helm, 1977), pp. 84–93.

6 Kenneth O. Morgan, *Labour People: Leaders and Lieutenants from Hardie to Kinnock* (Oxford: Oxford University Press, 1987), pp. 239–45.

7 Jon Lawrence, *Speaking for the People: Party, Language and Popular Politics in England, 1867–1914* (Cambridge: Cambridge University Press, 1998), pp. 157–60.

8 Pat Thane, 'Visions of gender in the making of the British welfare state: the case of women in the British Labour Party and social policy, 1906–1945', in Gisela Bock and Pat Thane (eds.), *Maternity and Gender Policies: Women and the Rise of the European Welfare States, 1880s–1950s* (London: Routledge, 1991), pp. 93–118.

9 Graves, *Labour Women*, pp. 59–64.

10 Mike Savage, *The Dynamics of Working-Class Politics: The Labour Movement in Preston, 1880–1940* (Cambridge: Cambridge University Press, 1987), pp. 167–80.

11 Amy Black and Stephen Brooke, 'The Labour Party, women and the problem of gender, 1951–66', *Journal of British Studies* 36 (1997), 443–47.

12 Black and Brooke, 'Labour Party', 430–3; Graves, *Labour Women*, pp. 23–7, 109–14.

13 Graves, *Labour Women*, pp. 95–6.

14 Black and Brooke, 'Labour Party', 431.

15 Graves, *Labour Women*, pp. 154–80.

16 Eleanor Gordon, *Women and the Labour Movement in Scotland, 1850–1914* (Oxford: Oxford University Press, 1991), p. 274.

17 Labour Party, *Discrimination Against Women: Report of a Labour Party Study Group* (London: Labour Party, 1972), p. 36.

18 Maeve Denby, 'Women in Parliament and government', in Middleton (ed.), *Women in the Labour Movement*, pp. 175–89.

19 'Women candidates in the Labour Party' (1974), quoted in Rachel Brooks et al., *Quotas Now: Women in the Labour Party* (London: Fabian Society, 1990), p. 8.

20 Maria Eagle and Joni Lovenduski, *High Time or High Tide for Labour Women?* (London: Fabian Society, 1998), passim.

Labour and gender

21 Quoted in Black and Brooke, 'Labour Party', 437.

22 Harold Smith, 'Sex vs. class: British feminists and the labour movement, 1919–1929', *Historian* 47 (1984), 19–37; Martin Pugh, *Women and the Women's Movement in Britain, 1914–1959* (Basingstoke: Macmillan, 1992), pp. 129–39; Joanna Alberti, *Beyond Suffrage: Feminists in War and Peace, 1914–28* (Basingstoke: Macmillan, 1989), pp. 174–90.

23 Graves, *Labour Women*, especially pp. 183–219.

24 For the conventional view, see Barbara Caine, *English Feminism, 1780–1980* (Oxford: Oxford University Press, 1997), pp. 182–97. For a more nuanced appraisal, see Cheryl Law, *Suffrage and Power: The Women's Movement, 1918–1928* (London: I. B. Tauris, 1999).

25 Edith Summerskill, *A Woman's World: Her Memoirs* (London: Heinemann, 1967), pp. 251–2.

26 Black and Brooke, 'Labour Party', 438.

27 Barbara Castle, *The Castle Diaries, 1964–70* (London: Weidenfeld and Nicolson, 1984), p. 373.

28 Barbara Castle, *The Castle Diaries, 1974–76* (London: Weidenfeld and Nicolson, 1984), pp. 22, 309.

29 For Lee's contempt for 'women's issues', see Patricia Hollis, *Jennie Lee: A Life* (Oxford: Oxford University Press, 1997), pp. 148–51.

30 Edward R. Pease, *The History of the Fabian Society* (London: Allen and Unwin, 1925), p. 177.

31 Martin Pugh, 'Labour and women's suffrage', in Kenneth D. Brown (ed.), *The First Labour Party, 1906–1914* (London: Croom Helm, 1985), pp. 233–53.

32 Savage, *Dynamics*, pp. 152–3.

33 Jonathan Schneer, *George Lansbury* (Manchester: Manchester University Press, 1990), pp. 110–17.

34 Quoted in Brian Harrison, 'Class and gender in modern British labour history', *Past and Present* 124 (1989), 158.

35 Marion Phillips (ed.), *Women and the Labour Party* (London: Headley Brothers, 1918), pp. 5–6.

36 Ibid., pp. 10–11.

37 Herbert Morrison, *Looking Ahead: Wartime Speeches* (London: Hodder and Stoughton, 1943), pp. 231–2 (my emphasis).

38 *Tribune*, 23 March 1945.

39 Susan Kingsley Kent, *Making Peace: The Reconstruction of Gender in Interwar Britain* (Princeton: Princeton University Press, 1993); Jon Lawrence, 'Violence in interwar British politics: the Olympia debate revisited' (Forthcoming).

40 Susan Pedersen, 'The failure of feminism in the making of the British welfare state', *Radical History Review* 43 (1989), 86–110.

41 Renee Frangeur, 'Social democrats and the woman question in Sweden', in Helmut Gruber and Pamela M. Graves (eds.), *Women and Socialism, Socialism and Women: Europe Between the Two World Wars* (Oxford: Berghahn, 1998), pp. 439–48.

Martin Francis

42 Pat Thane, 'The women of the British Labour Party and feminism, 1906–1945', in Harold L. Smith (ed.), *British Feminism in the Twentieth Century* (Amherst: University of Massachusetts Press, 1990), p. 139.

43 *Report of the 46th Annual Conference of the Labour Party* (London: Labour Party, 1947), p. 159.

44 Margaret Cole, *The Rate for the Job* (London: Fabian Society, 1946), p. 3. Cole's pamphlet also demonstrated the difficulty of defining what equal pay actually meant: was it equal pay for identical work, or equal pay for work of equal value?

45 For example, Juliet Mitchell, *Woman's Estate* (Harmondsworth: Penguin, 1971).

46 Hilary Wainwright, *Labour: A Tale of Two Parties* (London: Hogarth Press, 1987), p. 165.

47 Sheila Rowbotham, 'The beginnings of women's liberation in Britain', in Michelene Wandor (ed.), *The Body Politic: Writings from the Women's Liberation Movement in Britain, 1969–1972* (London: Stage One, 1972), pp. 91–7.

48 Beatrix Campbell, 'Proletarian patriarchs and the real radicals', in Vicky Seddon (ed.), *Cutting Edge: Women and the Pit Strike* (London: Lawrence and Wishart, 1986), pp. 250–82.

49 Ina Zweiniger-Bargielowska, 'Explaining the gender gap: the Conservative Party and the women's vote, 1945–1964', in Martin Francis and Ina Zweiniger-Bargielowska (eds.), *The Conservatives and British Society, 1880–1990* (Cardiff: University of Wales Press, 1996), pp. 194–223; Ina Zweiniger-Bargielowska, 'Rationing, austerity and the Conservative Party recovery after 1945', *Historical Journal* 37 (1994), 173–98.

50 Tony Benn, *Years of Hope: Diaries, Papers and Letters, 1940–1962* (London: Hutchinson, 1994), p. 155.

51 For example, *Report of the 47th Annual Conference of the Labour Party* (London: Labour Party, 1948), p. 136.

52 For example, Thomas Skeffington-Lodge, *Parliamentary Debates* (Commons), vol. 444 (28 November 1947), cols. 2355–7.

53 Quoted in James Ramsay MacDonald, *Margaret Ethel MacDonald* (London: Allen and Unwin, 1929), p. 200.

54 Harrison, 'Class and gender', pp. 143–4; 'Interim Outline of "Domestic Charter"' (n.d. but 1948–9), Fabian Society papers, fos. 78–84, Nuffield College, Oxford.

55 Jim Tomlinson, *Democratic Socialism and Economic Policy: The Attlee Years, 1945–1951* (Cambridge: Cambridge University Press, 1997), pp. 205–6.

56 Katherine B. Glasier, *Baths at the Pit Head and the Works* (London: Women's Labour League, 1912).

57 Katherine Bruce Glasier, 'The Labour woman's battle with dirt', in Phillips (ed.), *Women and the Labour Party*, p. 88.

58 Carolyn Steedman, *Landscape for a Good Woman: A Story of Two Lives* (London: Virago, 1986).

59 Chris Waters, *British Socialists and the Politics of Popular Culture, 1884–1914* (Stanford: Stanford University Press, 1990).

60 Jeffrey Weeks, *Sex, Politics and Society: The Regulation of Sexuality since 1800* (London: Longman, 1989), pp. 167–75.

61 Jon Lawrence, 'Class and gender in the making of urban Toryism, 1880–1914', *English Historical Review* 108 (1993), 629–52.

62 Graves, *Labour Women*, pp. 87–93.

63 Stephen Brooke, '"A new world for women"? Abortion law reform in Britain during the 1930s', in his *Gender, Class and Socialism, 1920–1980* (London: London Books, forthcoming), pp. 17, 29–30.

64 Summerskill, *Woman's World*, pp. 50–4.

65 Julie Grier, 'Eugenics and birth control: contraceptive provision in North Wales, 1918–1939', *Social History of Medicine* 11 (1998), 443–58.

66 *Labour Woman* (March 1924), 34; Marion Phillips, quoted in Cate Haste, *Rules of Desire: Sex in Britain, World War One to the Present* (London: Pimlico, 1992), p. 66.

67 Morrison, *Looking Ahead*, pp. 236–7; Summerskill, *Woman's World*, p. 77.

68 Peter Thompson, 'Labour's "Gannex conscience"? Politics and popular attitudes in the "permissive society"', in R. Coopey, S. Fielding and N. Tiratsoo (eds.), *The Wilson Governments, 1964–1970* (London: Pinter, 1993), pp. 136–50.

69 Richard Hoggart, *The Uses of Literacy* (Harmondsworth: Penguin edition, 1969), pp. 98–99; Robert Roberts, *The Classic Slum* (Harmondsworth: Pelican edition, 1973), p. 57.

70 Kenneth O. Morgan, *Callaghan: A Life* (Oxford: Oxford University Press, 1998), pp. 317–22.

71 *Report of the Annual Conference of Labour Women* (London: Labour Party, 1967), p. 37.

72 Keith McClelland, 'Masculinity and the "representative artisan" in Britain, 1850–80', *Gender and History* 1 (1989), 164–77; Lawrence, *Speaking for the People*, pp. 145–6.

73 Laura Ugolini, '"By all means let the ladies have a chance": *The Workman's Times*, independent labour representation and women's suffrage, 1891–4', in Angela V. John and Claire Eustance (eds.), *The Men's Share? Masculinities, Male Support and Women's Suffrage in Britain, 1890–1920* (London: Routledge, 1997), pp. 71–5.

74 The most famous of these eulogies is, of course, George Orwell, *The Road to Wigan Pier* (1937; Harmondsworth: Penguin, 1989), pp. 18–31. For a feminist critique, Beatrix Campbell, *Wigan Pier Revisited: Poverty and Politics in the 80s* (London: Virago, 1984), pp. 97–115.

75 These issues are explored more fully in Martin Francis, 'The Labour Party: modernisation and the politics of restraint', in Becky Conekin, Frank Mort and Chris Waters (eds.), *Moments of Modernity: Reconstructing Britain, 1945–1964* (London: Rivers Oram, 1999), pp. 152–72.

76 Jad Adams, *Tony Benn* (London: Macmillan, 1992), pp. 269–70, 388–9.

77 Ugolini, 'By all means', p. 78.
78 Deborah Thom, 'Free from chains? The image of women's labour in London, 1900–20', in David Feldman and Gareth Stedman Jones (eds.), *Metropolis London: Histories and Representations since 1800* (London: Routledge, 1989), pp. 85–99.
79 James Keir Hardie, 'Women and politics', in B. Villiers (ed.), *The Case for Women's Suffrage* (London: Fisher Unwin, 1907), pp. 81–2; Colin Cross, *Philip Snowden* (London: Bevrie and Rockcliffe, 1966), p. 26; MacDonald, *Margaret Ethel MacDonald*, p. 157.
80 Hoggart, *Uses of Literacy*, pp. 41–50. See also Amy Black and Stephen Brooke, 'Disruptive women? Sexuality, gender roles and the working classes in Britain, 1920s–1980s' (unpublished paper, 1996).
81 Graves, *Labour Women*, pp. 53–4.
82 George Thomas, *Mr Speaker: The Memoirs of the Viscount Tonypandy* (London: Century Publishing, 1985), pp. 11–37. See also, Deidre Beddoe, 'Munitionettes, maids and Mams: women in Wales, 1914–1939', in Angela V. John (ed.), *Our Mother's Land: Chapters in Welsh Women's History, 1830–1939* (Cardiff: University of Wales Press, 1991).
83 For Priestley and Orwell, see Sally Alexander, 'Becoming a woman in London in the 1930s', in Feldman and Jones (eds.), *Metropolis London*, pp. 245–6; for the 'shapeless' Mam, Hoggart, *Uses of Literacy*, p. 46. This issue requires further historical examination, but some suggestive findings are offered by Black and Brooke, 'Disruptive women?', and by Geoff Eley, 'The family is a dangerous place: memory, gender and the image of the working class', in Richard A. Rosenstone (ed.), *Revisioning History: Film and the Construction of a New Past* (Princeton: Princeton University Press, 1995), pp. 20–1.
84 Campbell, *Wigan Pier Revisited*, pp. 57–79.
85 *Guardian*, 1 June 1999. The former minister was Harriet Harman.

7 | Labour and the trade unions

Alastair J. Reid

At the end of its first century, the trade
unions play a much less prominent role in the Labour Party's affairs
than would have been thought possible at any earlier point in its history.
However, appearances can be deceptive. For trade unions in Britain continue to organise a higher proportion of the workforce than in other
advanced economies and thus continue to represent a very important
interest group in the country. They were widely felt to have wielded
excessive power during the long economic boom which followed the
Second World War, and it was the public reaction against this which
resulted in their currently reduced influence and status. However, as one
of their leading national spokesmen put it in the immediate aftermath of
the particularly troubled 1970s:

The issue is not who governs the country. Governments are elected to
govern, and in the last analysis they have the power to enforce decisions. The
issue is how they are to govern, and what sanctions are effectively available to
Government in a modern democratic society. Effective government rests on
acknowledging the pluralist basis of our democracy, accepting that there is a
variety of legitimate interests in our society, and finding means of reconcil-
ing these different interests.[1]

221

Alastair J. Reid

The sensitivity to pluralism in this statement reflects the diversity within the trade-union world itself. For, as organisations formed primarily to promote occupational interests, unions have been highly responsive to their members' immediate employment situations. Historically, this has given rise to an equally wide variety of types of union, each with its own conception of its members' interests, its own style of organisation and its own ways of coping with change. Thus political co-operation has generally only been possible around more general issues, above all the basic legal position of trade unionism, in which all such organisations have had an equal interest. Attempts by their opponents to exclude the unions from influence on national policy have tended only to strengthen their insistence on their right to representation, and also on their links with the Labour Party as the normal channel for the expression of their views. In general their political priorities have then focused on creating a framework within which each organisation could continue to pursue its distinctive interests: full employment, free collective bargaining and, more broadly, opposition to threats from foreign despotism. Around these core priorities the unions have tended to adopt a pragmatic approach to the Labour Party: above all they have wanted it to be in government, and they have been more ready than most politicians to recognise and abandon unpopular policies.

The trade unions' pragmatism also led to their unexpected willingness to accept a major reduction in their role within Labour's own constitution in the 1990s, when it was felt that public suspicion of their influence had become an electoral liability. This co-operative attitude undoubtedly contributed to Labour's landslide election victory in 1997, and its continuation will be vital if Labour is to achieve its ambitious goals in government. Thus, despite the seemingly continuous decline in their importance over the last twenty years, at the beginning of the party's second century understanding the complexities of the historical relationship between Labour and the trade unions remains just as relevant as it has ever been.

Trade unions and the origins of the Labour Party

Trade unions are among Britain's oldest and largest forms of voluntary association. Craft unions, such as the tailors in clothing and the masons in construction, could trace their long inheritance back through the medieval craft guilds to the parish guilds of Anglo-Saxon times: it was this which gave them their early grasp of effective organisational structures, their drive towards extensive welfare provision, and their strong commitment to local democracy. Indeed, because they were able to provide so much for their members through their own efforts, the involvement of the craft unions in politics tended to be directed against any external intervention and towards the protection of their own sphere of independence. As industrialisation proceeded in the nineteenth century, these traditions were handed on to new organisations such as the engineers and the electricians. Meanwhile, the rapid growth of other sectors was throwing up new conditions of employment and new types of trade unionism. Unions in the process industries, such as the spinners in cotton and the miners in coal, were faced with larger workplaces, greater regional concentrations of labour and more numerous junior assistants. The resulting difficulties of organisation made them turn towards the government for assistance, first for the humanitarian improvement of harsh working conditions and then for legislative support for trade unionism itself. As a result, these unions were more consistently involved in politics, more concerned to secure direct representation in Parliament and more favourably disposed towards state intervention, including public ownership of their industries. At the end of the nineteenth century similar attitudes were passed on to the general unions, such as the transport workers and the municipal workers, as the increasingly settled urban population made it feasible to organise larger numbers of the semi-skilled and the unskilled. However, these new unions developed as gigantic federations spanning very diverse types of workplaces: this made it harder for them to construct effective channels of internal democracy and coherent bargaining strategies and they tended to be dominated by more numerous and more powerful national officials. As a result, the general unions' involvement in politics was directed towards the improvement of workplace and labour-market conditions in the country as a whole rather than in any particular sector, and they became increasingly concerned about their relationship with governments and their influence on national strategies for industry and the economy.[2]

Given this range of types of organisation, each with its own attitude towards political activity, British trade unions would only be likely to come together in united action when the common foundations of their existence were involved. This could already be seen on a number of occasions during the nineteenth century, usually when the unions were at peaks of their organisational strength and prepared to tackle any legal obstacles in their way. For example, in 1824–5 the radical agitator and ex-trade unionist Francis Place was able to co-ordinate united action by the craftsmen in London and the cotton workers in Lancashire and Scotland, securing the repeal of a range of 'combination laws' which were inhibiting

Alastair J. Reid

industrial action. This involved regular meetings of a London committee to oversee parliamentary proceedings and resulted in the publication of a *Trades' Newspaper* which continued for several years. Similarly in 1867–71 the radical trade unionist Robert Applegarth was able to co-ordinate united action by the craft-run trades councils and the miners, securing legislation from a Liberal government to relieve the unions from inequitable applications of the law of criminal conspiracy. This involved not only regular meetings of another London committee to deal with the details of the legislation but also the establishment of the Trades Union Congress (TUC) which was thereafter to have a continuous existence as a national centre representing union interests. However, the legal foundations of union action were never permanently secure and new concerns arose as a result of a number of court cases at the turn of the century, in particular one in 1901 for damages from the railway servants, successfully taken as far as the House of Lords by the Taff Vale Railway Company. In 1900 the socialist agitator and ex-trade unionist Keir Hardie had already had some success in co-ordinating united action between the craftsmen on the parliamentary committee of the TUC and a number of socialist societies, to build up the political presence of the unions through the Labour Representation Committee (LRC). Under the even more acute threat of the Taff Vale decision the unions flocked into the LRC, helped to secure a Liberal election landslide, and were rewarded with another piece of parliamentary legislation protecting their funds from damages actions arising from industrial disputes. This time the lasting legacy was the Labour Party itself, as the LRC was renamed in 1906 after securing the election of twenty-nine MPs.[3]

Thus the Labour Party emerged out of a long tradition of united trade-union action to secure favourable legislation from Liberal governments. However, there was a new element in 1900 in the alliance with a number of small socialist societies, and this was to lead to significant frictions. For the trade unionists were generally pursuing improvements in their members' position within the existing social framework; the socialists, on the other hand, had a variety of visions of fundamental social reconstruction. Moreover, the trade unionists, having benefited repeatedly from Liberal governments, were generally content for Labour to function as a section of the Liberal Party; the socialists, on the other hand, saw Labour as the embryo of a new force in British politics which would challenge the Liberals for the leadership of progressive opinion. As a result, many trade unionists tended to be rather suspicious of the socialists, seeing them as deluded by unrealistic visions of the future and insufficiently grateful for the union contribution of most of the money for the new organisation. For their part, many socialists tended to be rather dismissive of the trade unions, seeing their activity not only as a diversion from longer-term aims but also as creating an unwelcome centre of power rivalling the state's conception of the public good. What brought the two wings together was that each for its own ends was prepared to support the 1899 resolution of the TUC:

That this Congress, having regard to its decisions in former years, and with a view to securing a better representation of the interests of labour in the House of Commons, hereby instructs the Parliamentary Committee to invite the co-operation of all the co-operative, socialistic, trade union, and other working organisations to jointly co-operate on lines mutually agreed upon, in convening a special congress of representatives from such of the above named organisation as may be willing to take part to devise ways and means for securing the return of an increased number of labour members to the next Parliament.[4]

The unions and party finances

For some time it was not clear if the new party would get off the ground after all, as a large body of trade-union opinion remained favourably impressed by the reforming Liberal governments of the years up to the First World War. Thus the miners remained quite separate from Labour at first, for they already had a dozen of their regional officials sitting as MPs within a parliamentary Liberal Party which was generally responsive to their demands. It was only their mounting dissatisfaction with local Liberal Associations' stubborn unwillingness to select even more union officials as candidates that led them to switch over to the Labour Party in 1909, in the belief that this would give them access to more seats in the mining districts. Similarly, there were significant minorities in other unions initially reluctant to abandon their habitual political loyalties. Even among the railway servants there were those who resented the spending of money on the new party, particularly as increasing numbers of its parliamentary candidates were drawn from the socialist societies. In 1907 a Liberal local official of the union, W. V. Osborne, began the pursuit of a successful legal action as far as the House of Lords, to restrain the railway servants from donating any of his subscription money to a political cause which he did not support. Nor was his attitude unique: 20 per cent of the union's members voting in an internal ballot agreed with him, and his legal action was given financial support by some sympathetic branches of other unions.[5]

However, the House of Lords went further in 1909 than Osborne and his supporters had intended when it ruled that the existing legal

Alastair J. Reid

definition of a trade union excluded any financial support for political parties. This posed problems for all MPs elected with union support, but in particular threatened to undermine the whole future of the Labour Party as it was so heavily dependent on union funding. Labour therefore played a leading role alongside the TUC in campaigning for the restoration of the unions' right to political involvement, with pressure on the Liberal government leading firstly to the introduction of the state payment of MPs in 1911, and secondly to the restoration of the unions' right to make financial payments to political parties in 1913. Thus, once again, the efforts of some Liberals to obstruct the political representation of the unions had backfired: not only had the Labour Party recovered its financial position but, because it had fought consistently for the restoration of the unions' political rights, it was also looking increasingly like the natural party for trade unionists to support.[6]

The 1913 Trade Union Act was, however, far from being the final word on the issue of trade unions and party financing, for its settlement included two key requirements: a membership ballot on the setting up of a separate political fund, and the individual right to 'contract out' of paying the political levy if out of sympathy with the party chosen by the majority. While this was a reasonable compromise between the collective and individual rights of trade unionists, the reliance of Labour on this source of funding made these legal requirements an irresistible target for the party's political opponents. The right wing of the Conservative Party in particular consistently pursued the alternative policy of positive 'contracting in' by individual union members from the early 1920s, in the belief that this would significantly reduce the numbers paying the political levy and thus limit the financial resources of what was now its main opponent. This aim had initial success in the difficult aftermath of the General Strike when the 1927 Trade Disputes and Trade Unions Act, among other things, prohibited civil service unions from setting up political funds at all and required regular 'contracting in' to all the other political funds. Naturally the unions campaigned consistently against this and one of the first actions of the 1945 Labour government was to restore the pre-1927 position. It has been estimated that this simple administrative switch led to an increase in the number of trade unionists paying the political levy by around two million or from around 50 per cent to around 75 per cent and, in combination with rising membership and rising levels of contributions, that this resulted in an increase in the combined annual political income of the unions from around £200,000 in 1945 to around £800,000 in 1958. However, a number of unions still remained without political funds: most of the civil service unions, because they wished to maintain a position as neutral public servants; many of the semi-professional associations such as the teachers, because political opinion among their members was too divided between the parties; and even some manual unions, because they felt they were too small to make any impact on Labour Party policy and could rely on the TUC to represent their industrial interests.[7]

The long post-war boom was accompanied by high levels of trade-union strength and a need for all governments to establish working relationships with union leaders. As a result, the Conservatives dropped the pursuit of 'contracting in' as early as 1951, at a time when their moderate wing was in the ascendancy. However, thirty years on, with rising unemployment and weaker trade unions, the right wing of the Conservative Party prepared to challenge Labour's main source of political funding once again. Moreover, it seemed likely that this would find significant support among trade unionists themselves, for in the early 1980s only around 40 per cent of them voted Labour in general elections and approved of the political levy in opinion polls. The Conservative government began by considering the reintroduction of 'contracting in' by individual members but calculated that this would be seen as too party political and that it could achieve its goals by requiring, in the 1984 Trade Union Act, that each union hold a ballot every ten years over the continuation of its political fund. In the ensuing campaign for a 'yes' vote in the ballots the Labour Party kept a low profile and a special Trade Union Co-ordinating Committee focused on the direct benefits of political representation to all members, without trying to disguise the historic link with Labour. As one of the white collar unions put it: 'the campaign is about preserving the traditional right of our Union to protect, advance and campaign for the well-being of our members and their families and for the union to be able to sponsor [MPs] who will be able to speak and pursue issues on behalf of *all* our members in Parliament'.[8] On this basis the campaign not only secured surprisingly large majorities in favour of the political fund in every union concerned but also succeeded in persuading twenty other unions to set up such funds for the first time, including all of the major civil service unions and some of the teachers' associations.

In general, then, challenges to the unions' political levy arrangements have not only failed but have tended to strengthen the links between Labour and the trade unions. Despite the large number of individual union members voting for the Liberal and Conservative parties, the Labour Party has regularly re-emerged as the champion of the unions' right to a collective political voice. Along with its greater willingness to pass legislation of direct benefit to trade-union members, this has repeatedly consolidated Labour's claim to be the major beneficiary of the unions' political contributions, as well as legitimising the unions' commitment of manpower and resources to Labour election campaigns. However, the relationship has not been all one way and, alongside their crucial financial and organisational support for the party, the unions have also exercised a considerable influence on its policies.

The unions and party policy, 1900–1950

Having seen moderate growth throughout the 1900s, British trade unions experienced a veritable explosion in their strength during the First World War, in terms not only of their membership and finances but also of the extent of consultation and concession from governments desperate to maintain war production. These wartime requirements also led to a major expansion of the sector of the economy controlled and regulated by the state, and this combination of growth in trade-union strength and the scale of public-sector employment gave the unions an increasingly important role in Labour Party policy-making. The overall significance of the adoption of the commitment to the 'common owner-ship of the means of production' in 1918 has probably been exaggerated: Labour remained an alliance of socialists and trade-unionists, so any general statement of aims which omitted socialism would have been controversial, and the new constitution also included a radical–liberal commitment to the 'emancipation of the people'. More significant was the channelling of a series of specific policies on post-war economic reconstruction from the TUC meetings of the previous two years, through the party conference, and into the 1918 election manifesto *Labour and the New Social Order*. This enhanced public role for the unions was further underlined by Labour's split away from the 'progres-sive alliance' with the Liberals over foreign-policy issues, in particular the lack of government attention to the rising threat of revolutionary Bolshevism in Russia. Indeed, the leading figure in the establishment of Labour as an independent national party and an international bulwark against despotism was Arthur Henderson, very much a traditional liberal in outlook and previously an official of the ironfounders.[9]

However, the potential of this new movement was not realised in the inter-war years, as rising unemployment weakened the unions and the consolidation of Conservative electoral popularity weakened Labour even when in government. The lowest point was undoubtedly the split in the Labour cabinet of 1931 when the increasingly aloof Prime

Minister, Ramsay MacDonald, felt obliged to pursue further cuts in welfare benefits to shore up the international position of the pound in the face of clear union opposition. Knowing that they would be unable to persuade the unions to accept this policy, Henderson led a majority of the cabinet into resignation and opposition to MacDonald's new National government. However, this was followed by a catastrophic defeat for the Labour Party in the next general election, when it lost over 200 seats and was left with only forty-six MPs.[10]

This disastrous weakening of the parliamentary wing of the party left the way open for another enhancement of the public role of the unions under the outstanding leadership of two younger men, Ernest Bevin, the leader of the transport workers, and Walter Citrine, the secretary of the TUC. The national offices of both Labour and the TUC had already been relocated to Bevin's headquarters at Transport House in 1928. The majority of Labour politicians who survived the 1931 election were union-sponsored MPs, more often than not from the traditional coal-mining seats. And in the immediate aftermath of the defeat, the National Joint Council (later renamed the National Council of Labour) was revived to co-ordinate the activities of the TUC, Labour's National Executive and the parliamentary party, with the TUC asserting its seniority by claiming both the chairmanship and half of the other seats. Thus, while the constituency parties were growing and the parliamentary leadership was becoming more rigidly socialist and pacifist, the unions were able to push overall policy in a more pragmatic direction. It was the TUC which formulated practical proposals for reducing unemployment before the transition to socialism, including a welcome for Roosevelt's 'New Deal' in 1933. And it was the TUC which renewed the commitment to the League of Nations and sanctions against foreign dictatorships, pressing for rearmament from 1937 and taking a clear anti-appeasement line during the Munich crisis of 1938.[11]

The Second World War saw a repeat of the first in the explosion of the unions' strength and public role. Indeed this was even more marked because of the greater threat of Germany's early military successes combined with the appointment of Bevin to head the Ministry of Labour from 1940, where he virtually transplanted the TUC's views into government manpower and industrial-relations policy. Because the coalition government also included a large group of Labour ministers running the rest of wartime domestic policy under the able leadership of Clement Attlee, the parliamentary wing was able to restore its position within the party and the role of the National Council of Labour was reduced. Nevertheless, through Bevin's central position in the government, the unions still exercised a considerable influence on the formation of Labour's programme of post-war reconstruction, which focused squarely on the limited but achievable goal of full employment in a mixed economy, combining expansionist demand management, public ownership of the utilities and free collective bargaining. This provided the core of the 1945 election manifesto *Let Us Face the Future* which helped the party to win its first overall majority in the House of Commons.[12]

The post-war government under Attlee was able to deliver on its central promises of full employment and public ownership of the utilities, which were indeed to remain as background assumptions across the party divide until the late 1970s. A third of the cabinet were union-sponsored MPs and the majority within the TUC gave the Labour government its loyal support, extending even as far as a voluntary wage freeze during a balance-of-payments crisis in 1948. With Bevin at the Foreign Office there was also a continuation of the close working relationship between the unions and the government to oppose overseas despotism, now in the form of a clear identification of the dangers of Soviet foreign policy and the need for a close alliance with the United States. As Bevin could rely on solid support not only from the majority of the unions but also from the majority of the constituency parties, the extreme left was defeated and restricted to a permanent minority position in British political life.[13]

This strong relationship between the trade unions and Labour ministers throughout the 1940s was accompanied by the emergence of a set of conventions governing the party's policy-making. The most fundamental of these was that the basic sphere of the unions' organisational autonomy would not be discussed at the Labour conference: if necessary, issues could be raised through special discussions between Labour ministers and the TUC, which had been able to establish itself in an unrivalled position as the unions' national representative body during the war. The second of these conventions was that the unions would generally have their own way on major industrial matters, regarded primarily as the concern of the specific organisations involved: Labour ministers were expected to consult directly and early with the relevant unions over any policies likely to affect their industries. The third convention was that the unions would leave the initiative on all other matters to the political wing of the party: they would be broadly loyal to the party leadership, and they would not use their formal domination of conference voting to oppose the policies of Labour ministers.[14]

Because this was Labour's first experience of real national power, these conventions began to evolve into strongly held assumptions about the proper sphere of activity for each wing of the party, obscuring the long-standing union interest in, and influence on, a much wider range of policies. As one union-sponsored MP asked rhetorically at the time:

Must we assume that the trade union movement exists exclusively to protect the industrial interests and meet the industrial needs of the workers? . . . Is that the limitation of the political responsibilities and the functions of the trade unions? Can the trade unions, the Trades Union Congress, and its General Council contract out of the political responsibilities that confront all the citizens, the whole community?[15]

Actually, for the first few decades of its existence the party's membership had been little but the unions. The link with the parliamentary leadership in the 1920s had been maintained through the central role of Arthur Henderson and his relationship of mutual respect with Ramsay MacDonald, and the crisis of 1931 had been caused by the increasing distance between the unions and the Labour leader. While the 1930s had been marked by an increase in the role of the constituency parties, the weakness of the parliamentary party had left policy-making largely in the hands of the unions on the National Council of Labour. The idea of a clear differentiation of functions between the industrial and political wings of the party was therefore a product of the peculiar circumstances of the 1940s: the severity of the international threats, the powerful personality of Ernest Bevin, and the effective partnership between Bevin and Clement Attlee. Even then the implicit rules characterising the relationship between the two wings worked strongly in the unions' favour: the basic framework of industrial relations was off limits, particular industrial issues were the province of the specific unions involved, and the unions' self-denying ordinance on wider political matters was no real burden with Bevin at the heart of government. Simultaneously, however, the unions had shown that, though they had their roots in particular sectional interests, they also had a wider social vision which could benefit the whole nation: indeed their pursuit of full employment at home and liberty abroad had taken on a powerful international significance during the Second World War and the post-war reconstruction of Europe.

The unions and party policy, 1950–2000

The wartime and immediate post-war unity of the parliamentary party began to break up after the 1951 election defeat, as the left grew in strength and rebelled against the commitment to rearmament, culminating in Aneurin Bevan's unsuccessful bid for the leadership in 1955. The union leaders still tended to follow the recently established conventions in leaving the definition of the main issues to the politicians, but could hardly be expected to abstain from voting on them at the party conference. However, the combination of the split in the political leadership with the absence of an outstanding trade-union statesman exposed the unions' domination of conference voting to critical scrutiny, all the more so as the frustrated Bevanites chose it as one of their major targets for abuse. In fact the left had always been a presence within the industrial wing and was now strong enough to ensure that up to a third of the unions' conference votes could be cast against the party leadership: the Bevanite image of a monolithic union vote orchestrated by 'four men in a smoke-filled room' was therefore increasingly detached from reality. Indeed the growth of support for the left among trade unionists began to affect even the largest organisations when Frank Cousins was elected as leader of the transport workers in 1956. By the end of the decade the parliamentary party under the dynamic leadership of Hugh Gaitskell found itself in the novel position of being defeated by union conference votes during an attempt to refocus the party's identity more sharply around what would traditionally have been regarded as a trade-union agenda of a mixed economy and a strong defence policy. Thus the sense that the party was moving into uncharted waters was perhaps due less to the unions' renewed involvement in wider policy-making and more to uncertainty about their broader political attitudes.[16]

In 1964, after thirteen years in opposition, an excited party under the left-leaning Harold Wilson scraped back into office, where it was faced with a difficult Conservative legacy of a balance-of-payments deficit and an overvalued pound. From the outset the new Labour ministers were inclined to take a significantly more interventionist line on industrial relations than the unions were accustomed to and, having increased their parliamentary majority in 1966, they imposed a statutory prices and incomes policy. This had some initial success, but soon provoked an explosion of local wage strikes which an already disillusioned trade-union leadership had neither the will nor the ability to control. A Royal Commission under Lord Donovan proposed the recognition of shop-floor representatives and the integration of productivity gains into local bargaining, but the government persisted in its more interventionist line: the White Paper *In Place of Strife* (1969) included not only compulsory strike ballots but also elements of compulsory arbitration. This was an unprecedented intervention by Labour ministers in the basic sphere of the unions' organisational autonomy, and it is probably significant that both Wilson and his Employment Minister, Barbara

Castle, were ex-Bevanites. In any case it should have been no surprise when the unions mobilised all their influence through the TUC and the parliamentary party, with James Callaghan becoming their main ally within the cabinet. As a result, the government was forced to drop these proposals and the friction between the unions and the party undermined Labour's campaigning ability and made a significant contribution to its defeat in the general election the following year.[17]

Jack Jones of the transport workers now pressed for the formation of a TUC–Labour Party Liaison Committee along the lines of the National Joint Council of the 1930s, made up of representatives from the TUC General Council, Labour's National Executive Committee and the parliamentary party, with a recognition of the senior role of the TUC. A chastened party leadership was forced to abandon its interventionist approach to industrial relations and move closer to the union position through acceptance of a 'Social Contract', combining voluntary wage restraint with progressive industrial legislation and redistributive social measures. This legitimised total resistance to Edward Heath's interventionist Industrial Relations Act of 1971, and his inability to handle two costly national disputes with the miners, and Labour's credibility as the party which could manage the unions and the economy, was sufficiently restored to ensure two narrow election victories in 1974. Overall, the Social Contract subsequently provided an effective framework for wage restraint in a series of national pay rounds, but international economic pressures led to cuts in the government's social spending, a significant rise in unemployment and growing union disillusionment. The Prime Minister James Callaghan and his Chancellor Denis Healey then made two significant miscalculations in the course of the notorious 'winter of discontent' of 1978–9: firstly in soldiering on without an overall majority when they would probably have won a general election in the autumn, and secondly in attempting to impose a strict 5 per cent ceiling on wage increases. It should have come as no surprise when this met head-on resistance from local union members, compounded by particularly disruptive disputes among low-paid public-service workers, effectively bringing down an already demoralised Labour government.[18]

After almost forty years of political influence and relative prosperity, the unions were completely unprepared for the impact of Margaret Thatcher's increasingly right-wing governments. In the course of the 1980s they were faced with declining membership as a result of national economic policies which produced persistent mass unemployment, a raft of legislative restrictions on their freedom to strike, and a series of

233

Alastair J. Reid

defeats in industrial disputes at the hands of a highly confrontational Prime Minister, most notably in the case of the miners in 1984–5. However, the reaction of the party membership to the early phase of Thatcherism was a simple rejection of Labour's recent record in government and a swing towards Tony Benn's left-wing campaign to reduce the autonomy of the parliamentary leadership, so as to ensure the enactment of Labour's already established programme when next in office. Enough of this was achieved at the conferences of the early 1980s, in particular the selection of the party leader by an electoral college instead of the parliamentary party, to provoke the damaging secession of a group of right-wing MPs to form the Social Democratic Party (SDP) and a very real electoral challenge to Labour from the Liberal–SDP Alliance. As in the 1950s, once a split had emerged within the political leadership the unions could hardly be expected to abstain from using their conference votes and, as these were bound to be decisive, all the defects of the party's constitution were once again exposed to critical public scrutiny. The union majority still tended to favour the traditional Labour mainstream rather than either the SDP or the Marxist left: they supported the 'right-wing' Denis Healey in a contentious deputy leadership election in 1981, as well as the 'soft-left' leader Michael Foot in the first rounds of the battle against the 'hard left' in the constituencies. However, neither this, nor the improved co-ordination provided by Trade Unions for a Labour Victory, was enough to prevent a disastrous election defeat in 1983 when the various divisions on the left were reflected in Labour's inability to secure more than 28 per cent of the poll, closely challenged by the Alliance with 25 per cent.[19]

Confronted with this potentially terminal decline of Labour's appeal, the unions began to face up to the weakness of the party in opposition and the extent of their own difficulties under the Thatcherite regime. The first priority was to reunite the party under the considerably strengthened parliamentary leadership of Neil Kinnock, who was thus able to take a series of policy and disciplinary initiatives against the 'hard left' and reintegrate the constituencies into the Labour mainstream. This also involved establishing a public distance between the unions and political decisions: a reduction in the size of the union share of conference votes was proposed by the union leaders themselves in 1989, and the principle of 'one member one vote' was introduced into the party constitution in 1993 in the arrangements for local candidate selection. However, this did not exclude trade unions from all influence on policy-making: indeed, under the leadership of John Edmonds of the municipal workers, a fresh bargain was struck in the late 1980s. Known as the

234

'New Realism', the unions now accepted the permanence of compulsory strike ballots and restrictions on secondary action, in return for the party leadership's commitment to improved employment rights, a statutory minimum wage and better union recognition. It was some time before this protracted reconstruction of the party reaped its electoral reward, but under the additional impetus of the dynamic leadership of Tony Blair and the explicit abandonment of the Clause Four commitment to public ownership, Labour finally won a landslide victory in the 1997 general election. One of the first actions of 'New Labour' in government was the symbolic signing up to the European Social Chapter, closely followed by the concrete implementation of a European Working Time Directive, a national minimum wage and provisions for union recognition wherever a majority of the workforce supported it. Moreover, this was alongside a package of economic policies designed to reduce unemployment and a 'New Deal' for the retraining of the young and long-term unemployed.[20]

The relationship between the unions and the Labour Party since the 1950s has therefore been a problematic one as a result of two main factors: the rise of the left within the political wing of the party and the impact of full employment on trade-union members. The origins of both the Bevanite revolt in the 1950s and the Bennite challenge in the 1980s lay in the relationship between a section of the political leadership and the members in the constituencies, but once underway such conflicts were bound to draw the unions into voting for one side or another at party conferences. Though the unions did not vote as a monolithic block, and indeed around 30 per cent of their votes usually went to the left, the decisiveness of their impact on the overall results of conference votes repeatedly attracted bitter attacks from the defeated factions within the party as well as critical scrutiny from the wider public. Meanwhile, the long period of post-war prosperity and full employment which began in the 1950s led to a scarcity of key workers and an explosion of their formal and informal bargaining power in the late 1960s and 1970s such as had previously only been experienced during the two world wars. Under peacetime conditions the union leaders were unable to restrain their members' demands for immediate improvements in wages and, since this also took place against the background of the declining competitiveness of British exports and recurring deficits in the balance of payments, strikes and trade unions became convenient scapegoats for the country's economic problems. This then led Labour ministers into significant errors of judgement, above all in the cases of the abandonment of voluntarism in 1969 and the imposition of a strict pay norm in 1978, the union response to which certainly played a significant part in the downfall of both governments. Under the combined impact of these two factors the traditional link with the trade unions came to be regarded for the first time as a significant liability by large numbers within the political wing, especially as the new context of high unemployment and hostile government action under Thatcherism in the 1980s undermined the unions' power and marginalised them in public life. As one of the more pragmatic union leaders of the period put it herself:

I don't necessarily think it's good for the Labour Party to be run by the trades unions. In fact, I think it's counterproductive . . . I'm a member of the Labour Party, I'll never vote any other way: but the people who put the party in are the five per cent 'don't knows'. If 'don't knows' see that the party is dominated by any one group that's going to hurt its election chances. Politics is about power, about being in government – and we've got to make sure we provide the means for the Labour Party to get elected.[21]

At the same time, most trade unionists felt that they had continued to act throughout these turbulent years as the mainstay of the Labour Party. They had generally cast their conference votes for mainstream candidates and policies; they had repeatedly come up with constructive proposals for combining free collective bargaining with economic efficiency; and, above all, they had always provided the bulk of the party's financial requirements for general election campaigns. Clearly the unions felt that they had a lot to gain from Labour in government, primarily in terms of labour legislation and full-employment economic policy. But if Labour was to survive and succeed it was clear that changes would have to be made in its link with the trade unions, in terms both of their role within the party constitution and also of their relationship with the party in office.

Reforming the party constitution

Within the Labour Party the trade unions have exercised their formal power through their 'block vote' at the annual conference, a system which has often been criticised and equally often misunderstood. Under this constitutional arrangement each union was originally given one conference vote for every one thousand affiliated members and the custom was for all the votes of each organisation to be cast in the same way, as one 'block'. However, it is important not to be misled by some of the overtones of this word, for the votes of all the unions have rarely if ever been cast together as one homogeneous 'bloc' within the party, and the

input of the unions into policy-making has been considerably more constructive than simply 'blocking' proposals they have not liked. It is also
worth noting that, though the functioning of the block vote has been
resented by many on the political wing of the party in periods of sharp
internal division, there was no conspiratorial motive behind its introduction during the formation of the Labour Representation Committee
in 1900: it was simply a transfer of the existing practice at the annual
conference of the TUC into what was at that time one of its sub-organi-
sations. There was some uneasiness about maintaining this system
during the reconstruction of the party constitution in 1918 to include
individual and non-union members, but the next general election was
approaching too quickly to engage in the extensive consultation which
would have been necessary, and it was another twenty years before the
constituency organisations were well enough established to begin to
demand a larger voice within the party.

The resulting legacy was, however, a problematic one for a party sensitive about democratic procedures, mainly because of the sheer predominance of the union share of conference votes. Never less than 80
per cent and rising to 90 per cent in the 1970s as a result of falling constituency membership, the high union share frequently frustrated initiatives from the political wing and tended to undermine the enthusiasm of
the individual members of the party. Moreover, it was often alleged that
this predominance was bought too cheaply, with the political levy for
each union member being only a fraction of the subscription for each
constituency member and the overall contribution of the unions to the
party's finances fluctuating between 50 per cent and 60 per cent.
However, it should be remembered that the party was more heavily
dependent on the unions in such key areas of funding as its national
headquarters and general election campaigns, respectively 70–90 per
cent and 80–95 per cent union-financed. In addition to the swamping of
the political wing, a second problem with the system of the block vote
was that it deprived the minority in each union of any voice within the
party. On a practical level this came about because of the customary procedure of issuing each organisation with a single voting card, but at a
deeper level it was also due to trade unionists' dislike of the rigid man-
dating of delegates which would have been implied by any system of
proportional representation of opinion within their organisations.
Because their own conferences determining the broad outlines of their
political positions usually took place months or even years before the
party conference, trade unionists preferred to have further meetings
during the party conference to allow their delegates to interpret their

237

Alastair J. Reid

organisations' positions in relation to current events and specific conference resolutions, and preferred to conclude these meetings with simple
majority voting to encourage a genuine discussion of the issues.[22]
It is therefore important to bear in mind that both of these problems
with the union block vote were problems connected with a particular
system of majority rule in a federal organisation, rather than with a fundamentally undemocratic constitution. As Clement Attlee noted wryly:

The real difficulty is one which is a necessary incident in any large organisation . . . In fact, the main objection is generally found to be less against the
method of voting than against the results of the voting. Those who make the
loudest song about the block vote are significantly silent when it happens to
be cast in accordance with their own views.[23]

In fact, there were always far more affiliated union members than individual constituency members: the question was whether all of these
union members should have a say in Labour Party policy-making when
many of them were supporters or even members of other political
parties and, on the assumption that most of them did wish to belong to
the Labour Party, whether they should not join on the same basis as the
constituency members and have their conference votes counted in the
same way. Meanwhile, since all members had their influence on party
policy mediated through a sub-organisation of some sort, even if it was a
constituency party or a socialist society, the principle of proportional
representation of minority opinion could not be confined to the trade-
union block vote: the question was whether some method of representation for the minorities within the largest unions might not in practice
produce quite different overall results.

Unfortunately, appropriate criticism of the party's constitution was
often hindered by a number of aspects of the annual conference which
gave a poor impression of internal procedures. For example, the unions
usually economised on the expense of the conference by not sending all
the delegates they were entitled to, and the delegates who were sent did
not always attend all of the debates, both of which made for large dis-
crepancies between the number of trade unionists present and the pre-
ponderance of their ultimate voting strength. Furthermore, when this
discrepancy was clarified through the examination of the casting of card
votes, this only highlighted the size of each of the union blocks, which
were growing ever larger as a result of the process of trade-union amal-
gamation: for example the transport workers' card was already equivalent to over half of the constituency party total in the 1950s and had
become almost twice as large by the 1980s. To cap it all, since there was

Labour and the trade unions

only one card for each union, it followed that in card votes it was presented by one person, usually the national secretary, who then looked as
if he had hundreds of votes at his personal disposal. None of this
implied that conference decisions were ultimately unrepresentative of
the balance of membership opinion, but the poor impression of internal
procedures added considerable fuel to heated attacks on the party's constitution by defeated factions and external critics.[24]

Challenges to the trade-union domination of the party conference
were mounted with varying degrees of support following the growth of
individual constituency membership during the 1930s. In the course of
an ultimately successful campaign to increase the constituency parties'
representation on the national executive, a proposal was made in 1935
for a separate constituency conference before the full party gathering.
However, this was unsuccessful because of the problem of how the decisions of such a pre-conference should be translated into voting at the full
conference. The obvious device would have been the creation of a constituency block vote, but this would only have spread the disadvantages
of that system, as well as risking a growing divergence between the two
wings of the party. All the same, this proposal for two parallel conferences can be seen to have survived as a loose notion whenever the leadership highlights its success in gaining majorities in both sections of the
party. The next proposal, in 1939, was that the unions should be represented through local branch affiliation to constituency parties, which
would then have become the main source of delegations to a national
conference without union block votes. This received the support of a
major figure during the Second World War when Aneurin Bevan became
increasingly frustrated with what he saw as the party's inability to keep
up with a leftward swing in the country, which he blamed on the conservatism of the national union leaders. Of course, in so far as this was true
the proposed remedy was bound to fail, for constitutional change would
have required a majority at a national conference run on the block vote
system, and indeed this notion never received any significant trade-
union support.[25]

However, the tendency towards increasingly factional disputes
between left and right from the early 1950s repeatedly put the block vote
under the spotlight. By the early 1980s some unions were willing to consider both a redistribution of conference votes towards the constituency
parties and the splitting of their own blocks to allow the representation
of minority opinion. Following another two election defeats in the
course of that decade and the acceptance of the unpopularity of excessive union power, a wide consensus emerged around reducing the union

Alastair J. Reid

share of the votes from 90 per cent to 70 per cent. This was passed by the party conference in 1990, in a package which included a provision for further increases in the constituencies' share in proportion to increases in their size, and a major drive was launched to double the membership from 250,000 to 500,000, including a special 'levy plus' arrangement to encourage those already affiliated through their unions to join as individual members at a reduced fee. By 1995 individual membership had passed the 300,000 mark which was the signal for the introduction of a straight 50:50 split of conference votes between the constituencies and the unions, with the number of affiliated members required for each union vote now set at 5,000. The question of splitting the union blocks was a more sensitive one, as it opened up the possibility of the party instructing its affiliated organisations on how to conduct their internal affairs. However, it was still decided in 1995 that the votes of each union were to be divided between its delegates and cast separately, without giving any instructions on how opinion among their members was to be assessed. It was assumed that a wide range of methods would survive along with the traditional party conference meetings of trade-union delegations to discuss specific resolutions.

Meanwhile, these changes in the role of the unions within the party conference were paralleled by another process of reform changing the role of the annual conference within the overall policy-making process. Again this was initiated in 1990 when the conference agreed to establish a new intermediate body known as the 'National Policy Forum', bringing together representatives of the parliamentary party, the National Executive Committee, the affiliated organisations and the constituency members for a more extensive consideration of policy. And again this reached its culmination in the run up to the 1997 general election when it was agreed that the National Policy Forum should supervise a set of two-year cycles of policy reviews and should eventually take over the role of presenting proposals to the annual conference from the separate affiliated organisations. It was hoped that this would replace the rather obscure process of 'compositing' numerous constituency resolutions and the rather ritualised statements of position which took place at the conference, with a more extensive programme of discussion and consultation of all types of members.[26]

The speed with which these major reforms of the party constitution were passed under the old block vote system in the 1990s belied the hackneyed image of the blinkered trade-union carthorse and the customary assumption that, however desirable constitutional proposals might be, trade-union conservatism would ensure that they were never

240

adopted. It broke decisively from the traditional assumption that the strength of the party's link with the unions was directly proportional to the scale of union domination of the annual conference votes; and it raised the question of whether formal power within the party was indeed such a central issue for the unions. Rather, it seemed that their main concerns were that the Labour Party should be electable and that they themselves should be seen as an acceptable interest group in public life. Having transformed itself so much and secured a massive parliamentary majority in 1997, 'New Labour' was now faced with the possibility that the role of the unions within the party's own constitution might not after all be the most troublesome aspect of the relationship.

Constructing a governing partnership

In approaching general elections when Labour has been fighting back from long periods in opposition, trade-union leaders have been publicly supportive of the party over issues such as pay and economic policy. Moreover, in long periods of high unemployment the unions have lost members, their members have lost confidence and together they have become increasingly cautious over the use of industrial action. However, when Labour has experienced long periods in office accompanied by fairly full employment the story has been a different one. At the very least, Labour governments have been faced with periodic strikes by key workers in strategic sectors, and these have required some measure of state intervention. More seriously, they have seen the long-term growth of workers' confidence and collective bargaining strength, and a tendency for rising wages to add to inflationary pressures. Attempts at direct control through statutory incomes policy or legal restrictions on trade-union action in such periods have usually ended in embarrassing government climb-downs. Attempts at indirect influence through voluntary agreement have been more successful, though they have often been followed by disorderly rushes to catch up on lost earnings. While the voluntary approach is therefore more promising it also has clear limitations, for whatever agreement a Labour government may reach with the TUC it has in the end no binding power over the mass of trade-union members. The TUC can only urge its affiliated organisations to follow guidelines with no real sanction other than expulsion. Similarly, the leaders of individual unions are elected to pursue their organisations' own sectional interests and, even if they wish to, have no real sanctions over their members within a decentralised collective bargaining system. Given the strength of Britain's voluntarist traditions, the co-ordination of state economic policy and trade-union industrial behaviour is unlikely to be

Alastair J. Reid

achieved through a simple government proclamation or even a national bi-partite agreement.[27]

The problem of constructing an effective governing partnership between Labour and the trade unions therefore has no easy solution, though past experience does suggest the importance of the central theme of communication. At the most fundamental level, periods of fairly full employment have tended to highlight any weaknesses of communication within the workplace. In recent decades the anti-union stance of Conservative governments has led to a collapse of national and industry-wide agreements. In the public sector the government itself has broken up bargaining units and introduced competition from external contractors, while in the private sector there has been a marked increase in single-employer bargains at the company and plant levels. During a long period of economic recession this has been imposed on relatively compliant workforces but, if the tide turns towards fuller employment again, trade unionists will regain their confidence and the fragmented nature of collective bargaining is likely to produce a turbulent period in industrial relations. Meanwhile the Conservative legislation removing immunity to damages actions arising out of unballoted and secondary strikes has placed a serious financial pressure on unions to increase the authority of their national officials at the expense of the independence of their shop stewards. However, as in the case of the new bargaining arrangements, this has only been seen in operation in a period of high unemployment and, if the tide turns, it is likely to produce a backlash to redistribute power towards the local membership. Thus Labour in government would be well advised to pay attention not only to such issues as union recognition and employment rights, but also to the need for improved channels of communication within the workplace: more sensitive attitudes on the part of management, more effective forms of joint consultation, and the sustained integration of shop-floor representatives within trade-union decision-making.[28]

At an intermediate level, periods of fairly full employment have tended to highlight weaknesses of communication between trade unions and their own members. Here, the anti-union stance of Conservative governments in recent decades has, both intentionally and unintentionally, brought about considerable improvements as the unions have struggled to maintain their role. The revival of interest in internal ballots for important decisions has been firmly underwritten by their statutory requirement for the initiation and conclusion of strikes, the election of national executive committees and the continuation of political funds. This has led the unions to computerise membership records, maintain up-to-date address lists, and experiment with new methods of communication such as regional consultations, internal opinion polling and focus groups. Meanwhile, high levels of unemployment have tended to undermine the unions' collective bargaining role and pushed them to provide a wider range of personal services for those still in work. As a result, their internal newsletters have not only switched the balance of coverage from general commentary to concrete examples of each organisation's successes, but have also begun to pay special attention to non-pay issues, such as individual employment contracts and financial advice. Finally, following the media furore around the 1978–9 disputes in the public sector and the subsequent repetition of images of the 'winter of discontent' in Conservative Party political broadcasts, the unions have become acutely aware of the extent to which their traditionally negative media image can seriously undermine their position. They have begun to move from a rather passive acceptance of poor publicity to an increasingly active handling of public relations, including the appointment of at least part-time press officers and the conscious channelling of information to industrial correspondents, though their influence is still weak in the cases of non-specialist newspaper journalists and the broadcast media. Thus the unions would be well advised to continue to increase their commitment of resources to communication both with their own members and with the wider public, for if they recover their industrial and political strength it will be vital not only to be as democratic as possible, but also to be seen to be so.[29] As an official of the country's largest union put it in a recent interview: 'The union has carried on a commitment to put its money where its mouth is. It recognises that members would be kept informed and the importance of its external influence for the public image of the union . . . the union recognises that without this sort of work, the union wouldn't grow, thrive or influence anybody.'[30]

At the level of national politics, the key issue naturally concerns the effectiveness of communication between the trade unions and the Labour Party itself. The reassertion of the predominance of the parliamentary leadership within the party in the course of the 1980s and 1990s has been accompanied not only by a reduction in the formal voting strength of the unions at the party conference, but also by an erosion of their informal influence on policy-making. While the front-bench spokesmen on employment have usually been sympathetic to the union position, there is no guarantee of their influence within the cabinet on the wider range of policies with implications for trade-union members. Meanwhile, the policy advisers and gate-keepers in the leader's office,

now the Downing Street policy unit, have had little or no personal expo-
sure to employment and trade-union issues, and are young enough to
have experienced nothing but decades of media myth-making on the
subject. Indeed the involvement of the trade unions in the modernisation of the party has depended mainly on key individuals on the union
side being prepared to follow and support an increasingly distant party
leadership. For example, Tom Sawyer of the public employees played
a central role in steering through the wide-ranging policy review of
the late 1980s and then, as party secretary, in developing the role of the
Policy Forum within the rolling programme. Equally important are the
numerous less well-known figures in the research and policy-making
units of individual unions who were able to exercise their influence at
vital moments, as well as the largely faceless union representatives on the
party's National Executive Committee who provided steady support for
the leaders' initiatives. This worked remarkably well in the hard-pressed
years of opposition, but it seems doubtful that such a one-sided relationship will guarantee effective communication in a period of fuller
employment and resurgent trade unionism.[31]

Indeed, if Labour has diverged from its origins in any way it has been
a result not of any 'betrayal of socialism', but rather of the declining role
of trade unionists within the parliamentary party. For trade unionists
provided the bulk of Labour MPs in the earliest years and, even after the
growth of the constituency parties, continued to provide around half of
the parliamentary wing in the 1940s. At first the trend towards an
increasingly middle-class profile for Labour politicians was offset by
Ernest Bevin and eight other trade unionists in the 1945 cabinet, but by
the end of the 1960s only Jim Callaghan was able to play a credible role
as a link between the two wings of the party. This decline was partly a
result of the unions' own reluctance to sponsor candidates outside safe
Labour seats, which in turn was a product of the thirty years of political
influence they enjoyed after 1945: when they could make successful
direct approaches to ministries it no longer seemed so important to
invest resources in parliamentary representation. Naturally there were
changes under the long period of right-wing Conservative rule in the
1980s and 1990s. As the Labour Party shrank back into its heartlands,
the share of union-sponsored MPs automatically increased; as the
various government ministries closed their doors, the unions began to
explore ways of making more use of their parliamentary representation.
However, the procedures for sponsoring individual MPs were eventually
abolished in 1996 as part of the modernisation of the party, and those
sponsored had in any case tended for some time to be middle-class career

politicians rather than ex-trade unionists. The result is that few leading Labour figures now have any direct experience of trade-union affairs, and the risk is that they may not always remember to consult their union counterparts or, if they do, that they may not always understand the full implications of what they hear. Perhaps, then, it is time for the unions to reconsider their unwillingness to allow their serving national officials to become MPs, and to commit the resources to building up a group of experienced trade unionists with influence in the parliamentary party and, in due course, an irresistible personal claim to sit in the cabinet. In the near future Labour is likely to remain highly sensitive to charges of union domination, but in the longer run the inclusion of significant trade union figures at the highest level could bring as many benefits to the party as to the unions.[32]

If the Labour Party and the trade unions, separately and together, can make further improvements in all of these areas of communication they may be able to reduce the problems which are likely to affect their relationship in periods of Labour government and fuller employment. However, even the best-maintained network of communication cannot always prevent significant misunderstandings, or indeed genuine conflicts of interest. 'Welcome to government' indeed!

Alastair J. Reid

Notes

1 Len Murray, general secretary of the Trades Union Congress, in 1980, quoted in Andrew Taylor, *The Trade Unions and the Labour Party* (London: Croom Helm, 1987), p. 289.

2 H. A. Clegg, Alan Fox and A. F. Thompson, *A History of British Trade Unions since 1889*, vol. I: *1889–1910* (Oxford: Oxford University Press, 1964), pp. 1–54.

3 Henry Pelling, *A History of British Trade Unionism* (Harmondsworth: Penguin, 1992), pp. 19–22, 52–65, 100–7, 113–17; Henry Pelling and Alastair J. Reid, *A Short History of the Labour Party* (London: Macmillan, 1996), pp. 1–15.

4 Quoted in Henry Pelling, *The Origins of the Labour Party, 1880–1900* (Oxford: Oxford University Press, 1965), pp. 204–5.

5 Roy Gregory, *The Miners and British Politics, 1906–1914* (Oxford: Oxford University Press, 1968), pp. 14–27; Henry Pelling, 'The politics of the Osborne Judgement', *Historical Journal* 25 (1982), 889–909; Pelling and Reid, *Short History*, pp. 16–31.

6 Pelling, 'Osborne Judgement', 895–6.

7 Martin Harrison, *Trade Unions and the Labour Party since 1945* (London: Allen and Unwin, 1960), pp. 21–31, 36, 60, 324–34.

8 Association of Professional, Executive, Clerical and Computer Staff, campaign bulletin, quoted in Taylor, *Trade Unions*, p. 226, and on these events more generally pp. 205–41.

9 Chris Wrigley, 'Trade unions and politics in the First World War', in Ben Pimlott and Chris Cook (eds.), *Trade Unions in British Politics. The First 250 Years* (London: Longman, 1991), pp. 69–87; Pelling and Reid, *Short History*, pp. 32–46.

10 Robert Skidelsky, *Politicians and the Slump. The Labour Government of 1929–1931* (London: Macmillan, 1967), pp. 367–83; Pelling and Reid, *Short History*, pp. 47–64.

11 Richard Shackleton, 'Trade unions and the slump', in Pimlott and Cook (eds.), *Trade Unions*, pp. 109–36; Pelling and Reid, *Short History*, pp. 65–79.

12 Alan Bullock, *The Life and Times of Ernest Bevin*, vol. II: *Minister of Labour, 1940–1945* (London: Heinemann, 1967), pp. 313–22, 336–40, 350–65; Pelling and Reid, *Short History*, pp. 80–8.

13 Kenneth O. Morgan, *Labour in Power, 1945–1951* (Oxford: Oxford University Press, 1984), especially pp. 45–93; Pelling and Reid, *Short History*, pp. 88–96.

14 Harrison, *Trade Unions*, pp. 195–203.

15 Sir Tom O'Brien MP, of the National Association of Theatrical and Kine Employees, in 1953, quoted in Harrison, *Trade Unions*, p. 202.

16 Harrison, *Trade Unions*, pp. 215–38; Pelling and Reid, *Short History*, pp. 97–114.

17 Robert Taylor, 'The trade union "problem" in the age of consensus, 1960–1979', in Pimlott and Cook (eds.), *Trade Unions*, pp. 173–99, especially pp. 181–9; Pelling and Reid, *Short History*, pp. 115–39.

18 Taylor, 'Trade union "problem"', pp. 189–97; Pelling and Reid, *Short History*, pp. 140–60.

19 Taylor, *Trade Unions*, pp. 115–51; Lewis Minkin, *The Contentious Alliance. Trade Unions and the Labour Party* (Edinburgh: Edinburgh University Press, 1991), pp 159–237; Pelling and Reid, *Short History*, pp. 161–74.

20 Minkin, *Contentious Alliance*, pp. 420–82; Pelling and Reid, *Short History*, pp. 175–92; Labour Party, *Fairness at Work* (London: Labour Party, 1999).

21 Brenda Deane of the Society of Graphical and Allied Trades in 1985, quoted in Taylor, *Trade Unions*, p. 293.

22 Harrison, *Trade Unions*, pp. 38, 67, 71, 97, 99, 107, 158–94; Minkin, *Contentious Alliance*, pp. 281–6, 306–10, 509.

23 C. R. Attlee, *The Labour Party in Perspective* (London: Victor Gollancz, 1937), p. 102, cited in Harrison, *Trade Unions*, p. 247.

24 Harrison, *Trade Unions*, pp. 206–9, 248–9; Minkin, *Contentious Alliance*, pp. 281–3, 298.

25 Ben Pimlott, *Labour and the Left in the 1930s* (Cambridge: Cambridge University Press, 1977), pp. 120–2; Michael Foot, *Aneurin Bevan, A Biography*, vol. I: *1897–1945* (London: MacGibbon and Kee, 1962), pp. 414–15; Harrison, *Trade Unions*, pp. 252–3; Minkin, *Contentious Alliance*, pp. 367–8.

26 Harrison, *Trade Unions*, pp. 252–4; Minkin, *Contentious Alliance*, pp. 367–84; *The Times*, 5 October 1995; Labour Party, *Labour into Power. A Framework for Partnership* (London: Labour Party, 1997).

27 Taylor, 'Trade union "problem"', passim.

28 H. A. Clegg, *The Changing System of Industrial Relations in Great Britain* (Oxford: Basil Blackwell, 1979), especially pp. 9–61; William Brown, 'The changed political role of unions under a hostile government', in Pimlott and Cook (eds.), *Trade Unions*, pp. 274–85.

29 Clegg, *Changing System*, pp. 226–7; Brown, 'Changed political role', pp. 275, 278, 284; Minkin, *Contentious Alliance*, p. 378; Jean Seaton, 'Trade unions and the media', in Pimlott and Cook (eds.), *Trade Unions*, pp. 256–73; Aeron Davis, *Trade Union Communications in the 1990s. A Report for the TUC and its Affiliate Unions* (London: Goldsmiths' College, 1998).

30 Interview with John Monks of Unison, quoted in Davis, *Trade Union Communications*, p. 5.

31 Philip Bassett, 'Unions and Labour in the 1980s and 1990s', in Pimlott and Cook (eds.), *Trade Unions*, pp. 307–27, especially pp. 312–13, 315.

32 Harrison, *Trade Unions*, pp. 262–306; Minkin, *Contentious Alliance*, pp. 241–76.

8 | Labour and its membership

Duncan Tanner

Since the 1920s, Labour has relied on com-
mitted volunteers amongst its mass membership and a small number of
professional activists to sustain its organisation. Labour's constitutional
and organisational structures gave some power to these activists at local
level and through party conference. Consequently, the actions of individual and affiliated members have always received considerable media
attention. Differences between members and leaders have been highlighted. The radicalism of some party members has been ruthlessly misrepresented and exploited by the media and by the party's opponents,
whilst the industrial actions of trade unions and the existence of the
block vote have been used to suggest the party's domination by groups
with no concern for the 'public interest'. As a result party leaders have
often sought to direct the views of party members in the interests of
electoral success, to limit their contribution to policy-making and policy
debate and to police the party's ideological boundaries in order to maintain its position as a moderate socialist force.

This chapter begins by suggesting that Labour has never been a mass
membership party on continental socialist lines. Party leaders tried and
partially succeeded in creating a mass membership during the 1930s.
The party recruited substantial numbers of women, expanded in the

south-east, but failed to turn the mass of male trade unionists in the party's traditional heartlands into active party workers. Moreover, after 1945 real membership levels fell and activism was restricted to an even smaller minority, ever-declining participation rates eventually leading to an organisational crisis. Subsequent sections examine the outlooks and politics of party members and activists. The heroes and heroines of this chapter are the party officials, election agents and intellectuals, the back-bench MPs and constituency activists who fought against local apathy and extremism to deliver a constructive and active socialism, often more in sympathy with the views of party leaders than popular opinion would suggest. The leadership's desire to remove power and influence from less constructive and representative activists is seen as understandable. Its failure to include and consider those who differed only in degree is shown to be a serious and recurrent weakness.

Labour Party membership in perspective

A mass membership can be more than a source of funds or a means of maintaining a party's local activities and persuading supporters to vote. In some countries, a large and socially disparate party membership prevented dependence on any one social group or faction. It was an indication of the party's roots in different communities, a source of legitimacy and ideas. Labour's membership has included those with knowledge of industry, of women's experiences, of issues concerning the young, elderly and minority groups. It has included those with expertise which could be beneficial when determining the likely impact of legislation. None the less, party leaders have seldom fully exploited this resource. Policy has at times reflected the interests of the most powerful members – male trade unionists – or the values of radical activists to the detriment of other groups. Consequently the party has suffered both electorally and as a vehicle for reform.

Unlike the position in most Western European social-democratic parties, most Labour members were affiliated to the party through their trade unions, paying a political levy but playing no direct part in local party activity. Individual membership has always been low, especially by comparison with the Swedish and German parties. Although their memberships peaked in the late 1940s, both of these parties recruited large numbers of new members during the 1960s and 1970s.[1] Individual membership of the Labour Party was lower even at its peak, continued to decline from the high point of one million achieved in 1952 and failed to recover in the 1960s and 1970s, despite some localised successes. Trade unions provided money for election campaigns, a practical and

Duncan Tanner

sometimes moderate counterbalance to the radicalism of party activists, skilled organisers in some seats, but handfuls of constituency workers rather than a mass membership. Official trade-union delegates totally dominated constituency executives in some highly unionised areas, but in the country as a whole the most active members were generally ward representatives and those holding executive office.

Labour Party individual membership figures are notoriously inaccurate. There are no national figures before 1928. From 1928 to 1956 all constituency parties were assumed to have a minimum of 240 members, and figures were compiled and published on this basis. In 1956 the minimum affiliation figure was raised to 800, despite the fact that in many parties membership was much lower. Figures for individual constituencies were no longer published. The minimum affiliation figure was raised to 1,000 in 1963 for financial reasons. Artificially inflated national figures became progressively more misleading as 'real' membership declined still further. Even during the period when constituency figures were reported, they were often inaccurate. Many parties lacked the bureaucratic machinery necessary to record membership. In times of financial hardship, some constituency parties affiliated only a proportion of their members to avoid paying affiliation fees to head office. It was not until Labour's computer-based and direct-membership system became firmly entrenched in the 1990s that accurate figures were published.[2]

The scale and pattern of party membership between the wars

Prior to 1918 most people participated in constituency Labour politics as union delegates or as members of the Independent Labour Party (ILP), which had affiliated in 1900. Some ILP branches had an active associational life, based around music, rambling, cycling and 'educative' political campaigning. A commitment to equality between the sexes encouraged women as well as men to join, though the latter predominated. More usually small branches relied on a few individuals. Most Labour activists served their communities, rather than preaching a socialist fundamentalism. None the less in most constituencies Labour was a small and struggling presence in 1914.[3]

The electoral and political opportunities which resulted from wartime circumstances occasioned a major review of the party's organisation and constitution in 1918. In order to exploit new opportunities, party leaders introduced individual membership of constituency parties. However, many leading figures within the constituency parties were unenthusiastic about the idea, fearing middle-class converts would take over hitherto union-dominated local parties. Initially most individual members were

women, drawn in the main from skilled working-class backgrounds. The
national party organisers actively sought this support. In 1926 they
organised a 'women's week'; in 1927 a 'women's month'. National and
regional organisers set up women's sections, regional women's advisory
committees and educational classes. Figures published in 1929 reveal that
in many safe or strongly unionised seats there were at best the minimum
240 members (and in reality far fewer). In Scotland, where individual
membership was low, Greenock's ninety-five individual members
seemed 'huge' by comparison to the position in many seats and even the
growth of women's sections was 'very slow'. In several Scottish seats the
position never really improved.[4] Across Wales and in many promising
English seats in the midlands, the north-east and Yorkshire, organisers
despaired. In South Shields, for example, there were just 150 members
even by 1929, most of these based in five active women's sections.[5] There
were of course exceptions. In Wales, Newport's Labour Party reported a
'huge increase' in membership in 1923, with women outnumbering men
by the following year. By 1929 it was the fourth largest party in the
country. Women's sections organised the social activities which sustained
most strong parties – notably bazaars and dances held at central and local
Labour halls, and outings for children – and contributed substantial
amounts to party funds both directly and through fund-raising activities.
In Newport (unlike many other areas) women were also strongly represented on the constituency executive. The Labour election agent's
journal produced numerous examples to show that agents with energy
could follow this example, even in rural seats.[6]

Labour achieved its highest individual membership in Woolwich. A
handful of other London seats had a substantial membership (notably
Poplar and Bermondsey), as did parties in working-class London
suburbs like Tottenham, which organised a successful 'thousand
members' campaign in 1924. Its network of social and political activities
utilised party halls and encompassed trips to the seaside ('nine chara-
bancs of Labour Ladies to Margate') and fund-raising for the miners (a
total of £3,000 being raised in 1926).[7] The south London seats of
Lewisham and Greenwich followed suit by canvassing on the new
housing estates, as did Labour parties in the suburban seats outside
London, such as Faversham in Kent and Romford in Essex (which had
the second highest membership of all).[8] Herbert Morrison's highly
organised London Labour Party lent support.[9]

The party had captured a series of seats for the first time in 1929,
often using members to distribute leaflets or newspapers tailored to the
local electorate.[10] Holding these seats – and gaining more like them – was

central to Labour's electoral prospects. In London, the *Citizen* news-paper (used to good effect in Tottenham and East Ham during the 1920s) was distributed in a growing number of constituencies. In Sheffield and Birmingham, borough newspapers were supplemented with localised news-sheets. A mass membership helped the party develop and deliver a broader political message, less dominated by the interests of male trade unionists, and more attentive to the needs of the whole electorate.

The party's desire to expand into areas outside its conventional heart-lands through active constituency campaigning of this kind, and espe-cially to create financially solvent constituency associations, encouraged the National Executive Committee to launch its 'million members' crusade in 1932. Whilst membership figures for individual constituen-cies during the 1930s are inaccurate in some cases, constituency records show that the decade saw a substantial and real increase, notably in the south-east. Labour threatened to become a mass party for the first time, with nearly half a million members by 1937.

Throughout the 1930s, head office tried to persuade local parties to canvass for members, and collect membership fees weekly to keep recruits in touch. It was easy to 'make' members, notoriously difficult to retain them. National party officials suggested paying a commission to collectors (or ward parties). There was local resistance to canvassing (a time-consuming business) and to paying collectors. Many believed this should be done voluntarily, individual involvement being an indication of serious intent and commitment to making socialism. However, the scheme was implemented in seats such as Bristol and Carlisle, and was especially successful as a means of recruiting women on the developing municipal housing estates. In Carlisle membership increased fourfold in two years, placing the party on a stable financial footing.[11] There were similarly large increases in other former blackspots – for example, across much of Lancashire and the industrial north-east. In the areas of strength already noted, individual membership soared. There were also respectable increases in such solidly working-class boroughs as East Ham, Deptford, Stepney and Shoreditch, as well as a series of more affluent suburban constituencies. By the late 1930s, there were around 2,000 party members in many of the Middlesex seats and over 1,000 in parts of Surrey, Sussex and Kent.

By contrast, in many solidly Labour areas the mass party never really materialised. Membership figures in safe, union-dominated Labour seats remained low. Although women's sections in some parts of the north-east and to a much lesser extent in parts of the South Wales coalfields were numerically strong, they did not generally wield much influence (despite the valiant efforts of some very forceful characters).[12] Parties seemed reluctant to canvass for members. In Tredegar, for example, the party had 'not encouraged nor promoted individual membership' for many years.[13] In Wrexham the executive committee called for a membership initiative in February 1932, but five months later the secretary reported 'a tremendous apathy and indifference existed almost everywhere in connection with this work'. Similarly, although Stockport's executive called for a 'centralised effort for new members . . . upon the Housing Estates' in 1936, it too reported five months later that 'activity is at a discount'.[14]

The national party's large affiliated membership did not entirely compensate for this. Trade unions regularly poured in money when sponsoring a candidate. Coalfield seats in particular were union fiefdoms. Elsewhere unions like the National Union of Railwaymen and in the 1930s the Transport and General Workers' Union regularly supplied a substantial number of active workers and local councillors, with railwaymen in particular acting as the backbone of many parties in weaker Labour areas.[15] Yet many local union branches could not find delegates to attend meetings. In 1936 the Sheffield Labour Party noted: 'whilst there are 346 [union] delegates on our register, the attendance at our delegate meetings is only about 30 per cent of this number'. In the South Wales coalfield many trade-union branches did not even affiliate, especially when money was scarce,[16] since a few mining lodges and the local officials dominated and organised activity so successfully themselves. The position was often no better where Labour really needed union support. Following the 1929 election the Birmingham Party reported that the trade-union section 'had done more than ever before', but not as much 'as we would expect', whilst in Tory-held Newport, activists complained throughout the 1920s that many local trade unions were uninterested in general party affairs.[17]

With neither a wealthy union nor a mass membership to support them, many weaker parties relied on a tiny active membership. Affluent parliamentary candidates were sought to provide for the association, finance an agent and mount campaigns. The Moss Side Labour Party told one prospective parliamentary candidate: 'it is absolutely necessary that the candidate should provide all the finance necessary for the election'.[18] Wealthy individuals – including some apparent dilettantes – made a significant and seldom-recognised contribution to local party affairs. The affluent ex-Tory Major Graham Pole ('the Beau Brummel of the Socialist Party') poured time and money into the mixed, sprawling, but winnable South Derbyshire constituency between 1925 and 1931, following his selection as parliamentary candidate. He paid an agent (adding the deposit for a house, removal expenses and a car), subsidised the constituency office, contributed an annual subscription, provided the agent with two funds, one for 'deserving causes', one for political work, and paid half the election expenses in 1929.[19] Pole's London office arranged meetings with the local press and his speaking tours. In 1926 he addressed forty meetings, wrote a press article every week and helped local miners and their families with personal and legal costs. Once elected in 1929 he was 'assiduous, painstaking and accomplished' at dealing with individual cases and kept in touch via a regular 'London letter', quarterly reports to the local party, speaking tours and the establishment of a monthly Labour news-sheet. Without him organisation had languished. When he left, it collapsed.[20]

Such largesse could create difficulties. In 1926 Oswald Mosley paid £350 to the Birmingham Ladywood constituency to pay towards the costs of establishing a Labour hall, £900 towards a house and salary for the agent and £150 towards the municipal election fund. He promised to continue helping the party if it released him to stand elsewhere. In 1927 he paid £450 towards maintaining the hall, a sum the local party found unsatisfactory. 'I am afraid I have made a great mistake', he wrote, 'in spending as much as I have, and this has done much to undermine the organisation'.[21]

Even in seats with large Labour majorities, a handful of people regularly kept the constituency machine in being. In seats with a union-sponsored candidate, branch officials and union organisers could be called on at election time, but even here the candidate and agent were generally the main contributors. In Llanelli, for example, branch activity was sustained by the election agent (Alderman Hughes) and the MP (Jim Griffiths). In 1937–8, Griffiths dealt with fifty constituency letters a week and held a hundred meetings in the division. Hughes dealt with 700 advice cases alone. The dedication of election agents was such that many accepted pay cuts or waited months for their salary to help stretch limited constituency funds. On occasions agents acted as the voice of party head office, but most did so from a position of total dedication to the party and its success.[22]

In safe seats, the 'mass membership' was only occasionally mobilised, notably at election times and for special 'theatrical' events (like May Day marches). Regular deliveries of leaflets and newspapers, or collections for moral causes (striking miners in 1926, the republican forces during the Spanish Civil War) were important as a means of creating participation.

These were the memorable, but exceptional, events and not the meat and drink of party life. For many, joining the party was an expression of their commitment to change, and greater involvement was either impossible or undesirable. Some who gave their lives to the party resented both this sporadic involvement and the 'social' activities which dominated much party life. Members of Labour clubs and Labour youth movements were regularly lambasted.[23] Yet often a mass membership was achieved and retained most successfully where the party's clubs enabled members to enjoy their membership through gambling, dancing and drinking, augmented by regular afternoon neighbourhood teas for wives with families. More cerebral activities were generally less popular with the bulk of members, although they too helped people stay within the party. The 'social side' reinforced the commitment of the most active and helped create a mass of occasional party workers.[24] If some leading local figures enjoyed and occasionally exploited their domination of the one-party Labour fiefdoms which were established in several areas by the 1930s, others were anxious to extend the party's membership. However, it was in the more marginal seats that Labour generally achieved its highest membership, not in those areas where it had the greatest popular support.

The absence of a mass membership did not necessarily indicate a 'failing' party. It could reflect a respect and support for local party leaders so deep that participation was unnecessary, or an organisational machine so perfect, successful and progressive in local government that more action was unnecessary. Yet it could also lead to complacency, a cumulative detachment from local views, and a policy agenda constructed by an entrenched, impermeable and overwhelmingly male Labour elite.

In weaker seats (where there was rarely an agent) branch secretaries, councillors, committee members and others – either trade-union officials or, as frequently, teachers, ministers and people from a variety of white-collar occupations – shouldered an inordinate, unpaid, burden. 'It is really surprising', reported the secretary of the Pembrokeshire Labour Party in 1918, 'to find the people who join our movement. Schoolmasters, tradesmen etc form a part of every District Committee'. A schoolteacher himself, he described the central role of such people in the establishment and development of the Labour Party: 'Addressing four meetings after school last week I had to cover over sixty miles in a side-car.'[25] None the less, the party as a whole remained rooted in the skilled working class. It was also reported in the 1920s that 90 per cent of women who joined the party were married, although oral testimony suggests their participation owed more to a family tradition of working-class activism than to their

Duncan Tanner

husbands' influence. Despite this, there is also evidence to suggest that those women who reached positions of local importance were generally single and affluent or married to supportive and political partners.[26]

The political issues of the 1930s helped broaden the social basis of party membership. Organisations such as the million-strong Left Book Club and the Peace Pledge Union prospered. In a climate of greater activism, Labour benefited from its practical and moral opposition to mass unemployment, fascism and war. This converted some to Labour and made others more active. The party's expanded membership in middle-class suburbs contained committees 'composed mainly of professional men and women'. In Southampton, Labour's membership was highest in the more affluent wards, a trend evident elsewhere.[27] There were new recruits within the universities. However, Labour did not become a party of protest and mass activism. Despite efforts to capitalise on an assumed youthful idealism, branches of Labour's youth movement collapsed or were closed down with considerable regularity. Nor was an active, passionate, commitment to these causes dominant amongst the educated even in the 1930s. In the universities, political activism – especially in the Labour Party – was seen as aberrant.

The scale and pattern of party membership since 1945

Following a decline during the war, membership increased substantially between 1945 and 1952, with the party finally achieving its million members in 1951. However, it was more difficult than ever to turn members into activists. In the aftermath of war, people naturally wished to get on with their lives. The problems were especially acute in safe Labour seats. For example, the Belper Labour Party tried to raise money and members' interest through a football pools sweep, a Labour newspaper and social activities. By 1955 failure had created despondency. Blaming the growth of television for its problems, the annual report noted: 'Our local and ward party stalwarts had a big job on their hands to keep a few interested members together.' Two women's sections had been organised 'in the hope it would strike a spark of enthusiasm', but both had failed. A League of Youth had been established but the majority who came 'were only interested in it as a youth club'. It too lapsed. 'A halt was called to public indoor meetings . . . due to poor attendances.'[28] Nor was this position unusual. In Coventry East, executive committee meetings were seldom quorate. Sub-committees were abolished as 'the same few faces were there to do the job whatever the business'. In Wrexham the same three trade-union officials dominated meetings. Most other delegates failed to turn up.[29] There were similar problems in

London and Durham, whilst in Nottingham there was 'hardly any organisation' in several wards and scarcely enough members to fill the available posts. None the less, recruitment campaigns were unpopular, one constituency chairman claiming 'he was opposed to enrolling members of the party who would not promise to attend all party meetings'.[30] Even in seats where membership once thrived, parties faced difficulties. Newport's Labour Party, one of the largest in the UK before 1945, tried hard to rekindle the old enthusiasm. There were familiar tensions when this involved social activities. In 1955 the party agent complained to one women's section that 'while many members are eager to take part in any social activities, not everyone could or would do the various jobs of work especially canvassing'. In a party with 2,000 or more individual members, annual meetings attracted around fifty and general party meetings fewer than thirty, most of these being officials.[31] In London, both Lewisham and Woolwich, seats with large memberships in the 1930s, were struggling by 1952.[32]

Successive election defeats led Labour to examine its organisation. The 1955 Wilson Report highlighted a 'progressive deterioration of the Party's organisation, especially at constituency level', commenting specifically on the limited numbers of 'voluntary workers willing and able to carry out election activities'. None the less, the report did not focus on recruiting members, but on the need for trained party workers. Other prominent Labour figures regarded television, opinion polls and groups of canvassers from the Labour students' organisation, strategically deployed in the marginal seats, as the key to victory. 'Modernisers' like Tony Crosland argued: 'the rank-and-file is less and less essential to the winning of elections. With the growing penetration of the mass media, political campaigning has become increasingly centralised; and the traditional local activities . . . are now largely a ritual'.[33]

The position was certainly serious. If officially membership stood at over 750,000 by the early 1960s, the real position was much worse.[34] A confidential survey of the East Midlands produced a depressing picture. Of the region's thirty seats only three had achieved the 1,000 minimum affiliation figure introduced in 1963, whilst over half had a membership of less than 500. In the West Midlands, many seats had both a low membership and many unaffiliated union branches.[35] The position declined still further during the 1966–70 Wilson government. The party lost 20 per cent of its membership in just four years. Sixty parties had over 2,000 members in 1965; just twenty-two by 1969. In Brixton real membership fell from 1,212 in 1965 to 212 in 1970. In the 1970s, reported party membership figures became a farce. Academics estimated 'real' party membership was 40–50 per cent of the reported figure (meaning membership had plummeted to 250–300,000 by 1979).[36]

The number of active members was even lower. In Bermondsey, a seat with a history of activism, only around 100 of the 3,000 members were regularly involved in the early 1960s. In Leicester, wards with memberships of between 80 and 213 produced between six and twelve active workers.[37] In one Manchester ward just 10–20 per cent of members attended meetings in the late 1960s. In 1969 an official investigation revealed that there were only 1,786 members in Glasgow, with the result that seven of the fifteen constituency organisations and thirty out of thirty-nine ward organisations were inert: 'the devoted work of two or three persons' prevented complete collapse.[38] In areas as diverse as Uxbridge and Salford local officials opposed membership campaigns because this would dilute their power or because there were too few workers to undertake the task.[39]

At the same time, the national party and many already overworked constituency activists attempted to address the problem. Regional Labour officials encouraged membership drives and promoted the involvement of local trade-union officials.[40] They encouraged attempts to recruit more working-class women members by focusing on the council estates. A different and more imaginative form of politics and less formal activities were suggested. Tea-groups, young mothers' clubs and discussion circles were set up. At least one party discussion paper (on discrimination against women) was drawn up following consultation with such groups. 'New' issues – unwanted pregnancies, the under-fives and related matters – were debated at Labour conferences.[41] Individual parties took recruitment within immigrant communities more seriously. The London Labour Party reported it could not 'describe itself as being fully representative of the community as a whole whilst the coloured membership of the Labour Party remains as low as it is at the moment'. This is not to argue that sexism (like racism) was absent; on the contrary. Women remained under-represented within the party and especially on constituency executives, whilst Labour's failure to recruit amongst the ethnic minorities, even in Coventry, Southall or Bradford, was hardly encouraging.[42]

In Wales – and probably elsewhere – a new generation of parliamentary candidates tried to reactivate the party during the 1960s.[43] Sometimes coming fresh from university politics, or with a history in protest groups, they encouraged a more campaigning approach. Helped by a core of existing party workers and new recruits, they sought to recreate features of party activity from the past – a vibrant social life, the support of Labour clubs, targeted campaigning using leaflets or news-sheets and educational classes to inform and involve activists. An influx of middle-class and generally younger members (often from the public sector) was reported even in working-class seats, such as Sheffield and Barnsley. At the same time, however, a number of party members – including moderates with a long history of social concern – felt deeply disappointed by what they saw as the Labour government's massive cuts in public expenditure after 1967. The party's failure to deliver its own agenda contributed to its problems.

The new enthusiasts recruited in the 1960s – often first-generation middle class – and existing party workers faced an uphill struggle. More expenditure cuts after 1976 were followed by a further drop in party membership. In many areas organisation shrivelled to nothing. Unrepresentative factions had gained control of a few ward committees during the 1960s.[44] In the 1970s supporters of the Trotskyite *Militant* newspaper claimed that a number of seats 'dominated by politically dead old men and women' were now 'ossified cliques'. There would be 'enormous opportunities' to infiltrate and control local parties.[45] A more liberal approach to party discipline after 1966 – including the abolition of the proscribed list – helped the left gain power, as did declining local trade-union participation, especially from the manual and craft unions. When one MP for a safe South Wales seat attempted to fight a Militant-backed attempt to de-select him, he found many 'moderate' unions were not even affiliated.[46] Of the six million affiliated trade-union members in the 1980s, only around 4,000 were active party members. Most of these were drawn from the white-collar or public-sector unions, which were shifting to the left.[47]

A major study conducted in 1989 revealed the impact of these changes and trends.[48] Membership was high in the south-east (with more than 30 per cent of the total) and low in Labour's heartlands (apart from the north-west). Forty per cent of Labour members were women (slightly lower than in the 1960s), and although less than 5 per cent were under twenty-five, 40 per cent were aged 26–45. Only a quarter of members were manual workers and very few belonged to ethnic minorities. Two-thirds worked in the public sector; a third had a higher degree; three-quarters owned their own home. Socially, the party's membership was hardly representative of its electoral base.

The values and politics of the rank and file before the Second World War

The earliest activists were frequently motivated by deep moral commitment, and by disgust at a capitalist system which deprived people of

Duncan Tanner

opportunity, enlightenment, pleasure and beauty.[49] Many had previously worked within the Liberal fold and had chapel roots. A puritanical approach to the evils of drink, gambling and popular culture permeated party rhetoric. Yet although many activists expressed their moral indignation at the injustice of capitalism (and its individual consequences), they also worked practically to ameliorate conditions, notably through local government, and to raise hopes and expectations. Nor did they simply accept Liberal values. Labour had its own reasons for supporting classic Liberal policies (such as free trade), never accepting that the market distributed resources fairly or efficiently. The party's commitment to nationalisation in 1918 was adopted without conflict. Across the party capitalism was seen as inefficient and unfair, pushing wages down and encouraging selfishness and greed. State intervention – as government policy during the war had demonstrated – was more efficient and equitable. Similarly, although Labour supported work over welfare, this stemmed from a belief in the dignity of labour and the morality of its reward. Intemperance too meant a loss of self-control and self-respect and an irresponsible attitude to the children and women whose survival depended on frugal use of a meagre income. (Although of course many also took a more relaxed approach. A list of Labour MPs whose careers were ruined by alcohol would fill a substantial appendix.) This was neither Marxism nor liberalism. It was a socialism rooted in experience. Many who imbibed these values were still leading the party in 1945.

Yet Labour also drew on a broader ideological tradition. In some areas – notably parts of Lancashire and the West Midlands – a substantial number of Labour activists came from Tory backgrounds.[50] Many more had no sympathy for a utopian socialist moralism. A number were practically minded trade unionists, some of whom clashed with socialist activists during the party's infancy. None the less, 'socialists' and 'trade unionists' were not distinct groups and did not always disagree. What divided members was often less significant than their common features – a stubborn nature, firm views and a commitment to creating real and practical changes in people's lives. Arguments conducted with conviction and energy often made small differences seem much larger. In the everyday realities of constituency politics, most found common cause in the pursuit of electoral success and the assault on class injustice, and later in the delivery of quality public services.

Many affluent rank-and-file socialists from the pre-war period played a significant part in defining the party's intellectual orientation before and after 1918. There were a fair number of little-known Fabian reformers in the mould of Sidney and Beatrice Webb – reformers motivated by a belief in 'Truth and Facts', with no faith in dogma and a strategy for change based on 'a new model army of vigilant administrators'.[51] However, others – including many women – were drawn from families with a history of unconventional radicalism, frequently religious in origin. They demonstrated their commitment by forming trade unions for the least skilled or through service on local Poor Law boards and councils.[52] Several formally educated activists, including some of the party's prominent early leaders and intellectuals (such as Clement Attlee, Arthur Greenwood, R. H. Tawney and E. F. Wise) worked for organisations such as Toynbee Hall, the Workers' Educational Association or Ruskin College.

The socially broader membership which Labour built up after 1918 did not necessarily dilute the party's radicalism or alter its ethical emphasis.[53] The gap between radical Liberals and some members of the ILP before 1914 was hardly substantial. Many shared interests in women's suffrage, democratic control of foreign policy and social reform. The circumstances of war allowed Labour to stress its commitment to moral reform and international brotherhood. These aspects attracted many former Liberals, reinforcing the 'socialist' element within the party. At the same time, some recruits – neglected until recently by historians – were attracted by the party's support for 'sensible' reform and progress. Some were former Tories, but not all Tory recruits were moderates, and not all ex-Liberal recruits gravitated to the left. Wartime experiences and attitudes to specific policies were just two elements governing an individual's ideological orientation.[54]

New members did, however, broaden the party's concerns. With more women members, issues relating to women's lives – such as birth control, nursery schools, state educational allowances for children and housing – gained prominence (although not as much as some wished). Frequently, Liberal and Tory converts focused on foreign and imperial policy, disarmament and peace, expanding Labour's expertise in these areas.

Whilst activists did not have a single conception of 'socialism', many believed that Labour should be more than an electoral machine. Almost instinctively doubting the validity of 'conventional' economic views, many were sympathetic to 'dissident' Labour programmes. As one ILP newspaper put it:

The official element in the Labour Movement also has 'experts' on the brain . . . They accept the spokesmen of the Banks being right every time. We must be controlled by Cunliffe Committees and Genoa Conventions, where the bankers' representatives laid down the principles of sane finance. The true revolutionary is never an expert. He does not know the truth, he feels it. He is instinctively right, he knows what is wrong because he is a revolutionary.[55]

Duncan Tanner

A simplistic version of Hobson's 'underconsumptionist' views seemed to be particularly prevalent amongst the rank-and-file.[56] Equally, leaders renowned for their idealism, such as Keir Hardie and George Lansbury, were venerated. Nor was such support confined to the party's 'heroes'. When H. N. Brailsford was removed as editor of the *New Leader* in 1926, he received a host of supportive letters. The *New Leader*'s 'aggressive policy', one supporter wrote, 'its brains and its human-ness [sic] . . . and its wide interests' had stood for 'a socialism that embraces the whole of life'. This reflected what many middle-class socialists wanted from their leaders.[57]

Rank-and-file radicalism became more visible in the 1930s. The left's hostility to fascism, imperialism, nationalism, xenophobic irrationalism, armaments and war again attracted many middle-class Labour members. Stafford Cripps (himself an affluent ex-Tory) developed a campaign of protest against the 'moderation' of Labour policy which received considerable support, both from middle-class socialists and others. It was passionate, active, inspiring, but not always very practical. Cripps' approach offered little as regards domestic policy and involved working with the Communist Party, and later others, in a 'Popular Front' against fascism. Conflict ensued. Throughout the 1920s Labour leaders had policed the ideological boundaries of the party through conference resolutions and the actions of party officials. In the 1930s they again used the party machine, this time to suppress Popular Front dissidents. However, they also provided a concrete alternative to the left. A policy of 'practical socialism' was outlined by Dalton, developed by Morrison and turned into a clear programme by 1937.[58] The appeal of such programmes to ordinary members has seldom been given sufficient recognition. Many of the most active wanted to make a difference. The papers of policy advisory committees established in the 1920s, of policy discussion groups in the 1930s, and of back-bench MPs all show a desire to be involved in the construction of practical schemes.

Party members at local level were no different. In the 1920s women's sections encouraged the adoption of a broader programme of welfare reforms. In the 1930s women *and* men wished to protect communities from the ravages of unemployment, to restructure the local economy, improve housing and to develop social services.[59] In more affluent areas, Labour stressed its desire to build better, more cohesive, communities. A practical, interventionist, socialism of the kind advocated by the national leadership gained substantial support from party members. In London, Labour's propaganda machine used newspapers to put over its message, extending the process which had operated so successfully in 1929. By

1935 the *Citizen* newspaper was being delivered to a million homes. In the syndicated pages of the paper, Labour stressed social services and amenities – welfare centres, council housing, public parks, nursery schools, good bridges and transport – as examples of its 'practical socialism'. In pages tailored to local circumstances, leaders reinforced the message, using local examples to claim that the 'main vehicle of national progress has been the development of social welfare through local government institutions . . . putting communal wealth, collected through rates, at the disposal of all who need what the community can give'. Rhetorical tirades and political inaction were equally inappropriate. The circumstances demanded 'sensible thinking, practical schemes which, put into operation, will quickly bring prosperity to the mass of the people'.[60]

Labour's collectivism was contrasted with the immoral, inefficient, selfish individualism of capitalism. Consumers were exploited by capitalist profiteers. Food was destroyed or hoarded to drive up prices. In opposing this, Labour stood not for the views of an active political minority, but for the whole community.[61] Addressing women, one woman councillor noted: 'Whatever our opinions, whether we are politically minded or not, we are forced against political problems by influences we cannot escape.' Labour avoided the rhetoric of class politics. Class division and inequality existed, but class war, on the other hand, was 'a consciously created state', nurtured by 'wretchedness and intolerable oppression; its product more often than not a Fascist state'.[62] Several parties involved members in petitions against war or in raising funds to help Spanish children and refugees. Whilst the aim was laudable, so too was the method of mass public collections. In mobilising humanity, Labour felt it was building socialism.[63]

There was not an inevitable gulf between the values and policies of 'party leaders' on the one hand and the views of 'rank-and-file' activists on the other. Where national policies were practical, ethical, involved collectivist solutions and were backed by a socialist vision, members and activists responded, as did the party's supporters. Although the Popular Front movement competed to represent the values of activists, simultaneously rousing the party and creating chaos in several constituency organisations, it was the leadership's conception of a practical socialism which triumphed overall.

The values and ideas of party members since 1945

A fuller if still incomplete picture of members' views can be drawn for the post-war years. A variety of studies indicate that, until the 1970s at least, there was considerable continuity with the pre-war position.

Members explained their political commitment not in complex ideological terms, but by referring to Labour as the party of the working class or
the disadvantaged. A radical family background, disgust at those
responsible for poverty and degradation and a commitment to doing
something about these injustices were still the dominant motivations.
Many took pride at their success in small but locally significant fights for
better conditions. Middle-class activists were probably no more dominant than they had been in the past.[64] At the same time, some oral testimony reinforces an academic emphasis on the rise of a 'constituency left'
after 1945 and the growth of conflict with party leaders. It has been
argued that a significant shift to the left during the post-war Labour
government resulted in up to a hundred constituency Labour parties
submitting radical conference resolutions, and warning that socialist
principles should not be abandoned.[65] The politics of the 1950s are often
portrayed as a conflict between Bevanite constituency activists, on the
one hand, and right-wing party leaders bent on redefining party philosophy on the other. Equally, historians have stressed rank-and-file radicalism in the 1960s, noting also that from the 1970s different types of
left-wing activists 'captured' constituency parties, most notably in
London and Liverpool. In the 1980s, the creation of an electoral college,
and proposals for the re-selection of MPs, strengthened the left.
Defections to the SDP enhanced its numerical strength and weakened
the political credibility of those moderates who remained. With a new
intellectual vitality, and a new leader in Tony Benn, the left mounted a
serious challenge. By the late 1970s rank-and-file views had shifted. A
belief in extra-parliamentary campaigning, in the need to control an
altered international capitalism through state regulation, and to address
injustice as it influenced women, gays, ethnic minorities and the young,
came to the fore. Moderate leaders received a hostile reception at party
conferences. In the aftermath of the party's defeat in 1979, constituency
radicals pushed forward. In 1983 the party adopted its most radical
manifesto ever.

Despite this emphasis, there is little to suggest the membership as a
whole was converted to a dissident radicalism. Members had applauded
the 1945–51 Labour government's achievements. Its combination of
collectivist and ethical aims, practical measures and a socialist vision
coincided with the values of many activists themselves. Throughout the
1950s and 1960s constituency parties seldom rebelled against the leadership in large numbers (except on public ownership, by now a party
article of faith).[66] Studies of local party activity in Wales and Salford
during this period indicate that unity around shared practical concerns

was far more common than ideological division. The 'Bevanites' never really presented a rival strategy and groups like Victory for Socialism tried without success to unify constituency dissidents.[67] Even during the 1970s and early 1980s, whilst there were seats where 'moderate' MPs were de-selected by radicalised constituency parties, around three-quarters of MPs were re-selected without opposition. Only eight were de-selected before the 1983 election, six before the 1987 campaign.[68] The Militant Tendency had some success – notably in Liverpool, where it obtained control of local Labour parties and the city council. The left also did well in London. Such parties had their own radical agendas. London's was designed to attract a 'rainbow coalition' of the disaffected, reflecting ideas absorbed from feminist and other groups. Yet many parties outside the south-east – including many led by and from 'the left' – continued to advocate more traditional policies, trying to defend services through their control of local government and attract jobs through local initiatives. Even London Labour parties adopted similar ideas. Official Labour policy also gradually incorporated some 'new' rank-and-file concerns.

The gap between 'leaders' and 'members' was also less pronounced than many have indicated. A limited number of genuinely critical activists gained disproportionate amounts of attention, creating a false impression of the rank and file as a whole. Moreover, the popular media constructed a distorted image of these activists, further exaggerating the apparent differences. Commitment was painted as fanaticism, a respect for minorities as faddism, a concern to end discrimination as 'extremist'. The activists' concern for inequality and injustice, their compassion and willingness to undertake dull and unpaid tasks within local communities, was ignored. In the early 1980s Labour activists were as popular as estate agents (though seemingly less numerous). As John O'Farrell writes of his experiences in London: 'Declaring that I was a socialist was like saying, "I am completely misguided and vaguely deviant – please be as hostile as you like".'[69]

'Hard left' activists tended to be concentrated in London, as were left organisations such as the Campaign for Labour Party Democracy and the Labour Co-ordinating Committee (LCC). Although *London Labour Briefing* tried to engineer the adoption of radical candidates in 1982, the main cause of the left's success was not its 'organisation' but the paucity of credible alternatives, the changed composition of the party, the contagious enthusiasm (and compelling emotionalism) of the left.[70] Less radical party members could also be swayed by elements of the left's programme. Many saw themselves as being 'on the left'. They supported

Duncan Tanner

particular protests against the leadership's actions (or inaction), especially when core party values (a belief in equality, collectivism and world peace) were seemingly abandoned by the party's leaders. The party contained many natural rebels. The left's support for unilateral disarmament in the 1970s and 1980s drew in many older activists who had supported CND (the Campaign for Nuclear Disarmament) in the 1960s (just as CND in the 1960s had drawn in many who supported the peace movement and anti-war movement of the 1930s). None the less, Labour's membership as a whole was not 'converted' to a radical agenda at odds with the leadership. By the mid-1980s there were even fewer differences between 'activists', 'members' and 'voters' (with the exception of nationalisation and nuclear disarmament).[71] Indeed, by the time Neil Kinnock became leader, even groups such as the LCC were moving away from a position on the oppositional left. Once the Conservatives were returned to office for a second term in 1983, the left's agenda seemed less attractive to those outside the ideologically committed core. Indeed, its failure both to grasp and adapt to shifts in public opinion now seemed dangerous. Only an effective opposition could save Labour's traditional supporters from a predatory right-wing movement. Items of rank-and-file faith – the national health service, the principle of public-sector provision – were under attack, whilst the poor and disadvantaged were paying the price of Britain's post-industrial renaissance.

The extent of this shift became evident when Neil Kinnock enfranchised ordinary party members through the introduction of individual voting (one member, one vote – OMOV) through a process of gradual – and contested – changes between 1984 and 1990. When Benn and Heffer challenged for the positions of leader and deputy leader in 1988, Kinnock won over 80 per cent of the vote in the constituencies section. Only 20 of the 112 constituency parties voting for Benn had balloted their members. In the deputy leadership campaign, Hattersley won support from three-quarters of parties which had conducted a poll.[72] Under Blair, a larger membership voted overwhelmingly in support of New Labour initiatives.

Despite the myths created by some radical activists and echoed by some historians, there has been a considerable area of agreement between ordinary Labour Party members and party leaders at most points in the party's history. Moreover, and as the following section indicates, when tensions have spread more widely, it has seldom been a direct consequence of formal ideological differences. Rather, past actions and suspicions became fossilised into a party tradition which exaggerated tensions between leaders and members and created a language of conflict which even some moderates found difficult to resist.

Leaders and members

By 1914 several leading Labour figures had developed an ambivalent attitude to the party's members. Ramsay MacDonald faced personal and hostile criticism from a section of the ILP, and whilst Labour conferences repeatedly endorsed MacDonald's practical emphasis and strategy, many activists shared his critics' reservations. MacDonald recognised rank-and-file fears. His response had two elements. First, he proposed devolving some responsibilities for administering party strategy, so that members could experience the constraints under which leaders operated. Second, he tried to construct an attractive and constructive programme which would 'rescue socialism entirely from the turning of phrases and impossible policies and make it a living and constructive thing'.[73] Members would thus be drawn away from the left's 'impossibilism'. Wartime and post-war conflict within the party confirmed his views. 'How much better it would be', he recorded in 1921, 'if people would honestly face the inevitable problems of political action and accustom their followers to realities'.[74]

MacDonald, Snowden and other leading figures faced further hostile attacks in the 1920s. During the second Labour government a section of the ILP turned every meeting of the parliamentary party into open warfare. MacDonald became even more distant from colleagues. He seemed to abandon the search for a 'constructive socialism' which would win over critics. Increasingly, all debate was seen as negative criticism. Members who railed against the system and constructive advocates of a more progressive reformism were tarred with the same brush, their views similarly ignored. Whilst he still expressed concern about the party's over-dependence on a few people, he was unwilling to accept its involvement in the policy process. 'Between the top and bottom of the movement', he noted, there was a 'silly, agitating, brainless' cohort, who frightened potential supporters with their impossible demands and encouraged popular expectations which could not be satisfied. He added: 'a certain number of us are not going to accept resolutions or pronouncements made by people or Conferences which are irresponsible or who are making decisions which they are not in a position to make with wisdom and which, indeed, are quite outside their business'.[75] MacDonald pounced on suggestions made by moderate experts from the party's advisory committees, noting in his diary that the whole party research system had 'let us down badly' and that poor advice in opposition would 'doom us as a government'.[76] In the end, he reacted to two decades of negative and often impractical opposition by abandoning his

Duncan Tanner

own, and his party's, attempt to create a constructive socialism and succumbed to the views of the economic establishment.

The 1931 debacle convinced leading trade-union and party figures that more concrete policies and a broader and a more effective campaigning base were essential. Whilst they were concerned that leaders should not in future abandon the party's agreed programme, they were even more concerned that the party programme should be popular and practical. As a result, party leaders attacked the left, often using the block vote, party rule book and pressure from party officials to marginalise the left's allegedly impractical ideas. An understandable concern over the left's capacity to repel support created a sense of paranoia which militated against any broader involvement, paradoxically at a time when the leadership was promoting a mass membership and trying to create an attractive and practical programme.

When the New Fabian Research Bureau and the Socialist League offered research assistance in the wake of the 1931 crisis, the leadership's own research units rebelled, warning of 'unofficial and it may be irresponsible policy-making by outside bodies'.[77] They also tried to stifle debate within Labour newspapers (notably the TUC-backed *New Clarion*), complaining that 'instead of emphasis being placed upon official policy and an attempt being made to get this over to the movement, more space is given to points of view which conflict with official policy'. A lengthy calendar of radical statements made in the *New Clarion*'s pages was sent to Bevin and Citrine.[78]

Other attempts to become involved received similar treatment. When moderate MPs and intellectuals formed the '1932 Club' in response to the trade unions' growing monopolisation of policy debate, TUC officials worked to undermine it.[79] The club's chief organiser commented that following these activities he faced a choice: 'if I continue to exercise my legitimate rights to improve and broaden the appeal of the Labour party, the whole weight of the Trade Union Congress would be used to exclude me from holding any responsible position in a party which I have done as much to serve during the last thirty years as any Trade Union leader'. The 'constituencies movement' of the later 1930s was viewed with equal suspicion by Labour leaders and officials. Originating in the home counties, the movement's leaders sought to create regional federations, organise constituency opinion and dilute the power of the block vote. Although there were links to critics of the leadership, the movement attracted support across the south-east from activists who felt under-utilised, including practically minded former MPs and candidates such as Charles Ammon and Patrick Gordon Walker.[80]

268

Whilst the party machine was used to attack these activities, under Hugh Dalton's direction, the party conference in 1937 allowed constituencies to elect an increased proportion of the NEC and rallied the party around a new programme.

The expulsion of Stafford Cripps and other dissidents in 1939 illustrates the tensions between activists and leaders. Even moderate party members felt the expulsion of 'good socialists' smacked of central domination. Radicals were more incensed. 'If this is the Executive's idea of democracy within the party', one ordinary member wrote, then 'it still has a good deal to learn'. Writing to the TUC secretary Walter Citrine in support of Cripps, another stated: 'the labour movement is mine as well as yours and in a democratic movement my voice ought to count just as much as yours'. None the less, Cripps' constant flouting of conference resolutions, and the membership's opposition to alliances with other parties, undermined rank-and-file sympathy.[81] He had breached too many elements of the party's operational ideology.

Party leaders displayed a similar fear of rank-and-file movements in the aftermath of war. When the Victory for Socialism movement attempted to establish pre-conference meetings of constituency activists, they were warned by party officials, who threatened to place the organisation on the proscribed list. Regional organisers and party officials played an increasingly substantial role in ensuring that local parties followed the national line, even if they were also capable of arguing against it (as they did in Wales over devolution).[82] As the political journalist Alan Watkins comments on the contribution of the party's National Agent, Sara Barker, in the early 1960s: 'a hint of heresy, a whiff of recalcitrance, and Sara's tanks would emerge at dead of night from the concrete garages deep under Transport House and move unstoppably towards the offending part of the country'.[83]

Party leaders faced many critical party conferences during the later 1960s and 1970s, and increasingly relied on the union block vote. Leaders abandoned the liberal approach to party discipline adopted in the 1960s, refused to endorse some prospective parliamentary candidates selected by constituency parties and launched enquiries into infiltration by the militant left. Alongside this, they once again tried to involve ordinary members and gain their support. One such exercise – termed 'Participation '69' – was based on similar campaigns conducted by Swedish socialists. On a number of subsequent occasions – notably in 1976 – MPs were sent on consultation tours to discuss policy with constituency delegates. In Wales party officials sent out questionnaires to gather opinions on the party's draft manifesto in 1980. There was little negative criticism. Indeed, as one party commented, members had 'welcomed the opportunity to become involved in the preparation of the manifesto at an early stage'.[84] None the less, the paucity of such initiatives fed the idea that party leaders were not to be trusted.

Members and leaders

Although the degree of conflict between members and leaders has been overstated, this is not to suggest that activists have been docile and compliant. A party so closely associated with 'fraternity' has shown precious little of this in its internal relations. Some conflict (at local level as in government) has resulted from the clash of strong and ambitious personalities and a tendency to destructive argument.[85] Parliamentary candidates contributing too little to their constituency, and local parties contributing little to the political survival of their MPs clashed on numerous occasions between the wars.[86] Genuine political differences have been regularly inflamed by social differences between 'new' and 'old' recruits. When Labour recruited articulate middle-class activists in the 1920s, young feminists in the late 1960s or Asian activists in the 1990s, sections of the party felt dispossessed, whilst the 'new' elements, charged with enthusiasm, found the baggage of Labour's past hard to accept. One Cambridge recruit in the 1920s expressed the position bluntly: 'working in the Labour movement is often a sordid job – one has to attend atrocious Jazz band socials [and] canvass among drink sodden, coarse folk'.[87] In 1969 it was reported that the 'posturing' of many radicals commanded 'little respect among hard working party members', whilst older women members objected to 'their' conference being taken over by feminists.[88] Young socialists were frequently told to behave like serious adults and could reply with similar disdain. The 'openness' of Labour politics in the 1970s and 1980s attracted recruits from new areas and ideological backgrounds. Some rapidly learnt the ways of the Labour machine, at times removing complacent, corrupt or inert traditionalists from key posts, at times alienating older members.[89]

The party's traditions also encouraged conflict. A distrust of leadership 'cabals' had been a feature of Britain's radical tradition since before the Chartists. It was a tradition turned into mythology after the events of 1931.[90] The desire to be consulted and for leaders to be accountable was a regular source of disputes. Between the wars, many individual Labour councillors proved reluctant to attend ward meetings. Activists expected to have their say. The result was conflict and suspensions. During the 1945–51 Labour government, parties were suspicious of the 'men at the top' and insisted on accountability in everything.[91] By the 1970s the

Labour left viewed all leadership actions with suspicion, pronouncing them undemocratic in a vitriolic and critical new version of an older Labour vocabulary. These arguments had a broader resonance, but party leaders only gradually recognised that radical activists were a small minority, and that members would support an electorally viable, constructive policy, presented as the outcome of Labour's values (as they had done in the past). Following Neil Kinnock's election as leader in 1983, centralised control over the presentation and management of strategy was accompanied by the devolution of power to ordinary members. The organised left – and many constituency activists – were cynical about these efforts, but direct enfranchisement was a credible means of drawing in less active members. It was certainly more 'democratic' than conference policy determined by the block vote or constituency decisions determined by a handful of activists. Internal communications improved. Under Kinnock, *Labour Party News,* the members' newsletter, provided (some) information and analysis.[92] The LCC's commission on party democracy produced a shrewd plan for increasing membership participation.[93] Further steps were taken under Smith and Blair. There was growing awareness of the party's imperfect organisation and democratic deficit. New party discussion groups such as the Labour Party Policy Forum, NEXUS ('Britain's first virtual think tank') and the Local Government Network, together with a variety of new and reborn party organisations (including a livelier Fabian Society) tried to make an educated and informed membership feel involved. The results of such changes were not merely cosmetic. The introduction of quotas and the 'pairing' of constituencies for candidate selection took power away from general management committees and ensured that more women became candidates. New Labour attracted new members, willing to accept the leaders' line. A constructive party, with power in its grasp, presenting its policies as part of a clear socialist vision, once again won support through the purchase of its ideas.

None the less, the strategy as a whole has not been entirely successful. Membership campaigns in the 1990s seemed concerned with improving party income, offering a plethora of 'membership benefits', including Labour Party credit cards, mobile phones, and a range of other 'stunning merchandise'. Those who hoped for more were initially disappointed. The 1988 'Labour listens' campaign, its organisers noted, was a 'mess'. Many of those attending the local discussion sessions were no more representative than general management committees. As Tom Sawyer noted at the 1989 party conference: 'The party isn't in a position to handle proper membership participation in policy-making.'[94] Under

Duncan Tanner

Blair, policy 'consultation' seemed to consist of plebiscites. On several occasions New Labour leaders failed to heed the feelings of members. Whilst a majority of party members in Wales voted for Rhodri Morgan to lead the party in the Welsh Assembly, Alun Michael (the candidate preferred by London) triumphed through the support of trade-union block votes. Many party members were subsequently reluctant to campaign for the party in the first National Assembly elections. Those who warned that the party could become 'de-energised' as a result of managerial centralism and the dissolution of constituency links seemed to have a point.[95] Membership started to fall. In the past, campaigns – and a capacity to influence matters through local government – gave Labour activists a purpose; a successful reforming agenda produced a sense of satisfaction and of progress. New Labour has yet to develop a full alternative means of embracing its potential rank-and-file sympathisers, regularly alienating even those willing to accept many of its aims.

Labour's membership has always been sympathetic to leaders who developed a successful, constructive, moral, programme. At the same time, the rank and file has contained many articulate critics, concerned to have their views respected and for the party to advance policies which reflect its compassionate ideals. At times dissident elements have constructed arguments which gained broader support, building on the values of activists and ingrained myths and fears about the proclivities of party leaders. Criticism, extremism and apathy from a section of the rank and file have reinforced the leaders' desire to keep control in the hands of a small group of professionals, committed to their line. However, by failing to mobilise potential sympathisers within the party, by relegating party activism to drudgery for the cause, leaders allowed the membership to shrink and in some constituencies to fall into the hands of those with little sympathy for a moderate and reforming agenda. In the 1990s constitutional changes and the party's successful return to power gave party leaders more power, overcoming the problems created by an unrepresentative group of activists in the 1970s and 1980s, and in theory at least giving individual members more direct say in party affairs. At the same time, the party's articulate and educated membership remains an under-utilised and potentially disaffected resource. This is not because the majority would prefer massively different policies to those proffered by party leaders, but because leaders still fail to employ the membership's knowledge, utilise their idealism, or create a coherent, socialist package of reforms which they can support with enthusiasm – and for some, because in the presentation of policy the language, traditions and values of the party as an institution are too

272

seldom heeded. A mass membership may seem less necessary now Labour is a modern, professional, organisation which can attract funding from the wealthy, use the mass media, telephone and internet to address the electorate, and focus groups and think-tanks to gauge and make opinion. It may also be that the values and expectations of party members had to change. However, it is not yet evident how recent changes will create the active and participatory citizenship, the local involvement and community development, which New Labour in opposition offered as its vision for a new country.

Duncan Tanner

Notes

I am grateful to Nick Tiratsoo and Steven Fielding for comments and references, to Cyril Parry for diligent attention to an earlier draft and to the University of Wales Bangor for research expenses.

1 See Berger, ch. 10 below.

2 Patrick Seyd and Paul Whiteley, *Labour's Grass Roots. The Politics of Party Membership* (Oxford: Clarendon Press, 1992), pp. 13–19. Official membership figures cited below are from the relevant *Report of the Annual Conference of the Labour Party.*

3 For the ILP, David Howell, *British Workers and the Independent Labour Party 1888–1906* (Manchester: Manchester University Press, 1983), pp. 327–42. For Labour, Duncan Tanner, *Political Change and the Labour Party 1900–18* (Cambridge: Cambridge University Press, 1990); Ian Hutchison, *A Political History of Scotland 1832–1924* (Edinburgh: John Donald, 1986), pp. 245–65.

4 Hutchison, *Political History of Scotland*, pp. 294–5; Hamilton Labour Party minutes, 1918–35 passim: D. Hatvany, 'Introduction to the minutes of Aberdeen Labour Party', p. 12. (These microfilmed minutes are part of Microform Limited's 'Origins and development of the Labour Party at local level' series. Where no other location is given, minutes cited are from this series.)

5 South Shields Labour Party minutes, 27 February 1928. For other examples, Llanelli Labour Party minutes, 18 March 1929, Carmarthenshire County Record Office; Sowerby Labour Party minutes, 23 December 1924, Calderdale Archives; Kenneth Dean, *Town and Westminster. A Political History of Walsall from 1906–1945* (Walsall: Walsall Libraries Department, 1972), pp. 77–9, 142–4; Jack Reynolds and Keith Laybourn, *Labour Heartland. A History of the Labour Party in West Yorkshire during the Inter-War Years* (Bradford: Bradford University Press, 1987), pp. 40–1.

6 Newport Labour Party papers, particularly *Annual Report and Balance Sheet*, 1923, 1924, University of Swansea; E. J. Alford, 'The problem of rural constituencies', *Labour Organiser* no. 84 (June 1928), 110–11.

7 *London Citizen*, Tottenham edition (August 1921), (February 1924), (March 1927), (July 1927).

8 'How we made our membership', *Labour Organiser* no. 102 (December 1929), 'Membership', *Labour Organiser* no. 188 (February 1937), 21; 'Romford. How they got over 7000 members', *Labour Organiser* no. 192 (June 1937), 101–2. For the context, Anrezej Olechnowicz, *Working-Class Housing in England between the Wars: The Beacontree Estate* (Oxford: Clarendon Press, 1997), ch. 4; and Tom Jeffrey, 'The suburban nation. Politics and class in Lewisham', in David Feldman and Gareth Stedman Jones (eds.), *Metropolis. Histories and Representations since 1800* (London: Routledge, 1989), p. 196.

9 Bernard Donoughue and George Jones, *Herbert Morrison. Portrait of a Politician* (London: Weidenfeld and Nicolson, 1973), pp. 70–8.

10 Duncan Tanner, 'Class voting and radical politics: the Liberal and Labour

274

parties, 1910–31', in Jon Lawrence and Miles Taylor (eds.), *Party, State and Society. Electoral Behaviour in Britain since 1820* (London: Scolar Press, 1997), pp. 120–2.

11 A. C. Powell, 'Labour individual membership', *Labour Organiser*, 9 (March 1931), 47; H. E. Roberts, 'How East Bristol makes its members', *Labour Organiser* no. 11 (May 1931), 84; A. C. Powell, 'How Carlisle got its 4430 members', *Labour Organiser* no. 128 (February 1932), 19. For Bristol see R. Whitfield, 'The Labour movement in Bristol 1914–39', M.Litt. thesis (University of Bristol, 1982), pp. 303–7, 349–50.

12 Huw Beynon and Terry Austrin, *Masters and Servants. Class and Patronage in the Making of a Labour Organisation* (London: Rivers Oram Press, 1994), pp. 258–9; Joyce Quinn, 'Introduction to Wansbeck Labour Party minutes', p. 6; Pauline Lynn, 'The shaping of political allegiance: class, gender, nation and locality in County Durham 1918–45', Ph.D. thesis (University of Teesside, 1999), pp. 74–5; Neil Evans and Dot Jones, '"To help forward the great work of humanity": women in the Labour Party in Wales', in Duncan Tanner, Chris Williams and Deian Hopkin (eds.), *The Labour Party in Wales 1900–2000* (Cardiff: University of Wales Press, 2000), pp. 220–1, 226.

13 G. A. Wilcox to W. Citrine, 16 June 1934, TUC Archives, MSS 292/79T/20, Modern Records Centre, University of Warwick (hereafter MRC).

14 Wrexham Trades Council and Divisional Labour Party minutes, 9 February and 16 August 1932; Stockport Labour Party minutes, 17 August 1936, 23 March 1937. See, similarly, Swansea Labour Association, *Annual Report 1933*, West Glamorgan County Record Office.

15 This point is made in a series of little-known local studies: e.g. Raymond South, *Heights and Depths. Labour in Windsor* (Windsor: Colophon Press, 1985), pp. 11–15; Peter Kingsford, *The Labour Movement in Hatfield 1918–70* (Hatfield: Hatfield Polytechnic, 1988), pp. 8–9, 16, 21; David Pretty, *The Rural Revolt that Failed. Farm Workers' Trade Unions in Wales 1889–1950* (Cardiff: University of Wales Press, 1989), pp. 89, 167, 171.

16 Sheffield Labour Party, *Annual Report 1936*; Duncan Tanner, 'The pattern of Labour politics in Wales 1918–39', in Tanner et al., *The Labour Party in Wales*, p. 120.

17 Tanner, 'The pattern of Labour politics', pp. 122–3; Birmingham Borough Labour Party minutes, 13 June 1929.

18 R. Graham and J. Jolly to J. Henry Lloyd, 14 October 1924, Lloyd MS DHL/7, University of Hull (hereafter Univ. Hull). Lloyd received similar letters from South Leeds, Hull North-West and other parties.

19 South Derbyshire Divisional Labour Party minutes, 15 August, 22 September 1928, Derbyshire County Record Office (hereafter DCRO); J. Loxton to L. Straw, 4 March and 14 April 1929, G. Pole to Pollard, 28 June 1930, Lewis Straw MS D2928/2/11, DCRO. Straw was the election agent.

20 South Derbyshire Divisional Labour Party, *Annual Report and Balance Sheet*, 1927 and 1930, DCRO. Labour Party minutes for Birmingham, Gloucester, Brecon and Radnor, Bedford and other seats suggest this was not unusual.

Duncan Tanner

Candidates continued to help financially after the war. See, for example, F. Lindop, 'Greenwich Labour Party 1920–1987' (Wakefield: Microform Academic Publishers, 1998), p. 7, noting a contribution of over £2,000 p.a. from Guy Barnett, MP during the 1980s.

21 O. Mosley to W. Whiteley, 25 January 1928, W. Whiteley MS UL 6/3 and for the financial details, O. Mosley to W. Whiteley, 23 June, 21 and 23 August, 9 November 1926, A. Young to W. Whiteley, 14 March 1927, W. Whiteley MS UL 6/4, Borthwick Institute, University of York (hereafter Univ. York).

22 Llanelli Divisional Labour Party, *Annual Report*, 1938, Carmarthenshire County Record Office. For agents helping to shoulder financial problems, see G. Pole to G. Lansbury, 22 May 1935 (re. Cardiff), Pole MS UL 5/4, Univ. York; Brecon and Radnor Labour Party minutes, 4 February 1933, National Library of Wales, Aberystwyth; Dean, *Walsall*, p. 79.

23 Steven Fielding, 'The Labour Party and the recruitment of the young, 1945–70', in Gaetano Quagliariello (ed.), *La formazione della classe politica in Europa* (Rome: Lacaita, 2000), pp. 577–98.

24 Duncan Tanner, 'The construction of the political elite, 1945–55', in ibid., p. 90. Dances and prize draws generally made money for the party. By contrast, in Stockport the drama society lost money and the orchestra had recruitment problems. See Stockport Labour Party, Fellowship Committee minutes, 15 September 1931, 24 April 1932.

25 Tanner, 'The pattern of Labour politics', p. 126. For a similar position in England see, for example, Jeffrey, 'Politics and class in Lewisham', pp. 196–7, Marie Dickie, 'Town patriotism and the rise of Labour 1918–39', Ph.D. thesis (University of Warwick, 1987), p. 118.

26 *Report of the 20th Annual Conference of the Labour Party* (London: Labour Party, 1920), p. 131; Pamela M. Graves, *Labour Women. Women in British Working-Class Politics 1918–1939* (Cambridge: Cambridge University Press, 1994), ch. 2; John Marriott, *The Culture of Labourism. The East End between the Wars* (Edinburgh: Edinburgh University Press, 1991), pp. 169–70. For ILP membership, see Howell, *British Workers*, pp. 330–5.

27 J. Fenning to Mr and Mrs Bridgeman, 12 May 1938 (re. Pinner Labour Party), Bridgeman MS DBN 8/2, Univ. Hull; Southampton Labour Party, 'Report on membership organisation in 1936' (copy in Llanelli Labour Party MS, D/POL/1/31, Carmarthenshire County Record Office). For the following, Duncan Tanner, 'The recruitment of the PLP in Britain, 1931–55', and 'The construction of the political elite', in Quagliariello, *La formazione della classe politica en Europa*, pp. 83–6, 90, 605–7.

28 Belper Labour Party, *Annual Report*, esp. 1955, DCRO.

29 Jonathan Schneer, *Labour's Conscience. The Labour Left 1945–51* (London: Unwin Hyman, 1988), pp. 177–8; Steven Fielding, Peter Thompson and Nick Tiratsoo, *'England Arise!' The Labour Party and Popular Politics in 1940s Britain* (Manchester: Manchester University Press, 1995), p. 171. Information from Wrexham Labour Party minutes courtesy of Judy Miles.

30 East Midlands' organisers' reports, 5 June 1952 (Nottingham), 17 September

1952 (North-East Derbyshire), Catermole MSS 9/3/14/104 and 9/3/14/173, MRC.
31 Andrew Walling, 'The structure of power in Labour Wales 1951–64', in Tanner et al., *The Labour Party in Wales*, pp. 211–12.
32 London organiser's reports, Catermole MSS 9/3/13/32, 9/3/14/48, 9/3/14/63, MRC.
33 Cited in Andrew Walling, '"Modernisation", policy and organisation in the Labour Party 1951–64', Ph.D. thesis (University of Wales Bangor, in progress), ch. 4.
34 Patrick Seyd, *The Rise and Fall of the Labour Left* (London: Macmillan, 1987), pp. 42–3.
35 Organiser's report, East Midlands Regional Council of the Labour Party, 21 June 1969, Catermole MSS 9/3/11/22, MRC; report of West Midlands' Labour organiser, MSS 6/3/1/252, 404, 477, 490, 514, MRC.
36 Seyd, *The Labour Left*, pp. 40–1.
37 Sue Goss, *Local Labour and Local Government. A Study of Changing Interests, Politics and Policy in Southwark from 1919 to 1982* (Edinburgh: Edinburgh University Press, 1988), p. 44; East Midlands' organiser's report, 1 February 1963, Catermole MSS 9/3/18/30, MRC.
38 Newton Heath Ward minutes, 1965–70, cited in Steven Fielding, *The Labour Party. Socialism and Society since 1951* (Manchester: Manchester University Press, 1997), pp. 80–1; Nick Tiratsoo, 'The May Day Manifesto Group', in R. Coopey, S. Fielding and N. Tiratsoo (eds.), *The Wilson Governments 1964–70* (London: Pinter, 1993), p. 165; Tom Forrester, *The Labour Party and the Working Class* (London: Heinemann, 1976), p. 80.
39 Steven Fielding, 'The "penny farthing" machine revisited: Labour Party members and participation in the 1950s and 1960s', in Chris Pierson and Simon Tormey (eds.), *Politics at the Edge* (London: Macmillan, 2000), forthcoming.
40 Welsh organiser's reports, cited in Duncan Tanner, 'Facing the new challenge: Labour and politics 1970–2000', in Tanner et al., *The Labour Party in Wales*, p. 283. See also meetings with regional TGWU officers and NUM officials in the East Midlands, 13 December 1963, 28 October and 19 November 1965, Catermole MSS 292/9/3/18/321, 9/3/20/282, 9/3/20/302, MRC.
41 Tiratsoo, 'May Day Manifesto', p. 167.
42 Steven Fielding, 'The evolution of "Wilsonism"', in Coopey et al., *The Wilson Governments*, pp. 35–6 and his 'Brotherhood and the brothers: responses to "coloured" immigration in the British Labour Party *c.* 1951–1965', *Journal of Political Ideologies* 3 (1988), 92.
43 The following derives from Tanner, 'Facing the new challenge', pp. 277–80 and Seyd, *The Labour Left*, pp. 44–6.
44 Organiser's report, 9 April, 28 October 1965, Catermole MSS 292/9/3/20/110 and 283, MRC; Eric Shaw, *Discipline and Discord in the Labour Party* (Manchester: Manchester University Press, 1988), pp. 130–3.

Duncan Tanner

45 Shaw, *Discipline and Discord*, p. 219.
46 Tanner, 'Facing the challenge', p. 283.
47 Colin Hughes and Patrick Wintour, *Labour Rebuilt. The New Model Party* (London: Fourth Estate, 1990), p. 110.
48 Seyd and Whiteley, *Labour's Grass Roots*, pp. 28–40.
49 For the following, Duncan Tanner, 'The development of British socialism', *Parliamentary History* 17 (1997), 48–66 and 'Ideological debate in Edwardian Labour politics: radicalism, revisionism and socialism', in Eugenio F. Biagini and Alastair J. Reid (eds.), *Currents of Radicalism. Popular Radicalism, Organised Labour and Party Politics in Britain 1850–1914* (Cambridge: Cambridge University Press, 1991), pp. 271–93.
50 The pre-war Tory inheritance is outlined in Howell, *British Workers*, pp. 373–88, Tanner, *Political Change*, chs. 5–6 and Jon Lawrence, *Speaking for the People. Party, Language and Popular Politics in England, 1867–1914* (Cambridge: Cambridge University Press, 1998), pp. 99–127, 246–8. For the post-war position generally, Martin Pugh, 'Class traitors: Conservative recruits to Labour 1900–1930', *English Historical Review* 113 (1998), 38–64.
51 The example cited here is F. H. Keeling: see E. Townshend (ed.), *Keeling. Letters and Recollections* (London: G. Allen and Unwin, 1918), pp. 59–60.
52 Charlotte Despard and Margaret McMillan, 'Why I became a Socialist', *Labour Leader*, 13 June, 11 July 1912. See also Jane Hannam, *Isabella Ford* (Oxford: Basil Blackwell, 1989).
53 Indeed, the ILP's alternative to MacDonald's gradualism in the 1920s (the 'Living Wage' programme) was largely drawn up by H. N. Brailsford, Frank Wise and J. A. Hobson, all educated and recent recruits to the party.
54 Some of these complexities are explained in David Blaazer, *The Popular Front and the Progressive Tradition. Socialists, Liberals and the Quest for Unity 1884–1939* (Cambridge: Cambridge University Press, 1992) and Pugh, 'Conservative recruits to Labour', pp. 43–60.
55 *Northern Democrat* (July 1928).
56 J. Boughton, 'Working class politics in Birmingham and Sheffield', Ph.D. thesis (University of Warwick, 1987), ch. 7; Dickie, 'Town patriotism', ch. 4. For the pre-war position, Tanner, 'Ideological debate', p. 292.
57 K. Wadsworth (Birmingham) to H. N. Brailsford, 19 October 1926, Brailsford MS HNB 1/24, Labour Party Archives, Manchester (hereafter LPA).
58 For the 1930s, Elizabeth Durbin, *The New Jerusalems. The Labour Party and the Economics of Democratic Socialism* (London: Routledge and Kegan Paul, 1985); Ben Pimlott, *Labour and the Left in the 1930s* (Cambridge: Cambridge University Press, 1977).
59 Tanner, 'The pattern of Labour politics', pp. 130–4; Reynolds and Laybourn, *Labour Heartland*, pp. 110–17, Dickie, 'Town patriotism', pp. 98–104.
60 *East Ham Citizen*, syndicated pages (October 1935), (March 1936).
61 For the central theme of capitalism and the price of food, *East Ham Citizen*, syndicated pages (August 1934), (September 1934), (March 1935), (May 1935), (August 1936).

62 *Central Southwark Citizen* (September 1937), *Beacontree Citizen* (September 1937).

63 *Acton Citizen* (January 1935).

64 Forrester, *The Working Class*, ch. 4, discussing studies of Greenwich, Newcastle-under-Lyme and his own work on Brighton; Hugh Jenkins, *Rank and File* (London: Croom Helm, 1980), pp. 36, 40, 54–6, 59, 74; Daniel Weinbren, *Generating Socialism: Recollections of Life in the Labour Party* (Stroud: Sutton Publishing, 1997), especially ch. 2.

65 Schneer, *Labour's Conscience*, p. 160.

66 Lewis Minkin, *The Labour Party Conference: A Study in the Politics of Intra-Party Democracy* (London: Allen Lane, 1978), p. 45.

67 Walling, 'Policy and organisation in the Labour Party', chs. 5 and 6. See also Goss, *Politics and Policy in Southwark*, p. 45.

68 Patrick Seyd and Paul Whiteley, 'Labour's renewal strategy', in Martin J. Smith and Joanna Spear (eds.), *The Changing Labour Party* (London: Routledge, 1992), p. 31.

69 John O'Farrell, *Things Can Only Get Better. Eighteen Years in the Miserable Life of a Labour Supporter 1979–1997* (London: Doubleday, 1998), p. 106.

70 For the London left's verve and its commitment to a new agenda, David Kogan and Maurice Kogan, *The Battle for the Labour Party* (London: Kogan Paul, 1982), ch. 10; Hilary Wainwright, *Labour. A Tale of Two Parties* (London: Hogarth Press, 1987).

71 Seyd and Whiteley, *Labour's Grass Roots*, pp. 214–18.

72 Hughes and Wintour, *Labour Rebuilt*, p. 94.

73 J. R. MacDonald to J. Bruce Glasier, 31 December 1908, Bruce Glasier MS JBG 08/78, University of Liverpool; W. C. Anderson to J. R. MacDonald, 31 March 1911, JRM 30/69/1155, Public Records Office (hereafter PRO).

74 JRM diary, 30 May 1921, JRM 30/69/1753, PRO.

75 J. R. MacDonald to P. Snowden, 25 October 1928, JRM 30/69/1173/fo. 573, PRO.

76 For example, David Marquand, *Ramsay MacDonald* (London: Jonathan Cape, 1977), pp. 417, 475–7, J. R. MacDonald to A. Greenwood, 4 March 1925, JRM 30/69/1170 and JRM diary, 25 September 1929, JRM 30/69/8/1, PRO.

77 W. Milne Bailey to W. Citrine, 3 December 1931, TUC MSS 292/756.1/3, MRC.

78 H. V. Tewson to E. Bevin, 16 May 1933, TUC MSS 292/784.6 and TUC Research Department memo 'extracts from the New Clarion', no date. There had been similar attempts to control the *Daily Herald* in the 1920s. See Huw Richards, *The Bloody Circus. The Daily Herald and the Left* (London: Pluto Press, 1997), pp. 73, 80.

79 W. Citrine to J. M. Kenworthy, 3 November 1932, H. Dunnico to W. Citrine, 10 November 1932, TUC MSS 292/753/4, MRC.

80 C. Ammon diary, 19 and 29 July 1933, Ammon MS 2/5, Univ. Hull; P. Gordon Walker diary, 12 July 1938, in Robert Pearce (ed.), *Patrick Gordon Walker Diaries* (London: Historians' Press, 1991), p. 75.

Duncan Tanner

81 E. Levy to Citrine, 28 January 1939, J. Jack to Citrine, 27 May 1938, TUC MSS 292/745/1, MRC. For constituency opinion see, for example, Reynolds and Laybourn, *Labour Heartland*, p. 144.
82 Shaw, *Discipline and Discord*, pp. 52–5, 113–14; Tanner, 'Facing the new challenge', pp. 278–80.
83 Cited in Shaw, *Discipline and Discord*, p. viii.
84 Tiratsoo, 'May Day Manifesto', pp. 167, 181; 'Constituency reports on draft manifesto 1980', Labour Party Wales MS 144, Nat. Lib. of Wales, Aberystwyth.
85 For example, in Gloucester arguments raged between 1928 and 1931, with regular resignations, allegations of 'sharp practice', refusals to 'forget the past and look to the future' or engage in criticism 'of a constructive rather than destructive character'. 'High words' rendered breaches 'wider still' (Gloucester Labour Party minutes, esp. 14 May, 26 November 1928, 10 June 1931).
86 For the activists' disquiet with candidates, Tanner, 'The pattern of Labour politics', p. 129 and fn 29 and for the candidates' disquiet with their constituency parties, Tanner, 'Recruitment of the PLP', p. 609.
87 E. M. Latimer to H. N. Brailsford, 22 October 1926, Brailsford MS HNB 1/63, LPA.
88 Tiratsoo, 'May Day Manifesto', p. 174.
89 Wainwright, *A Tale of Two Parties*, esp. chs. 3–4; Goss, *Politics and Policy in Southwark*, pp. 93, 96–7.
90 See Lawrence, ch. 11 below.
91 Schneer, *Labour's Conscience*, ch. 7. For councillors and accountability between the wars, Chris Williams, 'Labour and the challenge of local government 1918–39', in Tanner et al., *The Labour Party in Wales*, p. 152. For this in London during the 1970s, Goss, *Politics and Policy in Southwark*, p. 93.
92 See, for example, articles in *Labour Party News*, 7 January/February 1988. Disgruntled activists felt the publication was 'a mirror in which the leadership preened itself': see Richard Heffernan and Mike Marqusee, *Defeat from the Jaws of Victory, Inside Kinnock's Labour Party* (London: Verso, 1992), p. 82.
93 Labour Co-ordinating Committee, *The Forward March of Modernisation. A History of the LCC 1978–1998* (no publication information, but 1999). Tom Sawyer's intentions, noted in *New Labour, New Britain*, May 1996.
94 Cited in Hefferman and Marqusee, *Inside Kinnock's Labour Party*, pp. 100–1.
95 Eric Shaw, *The Labour Party since 1979. Crisis and Transformation* (London: Routledge, 1994), pp. 220, 223–4.

9 | Labour and the electorate

Nick Tiratsoo

> On the day of the election I took my little brother
> round the town in his toy motor, which my daddy
> decorated with Labour colours and Mr Ledbury's
> photo in a horseshoe. I was very disappointed that
> Mr Ledbury was not made MP. But my daddy says the
> people of Basingstoke are not awake yet.
> Winning entry, 'What I did in the election'
> competition for 'Young politicians', *Labour Woman* 11
> (1923), 15

In the early decades of the twentieth century, many in the Labour Party fervently believed that it was eventually destined to dominate British politics. The working classes were chafing at their subordinate position, while socialism seemed to provide answers for most of society's ills. It was only a matter of time before the people 'woke up' and the other parties were finally vanquished. Yet as the years passed, such hopes began to fade. Labour established a strong presence nationally and locally, but its overall performance fell well short of expectations. The twenty-one general elections between 1918 and 1992 yielded only two really emphatic triumphs, while the party only once came near to gaining 50 per cent of the votes cast at the polls.

This chapter begins with a detailed survey of Labour's record up to the early 1990s, and then examines why progress was so disappointing. Some of the party's difficulties were clearly beyond its control. Much of the British electorate remained unsympathetic to socialism. Moreover, the Conservative Party, in particular, was always a powerful competitor for the popular vote. But there were also self-inflicted wounds, for Labour developed an internal culture that was partly incompatible with its electoral ambitions. Indeed, activists sometimes thought and behaved in ways that actually alienated the ordinary voter. Of course, the

Blairites who took control of the party after 1992 were fully aware of this problem, and sought to bring it to an end. New Labour was to be made much more 'voter-friendly'. The extraordinary landslide victory of 1997 seemed to suggest that a major transformation had occurred. Whether or not this was the case is examined in a concluding section.

Labour's electoral record to 1992

It is easy to see why so many Labour members initially grew ever more optimistic about their prospects.[1] The party was very much an outsider in the elections of 1900, 1906 and 1910 and did not make much impression on either the Conservatives or the Liberals, winning at best a mere 7.6 per cent of the popular vote. But after 1918 the position changed rapidly.[2] Fighting a war had undermined much of the Edwardian order, while the Liberal Party's internal turmoil, various franchise reforms (including the granting of votes to women over thirty), and an enormous growth in trade-union membership allowed Labour new opportunities. The party gained 2.2 million votes in 1918, over 4 million votes in 1922 and 1923, and then 5.5 million votes in 1924, about one-third of the total, twice the Liberals' figure, and enough to allow the formation of a minority government. Unsurprisingly, exercising power in these circumstances proved impossible and the Conservatives quickly returned to office, but even so the momentum was not lost. Labour made impressive gains in local elections, capturing a string of county boroughs as well as its first city, Sheffield, in 1926. Arthur Henderson, the party's general secretary, talked excitedly of 'Labour's steady march to political power' and his optimism was finally rewarded at the 1929 election.[3] Labour's vigorous campaigning produced 8.4 million votes, 37 per cent of those cast, and only 300,000 less than the Conservative total. The Liberals had been pushed firmly back into third place. In Parliament, Labour now had the biggest block of MPs for the first time ever, and so once again agreed to form a minority administration.

The following two years were disappointing. The British economy was beset with difficulties and Labour found it almost impossible to implement coherent palliatives. The cabinet became beleaguered and divided. In the end, the Prime Minister, Ramsay MacDonald, and some of his key colleagues defected to form a National government with the Conservatives. Labour appeared discredited, and when an election was called, suffered the consequences, ending up with 6.6 million votes but only 52 MPs, 235 fewer than in the previous Parliament. Henderson spoke of a 'serious electoral reverse' though he considered that in the circumstances the party had performed 'little short of a miracle'. The

Labour Organiser, a journal aimed at agents and activists, was less san-guine. In the past few years, it noted, the party had expanded fast, mainly through trade-union affiliation, but there was nevertheless a 'gigantic margin' between 'the numerical strength of the Movement and the vote . . . attained'.[4]

During the following decade, Labour recovered, though only slowly. The election of 1935 yielded 8.3 million votes and 154 MPs, nowhere near enough to frighten the Conservatives. Later by-election victories, as Britain slid towards war, only reinforced the sense of frustration, since the swings involved did not suggest victory at a general election. Better results were achieved at local level, with the party capturing Glasgow in 1933 and London in 1934, but even here progress was hardly remark-able. By the end of the decade, Labour controlled only 60 of the 672 county and municipal local government units in mainland Britain, with its national agent complaining of the 'state of stabilisation, or stalemate' that had been reached in most other areas.[5]

Party politics were suspended during the war and most assumed that, when peace came, the Conservatives would once again dominate, but at the 1945 election Labour surprised even itself by recording an extraor-dinary victory. The party received nearly twelve million votes, 48 per cent of the total, and ended up with a 146-seat majority in the House. Important gains were made in every region except the south and south-west. Moreover, the swing to Labour was repeated at local elections shortly afterwards. By 1947, the party controlled fifty-two of the eighty-three most important cities. The LSE academic H. L. Beales predicted in *Political Quarterly* that Labour had come to stay: 'The government has only got to retain its unity, fulfil its very modest mandate, eschew alike factiousness and functionless authoritarianism and it will be renewed in due course'.[6]

In fact, events unfolded rather differently. Labour decided to hold an election in February 1950, polled well, but ended up with a paltry five-seat majority. Twenty months later, it failed to repeat the trick, and the Conservatives returned. Nevertheless, few in the party's ranks were really downhearted. Labour had again received enormous popular support and its 13.9 million votes still stands as an all-time record. Indeed, the general secretary, Morgan Phillips, was decidedly upbeat in his post-election report. Given the effort, the will and the determination, he concluded, 'final victory for democratic socialism' was 'assured'.[7]

However, hopes of a quick return to office failed to materialise. The Conservatives won in 1955 and then again in 1959, though Labour polled more than twelve million votes on both occasions. The second

Nick Tiratsoo

defeat produced a crisis of confidence. The Conservatives were riding an economic boom, which the left as a whole found difficult to deal with positively. Many commentators suggested that in future Labour might be doomed to perpetual opposition. A Penguin Special entitled *Must Labour Lose?* attracted much publicity, particularly because its expert authors seemed inclined to answer their own question in the affirmative.[8]

Nevertheless the pundits were again proved wrong. The Conservative government lost its way, and was wracked by indecision and scandal. Meanwhile, Harold Wilson, the new Labour leader, had begun projecting the party as a fresh and invigorating force that could transform Britain. Such developments were enough to give Labour a narrow victory at the 1964 election, and then a more substantial triumph two years later, based upon thirteen million votes or 48 per cent of the total. But this was to be a final high-water mark. Labour lost many local authorities in the late 1960s (including thirty-seven cities) and then suffered defeat at the 1970 election. The signs were ominous, as the party's share of the poll had fallen to 43 per cent, and in fact the next twenty years were to prove something of a hard slog.[9]

Labour returned to power in 1974, first as a minority government and then with a majority of three, though its vote was again down. But much worse followed. Capitalising on Britain's economic problems and the new phenomenon of 'stagflation', Margaret Thatcher's Conservatives regained power in 1979 and then won three further elections in succession. Labour was plagued by internal divisions and the breakaway Social Democratic Party, and saw its share of the poll collapse to a post-1922 low of 27.6 per cent in 1983, and then only slowly recover to 30.8 per cent in 1987 and 34.4 per cent in 1992. Relatively good results in European elections and some progress at the local level during the early 1990s proved little compensation. Writing after Labour's fourth consecutive defeat in 1992, a group of Britain's most prominent academic political scientists were pessimistic about the party's future. It had waged a good campaign in the recent election but still lost emphatically, humbled by the Conservatives' 42.3 per cent of the popular vote. The chances of victory at the next contest were slim. Labour might prevent a further Tory success but it had little chance of doing more. The prospect of a hung parliament was 'clearly a serious one'. In a letter to the *Independent*, Lord Skidelsky, biographer of Keynes and political critic, was more forthright. Labour, he declared, was now simply 'unelectable'.[10]

Assessed as a whole, Labour's record in the years to 1992 hardly impressed. Much of the electorate had remained resolutely Liberal or

Conservative. Even the less well-off were not necessarily sympathetic. The Conservatives consistently won about one-third of the working-class vote, and sometimes considerably more, as in 1951, when their share reached 44 per cent. In this situation, large swathes of the country never returned a Labour MP, a feature that was particularly true of non-metropolitan constituencies south of a line connecting the Wash to the Bristol Channel.[11]

Of course, the party could draw strength from the fact that it continued to dominate much of industrial Britain, and in particular the coalfields, but even here the situation was somewhat less favourable than it at first sight appeared. For if much of the urban working class remained loyal to Labour, levels of commitment were sometimes fairly perfunctory. Few could be persuaded to vote in local elections, and though a better number turned out at national polls, they did so without necessarily showing any great enthusiasm.[12] Indeed, voting was often given little thought at all, with choices being determined by custom, habit or instructions from a senior family member.[13] On the other hand, the number of Labour sympathisers who wished to do more than just vote for the party was always very small. Millions automatically enrolled as members through their trade unions, but far fewer actively sought to join their local constituency organisations. An internal report of 1949 suggested that individual membership was equivalent to one in nineteen of those who had supported Labour in 1945. Later estimates, based upon better data, produced even more unfavourable ratios, and underlined, too, that such figures were unusually low by European standards.[14]

Given this background, it is unsurprising to find that some of Labour's greatest electoral successes owed much to the failures of its opponents. The party was greatly assisted in the early 1920s by the divisions that plagued the Liberals. Later, in 1945, it benefited from a lacklustre Conservative campaign, which focused on Churchill's persona but failed to present relevant policy prescriptions for the problems of the time, notably the war-induced housing shortage. A similar pattern was observable in 1966. Harold Wilson was more popular than Edward Heath, his opposite number, but the result almost certainly turned on the public's perception that the Tories were unfit for office, 'tired, out of touch with ordinary people, [and] too much dominated by the upper classes'.[15] While Labour could obviously claim credit for amplifying this impression, the Conservatives had ultimately caused their own downfall.

In fact, Labour's problems with the electorate were serious enough to steadily erode much of the early optimism about ultimate victory. Party loyalists continued to be puzzled about their lack of appeal. Some rededicated themselves to the struggle, but others lapsed into cynicism or criticised the voters for their ignorance or perfidy. The *Labour Organiser*'s headline in the wake of the 1931 result was 'Forty Millions – Mostly Fools'. Five years later, the Labour peer Lord Snell explained working-class attitudes by reference to the farmyard: 'They have been driven like cattle, they have often been housed worse than cattle, and they carry with them the marks of their history.' By the end of the 1950s, judgements were becoming even less sympathetic. Seeking to explain Labour's third successive election defeat, the MP Renee Short told the party conference: 'Women in this country . . . are by and large . . . politically illiterate.' Her radical colleague Michael Foot was equally forthright: 'The Tories caught the mood of the public. Their votes prove it. But that mood was blind, smug, somnolent, and, in some respects, evil.'[16] A section of the left's later fixation with '*Sun* readers' – apparently xenophobes and misogynists to a man – was very much in keeping with this tradition. From such a perspective, the party's conscience was clear: it had advanced sensible programmes but had then been let down by the electorate.

Popular conceptions of politics

What explains Labour's relatively poor showing at the polls? One central difficulty for the party was that relatively few intuitively shared its fundamental values. Labour stood for public welfare against private interest, the collective as opposed to the individual. It wanted a society where citizens focused on wider goals than their own immediate material interests. But for many, these were unattractive propositions, which cut across the grain of ordinary life. In the prevailing view, politics had its place, but it was essentially seen in instrumental terms, as a means of improving everyday conditions, not as a vehicle for promoting some kind of social transformation.

Working-class ambitions centred on job, family and home. The widely shared aspiration was to maintain independence and attempt a modicum of self-improvement. Fear of a descent into poverty, with its accompanying humiliations at the hands of 'the authorities', was ever present. This coexisted with a belief that something could usually be done to make life better, especially when it came to the lives of children. Many parents wanted their offspring to 'have a chance', avoid the most degrading or physically dangerous jobs, and perhaps take up whatever educational opportunities were on offer. The hope was that they would 'get on'. By comparison, views about society as a whole were more complicated and embraced several tensions. There was a widespread feeling of resentfulness towards 'them' – an elastic amalgam of those who were understood to control the system, probably for their own benefit. Strong feelings often lurked just below the surface. During the second half of the 1940s, the Labour government exhorted Britons to 'work or want' in a bid to overcome the depredations of war. Interviewing workers in a café, one social investigator touched upon the campaign, and was immediately assailed with the following tirade:

If you want an argument, you just put down 'Work or want', that's what Mr Bevin said isn't it, Well all that lot is hard on the miner isn't it, tell him work or want, well tell them to go up to London, to Oxford street and Fleet street where I've been today and see all the people walking about doing nothing, only spending money. We're working to keep them . . . you can tell this Government and the whole houses of Parliament they can be blown up with an atom bomb.[17]

Such anger sometimes produced a consciousness of class, and a belief that all those who worked with their hands were 'in it together'. Nevertheless, these impulses were usually highly qualified by a variety of other prescriptions and prejudices. Working-class communities tended to be rather parochial, and there was a general suspicion of 'foreigners', whether they came from a neighbouring district, a different region of Britain, or overseas. Moreover, profound divisions existed between the 'rough' and the 'respectable'. Indeed, 'keeping up standards' was habitually viewed as of paramount importance, and formed the basis for evaluating workmates and neighbours. Writing of life in Shoreham-by-Sea during the 1950s, one woman recalled that her parents never spoke to the family next door. She explained: 'Just after Mum moved in, she was redding the top of her gate post and Mrs Clough came out saying "Are you trying to show me up, redding your gateposts?" and after that, those two women ignored each other for over thirty years.'[18] The prevailing ethos was particularly clearly apparent in attitudes towards welfare provision. Here, the Victorian distinction between the deserving and undeserving poor remained potent, despite the vigorous efforts of social reformers and politicians to cultivate more generous sentiments and a greater compassion for those in need.[19]

These various dispositions coloured attitudes to party affiliations. Most ordinary people showed only passing interest in the electoral struggle, while knowledge about politics was inversely related to income and social position.[20] What working-class voters wanted above all were measures that would improve their lives in practical ways. For many, this

Nick Tiratsoo

meant favouring Labour, since it was popularly believed to be the party that stood for the worker against the boss, for the poor against the rich, and for equality as opposed to privilege. Nevertheless, such support was rarely given unconditionally. The nature of popular priorities was well described by John Barron Mays, a social worker and schoolteacher who observed inner-city Liverpool during the 1950s and 1960s. As he concluded, the local population was most concerned with personal or family problems, particularly those relating to employment and accommodation, and as a result would 'flock to the doors of their city councillors' committee rooms, expecting them to use their civic influence on their behalf'. However, if the desired outcome was not forthcoming, many would simply fall back on the traditional local view that all politicians were 'racketeers'. Hence, the area as a whole was notable for its 'air of political apathy'.[21]

Middle-class attitudes followed a somewhat similar pattern. The central consideration, once again, was with 'getting on', for example with obtaining the educational or professional qualifications that would allow a better lifestyle. Families worried about falling down the social scale, and did all they could to maintain outward respectability. However, the great fear here was not poverty but contamination by the working classes. The battle lines were drawn wherever this appeared possible, with complex rules to prevent encroachment in speech, dress, recreation and habitation. On occasion, residents of up-market estates actually connived in blocking off streets to separate themselves from nearby council tenants.[22] The masses were seen as uncouth and ill mannered, ignorant, indolent yet spendthrift, and perhaps prone to violence. Encounters with workers could prove traumatic. The historian Richard Cobb remembered one of his friends who had left his genteel home town of Tunbridge Wells in the Second World War to become a volunteer miner. The youth had quickly reappeared, pale, drawn, and 'quite shattered' by his experiences:

It had – he said to me . . . been absolutely *awful*: the digs, the food, something called High Tea and involving no silver and thinly cut cucumber sandwiches, getting up early in the morning . . . the actual working conditions . . . above all, the language and attitudes of his work-mates; they had made fun of his accent, had ribbed him incessantly, had taken him out to the pub and made him drink *beer* . . . and they had never heard of Tunbridge Wells ('What did they make there?').[23]

The subject of party politics was rarely discussed in such circles, but many knew exactly where they stood, and were almost instinctively

288

Conservative. Writing of his neighbours in the Surrey town of Farnham during the early 1990s, Richard Hoggart commented: 'They vote Tory because they believe – "assume" would be more accurate – that the Conservatives are the natural party of government.' By contrast, Labour continued to be castigated as controlled by the unions, addicted to bureaucracy and regulation, and untrustworthy when it came to safeguarding Britain's interests overseas. Identification with the party was taken to be a sign of wilful malevolence. After studying mid-century Banbury, the sociologist Margaret Stacey reported: 'When the middle class do come across a member who is a Labour supporter, they are surprised and shocked. They avoid social relations with the recalcitrant.' In Farnham, according to Hoggart, to be a socialist was 'almost unthinkable'. Labour members were dismissed as 'loud-mouthed demagogues driven by rancour and envy'.[24]

Of course, these well-established patterns appeared less secure in some periods than in others. Working-class solidarity grew at times of major industrial unrest, for example during the General Strike of 1926 and, to a lesser extent, when the miners confronted the government in 1974 and 1984–5. Moreover, there were one or two occasions when sizeable parts of the country as a whole flirted with radicalism. Yet these deviations were all in the end remarkably short-lived. For though socialist agitators always hoped differently, there was simply little widespread or sustained popular appetite for fundamental change. In this respect, events in the later 1940s are especially instructive.

The prosecution of a 'people's war' between 1939 and 1945 inevitably encouraged questioning of the status quo. Workers knew that they were making great sacrifices in order to secure victory, remembered the broken promises that had followed the peace in 1918, and vowed that they would not be fooled again. Some middle-class consciences were pricked when bombing and evacuation revealed the extent of poverty in Britain's inner cities. As a consequence, the mood of the country began to alter. There were demands that Britain should be re-built on more egalitarian and democratic lines, and a greater willingness to consider novel solutions, factors that obviously helped Labour win the 1945 election. But it is also notable that this upsurge dissipated much more quickly than almost anyone had expected. Many working-class voters stayed loyal to Labour, appreciating practical reforms like the welfare state and full employment, but only a tiny minority wished the government to pursue further socialist advances. Writing in 1952, the pioneering sociologist Ferdinand Zweig commented: 'There is not a shred of revolutionary feeling in British socialism. The British worker believes in

Nick Tiratsoo

gradualism; he does not want to overthrow the existing social structure. As a matter of fact, he does not feel very strongly or think very often about it.' Indeed, he added, 'the average man' was 'far more interested in sport than politics'. Meanwhile, middle-class radicalism proved even less durable. The better-off disliked rationing and the administration's determination to redistribute wealth, reacting with emotions that ranged from 'hurt bewilderment' to 'white fury'. In this situation, it was not long before almost all had returned to their traditional political affiliations. Indicatively, at the 1951 election, the Conservatives won as much as 73 per cent of the middle-class vote, up from 61 per cent in 1945.[25]

In these circumstances, dedicated socialists usually remained isolated within their local communities, atypical figures whose interests and passions found only faint echo in the wider population. The Independent Labour Party organiser John Paton recalled of his youthful proselytising in Edwardian Aberdeen: 'Our ideas were poured out at continual open air meetings, usually at small gatherings of very casual onlookers with an appearance of having stopped to listen because they were too early for important appointments.' Socialists, he admitted, were 'in a similar category to the strange beings who tore their beards and confessed their sins in public at religious meetings'. The veteran policeman turned radical journalist C. H. Rolph made a similar point in an autobiography of the 1980s. Being an activist, he concluded, 'all too often seemed to mean shuffling about under banners, preceded by buglers or pipers, ignored by all except the ambiguous policemen marching alongside, by the absurd groups of unwelcome and uninvited camp-followers, and by the Press and television photographers concerned only to get pictures of the camp-followers'.[26]

Opponents and competitors

A second difficulty for Labour was that many organisations were determined to thwart its progress. The opposition included political parties, several well-funded propaganda organisations, and a cohort of right-wing newspapers. All aimed to limit Labour's electoral capabilities and perhaps neutralise its ideology. Some wanted a Britain that was free forever from what was referred to as 'the cancer of socialism'.

Labour's electoral opponents varied in strength and effectiveness. Organisations further to the left remained largely impotent. The Communist Party stood candidates at every election between 1922 and 1987 and polled an average of only 42,000 votes, or never more than 0.5 per cent of the electorate. Nationalists were sometimes more of a threat,

Table 9.1. *Party central income 1967–1976, at constant (1970) prices (£000)*

	1967/8	1968/9	1969/70	1970/1	1971/2	1972/3	1973/4	1974/5	1975/6
Conservative	1041	2413	1076	1823	816	967	2043	950	801
	1967	1968	1969	1970	1971	1972	1973	1974	1975
Labour	457	414	403	1072	552	645	707	1291	584

Source: Cmnd. 6601, *Report of the Committee on Financial Aid to Political Parties,* Parliamentary Papers (1975–6), vol. XIII, p. 90. It should be noted that this table underestimates Conservative income because it excludes sums raised in Scotland between 1971 and 1975.

though they found it difficult to establish a consistent presence even in their heartlands. The real challenge was always from the centre and right. The Liberal Party's fortunes fluctuated. It had a strong working-class following in the early years of the century, but quickly lost ground in the 1920s, and thereafter languished for several decades outside a few local strongholds (for example, the south-west). A revival began in the early 1970s, and picked up momentum following the creation of an alliance with the Social Democrats in 1981, but though the two parties received 25.4 per cent of the vote in 1983, they found it difficult to make further progress, and subsequently saw their share of the vote decline. The most enduring and effective opposition came from the Tories.

Conservative strength was built on firm material foundations. The party had longstanding links with both business and the aristocracy and so could almost always deploy far larger sums on electioneering than any competitor. Tory finances remain shrouded in mystery,[27] but the figures produced for the Houghton Committee on political funding in the early 1970s, summarised in table 9.1, give some idea of the party's advantage. In practical terms, this meant that the Conservative machine was always well staffed and provided with resources. During the early 1960s, for example, the Tories employed 677 national and constituency workers compared with Labour's 286. In addition, the party also benefited from having a large rank and file. Accurate returns are again unavailable, but it has been credibly estimated that membership rose from about 1.25 million during the inter-war years to a peak of 2.8 million in the early 1950s, and was still probably near the one million mark as late as 1982.[28]

Nick Tiratsoo

As well as possessing an impressive institutional weight, the Conservatives were imbued with a will to win, a determination to gain and hold power at all costs. The party's ideology was elastic and embracing, allowing it to reach out to all sections of the community. Emphasis was placed on patriotism, prosperity and freedom, values that had obvious and widespread appeal. Great efforts were made to blend serious political activity with a wide variety of social events and entertainments. Special sections catered exclusively for women, trade-unionists and the young. Moreover, the Tories were always ready to embrace the latest campaigning techniques. They pioneered film propaganda in the 1920s, seized on the opportunities offered by television and the computer, and were early and enthusiastic users of public relations professionals to help them put over policy. All in all, as the historian Richard Cockett concludes, their record here was one of 'extraordinary innovation – certainly compared to that of the other British political parties'.[29]

These attributes meant that the Conservative challenge in constituencies was frequently very potent. A report on the London area for 1926 noted typically high activity levels. There had been numerous indoor and outdoor meetings, especially in working-class areas like the East End; an extensive canvass of some 74,017 households in eight marginal seats; as well as a large sale of literature. Women's sections existed in all but three of the city's sixty-one constituencies, and boasted a total of 35,686 members. In some cases, the party was able to go beyond mere campaigning and become the central hub of local life. A correspondent to the *Economist* in 1949 remarked of his suburb:

The social activities of about 20,000 people are, apart from the local cinema, now largely organised openly or at second-hand by Tory interests. Dances, lectures, outings, sports events and so forth are extremely well organised. The young men and women in their early twenties – those on the electoral register for the first time – are, almost without knowing it, Tory voters. A slick little magazine giving all the details of the social events drops through the letter box each month. It is, of course, strongly supported by local shop advertising.

In these conditions, Conservatism was being promoted as a way of life, much more than a choice made every few years at the ballot box.[30]

The Tory cause was aided by a group of allegedly entirely independent organisations which argued its case in specific contexts. Ratepayers' associations spread rapidly in the south during the 1920s and 1930s, and campaigned vociferously against 'socialist waste and extravagance' in local government. About 500 were still in existence thirty years later.[31]

Aims for Industry and the Economic League, founded in 1919 and 1942 respectively, took the free market case to the shop floor and tried to influence the ordinary worker. Amongst other things, they asserted that 'class warfare is ass warfare'. Their promotional efforts were prodigious: in 1947 alone, the League held 14,110 meetings, ran 63,071 group talks and distributed seven million leaflets, while Aims placed 61,000 column inches of stories in the provincial and national press. Finally, many ad hoc trade and professional organisations periodically campaigned in favour of particular policy goals. For example, private steel companies and their trade association spent £1,298,000 on anti-nationalisation propaganda in the months immediately before the 1964 election, four times more than Labour's total outlay on publicity in the same period.[32]

The Conservatives were also able to count on strong backing from much of the press. Papers like the *Daily Mail*, the *Daily Express*, and the *Daily Telegraph* were almost completely loyal, and also had large circulations. In 1945, the dailies sympathetic to the Tories were selling 5.8 million copies each morning, one third more than their Labour equivalents. Subsequently, with the success of the *Sun*, the position tilted even further out of balance. During the early 1970s, the Conservatives were supported by papers with 57 per cent of the national circulation total, while by 1992 this figure had reached a record 70 per cent. A similar bias was also noticeable in provincial evening and weekly publications, though its dimensions were probably less pronounced.[33]

Taken together, many saw this as amounting to a formidable combination, which should in normal circumstances dominate elections. But as more informed commentators recognised, the Tory effort was in fact rather less impressive than it at first sight appeared. To begin with, like their competitors, the Conservatives on occasion suffered from inferior leadership, political divisions and poor policy formulation. Margaret Thatcher's final years in office offer recent and telling examples. In addition, there were more enduring problems relating to electioneering. The Tories wanted to appeal to all sections of the community yet often found this difficult to achieve. Officials and activists usually came from a fairly restricted range of middle-class backgrounds and frequently knew little of the ordinary elector. Interchanges could therefore be tense or even counterproductive. Looking back over his political career, the one-time Labour MP for Romford, John Parker, remembered that a Conservative opponent at the general election in 1935 had surrendered many votes because of his arrogance: 'He was a great help to me during the campaign! For he lost his temper when heckled. A strong woman supporter of mine was cross-eyed. She followed him around asking awkward questions.

Nick Tiratsoo

"Thank the Lord I am not your husband and don't have to look at your face every morning at breakfast" was a reply which circulated round the neighbouring pubs.' Indeed, anecdotes about Tory insensitivity were much repeated in working-class areas. The fenland poet Edward Storey remembered his father harping upon a local MP who had publicly declared in the inter-war years: 'The working class are like potatoes; they should be buried in winter and dug up when needed.'[34]

Nor were the Conservatives as positive in their reactions to women as was sometimes imagined. The party flattered female voters but rarely allowed women much power in its organisations. Only 4 per cent of the 11,900 Tory candidates who stood in general elections between 1918 and 1987 were women. In fact, there was a general feeling in the party, shared by both sexes, that politics was a male pursuit. Women seeking adoption in the comparatively liberal 1990s still felt discriminated against. One complained: 'At each meeting a small but determined group of women told me . . . that it was quite wrong for any woman with a small child to apply for such a demanding job.' Needless to say, unconventional men could fall victim to similar intolerance. The candidate at the Christchurch by-election of 1993 was disliked in local Tory circles because of his droopy moustache. A woman activist inquired: 'Can't you make it grow upwards?'[35]

The party's various allies were also less effective than they liked to admit. Ratepayers' organisations regularly fell prey to factional divisions and personality politics. Aims for Industry and the Economic League inevitably claimed great influence, but produced little substantiating evidence other than endless lists of their own activities. Even the power of the Tory press was clearly circumscribed. Labour loyalists frequently blamed the newspapers for their lack of success. One party pamphlet concluded in 1952 that the press 'acted as a vast amplifier of Conservative views' and had 'immense' sway. Thirty years later, it was commonly asserted in left-wing circles that 'if the media all disappeared tomorrow Mrs Thatcher would not last a week'. Newspaper editors with links to the Tory establishment made similar claims. The *Sun* declared after the 1992 election that it was 'the *Sun* wot won it'. Yet the evidence remained inconclusive. Much of the electorate took little notice of newspapers. Readers often turned to the entertainment or sports pages first and virtually ignored political and editorial comment. Substantial minorities who read Tory-leaning papers were Labour voters. The *Sun* may have helped John Major win in 1992, but academic experts were by no means unanimous that this was so. And, most significantly, it was unarguable that Labour had been able to achieve clearcut victories in both 1945 and 1966 despite the biases that existed.[36]

Because of these factors, the Conservatives' popularity inevitably varied considerably by area and over time. There were middle-class Tory strongholds, as has been suggested, but also working-class localities where the party was widely despised. Standing as a Conservative in the Rhondda at the 1951 election, Oliver Stutchbury was treated with more or less open contempt. People told him: 'We haven't got anything to conserve', 'Its Labour we are', or 'Churchill's a warmonger'. Even the local Conservative club offered no succour, having been taken over surreptitiously by thirsty but militant Communists.[37] Tory influence amongst women also fluctuated, though the so-called gender gap was declining continuously from 1955, and had nearly disappeared altogether by the 1983 and 1987 general elections.[38] All in all, the Conservative's electoral superiority was frequently hard won, and delivered by a machine that had pulled out all the stops to gain victory. As this suggests, the fact that the party was so blessed with material wealth continued to be of considerable significance.

Labour campaigning

The circumstances that have been outlined obviously imposed limits on Labour's scope for advance, but they did not of course rule it out altogether. British politics continued to be marked by a degree of fluidity. There was always at least some potential for leftward change. Though few in the electorate appeared interested in socialism, many desired social reform. Moreover, Conservative weaknesses were there to be exploited. What this meant was that Labour could always to some extent shape its own destiny. Yet the party's response to this challenge was rarely fully convincing. The problem was that though Labour strategists saw clearly how to maximise popular support from the 1920s onwards, their prescriptions were never rigorously applied, and campaigning suffered as a result. Lack of finance was invariably an important impediment, but what held the party back most, perhaps surprisingly, were some of its own members' attitudes and practices.

In the years immediately following the First Word War, Labour's election specialists had to decide how to build on their party's sudden and unexpected breakthrough at the polls. The solution recommended was based upon a frank appreciation of psephology. Labour could count on good and improving support amongst the urban working classes, but this would never be enough to ensure majority government. The party had to make inroads where it was presently weak, in rural areas and middle-class suburbs.[39] Winning votes here was not going to be easy, but it could be accomplished if various principles were established. The party of course needed to ensure that adequate resources were at hand. Indeed, there was a strong case for actually prioritising less well-developed local organisations. But the most important requirement was an appropriate style of politics. In the recent past, too many had assumed that electioneering meant simply sloganising about capitalism's iniquities. This would no longer suffice. Labour must be more discerning about the electorate, accept that there was diversity of experience, and generate propaganda to suit. The point was made particularly cogently by the chief women's officer, Marion Phillips, in an article about how the party should set about attracting the newly enfranchised female voter:

She should be made to feel from the very beginning that the Labour Party recognises her position and knows her needs, and that on every side throughout the campaign women are given a prominent and honoured position. There is no greater error than to treat the wife as giving a vote automatically to whichever candidate her husband favours. The woman elector must be treated as a free individual responsible to herself alone for her decision and having special difficulties in her life for which Labour policy provides a remedy.[40]

As this implied, Labour activists could not afford to be dismissive about any section of the public. One contributor to *Labour Organiser* cautioned: 'Don't denounce as parasites all who do not happen to be manual workers. The idea that those who don the black coat and high collar are "snobs" is a mistake. To be well dressed, is, to one class of the community, as essential as the bag of tools and the overall to another.' The watchwords of effectiveness were care and sensitivity in everything, from policy right down to addressing envelopes.[41]

In later years, many stressed similar themes. Labour would not prosper if it ignored social realities. Nor were solutions, as Harold Wilson told the 1966 party conference, to be found by communing with Marx's remains in Highgate cemetery.[42] The need was always for a creative politics that responded to the spirit of its times. Yet talking about such a strategy was one thing, implementing it quite another. Part of the problem was financial for, unlike the Tories, Labour continued to be largely impecunious.[43] The head office organisation raised funds from individual members and affiliated trade unions but found that this income was usually barely sufficient to cover minimum possible expenditure. Local parties were largely left to fend for themselves in financial matters and coped as best they could. In these conditions, it was all too easy to fall back on dogma and rhetoric when electioneering. Working long hours at low pay, party officials and agents struggled against heavy odds to maintain a public presence.[44] At constituency level, the endless round of bring-and-buys, socials and whist drives inevitably sapped energy. Near poverty was not a condition that encouraged the imagination.

In addition to this, much of the party remained unsure about, or even opposed to, what was being suggested. Intransigence started at the top. Many Labour leaders broadly endorsed a progressive campaigning stance, but national executive members and senior MPs sometimes took an entirely different view. Left-wingers in particular continued to argue that protecting the party's spiritual integrity must always be given priority. Labour was nothing if not a moral crusade. The business of winning elections was really a secondary consideration. In a 1960 pamphlet reflecting on Labour's recent years in the wilderness, the MP Dick Crossman warned: 'politicians whose sole object, or even whose main object, is to regain office tend to be opportunists, to hedge and to equivocate in order to appease the voter'. If a socialist party thought only of the polls, he added, it would 'destroy itself'. Thirty years later, one-time minister Tony Benn declared in similar vein: 'We may win elections from time to time. But all that is worthless unless our thoughts and actions are firmly grounded in moral truth.'[45] The practical consequences that flowed from this fundamentalism were inevitably uncompromising. Left-wingers typically insisted that policy should reflect 'socialist principles', almost regardless of public opinion. A well-documented example occurred in the early 1970s, when the left-dominated National Executive Committee adopted sweeping nationalisation proposals even though it knew from specially commissioned research that these were only supported by a tiny minority in the electorate.[46] Similar concerns marked discussion about the mechanics of electioneering. The left believed that its duty was to put over political truths as plainly and clearly as possible. This was best achieved through the spoken word, judged the most authentic medium for politics.[47] Innovations like opinion polls and television broadcasts were frowned upon, distrusted because of their American origins and commercial connotations.[48]

In the party at large, attitudes were more complex though sometimes just as unhelpful to the development of an enlightened electoral politics. On the plus side, Labour activists were renowned for their keen sense of social justice. Many had first-hand experience of inequity and were determined to produce a fairer world. Two members of the Lowestoft

297

constituency party in the inter-war years, a Mr and Mrs Harris, established such a reputation that they were subsequently remembered as
'saints'. The local stories about their concern for the under-privileged
were legion – 'The occasion Joe gave his overcoat to an unemployed man
when it was raining heavily; the teas for the children of the poor; Mrs
Harris' clothes cupboard at home, filled with garments wrung out of the
better-off to be handed out to any needy callers; their work on the Board
of Guardians'.[49] Such selfless dedication was inevitably remembered at
the ballot box. But activists could repel as well as attract.

Running the Labour Party machine took time and effort, and sometimes became an end in itself. Rules and procedures dominated, leaving
little time for other political activity. Visiting Nottingham in the mid-
1960s, a Labour official sat through a general management committee
meeting that developed into the epitome of tedium:

It took 30 minutes to dispose of the Minutes of the last meeting, 30 minutes
for the report of the special emergency meeting, which was finally approved
as Minutes, 21 minutes to discuss the letter from Head Office regarding conference decision that delegates from affiliated organisations should be
members of the Party, 12 minutes to receive the report of the Labour Group
meeting held in September, and 24 minutes to receive reports of Group
meetings held in October and November. By this time it was twenty-nine
minutes past nine. Standing Orders say meetings should close at 9.30pm,
and the meeting refused to accept a motion for suspension of Standing
Orders . . . and the Treasurer had one minute to get the approval of the
meeting to draw £250 from their reserve fund to meet outstanding commitments.[50]

Needless to say, such 'resolutionary socialism' could prove deeply off-
putting, particularly to new recruits and outsiders. At times it seemed as
if local parties were being run for the benefit of pedants and incorrigible
bureaucrats.

In addition, Labour activists often had their own repertoire of alienating prejudices. Male trade-unionists usually asserted considerable
authority in local organisations and perpetuated a particular proletarian
ethos. Their reference points were work and leisure, with a particular
emphasis on drinking and sport. Argument could be brutal and unfor-
giving. Birmingham socialists of the inter-war years debated strategy in
a city-centre café where it was not uncommon to hear comments like
'Your opinions are based on ignorance and are of no value whatsoever.'
One recalled: 'if you could hold your own in this circle, then you could
hold your own anywhere'.[51] Members from other backgrounds were

expected to fit in. The party as a whole was keen to recruit women and
helped a good number to gain public office but progress towards equality
of treatment and opportunity was slow. 'Why is it the *woman* member', a
correspondent to the *Labour Organiser* asked in 1947, 'who is always
chosen to wield the mop?'[52] Middle-class socialists experienced similar
problems. Some colluded in an 'inverted snobbery', mimicking what
were conceived of as popular idioms. During the 1930s, undergraduates
in the Oxford party apparently called each other 'comrade' and avoided
being seen entering the most expensive restaurants. Another strategy
was to remain aloof. John Strachey, the intellectual MP for Dundee, had,
according to his wife, 'no energy for ordinary people, and no common
touch'. When forced to visit his constituency at election times, Strachey
would deign to campaign during part of the day but then retreat to the
Royal British Hotel, dining in a private room screened off from his supporters. One of the Labour candidates for Luton at the 1970 election
took a similar view, arriving in the town from Hampstead just ten days
before the poll, and then publicly declaring that this 'was quite long
enough for anybody'. Again, much of this simply appeared baffling or
unattractive to both sympathisers and the electorate at large.[53]

Finally, there were more than a few Labour activists who used the
cloak of politics to pursue their own nefarious purposes. Some branches
and council groups were little more than vehicles for patronage and personal gain. Local 'barons' controlled decision-making, and reaped the
benefits.[54] Malpractice could be extensive. In a confidential review of
the late 1970s, Glasgow District Council Group was forced to admit:
'One of the most disturbing aspects of housing allocation is that many
people are convinced that it is crooked. Many tenants maintain that they
know of irregular house lets . . . [and] there is a general atmosphere of
mistrust.'[55] Elsewhere, the threat came from far-left groups determined
on their own conspiratorial agendas. Most Communist and Trotskyist
parties attempted 'entryism' at one time or another, with the semi-clan-
destine Militant organisation using the tactic particularly successfully in
the 1970s and 1980s.[56] When Labour loyalists fought back, the outcome
was frequently chaotic and acrimonious. Conflict between Militant supporters and their opponents in one of the Newham seats eventually led
to a court case, where the presiding judge, Lord Denning, provided a
vivid picture of what had ensued:

There are within Newham North-East a number of small branches of the
Labour Party. They send delegates to the local general committee . . . The
rules prescribe the number of delegates . . . Usually there are only about 150

to 200 delegates present. Some favour one faction. Others the other. They are fairly evenly divided. So a switch-over of a few delegates may alter the whole pattern of voting. Each faction strives hard, therefore, to increase its own delegates and reduce those of the other faction . . . Each faction has done this to some extent by 'infiltration'. That is, the faction will bring in a new-comer to live in the constituency. He joins the local constituency Labour Party. He is active as a branch member and becomes a delegate. Other new-comers do the same. Just a handful of such newcomers may make all the difference to the voting and the result.[57]

Where such conditions prevailed, normal political activity was obviously almost impossible, and the party's reputation suffered as a result.

Shaped by these various pressures, Labour's actual performance at elections inevitably tended to be uneven. The party was good at mobilis-ing its activists' enthusiasm, and there were some extraordinary feats of campaigning. In the record year of 1951, Labour distributed fourteen million leaflets and manifestos, and allegedly canvassed as many as two-fifths of all households.[58] But there were also enduring weaknesses and blindspots. The party remained addicted to voluntary effort and suspi-cious of any measure that involved bringing in expert advisers. Fairly typically, a comprehensive report on organisation in 1955 rejected devel-oping 'a streamlined professional machine' because it would be 'offensive' to party traditions and principles.[59] As a result, Labour con-tinued to be poor at planning and organisation, often amateurish at developing activity. After attending a campaign committee meeting shortly before the 1959 election, Tony Benn wrote in his diary: 'The simple fact is that they had not thought out tactics for the next months at all and were just muddling through without proper documentation or briefing. There was no co-ordinated plan of any kind and everyone was junking in with their own schemes.'[60] Moreover, innovations in election-eering techniques were rarely applied to their full potential. The party was inept at marketing itself and relatively slow to appreciate opportu-nities offered by the electronic media. Only sporadic use was made of opinion polling.[61] Finally, the targeting of voters was never carried out systematically. Labour activists were always happiest campaigning in working-class constituencies, where they could focus on familiar themes like housing and employment. On the other hand, the need to win support in the more affluent suburbs was sometimes acknowledged but rarely systematically acted upon.[62] There was a widely held suspicion that anybody who owned a house was likely to vote Tory.[63] Assessed as a whole, therefore, Labour's record was hardly dazzling. Outside com-mentators often remarked upon the party's shortcomings. Writing in the wake of the disastrous 1983 defeat, the psephologist Peter Kellner was particularly scathing: 'Almost nothing went right for Labour . . . In virtually every respect – personal, political, tactical, organizational – the campaign was a disaster.'[64]

New Labour

From the early 1990s onwards, it was increasingly recognised in Labour circles that the party had reached some kind of crossroads. The electoral position appeared critical. A period of strong Conservative government had responded to and then reinforced the popular aspiration to 'get on'. Yet Labour had largely failed to react, simply reiterating its traditional nostrums about the importance of collective solutions. As a consequence, many ordinary voters now viewed the party as hostile to talent and opportunity, apparently intent on punishing those who made a success of their lives. If these trends continued, some predicted, there was a real danger that Labour would lose its status as a national political force and become merely a pressure group for the economically marginal and dispossessed – the unskilled, council tenants, the unemployed, and welfare dependants.[65]

The party was initially uncertain in its response to this predicament, but after some sharp internal debate, a group of modernisers gained control and embarked upon a programme of thoroughgoing internal reform. When Tony Blair became leader in 1994, the pace of change quickened. The overriding objective was to make Labour less inward looking and more in touch with the electorate. Blairites emphasised that Labour's core values were still relevant, but argued that they needed to be applied with greater sensitivity to the current context. Means should not be confused with ends. In addition, they were determined to break with the incompetence that had dogged so much of the party's previous electioneering. The upshot was a renewed emphasis on opinion research, the targeting of marginal seats, and the effective use of the media. By 1996, outside observers were concluding that against all expectations Labour had transformed itself into a formidable electoral machine.[66]

The 1997 election seemed to vindicate the Blairite approach. Labour won 13.5 million votes, 2 million more than in 1992, 43.2 per cent of the total, and enough to produce a Commons majority of 179. Moreover, the party's advance was spread across every region and social group in Britain. It had made especially impressive gains amongst the lower middle class, and in Greater London and the rest of the south-east. The extent and direction of the turnover of votes and seats was comparable to 1945.[67] Yet when the dust had settled, it was apparent that Labour euphoria needed to be qualified. The Conservatives had performed very poorly both before and during the election. The Major government was widely seen as incompetent, while the Tories' once impressive electoral machine had been allowed to languish. One insider went so far as to dismiss Conservative headquarters as 'a 1950s office with a 1950s culture'.[68] On the other hand, there was also room for debate about exactly what Labour's new stance had actually achieved. Party modernisers were bullish, claiming that they had won over large sections of the electorate, but independent experts were less convinced. One team of prominent political scientists and psephologists concluded: 'Labour's campaign machine failed to mobilise anything like Labour's support. Arguably, it consolidated Labour's pre-campaign position . . . was effective as a "banana-skin" avoidance machine, and helped catalyse effective tactical voting.'[69] In this view, the 1997 result was best understood by reference to the tried and tested maxim that elections in Britain had usually been lost rather than actively won.

Whatever the truth of such claims, the Blairites had certainly made Labour more proficient at fighting elections than at any time in its history. Yet whether the party as a whole was prepared to sustain this development remained open to question. For though many ordinary members strongly identified with the new leadership, traditional reflexes and modes of thinking also persisted. Thus, though Labour had more female MPs than ever before, few believed that discriminatory practices had altogether disappeared. Writing in 1998, Helen Wilkinson, think-tank project director and one-time Blair admirer, claimed: 'The men remain in charge with old Labour's macho labourist culture replaced by a subtler, covert and insidious laddishness.' Moreover, social prejudices, too, endured, with self-styled 'traditionalists' railing against what they saw as the party's capitulation before 'middle-class' sensitivities. Finally, and most seriously, local Labour organisations still seemed worryingly prone to nepotism and corruption. Before the new government was one year old, such strongholds as Doncaster, Hull, South Tyneside and Renfrewshire all found themselves under investigation.[70] In this sense, the Blairites had some way to go before they could claim to have finally harmonised the historic tension between their party's internal and external faces.

Notes

The author is grateful to Steven Fielding, Jim Obelkevich, Duncan Tanner and Pat Thane for perceptive comments on an earlier draft of this chapter; Lawrence Black, Alan Mckinlay, Dilwyn Porter and Jim Smyth for generous advice regarding sources; and Luton University for research support.

1 For a detailed statistical summary of Labour's electoral performance, see appendix 1.
2 Labour's fortunes during this period are comprehensively analysed in Duncan Tanner, *Political Change and the Labour Party 1900–1918* (Cambridge: Cambridge University Press, 1990).
3 *Daily Herald*, 21 July 1928.
4 The Secretary, 'Report on the General Election', 10 December 1931, pp. 3–4, National Executive Committee minutes, Labour Party Archive, Manchester (hereafter LPA); 'The morning after. An editorial review of the General Election', *Labour Organiser* no. 126 (1931), 202.
5 Mary Agnes Hamilton, *The Labour Party To-Day* (London: Labour Book Service, 1939), pp. 88–9; National Agent, 'Memorandum on Municipal Elections', p. 2, National Executive Committee minutes, 23–4 November 1938, LPA.
6 Steven Fielding, Peter Thompson and Nick Tiratsoo, *'England Arise!' The Labour Party and Popular Politics in 1940s Britain* (Manchester: Manchester University Press, 1995), pp. 58–68 and 170; H. L. Beales, 'Has Labour come to stay?', *Political Quarterly* 18 (1947), 59.
7 Fielding, Thompson and Tiratsoo, *'England Arise!'*, pp. 191–20; 'General Election Campaign 1951. General Secretary's Report', National Executive Committee minutes, 7 November 1951, p. 6, LPA.
8 N. Tiratsoo, 'Popular politics, affluence and the Labour Party in the 1950s', in Anthony Gorst, Lewis Johnman and W. Scott Lucas (eds.), *Contemporary British History 1931–1961* (London: Pinter, 1991), pp. 44–61; Mark Abrams, Richard Rose and Rita Hinden, *Must Labour Lose?* (Harmondsworth: Penguin, 1960), p. 119.
9 N. Tiratsoo, 'Labour and its critics: the case of the May Day Manifesto Group', in R. Coopey, S. Fielding and N. Tiratsoo (eds.), *The Wilson Governments 1964–1970* (London: Pinter, 1993), pp. 163–83.
10 Anthony Heath, Roger Jowell and John Curtis, 'Can Labour win?', in Anthony Heath, Roger Jowell and John Curtis, with Bridget Taylor (eds.), *Labour's Last Chance? The 1992 Election and Beyond* (Aldershot: Dartmouth, 1994), pp. 275 and 295; *Independent*, 11 April 1992.
11 Henry Durant, 'Voting behaviour in Britain, 1945–64', in Richard Rose (ed.), *Studies in British Politics. A Reader in Political Sociology* (London: Macmillan, 1966), p. 123; Ivor Crewe, Anthony Fox and Neil Day, *The British Electorate 1963–1992* (Cambridge: Cambridge University Press, 1995), p. 19; Margaret Cole, *The General Election 1945 and After* (London: Fabian Society, 1945), pp. 4–5.

Nick Tiratsoo

12 See, for example, Steven Fielding, '"Don't know and don't care": popular political attitudes in Labour's Britain, 1945–51', in N. Tiratsoo (ed.), *The Attlee Years* (London: Pinter, 1991), pp. 108–9.

13 See, for example, Stanley Oreanu, 'Why did we vote?', *Current Affairs* no. 123 (1951), 11.

14 Campaign Sub-Committee report, 'Tasks ahead', p. 1, National Executive Committee minutes, 29 June 1949, LPA; Patrick Seyd and Paul Whiteley, *Labour's Grass Roots. The Politics of Party Membership* (Oxford: Clarendon Press, 1992), p. 56; Stefano Bartolini, 'The membership of mass parties: the social-democratic experience, 1889–1978', in Hans Daalder and Peter Mair (eds.), *Western European Party Systems* (London: Sage, 1983), pp. 188–91.

15 D. E. Butler and Anthony King, *The British General Election of 1966* (London: Macmillan, 1966), pp. 265–7.

16 *Labour Organiser* no. 125 (1931), 201; Lord Snell, *Men, Movements and Myself* (London: Dent, 1936), p. 268; *Report of the 58th Annual Conference of the Labour Party* (London: Labour Party, 1959), p. 142; *Daily Herald*, 16 October 1959.

17 Report by 'K. B.' on 'Non-membership of groups – Tottenham', 30 July 1947, Beveridge enquiry, box 2, file A, Mass Observation Archive, University of Sussex.

18 Terry Jordan, *Growing Up in the Fifties* (London: Macdonald Optima, 1990), p. 72.

19 Rudolf Klein, 'The case for elitism: public opinion and public policy', *Political Quarterly* 45 (1974), 411.

20 See, for example, Mark Abrams, 'Social trends and electoral behaviour', *British Journal of Sociology* 13 (1962), 232–3; and Royal Commission on Local Government in England, *Research Studies 9. Community Attitudes Survey: England* (London: HMSO, 1969).

21 John Barron Mays, *Growing up in the City* (Liverpool: Liverpool University Press, 1964), p. 61.

22 Peter Collison, *The Cutteslowe Walls. A Study in Social Class* (London: Faber and Faber, 1963).

23 Richard Cobb, *Still Life. Sketches from a Tunbridge Wells Childhood* (London: Hogarth Press, 1984), pp. 110–11.

24 Richard Hoggart, *Townscape With Figures. Farnham: Portrait of an English Town* (London: Chatto and Windus, 1994), p. 170; Margaret Stacey, *Tradition and Change: A Study of Banbury* (Oxford: Oxford University Press, 1960), p. 53.

25 Ferdinand Zweig, *The British Worker* (Harmondsworth: Penguin, 1952), p. 189; Roy Lewis and Angus Maude, *The English Middle Classes* (London: Phoenix House, 1949), pp. 92–7; Durant, 'Voting behaviour', p. 123.

26 John Paton, *Proletarian Pilgrimage. An Autobiography* (George Routledge: London, 1935), pp. 115–16; C. H. Rolph, *Further Particulars* (Oxford: Oxford University Press, 1988), p. 204.

27 See Colin Challen, *Price of Power. The Secret Funding of the Tory Party* (London: Vision Paperbacks, 1998).
28 S. E. Finer, *The Changing British Party System, 1945–1979* (Washington D.C.: American Enterprise Institute for Public Policy Research, 1980), p. 102; Stuart Ball, 'Local Conservatism and party organisation' in Anthony Seldon and Stuart Ball (eds.), *Conservative Century. The Conservative Party since 1900* (Oxford: Oxford University Press, 1994), p. 292.
29 David Jarvis, 'The shaping of the Conservative electoral hegemony, 1918–39', in Jon Lawrence and Miles Taylor (eds.), *Party, State and Society. Electoral Behaviour in Britain since 1820* (Aldershot: Scolar Press, 1997), pp. 131–52; John Turner, 'A land fit for Tories to live in: the political ecology of the British Conservative Party, 1944–94', *Contemporary European History* 4 (1995), 189–208; Richard Cockett, 'The party, publicity and the media', in Seldon and Ball (eds.), *Conservative Century*, pp. 576–7.
30 '15th Report by Lord Jessel to the Chairman of the Unionist Party on the London Department', 1 July 1926, ARE/1/29/1, Conservative Party archive, Bodleian Library, Oxford; *Economist*, 10 December 1949.
31 Ken Young, *Local Politics and the Rise of Party* (Leicester: Leicester University Press, 1975), pp. 168 and 227–30; Neill Nugent, 'The ratepayers', in Roger King and Neill Nugent (eds.), *Respectable Rebels: Middle Class Campaigns in Britain in the 1970s* (London: Hodder and Stoughton, 1979), p. 25.
32 Arthur McIvor, '"A Crusade for Capitalism": the Economic League, 1919–39', *Journal of Contemporary History* 23 (1988), 631–55; S. E. Finer, 'The political power of private capital. Part two', *Sociological Review* 4 (1956), 12; '12 Carteret Street', *Scope* (May 1948), 80–2; and Richard Rose, *Influencing Voters. A Study of Campaign Rationality* (London: Faber and Faber, 1967), p. 130.
33 Samuel J. Eldersveld, 'Communication media and the 1950 British election', in James K. Pollock et al., *British Election Studies, 1950* (Ann Arbor, Mich.: George Wahr, 1951), p. 32; Dennis Kavanagh, *Election Campaigning. The New Marketing of Politics* (Oxford: Blackwell, 1995), p. 185; Ian Jackson, *The Provincial Press and the Community* (Manchester: Manchester University Press, 1971).
34 John Parker, *Father of the House. Fifty Years in Politics* (London: Routledge and Kegan Paul, 1982), p. 32; Edward Storey, *Fen Boy First* (London: Robert Hale, 1994), p. 131.
35 F. W. S. Craig, *British Electoral Facts 1832–1987* (Aldershot: Gower Publishing, 1989), pp. 51 and 114; *Independent*, 6 January 1994 and 23 July 1993.
36 Nugent, 'The ratepayers', pp. 25–6; Peter Shore, *The Real Nature of Conservatism* (London: Labour Party, 1952), p. 26; Tony Benn, quoted in *South London Press*, 2 April 1982; Advertising Services Guild, *The Press and its Readers* (London: Art and Technics, 1949); Rose, *Influencing Voters*, p. 169; and John Curtice and Holli Semetko, 'Does it matter what the papers say?', in Heath et al. (eds.), *Labour's Last Chance?*, pp. 43–61.

Nick Tiratsoo

37 Oliver Stutchbury, *Too Much Government? A Political Aeneid* (London: Boydell Press, 1977), pp. 11–12.

38 Joni Lovenduski, Pippa Norris, and Catriona Burness, 'The party and women', in Seldon and Ball (eds.), *Conservative Century*, pp. 614–17.

39 See, for example, S. J. Gee, 'The problem of rural constituencies', *Labour Organiser* no. 35 (1923), 9; Herbert Morrison, 'Can Labour win London without the middle classes?', *Labour Organiser* no. 35 (1923), 16–19; and 'National Agent's Report', National Executive Committee minutes, 7 November 1924, LPA.

40 Marion Phillips, 'Organising women electors', *Labour Organiser* no. 19 (1922), 21.

41 Frank Smith, 'About propaganda', *Labour Organiser* no. 29 (1923), 2–3; Frank H. Edwards, 'Hints on the addressing of envelopes', *Labour Organiser* no. 31 (1923), 16–17.

42 *Report of the 65th Annual Conference of the Labour Party* (London: Labour Party, 1966), p. 163.

43 See, for example, 'JSM', 'The Labour Party', (n.d. but 1929), confidential memorandum inserted into National Executive minutes, LPA; 'Interim Report of the Sub-Committee on Party Organisation', in *Report of the 54th Annual Conference of the Labour Party* (London: Labour Party, 1955), pp. 83–8; Stutchbury, *Too Much Government?*, pp. 35–49.

44 For one agent's struggles, see Cliff Prothero, *Recount* (Ormskirk and Northridge: G. W. and A. Hesketh, 1982).

45 R. H. S. Crossman, *Labour in the Affluent Society* (London: Fabian Society, 1960), p. 6; Tony Benn, *A Future for Socialism* (London: HarperCollins, 1991), p. 64.

46 Michael Hatfield, *The House the Left Built* (London: Victor Gollancz, 1978), pp. 228–9.

47 Even the modernising Neil Kinnock was apparently haunted by the 'hunt for elusive words': see Philip Gould, *The Unfinished Revolution. How Modernisers Saved the Labour Party* (London: Little Brown, 1998), p. 147.

48 See, for example, Mark Abrams, 'Public opinion polls and political parties', *Public Opinion Quarterly* 27 (1963), 13–18.

49 Don Mathew, *From Two Boys and a Dog to Political Power. The Labour Party in the Lowestoft Constituency 1918–1945* (Lowestoft Constituency Labour Party, 1979), pp. 43–4.

50 Organiser's report on 'Nottingham City Party, 9 December 1965', Catermole MSS 9/3/20/321, Modern Records Centre, University of Warwick.

51 Denis Howell, *Made in Birmingham* (London: Queen Anne Press, 1990), p. 54.

52 'Forward to socialism!', *Labour Woman* 22 (1934), 186–7 and Fielding, Thompson and Tiratsoo, *'England Arise!'*, pp. 183–4. See also, Pamela M. Graves, *Labour Women. Women in British Working-Class Politics 1918–1939* (Cambridge: Cambridge University Press, 1994) and Pat Thane, 'The women of the British Labour Party and feminism, 1906–1945', in Harold L. Smith

(ed.), *British Feminism in the Twentieth Century* (Aldershot: Edward Elgar, 1990), pp. 124–43.

53 Christopher Mayhew, *Party Games* (London: Hutchinson, 1969), p. 26; Hugh Thomas, *John Strachey* (London: Eyre Methuen, 1973), pp. 224 and 303; *New Society*, 18 June 1970.

54 See, for example, Edward Milne, *No Shining Armour* (London: John Calder, 1976); Joe Morgan, *Eastenders Don't Cry* (South Woodham Ferrers: New Author Publications, 1994); Graham Turner, *The North Country* (London: Eyre and Spottiswoode, 1967), pp. 313–31; and Chris Williams, *Democratic Rhondda. Politics and Society, 1885–1951* (Cardiff: University of Wales Press, 1996), pp. 173–81 and 193–5.

55 Glasgow District Council Labour Group, 'New horizons for housing', February 1978, p. 2, Kelvingrove Constituency Labour Party Records, Mitchell Library, Glasgow.

56 Michael Crick, *Militant* (London: Faber and Faber, 1984); Sue Goss, *Local Labour and Local Government. A Study of Changing Interests, Politics and Policy in Southwark from 1919 to 1982* (Edinburgh: Edinburgh University Press, 1988), pp. 83–105; Eric Shaw, *Discipline and Discord in the Labour Party* (Manchester: Manchester University Press, 1988).

57 *The Weekly Law Reports*, vol. I (London: Incorporated Council of Law Reporting for England and Wales, 1978), p. 1065.

58 'General Election Campaign 1951', appendix 9, LPA; D. E. Butler, *The British General Election of 1951* (London: Macmillan, 1952), pp. 142–3.

59 'Interim Report', *Report of the 54th Annual Conference of the Labour Party*, p. 65.

60 Tony Benn, *Years of Hope. Diaries, Papers and Letters 1940–62* (London: Arrow Books, 1995), p. 306.

61 Kavanagh, *Election Campaigning*, pp. 77–109.

62 See, for example, 'Interim Report', *Report of the 54th Annual Conference of the Labour Party*, p. 82.

63 See, for example, Leah Manning, *A Life for Education* (London: Victor Gollancz, 1970), p. 193.

64 Peter Kellner, 'The Labour campaign', in Austin Ranney (ed.), *Britain at the Polls 1983. A Study of the General Election* (Durham, N.C.: Duke University Press, 1985), p. 65.

65 Giles Radice, *Southern Discomfort* (London: Fabian Society, 1992); Ivor Crewe, 'Labor force changes, working class decline, and the Labour vote: social and electoral trends in postwar Britain', in Frances Fox Piven (ed.), *Labor Parties in Postindustrial Societies* (Cambridge: Polity Press, 1991), pp. 20–36.

66 Gould, *Unfinished Revolution*; Tony Blair, *Let Us Face the Future – the 1945 Anniversary Lecture* (London: Fabian Society, 1995); Steven Fielding, 'Labour's path to power', in Andrew Geddes and Jonathan Tongue (eds.), *Labour's Landslide* (Manchester: Manchester University Press, 1997), pp. 23–35; David Butler and Dennis Kavanagh, *The British General Election of 1997* (London: Macmillan, 1997), pp. 46–67.

Nick Tiratsoo

67 Butler and Kavanagh, *The British General Election of 1997*, pp. 244–7
68 *Financial Times*, 22 August 1998.
69 John Bartle, Ivor Crewe and Brian Gosschalk, 'Introduction', in Ivor Crewe, Brian Gosschalk and John Bartle (eds.), *Political Communications. Why Labour Won the General Election of 1997* (London: Frank Cass, 1998), p. xix. See also Robert Worcester and Roger Mortimore, *Explaining Labour's Landslide* (London: Politico's Publishing, 1999).
70 *New Statesman*, 7 August 1998, 11 September 1998; *Economist*, 15 August 1998.

10 | Labour in comparative perspective

Stefan Berger

'The leading candidate for the position of "most anomalous Left" in Europe was and perhaps remained the British.'[1] 'Since labour movements arise as a human response to external social and economic conditions the labour movements of Europe in their turn come to assume forms significantly different from those of either Britain or the US.'[2] 'I do not want to get mixed up with the English any more. Not only do they speak a different language, they also think differently. Insular isolation has made them special human beings.'[3] These are the voices of distinguished comparative labour historians Donald Sassoon, Walter Kendall and August Bebel, and it would not be difficult to add many more quotations of this sort from, amongst others, Julius Braunthal, Dick Geary, Carl Cavanagh Hodge, Hans Mommsen, Tom Nairn, Douglas Newton, Perry Anderson and Stephen Yeo.[4] For a long time the prevailing view on the Labour Party has been that it was an inward-looking, isolationist, 'Little-Englander' party which was following a different trajectory from the working-class parties on the continent and which was influenced almost exclusively by peculiarly British antecedents.

This impression was, if anything, re-enforced by the portrayal of important Labour Party leaders as anti-foreigner and, in particular,

Stefan Berger

anti-European patriots with little understanding of foreign languages and even less taste for foreign customs. So, for example, Denis Healey described the head of the Labour Party's International Department in the inter-war period, William Gillies, as a 'catankerous Scot who distrusted foreigners and hated all Germans'.[5] According to both Ken Morgan and Alan Bullock, Ernest Bevin's commitment to British national interests far outweighed his internationalism, not to speak of his anti-Germanism.[6]

But it is also possible to construct a very different narrative about the Labour Party's stance towards internationalism generally and European social democracy in particular. In a nutshell, the arguments about British insularity and peculiarity have prevented recognition of the simple fact that the Labour Party was not so different a political animal from its north-west European sister parties. During important spells of its history, the Labour Party even stood at the heart of this north-west European social-democratic project.[7] It often had to be cautious about emphasising its internationalist links and commitments. After all, they laid the party open to the charge of anti-patriotism, for example in 1924, the affair over the Zinoviev letter, and 1998, the attacks of the Conservative opposition on the Labour Party's position *vis-à-vis* monetary union. Furthermore, the paths that the Labour Party travelled were not identical to those trodden by European social democracy. Many differences remained. However, no working-class party in Western Europe followed exactly the same road. Each and every one had its peculiarities: peculiar class alliances in Sweden, the precocious winning of universal male suffrage combined with the continued social exclusion of workers in France, the lack of political and social integration of organised workers in Germany, the linguistic split in Belgium, and the strength of anarchism in Spain. The Labour Party also had its peculiarities, but, as will be argued, it should nevertheless be firmly placed within the European mainstream. Klaus Tenfelde is right to be 'struck by the relative uniformity of developments across national frontiers'. He adds: 'This makes it look as if there is still a "European" type of labour movement, which historically has converged sometimes to a greater, sometimes to a lesser extent, but which has by and large traced and continues to trace the same path.'[8]

Perhaps one should be more exact: a north-west European type of labour movement. For social democracy in southern and eastern Europe was, to a significant extent, a different story. Before the Second World War, many countries of south-eastern Europe had repressive political regimes in which social democracy could only develop under clandestine conditions. Although the social democracies in south-eastern Europe, in so far as they were allowed to exist, followed, by and large, the model provided by the West European parties, they did not have the same scope for development. More importantly, after 1945 they became submerged in the communist regimes which were established in Eastern Europe under Soviet tutelage. And after 1989, the re-emerging social democracies in Eastern Europe struggled to define their image in the context of the crises of their West European counterparts and the rapid 'social-democratisation' of the former communist parties of Eastern Europe.[9] Hence, whilst it will be important to take brief side glances at the attitude of the Labour Party towards East European and in particular Soviet communism over time, the main emphasis of the comparison will lie with north-western Europe.

Nevertheless, it will also be important to take glimpses at the Labour Party's connections with non-European progressive and socialist movements. The fact that Britain commanded a huge empire did matter.[10] The Labour Party had strong personal links to labour movements in the colonies, in particular to those of white-settler societies. Colonial and Commonwealth affairs played an important part in the Labour Party, and some of its leaders, notably Hugh Gaitskell, felt much closer to the Commonwealth countries than to continental European socialism. The relationship of the Labour Party with working-class parties in the US and parts of the British empire were, however, of a different character. Whilst ties of language and culture were obviously strong and whilst interest – in particular in the Australian Labor Party – could be intense at times, continental European working-class parties in many ways proved to be far closer to home for the British Labour Party.

The above themes and arguments need to be unfolded in relation to the various phases of the Labour Party's development. The first phase, from its inception to the end of the second Labour government in 1931, saw the development of a party which followed a distinctly European trajectory. In the second phase, which witnessed the Labour Party's rise from the political ashes to the heroic period of the immediate post-Second World War Labour government, the outlook and development of the party kept in line with that of other major north-west European working-class parties. The third phase, lasting from 1951 to 1983, saw the party go from high hopes for a socialist millennium to disillusionment and despair. Finally, from the second half of the 1980s onwards, the Labour Party, in line with other social-democratic parties in Europe, has been searching to redefine its ethos, reformulate key ingredients of social-democratic ideology and remodel its organisation.

Stefan Berger

From foundation to the end of MacDonaldism (1900–1931)

When the Labour Party was founded in 1900 it was firmly rooted in national traditions. It is common to assert that the years before 1914 were characterised by the forging of strong organisational links with the powerful trade-union movement, and, to a lesser extent, attempts to build bridges to the co-operative movement. Yet the Labour Party was never *just* a trade-union creature with narrow trade-union concerns. The smaller socialist parties and societies, such as the Independent Labour Party, the Fabian Society, the Social Democratic Federation (SDF), the Socialist League and the Clarion movement all impacted on the outlook and shape of the party – especially on its leaders. Furthermore, the Labour Party was in many respects formed in direct response to and clashed with the established political parties in Britain. Its outlook and organisation were also vitally influenced by Nonconformity.[11]

Any such exclusively national interpretation would have to overlook the longstanding concern of the party with internationalist aspirations and ideals. In its formative period the Labour Party was more interested in the continental working-class parties – and in particular the German Social Democrats – than it was in working-class parties of the English-speaking world. This may be surprising because of the obvious ties of language and culture, but, with the exception of Australia, none of the English-speaking countries had developed powerful working-class parties around the turn of the century. Whilst pan-Anglo-Saxonism was influential amongst the Liberal and Conservative parties of Britain, the quasi-racialist overtones inherent in this concept made it less attractive for British socialists. The transatlantic flow of radical and socialist ideas was important at times. So, for example, as Max Beer put it in 1920, 'four fifths of the socialist leaders of Great Britain in the eighties passed through the school of Henry George'.[12] The theories of the American socialist, writer and founder of the Socialist Labor Party, Daniel de Leon, had a distinct influence on radical socialism in Scotland before 1917.[13] While Keir Hardie and Tom Mann wrote regularly for the trade-union press in America, Sam Gompers was in contact with many British activists whom he accepted as 'true socialists' committed to building up a mass labour movement and whom he contrasted to 'fake socialists' like de Leon in his own country.[14] Yet, overall, there was much vague and general unease about the United States amongst British mainstream socialists who tended to perceive America as the bastion of world capitalism.[15] The fact that an American version of the Labour Party did not seem to be forthcoming also contributed to the negative perception of the fortunes of American socialism, as did the rivalry and infighting among American socialists. Like Keir Hardie on his tours of the United States in 1895 and 1912, British Labour politicians were mostly intent on lecturing the Americans on how to build socialism rather than being prepared to learn from any American experience.

Australia was different. In 1905 the Australian Labor Party (ALP) formed the first national Labour government in the world. It contributed significantly towards Australia's progressive legislation in the areas of social welfare and education and thus helped to shape the country's reputation as an early laboratory for the welfare state. The successes of the ALP were keenly followed in the British Labour Party. At the 1905 Labour Representation Committee (LRC) conference, for example, Isaac Mitchell, the fraternal delegate of the Amalgamated Society of Engineers, referred to the Australian party's successes as a model for the Labour Party: 'He hoped that the claims of the LRC for political organisation would succeed, and that in the very near future they would occupy as high a position in the political affairs of the country as their colleagues in Australia reached some months ago.'[16] Many Australian labour movement leaders were British in origin, and they retained strong bonds of language and culture with the country of their birth. In organisation and outlook the ALP came to be an inspiration for the Labour Party. The Australian unions had formed the backbone of the ALP. The Australian party had instituted women's branches within local parties after 1904, a policy adopted by the Labour Party after 1918. Many British socialists were impressed with the ALP's legislative reforms, in particular with respect to state wages boards, the minimum wage and compulsory arbitration. The ALP stood for gradualism, reformism and pragmatism – a position that the Labour Party was to inherit and represent within a European context. Yet the geographical distance between the ALP and Labour Party, as well as the ALP's peculiarities, such as its racialist 'White Australia' policy, its unashamed championing of nationalism, its pro-tariff stance and the strong support it received amongst non-working-class sections of the Australian population, all set it apart from the Labour Party. Furthermore, many of the socialists and trade-unionists who went to Australia (and other parts of the empire) did so with the express intention to teach socialism rather than to learn from an indigenous working class, which was often perceived as raw and underdeveloped. Arthur Henderson, returning from a visit to Australia in the mid-1920s, wrote admiringly about the achievements of the ALP, about the fine Australian cities, the low unemployment figures, the high wages and 'the dozens of profit-making publicly

Stefan Berger

owned enterprises'. At the end of his article, however, he rather patron-
isingly concluded: 'Australia may yet become the Greater Britain of the
Southern Seas.'[17]

While perceptions of and relations to the ALP were important, the
Labour Party was keen to join the socialist Second International which
was dominated by the major north-west European parties and, before
1914 in particular, by the Social Democratic Party of Germany (SPD).
The biggest obstacle the Labour Party had to overcome was the rigorous
opposition of the SDF to its application for membership. The SDF
leader Henry Hyndman, who sat on the executive of the International,
argued that the Labour Party did not accept the class struggle as the
basic principle of its organisation and therefore could not be admitted to
the International. It was a measure of the keenness of continental socialists to bring the Labour Party on board that eventually Karl Kautsky's
ingenious compromise formula for accepting the Labour Party's membership was approved by a large majority. It read: 'The British Labour
Party is admitted to the International Socialist Congresses, because,
while not expressly accepting the proletarian class struggle, in practice
the Labour Party conducts this struggle, and adopts its stand-point,
inasmuch as the party is organized independently of the bourgeois
parties.'[18]

The Labour Party did indeed share what can be described as the programmatic core of north-west European social-democratic parties: a belief
in class solidarity, state planning of a socialised economy, and security of
life as well as equality of opportunities for all. Second International
Marxism, just like labourist socialism in Britain, was much more important as a utopian unifying myth than a concrete orientation for specific
policies.[19] The socialist millennium fulfilled an important spiritual function for the parties' rank and file everywhere in Europe, but what the
social-democratic parties did in terms of their specific policies was quite
a different matter. In the years before 1914 the Labour Party was to par-
ticipate strongly in the activities of the International, notably in its campaigns against war and its debates surrounding the general strike. 'After
1905', as Chris Wrigley has written, 'the Parliamentary Labour Party
leaders – Hardie, MacDonald and Henderson – became major figures in
the international movement.'[20] Within the International, the Labour
Party was widely perceived as the model party of the reformist wing of
European social democracy. Already by 1900 Kautsky was pointing out
that German revisionism was following an 'English model'.[21] And, in the
late 1920s, Egon Wertheimer of the SPD praised the British Labour
Party for its tolerance and individualism.[22]

314

Yet this was not just a one-way relationship. For many Labour Party leaders were enamoured of the successes of continental socialism and in particular with the spectacular growth of the biggest working-class party in the world, the German SPD. With respect to developing a powerful organisational machine, to emulating the electoral success of the SPD, to building up a strong individual membership after 1918, to maintaining and expanding the socialist press and to constructing the 'communities of solidarity' which were so characteristic of the German Social Democrats, the SPD became a powerful influence on the organisational outlook adopted by the Labour Party leadership in the first three decades of its existence.[23] Arthur Henderson and Ramsay MacDonald were amongst those who travelled to Western Europe, and Germany in particular, in order to learn about organisational efficiency and social policy. Many socialist women such as Dora Montefiore and Margaret MacDonald were keen delegates at socialist women's conferences and forged strong relationships to leading socialist women in Western Europe.[24] Herbert Morrison's London Labour Party was largely built on his perception of the Berlin SPD. He wrote in 1929:

I have never forgotten what Stephen Sanders, MP, told us before the war with regard to Berlin: 'That the Social Democratic Party Executive could sit on the top floor of the *Vorwärts* building, pass a manifesto paragraph by paragraph, have it put into type and circulated to every tenement in the city of Berlin by the next morning.' We cannot quite do this yet in London, but we ought to be able to do it. And some day we will do it.[25]

And just before the outbreak of the First World War, Tom Fox, who was to become the first Labour mayor of Manchester in 1919, in his presidential address to the Labour Party conference, blamed 'the deplorable inefficiency of our methods of organisation' for the failure of the party to achieve substantial social progress, and added: 'Our German brethren have learned their lesson better and are using their experience to better purpose in spite of the greater political handicap they have to bear.'[26]

The First World War left West European socialist internationalism in tatters. In almost every social-democratic party, including the British Labour Party, divisions occurred between those who, for very different motives, supported the war efforts of their respective countries, and those who, again for very diverse reasons, opposed the war effort. Yet, in many countries, the war rapidly accelerated the firm integration of social-democratic parties into the mainstream of the national political arena. Without the First World War, the speed and the extent with which the Labour Party was to replace the Liberals as one of the two

Stefan Berger

main parties in the British party political system would in all probability have been much slower. Socialists in Britain as well as in France, Belgium and, towards the end of the war, even in Germany, joined governments and were remarkably successful in obtaining at least some of the economic and political reforms they had been struggling for in the years before 1914. At the end of the war, they were rewarded by the democratisation of the political system and the growing recognition of the trade-union movement. A corporatist restructuring of Europe was on the cards, including in Britain.[27]

However, the widespread hopes and enthusiasm found right across the social-democratic spectrum about the prospects for social and economic reform soon gave way to disillusionment and disappointment. Clashes over nationalisation occurred in France, Germany and Britain after 1918, but nowhere did socialists manage to push through any such measures. The implementation of 'economic democracy' was widely discussed, but soon the old antagonism between unions and employers resurfaced. Although a wide-ranging attempt was made in Germany, nowhere did a sustainable welfare state emerge which was based on a broad consensus of different sections of the population. As John Horne has pointed out, the war left similar ideological legacies in Britain and France (and, one could add, in several other Western European countries):[28] a moral condemnation of capitalism combined with the programmatic search for collectivist alternatives to produce similar agendas for reforming capitalism. The language of productivism, so familiar to pre-war European social democracy, became overlaid with the language of consumption to produce a social-democratic vision of modernity.[29] The formation of communist parties facilitated the move of social-democratic parties to reformist agendas almost everywhere. The ideological gap between continental European social democracies and the British Labour Party was thus further reduced in the inter-war period.

As before 1914, social-democratic parties hoped to achieve any readjustments to capitalism within an internationalist framework.[30] The British Labour Party was instrumental in rebuilding the Socialist International after 1918. As Beatrice Webb noted in her diary in December 1918: 'the one outstanding virtue of the Labour Party, a virtue which is its very own, not imposed upon it by intellectuals, is its high sense of international morality. Alone, amongst British politicians, the leaders of the Labour Party do honestly believe in the brotherhood of man.'[31] For Arthur Henderson, Ramsay MacDonald and many others, internationalism was the soul of socialism. In line with reformist social-democratic thought (and in opposition to Leninism, Luxemburgism or anarchism) they saw no contradiction between internationalism and patriotism. On the contrary, following Eduard Bernstein, they argued that any genuine internationalism could only be built on a self-confident patriotism.[32]

The International Department of the Labour Party, set up at the end of the First World War, played a crucial role in fostering and developing the party's outlook in the inter-war period. Its head, William Gillies, was 'the major route for information from Britain to Europe and vice versa'.[33] As far as 'his knowledge of European socialism' was concerned, it was 'only outmatched by that of Henderson and MacDonald'.[34] The crucial role of the Labour Party in rebuilding socialist internationalism after 1918, in re-unifying the rump of the Second International with the Vienna Union in 1923, and, subsequently, in the Labour and Socialist International, was paralleled by the strong interest of British socialists in the Women's International, the Youth International and a wide variety of subject-based Internationals.[35] The Labour Party's commitment to a Eurocentric internationalism went hand in hand with pro-European sentiments. The German Social Democrats' call for 'the creation of the United States of Europe'[36] was mirrored by Ernest Bevin's desire to promote within the British labour movement 'the spirit of a United States of Europe'[37] or by Clement Attlee's dramatic exclamation: 'Europe must federate or perish.'[38]

The Labour Party showed not only an acute internationalism in the inter-war period, it also followed a similar trajectory to that of other north-west European social-democratic parties. Electorally, they could not move decisively beyond their traditional stronghold in the industrial working class. To make matters worse, in mainland Europe they often could not find suitable coalition partners. The combined effect of these two handicaps kept social-democratic parties out of power. Where they did succeed in forming governments, such as in Britain and Germany, they did so either as minority governments (Britain) or in unstable coalition governments (Germany). A further problem surfaced as soon as the working-class parties were in power, for they seemed to be totally bereft of any immediate programmes and tended to follow the economic orthodoxies of the day. A comparison of the political actions of the SPD Finance Minister Rudolf Hilferding in the late 1920s and Philip Snowden's efforts in 1931 shows how both social democrats rejected the idea of deficit-financed employment programmes and underlined the importance of balancing budgets. Scandinavian social democracy was the only modest exception from this rule. So, for example, the Swedish Socialist Workers' Party (SAP) was not only successful in finding a powerful coalition

Stefan Berger

partner in the Agrarian Party (which represented agricultural interests), but also began experimenting with forms of Keynesian anti-cyclical economic policies in the early 1930s, well before other parties took Keynes seriously. Yet such new beginnings were rare amongst the social-democratic parties in Western Europe. Drawn between the longing for an altogether different politics and the pressures of pragmatic policy-making whilst in office, social-democratic parties found it difficult to steer a clear political course. In Britain, the tensions between these two different sets of priorities ultimately culminated in the crisis of 1931, when Ramsay MacDonald and some of his cabinet colleagues did the unthinkable and went 'agin the party' in order to do what they regarded as right for their country in the midst of a desperate economic situation.

From political wilderness to pacesetter for European social democracy (1931–1950)

The elections of 1931 saw Labour representation in the Commons slashed from 287 to just 52 members. And although the Labour Party managed to recapture about two million votes in the 1935 general elections, it found itself in the political wilderness for the remainder of the decade. In line with other West European social democracies, sections of the Labour Party became more radical as a result of domestic political isolation and the rise of right-wing authoritarian regimes across Europe in the 1930s. The Socialist League, founded in 1932, gave a voice to all those who were disappointed by the parliamentary road to socialism and by piece-meal gradualism. Instead, some of the most powerful Labour Party intellectuals and leaders such as Harold Laski, Stafford Cripps, Aneurin Bevan and R. H. Tawney became outspoken proponents of more direct action by workers – occasionally even arguing for a confrontationist 'class against class' stance in politics. Such a return to the more revolutionary origins of West European social democracy could be found in a number of European parties in the 1930s and was often connected to the necessity 'to respond to fascism'.[39]

Given the Labour Party's position on the reformist wing of pre-1914 European social democracy, there was a surprising amount of sympathy with the Soviet Union after 1917. The British labour movement mounted a stark challenge to the British government over the Allied intervention in the Russian civil war, culminating in the threat of a general strike in 1920. The Webbs even discovered in the Soviet Union the promise of the future socialist utopia and heartily endorsed the communist experiment.[40] Many in the British Labour Party had a kind of instinctive sympathy for a government which had abolished capitalism and claimed to represent working-class interests. Roy Jenkins, himself quite immune to such feelings, has referred to the Labour Party's 'wallowing in vague, emotional feelings of solidarity with the Soviet Union',[41] whilst a more sympathetic Richard Crossman spoke of the party's 'Russian complex'.[42]

The Labour Party leadership, however, like the leadership of the German Social Democratic Party in Exile (SOPADE), opposed an official united front stance of social democrats and communists against fascism. In the 1930s, Gillies, for example, coined the term 'Communazis' to indicate that, as far as he was concerned, communists and Nazis were alike.[43] At the 1933 Labour Party conference the totalitarianism of both left and right was condemned in equal measure. Much of the unease of British Labour leaders with the Spanish Civil War stemmed from their mistrust of any social-democratic alliance with communists. While there were considerable pro-republican sentiments amongst the labour movement's rank and file, the majority of the party leaders restricted official party policy to a concentration on humanitarian relief efforts.[44] In its overall lack of support for the Spanish republic, British Labour was, however, hardly exceptional: after all, the Popular Front government of Léon Blum in France also subscribed to the non-interventionism which ultimately sealed the fate of the Spanish republic.[45] Possibly the most important legacy of the Spanish Civil War for the British Labour Party was its crucial role in overcoming intra-party opposition to rearmament. Leading trade-unionists such as Bevin and like-minded Labour Party leaders came to endorse rearmament in the 1930s because they knew full well what had happened not only to the Spanish socialists but to powerful social-democratic parties in Germany and Austria. As Bevin pointed out at the 1936 party conference: 'Which is the first institution that victorious Fascism wipes out? It is the trade union movement . . . we saw our Movement go down in Germany . . . our men shed their blood in Austria – and nearly every one of them was a trade-unionist.'[46]

Its anti-united front stance and its timid response to the Spanish Civil War confirmed the Labour Party's position on the reformist wing of West European social democracy. If there was some interest in the communist experiment in the Soviet Union, there was much more interest in Scandinavia, and in particular Swedish social democracy.[47] Gillies was in correspondence with various Scandinavian socialists over their policies on public works programmes, housing policies, a national health service and trade-union–party relationships, while he also facilitated contacts between Scandinavian social democrats and Labour Party politicians such as F. W. Pethick Lawrence. The advances made by Swedish and Scandinavian social democrats in the 1930s by a combination of success-ful coalition-building and reformist policy packages were noted and admired by many in Labour Party circles.[48] There were laudatory articles about Swedish social democracy in the official journal of the party, *Labour*. And the publication *Notes for Speakers* of 2 October 1936, under the heading 'What Socialism has done for Sweden' noted: 'Today Sweden is in a position of stability which is the envy of other countries, her progress towards economic recovery has been greater than that of any other country, and the good work of the Socialist Government has been acknowledged even in the anti-Socialist press of this country.'[49] The New Fabian Research Bureau took an active interest in Scandinavian social democracy as well. It sent a delegation to Sweden in the summer of 1937, which included, among others, Evan Durbin, Hugh Gaitskell, G. D. H. and Margaret Cole as well as Raymond Postgate. On its return a laudatory conference was held and its proceedings were published.[50] Elsewhere Hugh Dalton praised Gunnar Myrdal and Ernst Wigforss as the brains behind the Swedish recovery and argued that the Swedish model had much to recommend it to Britain.[51] The Fabians also facili-tated official contacts between the Swedish SAP and the Labour Party, leading to the visit of George Dallas as fraternal delegate to the SAP party conference in 1936.[52]

As in 1914–18, the Second World War saw a further push towards the integration of working-class parties in a variety of European countries including Britain. Having been part of national coalition governments (or, in continental Europe, national resistance movements) brought social-democratic parties recognition and respectability, and at the end of the war, when issues of social justice and equality stood high on the European political agenda, social democrats found themselves in government in most West European countries. However, whereas they had to share power with diverse coalition partners almost everywhere, it was only in Norway and Britain that they had a majority. Both parties became stalwarts of economic planning, nationalisation, the welfare state and full employment. Their policy goals were strongly influenced by a social–liberal tradition within both parties. In Britain this was epi-tomised by the influence of the Beveridge Report on the post-1945 Labour government. The Norwegian and the British Labour parties were forced into making some compromises with the liberal capitalism espoused by the United States in exchange for American financial help, which was badly needed by both countries after the war. In particular the British party became a pacesetter for other social-democratic parties in post-war Europe which had to balance their adherence to the emerging *Pax Americana* with their long-term aim of searching for a capitalism with a human face.

In 1945, many European social democrats lived in hope that a social-democratic Europe would emerge out of the ruins of the Second World War to form a third major power bloc between the capitalist United States and the communist Soviet Union. These concepts were sometimes connected to the idea that European social democracy could form a bridge between the opposing systems of liberal capitalism and state communism. In Britain such notions found expression in the 'Third Force' movement which combined demands for neutralism in foreign policy with the hope that a bloc of socialist West European nations would soon emerge, among which Britain would take a prominent place.[53] In subsequent decades, neutralist residues were to resurface in most social-democratic parties across Western Europe. The Campaign for Nuclear Disarmament in Britain, for example, had its parallels in the Anti-Atomtod movement in the Federal Republic of Germany (FRG), and the support of the left for the peace movement of the late 1970s and early 1980s was very strong across Western Europe. Yet the overwhelming support for Ernest Bevin's brainchild NATO amongst almost all West European social democracies indicated that, in the emerging Cold War, 'Atlanticist' sentiments were to win the day.

Immediately after the war, left-wing sympathies with the Soviet Union were still considerable. After all, Labour in 1945 used the campaign slogan 'Left understands Left' – indicating that the antagonistic stance between Churchill and the Soviet leadership could give way to better mutual understanding under a Labour government. Yet, eventually, the strong pro-Americanism in the parliamentary Labour Party (PLP) and amongst the trade-union leadership was given nourishment by the Berlin airlift and the Marshall Plan. These events ultimately ensured that pro-Soviet feelings were marginalised. The 'soft left' gathered around *Tribune* now contributed to a major campaign of 'anti-anti-Americanism' which was to be much more powerful than any residues of anti-Americanism in post-war British Labour circles.[54]

Social-democratic parties in the 1930s had still been torn between their immediate reformist ambitions and their long-term transformatory aims. In the 1950s, they abandoned any fundamental opposition to capitalism for a more accommodationist stance. The record of the post-war Labour government was firmly based on the ultimate goal of modernising the British economy and society in conjunction with capital rather than in opposition to it. The relationship between West European social

Stefan Berger

democracy and capital became one of 'critical partnership' – with social-democratic governments by and large abstaining from structural reforms at any level of the state or the economy.[55] State interventionism was proposed on the basis that capitalism could be more effectively run by social-democratic parties. When Labour had pushed nationalisation to its erstwhile limits (and nowhere in Western Europe was it pushed any further), and when the welfare state based on the principle of universality had been created, most Labour Party leaders and their followers had no clear idea where the party was heading, particularly as the political balance of power in Britain did not seem favourable to more radical reform policies. That is also why, by 1950, some, like Herbert Morrison, argued strongly in favour of consolidating what had already been achieved.

What had been accomplished did indeed look impressive by the standards of other West European states, and in the 1950s, in a period when most social-democratic parties found themselves facing a prolonged period of opposition, their search for programmatic reform centred on the models and ideas provided by the Labour Party. In the first half of the 1950s, Anthony Crosland became the guru of growth-oriented West European social democracy. His authority was invoked time and again in the many programmatic reforms initiated by a whole string of social-democratic parties. And Crosland, like many others in the Labour Party, remained in touch with mainland European reformism, in particular in the Scandinavian countries.[56] A Labour Party delegation went to Sweden in 1951 'to study the achievements of the Swedish labour movement'. It reported back highly favourably on housing, social services, industrial relations and attitudes to public ownership and concluded that Sweden was 'a laboratory of social progress' and that it 'provides many lessons which other nations might well learn, mark and inwardly digest'.[57]

As at the end of the First World War, the Labour Party was crucial in rebuilding the Socialist International. The patriotic wartime stance of the party had not fundamentally undermined its internationalism. Anti-German feelings in Labour circles were no stronger than in other West European parties at the time. In fact, they were probably weaker than amongst French and Belgian socialists. The activities of organisations such as Fight for Freedom were therefore not necessarily a sign of any deep-rooted adversity to Germany and the German Social Democrats in particular.[58] Rather, it was a reflection of the fact that significant sections of the Labour Party continued to support a conciliatory stance towards the German Social Democrats despite the almost complete break-up of official relationships during the Second World War.[59] It was indicative that the difficulties which existed between leading Labour Party and SOPADE politicians were never widely advertised within the party for fear that they would exacerbate the rifts that already existed within the Labour Party leadership. After all, the relationship of the two parties had been of significant importance before 1933.[60] Leading members of the Socialist Union (SU) and its precursor, the Socialist Vanguard Group, such as Allan Flanders and Rita Hinden, had been in close contact with leading members of the German International Socialist Fighting League. Flanders, who was the head of the political division of the Allied Control Commission in post-war Germany, spoke fluent German and was a close friend of Willi Eichler, a leading post-war Social Democrat and author of the SPD's 1959 Bad Godesberg programme. The SU's publications such as *A New Statement of Principle* rivalled the *New Fabian Essays* in their importance for the programmatic reorientation of the Labour Party in the 1950s.[61]

In the years following the end of the Second World War, close contacts were established between the Labour Party and the French and Belgian social-democratic parties – in particular through the Labour Europe Group.[62] By contrast, the relationship with the German Social Democrats was difficult, not the least because of the stringent nationalism of Kurt Schumacher. After Schumacher's death, however, relations began to improve.[63] Even before that, the head of the Labour Party's International Department, Denis Healey, who spoke fluent German, had excellent contacts with German socialists, in particular with Herta Gotthelf. She provided much background information which was circulated by Healey amongst the Labour Party leadership as a 'letter from Germany'. Ultimately it was the Labour Party's constant efforts to mediate between the German Social Democrats and other continental social democrats which allowed the SPD to return to the International at its Antwerp conference of 1947. Furthermore, British efforts were paramount in formally reconstituting the Second International at Frankfurt-am-Main in 1951. Since then the Socialist International has become an important forum for the exchange of ideas between the leaders of West European social democracy, and it has taken notable steps in bringing about *détente* between East and West as well as initiating a dialogue between the developed and developing world. Last, but not least, it played a significant role in supporting socialist parties in exile, in particular the Greek, Spanish and Portuguese social democracies.

The positioning of the Labour Party *vis-à-vis* the post-war European project was ultimately one of caution. In line with leading German

Stefan Berger

Social Democrats, many in the British Labour Party perceived the emerging European Economic Community as dominated by conservative, Catholic and capitalist forces. In view of the almost in-built anti-socialist majority in such a Europe, the Labour leaders feared giving up any national sovereignty and opted for the possibility of building socialism in one country. Much has been written about Ernest Bevin's preference for Atlanticism over Europeanism, yet in effect he worked very hard to strengthen European co-operation between 1948 and 1951. However, his plans, in particular those for a strengthened Western European Union, found little sympathy with leading European federalists.[64] The language of trade was more important than an alleged anti-European mentality in explaining the ultimate reluctance of the post-war Labour (and Conservative) governments about entering any European economic alliances. In its organisational and ideological development, the Labour Party was following a European trajectory, but British trade continued to be primarily extra-European. Anyway, the Labour Party was not the only social-democratic party in Western Europe to show a lack of commitment to the emerging European Union. In fact, the social-democratic parties in the Benelux countries were almost exceptional in the interest they took in closer European co-operation.

Disenchantment, strife and division (1950–1983)

From 1945 to the early 1980s, the Labour Party's position on Europe underwent several violent and abrupt changes, from Euro-scepticism to pro-European commitments and back. In the 1950s hostility prevailed and in 1961 the party abstained in the Commons vote on Britain's application for membership of the European Economic Community (EEC). Yet Gaitskell's less than pleasant interchanges with European social democrats at meetings of the Socialist International are only one side of the coin. Leading Labourites including Cole, Brockway and Healey continued to speak in favour of closer European co-operation. An increasing number of back-bench MPs joined 'contact' organisations and took trips to mainland Europe in search of lessons to be applied to Britain. As in the SPD under Schumacher, there was an important pro-European minority tradition in the British Labour Party.

The Wilson governments of the 1960s were committed to seeking entry into the EEC, but when the party returned to the opposition benches after the 1970 general election, it campaigned against entry for largely tactical reasons. Yet those who supported European entry inside the PLP (organised efficiently in the Labour Committee for Europe) had nothing but distaste for such a tactical game over an issue to which they attributed the greatest historical significance, and, in October 1971, sixty-nine Labour MPs defied a three-line whip to support the Conservative Party on British entry.[65] When Labour returned to government in 1974 it successfully renegotiated Britain's terms to enter the EEC, only to move back to anti-European policies after Michael Foot became leader of the party in 1980. This ultimately led to the breakaway of the pro-European faction in the Labour Party and the creation of the Social Democratic Party (SDP) in 1981.

In its violent mood-swings and policy U-turns concerning Europe, Labour was not alone. The Scandinavian social democracies also had grave doubts about the European project.[66] By the time of the 1983 general election, the Labour Party was committed to withdrawal from the EC. However, that election saw Labour lose almost three million votes. The 'Liberal–SDP Alliance' polled almost as well as the Labour Party, and the Conservative government was returned with a huge majority. The 1983 election, more than any other in the party's history, indicated that Labour seemed in terminal decline. For many inside the party, it appeared that after 1951 everything had gone wrong. For, whereas many West European social-democratic parties suffered electoral reverses in this period, nowhere was this as marked as in Britain, where Labour's share of the vote fell from an average of 44.5 per cent between 1944 and 1978 to an average of 31.8 per cent between 1979 and 1988 – a 12.7 per cent drop compared with an average for West European social democracies of just 0.6 per cent over the same period.[67]

All West European social democracies had to adjust to massive social change, in particular the increasing deproletarianisation of West European societies. Male industrial workers who performed hard physical labour were increasingly finding themselves in a minority position among the total number of wage earners. In line with these developments many social-democratic parties deproletarianised their images in the 1950s and 1960s and transformed themselves from parties whose appeal rested almost exclusively on class into people's parties. There was significant pressure to demonstrate their social openness and win new converts amongst non-working-class sections of the population. This restyling of social democracy's traditional image was marked in countries such as Germany, Austria, Sweden and the Netherlands, though it was less noticeable in Belgium, France and Italy.

Under Gaitskell, the Labour Party also attempted a sweeping remodelling of the party's programme and image. However, in contrast to the

German SPD, Gaitskell was not successful in abandoning key symbolic features connected to the old class party, notably Clause Four. Such failure had much to do with the Gaitskellites' complete disregard for the party's sense of tradition and history. Hence they managed to antagonise both the right-wing trade-union leadership and the Labour left.[68] Despite the official defeat of the Gaitskellites, the Labour Party remained what it had always been in its majority: a reformist social-democratic party in the West European mould. In fact *Signposts for the Sixties*, which was adopted by the 1961 Labour conference without much dissent, amounted to 'the British equivalent of Bad Godesberg'.[69] David Ennals, secretary of the Labour Party's International Department, confirmed the similarity in outlook between the British and German parties in a report about the sixth congress of the Socialist International held at Hamburg in July 1959. The debate on 'democratic socialism today', according to Ennals, 'showed variations between the bourgeois attitude of parties such as the SFIO (France) and the PSDI (Italy) and parties such as the SPD (Germany) and the Labour Party which have their roots in the working-class movement'.[70] Contrary to much received party opinion of the 1990s, the Gaitskellite defeat cannot be seen as the moment when Labour Party history failed to turn.

In fact, in Britain as elsewhere in Western Europe, the period from the 1950s to the 1970s can indeed be seen as 'the golden age' of social democracy.[71] Centre-right parties everywhere rapidly social-democratised their ethos. In Britain, 'Butskellism' marked the specific form this social-democratisation took for the Conservative Party. In the 1960s social-democratic leaders such as Willy Brandt in Germany, Olof Palme in Sweden, Bruno Kreisky in Austria and Harold Wilson in Britain set the intellectual agenda. Across Western Europe, social democracy was perceived as a movement in line with modern times, youth and progress. The Labour Party in this period was in discussion with its continental sister parties over a variety of policies. So, for example, there was much interest in French 'indicative planning' in the mid-1960s, while Barbara Castle's famous *In Place of Strife* sought to reformulate British industrial relations' culture following what many perceived as a German/Scandinavian model. Wilson's attempt to 'modernise' Britain through a 'white hot technological revolution' was part and parcel of the seemingly boundless belief of West European social democracy in forms of social engineering and economic steering by a strong state within vaguely defined frameworks of liberal corporatism. Whilst British-style corporatism, like its German variant, never got involved in joint policy-making (beyond feeble attempts to arrive at some form of voluntary wage determination), and hence was fundamentally different from the more developed corporatist frameworks in countries such as Sweden and Austria, a 'corporatist bias' was still observable in Britain during these years.[72]

There are significant similarities between German-style 'concerted action' in the late 1960s and 1970s and Callaghan's attempts to implement a 'social contract' in the late 1970s. They were both attempts at a Western European crisis management which heavily relied on state intervention in the economic sphere. It was, in Esping-Anderson's memorable phrase, 'politics against markets' which was to lead the West European national economies out of economic crisis in the 1970s.[73] However, the perception of success rates of national governments in this undertaking differed widely. The British Labour Party and the German Social Democrats were probably at opposing ends of the spectrum. Whereas the SPD government under Helmut Schmidt appeared to succeed in controlling inflation and guaranteeing modest growth rates, the Labour government under Jim Callaghan appeared to fail in its attempt to build 'social contracts'. Whereas the 'winter of discontent' became a lasting symbol of the 'British disease', 'model Germany' became a powerful election slogan for the SPD.[74]

Yet if the outcome of these two attempts to organise capitalism in crisis differed enormously, the similarities were equally striking. Both governments were ultimately forced to prioritise the containment of inflation over the creation of jobs. Unsurprisingly, both policies led to serious conflict with the unions. In effect, wherever social-democratic parties found themselves in government in the 1970s and 1980s, they ultimately had to accept the economic orthodoxies of the day. Callaghan abandoned Keynesianism in the mid-1970s at about the same time as Schmidt began to turn to monetarism. Craxi's economic policies in Italy were virtually identical with the neo-liberalism of centre-right governments elsewhere. In Spain and Portugal social-democratic parties initiated major austerity programmes in the 1980s. After the failure of the programme of nationalisation and economic planning started by the French Socialist and Communist coalition government of the early 1980s, French social democrats moved to the right in their economic thinking. Even in Sweden, there was increasing pressure on the Social Democrats to conform to the international neo-liberal agenda. Given the readiness of social-democratic parties across Western Europe to 'play the game', it is indeed questionable whether 'politics against markets' accurately described the social-democratic position in the 1970s and 1980s.

Stefan Berger

Almost everywhere social democrats adopted neo-liberalism at a cost. It produced serious internal rifts, as well as divisions between social-democratic governments and the parties at large. So, for example, the 1976–77 split between the Labour government and the Labour Party was paralleled by the inability of Helmut Schmidt to find broad support for his policies among his own party ranks at subsequent party conferences in the early 1980s. Social-democratic parties across Western Europe became characterised by vicious factional strife. In countries such as Britain, Germany, Spain and France, where social democrats enjoyed prolonged periods in government and where they adopted neo-liberal policies, it left them either internally divided (Britain, Germany) or without any kind of positive vision and programme which would have distinguished them from the political right (Spain under Gonzales; France under Mitterrand).

The trade unions in particular became increasingly dissatisfied about the apparent inability of social-democratic governments to tackle rising unemployment. Furthermore, the traditional left wing of social democracy was concerned about 'their' governments abandoning the aim of a more equal distribution of wealth and opportunities. The New Left, which had initially developed outside the traditional social-democratic parties now entered social-democratic politics from the late 1960s onwards, in order to gain influence on the political process. It often introduced a high dosage of feminism into this traditionally male-dominated sphere. Already in the inter-war period, the coming together of socialism and feminism had inspired great hopes and aspirations. Socialists across Western Europe had been committed to gender equality and the socialist women's groups within social-democratic parties produced very similar programmes and agendas in the 1920s and 1930s. However, the discourse of domesticity, welfare and maternalism prevailed everywhere, and the policies of European social democracy continued to perceive women mainly through their role in the family.[75] Second-wave feminism in the 1960s and 1970s set out to change that. Furthermore, the impact of the New Left accentuated social democracy's latent anti-Americanism and strengthened the links to pacifist and peace groups. The outcome of the ensuing power struggle between new and old left-wing programmes and cultures differed from country to country, but was played out across Western Europe.

In most social-democratic parties the dominance of the reformist centre-right was retained, but in Britain the left was able to capture the party for a brief period between 1979 and 1983. This was due to the importance of the trade unions in the formal processes of the party and the relatively decentralised character of decision-making which allowed left-wing activists to take over local parties in a way that was much more difficult in centralised, hierarchically organised parties like the German SPD.[76] The dominance of the centre-right in the SPD under Helmut Schmidt contributed to rising levels of dissatisfaction inside the party and to the emergence of the Green Party to the left of the SPD in 1980. The Social Democrats lost almost an entire generation to the Greens. In Britain, the Labour Party did not lose its traditional left wing, but the left ultimately prompted the right wing to secede and form the SDP in 1981.

Yet the real challenge to the social-democratisation of British politics did not come from an anti-capitalist Labour Party. It arrived rather in the form of Margaret Thatcher who was to destroy the foundations of the social-democratic consensus in such a radical way as to make Britain almost unrecognisable from the viewpoint of continental West European countries. As Claus Offe has recently argued, nowhere else did the conscious demolition of the state, and of public responsibilities more generally, go as far as it did in Britain under Thatcher.[77] The Labour Party went from defeat to seemingly inexorable decline. This impression was re-enforced by the peculiarities of the majority voting system. This allowed the Conservatives to rule with massive majorities of MPs despite having gained well below 50 per cent of the overall vote. In other West European countries, which had a more equitable voting system, social-democratic parties were either able to cling to power through forging successful alliances with other parties or at least to prevent the radicalisation of right-wing political thinking which Britain underwent in the late 1970s and early 1980s.

Of course there were other reasons for Labour's electoral decline. First, the general fall in the numbers of industrial manual workers combined with an increase in upward, intergenerational social mobility produced a major shift of the social foundations on which the Labour Party had been built. Second, the party was unable to win over the unemployed and other marginal workers whose fatalism and mistrust in all formal politics made them more likely to abstain rather than vote Labour. Third, the working-class base of the party felt alienated from its increasingly middle-class activists.[78] Fourth, the rapid decline of trade-unionism during the 1980s contributed to the increasing de-alignment of workers from the Labour Party. Finally, skilled workers turned away from the Labour Party, as they were the main beneficiaries of the increasing housing tenure made possible by the Conservatives' privatisation of council housing.[79] They perceived the Conservative Party as

Stefan Berger

better qualified to deliver on promises of rising living standards than the
Labour Party, which increasingly seemed the party of the marginal.

Towards a definition of New Labour (1983–1999)

The late 1970s and early 1980s was a period of much recrimination and
frustration, and not only for the Labour Party. In the last years of the
socialist–liberal coalition in Germany, the gulf between the Social
Democrat Chancellor Schmidt and his party widened. The SPD seemed
almost relieved when it entered the opposition in 1982. In France, the
Socialist–Communist coalition government of the early 1980s had initiated what in hindsight appears as the last stand of old-style social-
democratic statism. Within two years, the experiment collapsed, and it
discredited 'old labour politics' across Western Europe. A 'post-Fordist'
globalising economic order further eroded old class identities and,
together with a series of election defeats, forced social-democratic
parties to rethink their programmatic and organisational profile. In the
1980s and 1990s, social-democratic parties in Western Europe went on
the search for a second historic realignment between capitalism and
social democracy.[80] They attempted to find a bridge between what was
necessary to ensure economic growth and what was desirable to maintain
social solidarity. The 1989 Policy Review in Britain should therefore be
seen in the context of the 1990 Berlin Programme of the SPD, the 1990
Swedish 90-talsprogrammet, the Norwegian Freedom Debate of the
1980s, the 1990 Programma 2000 of the Spanish Social Democrats and
the Austrian party's Perspektiven-90.

Labour Party leaders from Neil Kinnock to Tony Blair embarked on
a long, step-by-step process of programmatic and organisational reform
which was to bring the party back into the mainstream of European
social democracies, where it had belonged since the heyday of
MacDonaldism in the 1920s. By the mid-1990s, Tony Blair was declaring: 'the ultimate objective is a new political consensus of the left of
centre, based around the key values of democratic socialism and
European social democracy'.[81] Once again, the development of the
Labour Party and SPD show remarkable similarities: greater democratisation in the form of more participation for the grass-roots members in
decision-making processes, and an increasing professionalisation of the
parties' campaigns and images with a strong theme of organisational and
programmatic renewal. If the 1950s had witnessed the withering away of
the old class parties and the emergence of the new people's parties, the
1990s have seen a new variant of the people's party, perhaps best characterised by the phrase 'media communication party'.[82]

By the mid-1990s, West European social democracy was making a spectacular comeback. In January 1999 social democrats were in government in thirteen out of the fifteen member states of the European Union. Only in Spain and Ireland did they belong to the opposition. In Britain, Greece and Portugal they governed on their own, whilst they were senior coalition partners in Sweden, Finland, Germany, the Netherlands, France, Italy and Austria. In Belgium and Luxembourg they were junior partners in coalition governments with Christian-democratic parties. Ralf Dahrendorf, who, in 1987, had famously declared the death of European social democracy,[83] was in 1998 one of the first to analyse its rebirth.[84] But what has been reborn? Is it still the same old social democracy, defined by state interventionism in economic and social affairs, as well as a commitment to social equality (i.e. the welfare state and redistribution of wealth)?

According to Herbert Kitschelt, what occurred in the 1980s and 1990s amounts to the emergence of a new 'liberal socialism', i.e. a merger of the classical values of social democracy with the triumphant neo-liberalism of the 1970s and 1980s.[85] Liberal socialists tend to portray themselves as 'modernisers' intent on 'modernising' their parties and, once in power, their countries. Under the catchword of 'modernisation', social-democratic parties reclaimed some of their forgotten traditions. In Britain, Blairism stands for a re-evaluation of pre-1914 New Liberalism and a more positive re-examination of the Gaitskellites as well as the Wilson years.[86] Not for nothing did Blair choose to emphasise the remodelling of Clause Four: this was, after all, the stumbling block when the Gaitskellites had allegedly failed to modernise the party in the 1950s. Blair could now successfully demonstrate that he had ended the legacy of the late 1970s and early 1980s and had returned to the reformist traditions of the party. In a similar attempt to move German social democracy back to the centre ground and win over sections of the middle classes, Gerhard Schröder in Germany has consciously harked back to the legacies of technocratic modernisation under Karl Schiller and Helmut Schmidt in the 1960s and 1970s. Liberal socialism thus appeals to those largely middle-class voters who lack a collective occupational biography and whose lifestyles have been characterised by increasing individualisation. They are socially and geographically highly mobile and well educated and tend to change their jobs frequently.

Liberal socialists have given up the idea of economic planning and nationalisation. The Labour Party, more so than its continental sister parties, has accepted economic globalisation as fate. The first measure of the New Labour government gave independence to the Bank of England, which symbolised the liberal socialists' belief in the autonomy of economics from politics. They tend to accept the increasing deregulation and flexibilisation of labour markets in the name of economic necessity and the competitiveness of national economies in a global market-place. Classical Keynesian unemployment programmes are regarded as things of the past, although liberal socialists advocate more state interventionism in the employment markets than their Conservative predecessors. The French Social Democrats' introduction of a thirty-five-hour week, the German Chancellor's stress on his 'Alliance for Work' programme, and the British Labour government's 'Welfare to Work' scheme all testify to the desire of liberal socialists to take a more proactive role in combating unemployment. In France and Germany, social democrats are probably more willing to consider active state intervention in the economy than in Britain. This reflects the much stronger tradition of state interventionism in those two countries.

However, even in countries with strong state traditions, liberal socialism has made important inroads. Wim Kok, head of the Dutch government and the Dutch Labour Party, demonstrated to his liberal socialist comrades how to pursue prudent financial policies, cut state expenditure and initiate successful employment policies in partnership with capital and labour. Swedish and Austrian Social Democrats have won elections in the 1990s on the basis of their reputations as governmental parties which can successfully cut state expenditure and yet maintain the commitment to social policies.

Like their reformist predecessors in the 1950s, liberal socialists refute any fundamental opposition towards capitalism. Instead they seek regulatory frameworks in which capitalism can be made to work for the good of the greatest possible number of people. Hence, liberal socialists stress their commitment to social-democratic norms and values – nowhere more so than in Britain. They talk about increasing life chances, equality of opportunities, being concerned about social justice, reviving the spirit of solidarity, a fair deal and giving a new ethical basis to society. They derive comfort from the fact that the belief in universal welfare ethics and collectivism still runs deep in the West European populace.[87] And their actual policies reflect the rhetoric. In Britain, for example, the 1998 Labour budget was widely credited with producing a more equal distribution of wealth, indeed of being redistributive in the old social-democratic sense.

Liberal socialists across Western Europe are trying out, in Blair's words, 'permanent revisionism' in the sense that they pragmatically merge and mix policies without much regard for ideological demarcations and taboo topics. In the process of such experimentation, social-democratic parties have injected market-liberal elements into their traditional programmes and accepted the tendency of modern societies to pluralise their modes of organisation. Whilst some, notably the SPD, have sought to find answers to the challenges of environmentalism and feminism (the Labour Party cannot be seen as a trendsetter in these two areas), the traditional strong links between the trade-union movement and social-democratic parties have been loosened in many countries (with notable exceptions such as Sweden and Austria). In post-industrial societies, trade unions have been increasingly regarded as more of an electoral liability than an asset.

If New Labour spearheads the liberal socialist movement in Western Europe, the framework in which these debates are taking place is a genuinely European one. The problems discussed are similar everywhere, the answers given might vary from state to state, but the discussions have moved beyond national borders.[88] Schröder's 'New Centre' (*Neue Mitte*) resembles Blair's 'Third Way' in more than terminology. Hence, it is a sign of the continuing Europeanisation of social democracy that Anthony Giddens' book on *The Third Way* is presented in its German translation by Gerhard Schröder and that, in June 1999, the British and German parties published a joint manifesto on the future of social democracy in Europe.

Stefan Berger

Notes

1 Donald Sassoon, *One Hundred Years of Socialism. The West European Left in the Twentieth Century* (London: I. B. Tauris, 1996), p. 15.

2 Walter Kendall, *The Labour Movement in Europe* (London: Allen Lane, 1975), pp. 3 f.

3 Bebel to Molkenbuhr, 28 September 1908, NL22/132, 23, Bebel papers, Stiftung Archiv der Parteien und Massenorganisationen der DDR im Bundesarchiv, Berlin.

4 See the review of the literature in Stefan Berger, *The British Labour Party and the German Social Democrats 1900–1931. A Comparative Study* (Oxford: Oxford University Press, 1994), pp. 12–16.

5 Denis Healey, *The Time of My Life* (Harmondsworth: Penguin, 1990), p. 57.

6 Alan Bullock, *Ernest Bevin. Foreign Secretary* (Oxford: Oxford University Press, 1983), p. 90, cites Bevin on the Germans: 'I tries 'ard', but I 'ates them.' See also Kenneth O. Morgan, *Labour in Power 1945–1951* (Oxford: Oxford University Press, 1984), pp. 255–7.

7 I use the term social democracy to refer to those parties which were united in the International after 1889, the Labour and Socialist International after 1923 and the Socialist International after 1951. These were sometimes called social democratic, sometimes socialist, and, in the case of the Labour Party, neither. However, it is my contention that such linguistic differences, while important in their own right, should not deflect from the fact that the parties shared a wide range of ideological and organisational features.

8 Klaus Tenfelde, 'The European labour movement: decline or regeneration?', *Contemporary European History* 5 (1996), 432.

9 Michael Waller, Bruno Coppieters and Kris Deschouwer (eds.), *Social Democracy in a Post-Communist Europe* (London: Frank Cass, 1994).

10 See, in particular, Henry Pelling, 'British labour and British imperialism', in Pelling, *Popular Politics and Society in Late Victorian Britain* (London: Macmillan, 1968), pp. 82–100, and Roger Price, *An Imperial War and the British Working Class* (London: Routledge, 1972).

11 Stefan Berger, 'The belated party. Influences on the British Labour Party in its formative years', *Mitteilungsblatt des Instituts zur Erforschung der europäischen Arbeiterbewegung* 18 (1997), 83–111, summarises the national influences on the Labour Party but equally insists on the importance of hitherto neglected international links. 'Heretical counter-arguments' to the prevailing national perspective in British labour history are also presented in Duncan Tanner, 'The development of British socialism, 1900–1918', *Parliamentary History* 16 (1997), 48–66.

12 Max Beer, *A History of British Socialism*, vol. II (London: G. Bell and Sons, 1920), p. 245. The American economist Henry George (1839–97) in his best-selling *Progress and Poverty* (1879) had argued for a single tax on land as the best remedy for the social question.

13 John R. Frame, 'America and the Scottish left. The impact of American ideas

on the Scottish labour movement from the American Civil War to World War One', Ph.D. thesis (University of Aberdeen, 1998), especially chs. 5, 6 and 7. See also James J. Young, 'H. M. Hyndman and Daniel de Leon: the two souls of socialism', *Labor History* 28 (1987), 534–56.

14 Neville Kirk, 'Transatlantic connections and American peculiarities: the shaping of Labour politics in the United States and Britain, 1893–1908', paper presented at 'New Directions in Comparative and International Labour History', Manchester, 18–19 March 1999.

15 This has already been stressed in Henry Pelling, *America and the British Left. From Bright to Bevan* (London: Adam and Charles Black, 1956). Pelling also argued, correctly in my view, that such feelings tended to be particularly strong among Labour intellectuals, while they were less marked among trade unionists.

16 *Report of the 5th Annual Conference of the Labour Representation Committee, 26–28 January 1905* (London: Labour Party, 1905), p. 40.

17 Arthur Henderson, 'Life and Labour in Australia', *Labour Magazine* 5 (1927), 435–8.

18 National Executive Committee minutes, 15 December 1908, Labour Party Archive, Manchester (hereafter LPA).

19 For a subtle critique of the concept of labourism, see Steve Fielding, '"Labourism" and locating the British Labour Party within the European left', *Working Papers in Contemporary History and Politics* 11 (1996). Very stimulating on the comparative weakness of Marxism in Britain is Ross McKibbin, 'Why was there no Marxism in Great Britain?', *English Historical Review* 99 (1984), 297–331.

20 Chris Wrigley, 'Widening horizons? British Labour and the Second International 1893–1905', *Labour History Review* 58 (1993), 12.

21 Karl Kautsky, 'Akademiker und Proletarier', *Neue Zeit* 19 (1900/1), 89–91.

22 Egon Wertheimer, *Portrait of the Labour Party* (London: G. P. Putnam's and Sons, 1929), p. xi.

23 I have argued this at much greater length in Berger, *The British Labour Party*, chs. 3 and 4,

24 Karen Hunt, 'British women and the Second International', *Labour History Review* 58 (1993), 26.

25 Herbert Morrison, 'London's Labour majority', *Labour Magazine* 8 (1929/30), 68.

26 *Report of the 13th Annual Conference of the Labour Party* (London: Labour Party, 1914), p. 91.

27 Charles Maier, *Recasting Bourgeois Europe. Stabilisation in France, Germany and Italy in the Decade after World War I* (Princeton: Princeton University Press, 1975).

28 John N. Horne, *Labour at War. France and Britain 1914–1918* (Oxford: Oxford University Press, 1991), p. 393.

29 For Germany this has been investigated by Mary Nolan, *Visions of Modernity. American Business and the Modernisation of Germany* (Oxford: Oxford

Stefan Berger

University Press, 1994). Similar processes of economic rationalisation were taking place in inter-war Britain, and sections of the British labour movement were equally fascinated by the promises of consumptionism. A detailed cross-national comparison of the (partial) replacement of the productivist ethos by consumptionism in the inter-war period is still outstanding.

30 The importance of working-class internationalism for a socialist foreign policy in Britain has been stressed by Michael R. Gordon, *Conflict and Consensus in Labour's Foreign Policy 1914–1965* (Stanford: Stanford University Press, 1969).

31 Norman and Jean MacKenzie (eds.), *The Diary of Beatrice Webb*, vol. III: *1905–1925* (London: Virago, 1983), p. 326.

32 For a comparative view on the pitfalls of these assumptions, see Stefan Berger, 'British and German socialists between class and national solidarity', in Stefan Berger and Angel Smith (eds.), *Nationalism, Labour and Ethnicity, 1870–1939* (Manchester: Manchester University Press, 1999), pp. 31–63.

33 Christine Collette, 'Internationalism and officialdom in the British labour movement: Labour's attitude to European socialism 1918 to 1939, with special reference to the role of the International Secretary of the Labour Party', M.Litt. thesis (University of Oxford, 1992), p. 109.

34 Christine Collette, *The International Faith. Labour's Attitudes to European Socialism, 1918–1939* (Aldershot: Ashgate, 1998), p. 58.

35 For details see ibid., pp. 99 ff.

36 Dieter Dowe (ed.), *Programmatische Dokumente der deutschen Sozialdemokratie*, 2nd edn (Bonn: J. W. H. Dietz Nachf., 1984), p. 224.

37 *Report of the 1927 TUC Congress* (London: TUC, 1927), p. 392.

38 Clement Attlee, *Labour's Peace Aims* (London: Labour Party, 1939), p. 13.

39 Gerd-Rainer Horn, *European Socialists Respond to Fascism. Ideology, Activism and Contingency in the 1930s* (Oxford: Oxford University Press, 1996).

40 Beatrice and Sydney Webb, *Soviet Communism: A New Civilisation?* (London: Longmans, Green and Company, 1935).

41 Roy Jenkins, *Pursuit of Progress. A Critical Analysis of the Achievement and Prospect of the Labour Party* (London: Labour Party, 1953), p. 15.

42 *Report of the 1937 TUC Congress* (London: TUC, 1937), pp. 472–4.

43 Collette, *The International Faith*, p. 78.

44 Tom Buchanan, *The Spanish Civil War and the British Labour Movement* (Cambridge: Cambridge University Press, 1991).

45 Although it has to be said that leading French socialists, including Blum himself, were initially in favour of helping the republican forces in Spain. However, faced with diplomatic pressure by the British government and with bitter divisions in his own party as well as his government coalition, he finally committed himself to non-intervention as the best way of averting another European war. See Nathanael Greene, *Crisis and Decline. The French Socialist Party in the Popular Front Era* (Ithaca: Cornell University Press, 1969), pp. 78–90.

46 *Report of the 35th Annual Conference of the Labour Party* (London: Labour Party, 1936), p. 203.

47 This was, of course, an interest shared by almost all other social-democratic parties in Western Europe, and also by non-socialist progressives. Scandinavia became a by-word for hope at a time when democracy and democratic variants of socialism were threatened by fascism and communism. For Britain, an example of this perspective is provided by E. D. Simon, *The Smaller Democracies* (London: Victor Gollancz, 1939), p. 175: 'Most important of all, the Scandinavian countries are the only countries in Europe which, since the war, whilst elsewhere the newer democracies have been destroyed and the older ones are on the defensive, have become steadily more democratic, steadily more prosperous and more contented.'

48 Gillies papers: box 12 on Sweden and Scandinavia in the 1930s, LPA.

49 Ibid., box 12, file 4, WG/SWE/80, LPA.

50 Margaret Cole and Charles Smith (eds.), *Democratic Sweden* (London: Routledge, 1938).

51 Dalton's fascination with the Swedish socialists' economic and financial policies has been investigated in great detail by Elizabeth Durbin, *New Jerusalems. The Labour Party and the Economics of Democratic Socialism* (London: Routledge, 1985), ch. 10.

52 International Committee minutes, 26 November 1934 and 19 February 1936, LPA.

53 Jonathan Schneer, 'Hopes deferred or shattered: the British Labour left and the Third Force movement, 1945–1949', *Journal of Modern History* 56 (1984), 197–226.

54 Giora Goodman, '"Who is anti-American?": the British left and the United States, 1945–1956', Ph.D. thesis (University of London, 1996).

55 Stephen Padgett and William E. Paterson, *A History of Social Democracy in Postwar Europe* (London: Longman, 1991), p. 186. It should, however, be noted that in Britain some of Labour's economic plans were thwarted by a powerful coalition of opposition forces. See, for example, Jim Tomlinson, 'The iron quadrilateral: political obstacles to economic reform under the Attlee government', *Journal of British Studies* 34 (1995).

56 For which he was criticised by the New Left. See, for example, Perry Anderson, 'Sweden: Mr Crosland's Dreamland', *New Left Review* 7 (1961), 4–12 and 9 (1961), 34–45. Anderson was critical of the Swedish Social Democrats' alleged indifference to issues of social equality and adamant that Swedish conditions could not be reproduced in Britain. However, even Anderson was full of praise for the many achievements of the SAP in the areas of welfare policies, education and housing.

57 The report is contained in the Healey papers, Sweden 1946–1952, LPA. Specifically on industrial relations see also Jack Cooper, *Industrial Relations: Sweden Shows the Way* (London: Fabian Society, 1963), p. 31: 'there is a basic lesson to be learned from the Swedish experience . . . It is that the foundation of improved industrial relations is acceptance of the fundamental proposition

Stefan Berger

that the purpose of industrial relations is to reach agreement by negotiation.' For a 1980s' call to learn from Sweden, see Martin Linton, *The Swedish Road to Socialism* (London: Fabian Society, 1985).

58 For such a view see Isabel Tombs, 'The victory of socialist "Vansittartism": Labour and the German question 1941–1945', *Twentieth Century British History* 7 (1996), 287–309, especially p. 307. Fight for Freedom was set up in December 1941 by British and exiled socialists. One of their main aims was to fight the, in their view, illusory assumption of a 'good Germany' different from and opposed to Nazi Germany. Tombs' characterisation of the group's viewpoint as Vansittartist is, however, misleading, as their arguments were not based on biological essentialism but on (rather sound) historical argument.

59 Anthony Glees, *Exile Politics during the Second World War. The German Social Democrats in Britain* (Oxford: Oxford University Press, 1982).

60 Berger, *The British Labour Party*, ch. 6.

61 On the SU and its close contacts with German Social Democrats see Mark Mignion, 'The Labour Party and Europe during the 1940s: the strange case of the Socialist Vanguard Group', *South Bank European Papers* 4 (1998), and Lawrence Black, 'Social democracy as a way of life: fellowship and the Socialist Union, 1951–1959', *Twentieth Century British History* 10 (1999), 499–539.

62 James P. May and William E. Patterson, 'Die Deutschlandkonzeption der britischen Labour Party 1945–1949', in Claus Scharf and Hans-Jürgen Schröder (eds.), *Politische und ökonomische Stabilisierung Westdeutschlands 1945–1949* (Wiesbaden: Franz Steiner, 1977), pp. 80 f.

63 Rolf Steininger, 'British Labour, Deutschland und die SPD 1945/46', *Internationale Wissenschaftliche Korrespondenz zur Geschichte der deutschen und internationalen Arbeiterbewegung* 15 (1979), 226.

64 Geoffrey Warner, 'Die britische Labour-Regierung und die Einheit Westeuropas 1948–1951', *Vierteljahreshefte für Zeitgeschichte* 28 (1980), 310–30.

65 See the interesting account given by Roy Jenkins of a meeting with Michael Foot in early January 1971 when Foot argued that the issue of Europe was a unique opportunity for Labour to defeat the government, in 'The Labour Committee for Europe', *Contemporary Record* 7 (1993), 391.

66 For a detailed comparison between the British and Norwegian Social Democrats on this issue, see Robert Geyer, *The Uncertain Union: British and Norwegian Social Democrats in an Integrating Europe* (Aldershot: Avebury, 1997).

67 Frances Fox Piven, 'The decline of labor parties: an overview', in Fox Piven (ed.), *Labor Parties in Postindustrial Societies* (Cambridge: Polity, 1991), pp. 10 f. Next to the British Labour Party the harshest decline was faced by social-democratic parties in Luxembourg (minus 5 per cent) and Denmark (minus 4.7 per cent), whereas France saw a staggering 12.3 per cent rise in the social-democratic vote over the same period.

68 For illuminating comparisons see Carl Cavanagh Hodge, 'The long fifties: the

politics of socialist programmatic revision in Britain, France and Germany', *Contemporary European History* 2 (1993), 17–39, and Tony Nicholls, 'Zwei Wege in den Revisionismus: die Labour Partei und die SPD in der Ära des Godesberger Programms', in Jürgen Kocka, Hans-Jürgen Puhle and Klaus Tenfelde (eds.), *Von der Arbeiterbewegung zum modernen Sozialstaat. Festschrift für Gerhard A. Ritter* (Munich: K. G. Saur, 1994), pp. 190–204.

69 Sassoon, *One Hundred Years*, p. 304.

70 The report is included in the International Committee minutes, July 1959, LPA.

71 Eric Hobsbawm, *Age of Extremes. The Short Twentieth Century 1914–1991* (London: Michael Joseph, 1994), part 2: 'The Golden Age', in particular chs. 9 and 10.

72 Keith Middlemas, *Politics in Industrial Society: The Experience of the British System since 1911* (London: André Deutsch, 1979), p. 391. For a telling comparison between British difficulties with the corporatist concept and Swedish success see James Fulcher, *Labour Movements, Employers and the State. Conflict and Co-operation in Britain and Sweden* (Oxford: Oxford University Press, 1991).

73 Gosta Esping-Anderson, *Politics Against Markets: The Social Democratic Road to Power* (Princeton: Princeton University Press, 1985).

74 For a comparison of the reasons behind these divergent experiences, see Sassoon, *One Hundred Years*, pp. 499 ff.

75 Helmut Gruber and Pamela Graves (eds.), *Women and Socialism. Socialism and Women. Europe Between the Two World Wars* (Oxford: Berghahn, 1998).

76 For a comparison of the New Left challenges within the British Labour Party and the German Social Democrats, see Thomas A. Koelble, *The Left Unravelled. Social Democracy and the New Left Challenge in Britain and West Germany* (Durham, N.C.: Duke University Press, 1991).

77 Claus Offe, 'Die Aufgabe von staatlichen Aufgaben: "Thatcherismus" und die populistische Kritik der Staatstätigkeit', in Dieter Grimm (ed.), *Staatsaufgaben* (Frankfurt-am-Main: Suhrkamp, 1996), p. 342.

78 By 1989 only one in four members of the Labour Party was a manual worker: see Patrick Seyd and Paul Whiteley, *Labour's Grass Roots. The Politics of Party Membership* (Oxford: Oxford University Press, 1992), p. 34. Again this was not exceptional: the SPD had already reached a similar ratio by 1972!

79 On the unusually high correlation between the voting behaviour of skilled workers and Conservative preferences in Britain, see the illuminating comparison by Herbert Döring, 'Wählen Industriearbeiter zunehmend konservativ? Die Bundesrepublik Deutschland im westeuropäischen Vergleich', *Archiv für Sozialgeschichte* 29 (1989), 225–71.

80 Richard Gillespie and William E. Paterson (eds.), *Rethinking Social Democracy in Western Europe* (London: Frank Cass, 1993).

81 Tony Blair, *New Britain. My Vision of a Young Country* (London: New Statesman, 1996), p. 4.

82 Uwe Jun, 'Inner-party reforms: the SPD and Labour Party in comparative

Stefan Berger

perspective', *German Politics* 5 (1996), 58–80. Democratisation has in fact strengthened the hand of the parties' respective leaderships *vis-à-vis* the more left-wing activists within the party, who were often unrepresentative of the rank and file as a whole.

83 Ralf Dahrendorf, 'Das Elend der Sozialdemokratie', *Merkur* 41 (1987), 1021–38. Dahrendorf argued that – its historic mission having been fulfilled – social democracy had lost both purpose and direction.

84 *Die Zeit*, 3 July 1998.

85 Herbert Kitschelt, *The Transformation of European Social Democracy* (Cambridge: Cambridge University Press, 1994).

86 See especially Steven Fielding, ch. 12 below.

87 For Britain, in particular, this is argued by Ivor Crewe, '1979–1996', in Anthony Seldon (ed.), *How Tory Governments Fall. The Tory Party in Power since 1783* (London: Fontana, 1996), pp. 406 f.

88 On comparisons between the Labour Party and other left-wing parties in the 1990s, see Thomas Meyer, *Die Transformation der Sozialdemokratie. Eine Partei auf dem Weg ins 21. Jahrhundert* (Bonn: Dietz, 1998), pp. 201–28; Frank Unger, Andreas Wehr and Karen Schönwälder, *New Democrats, New Labour, Neue Sozialdemokraten* (Berlin: Elefanten Press, 1998); René Cuperus and Johannes Kandel (eds.), *European Social Democracy: Transformation in Progress* (Bonn: Friedrich Ebert Stiftung, 1998).

11	Labour – the myths it has lived by

Jon Lawrence

Across its history Labour has gone through a number of distinct incarnations. Before the First World War, the party can be seen as an uneasy coalition between socialist prophets of the 'new social order' and political pragmatists whose understanding of the 'labour interest' remained extremely narrow. By mid-century, in contrast, trade-union leaders and middle-class 'progressives' had forged a fruitful *modus vivendi* that underpinned the construction of the post-war 'welfare state'. By the 1970s and early 1980s, with the prestige of trade-union leaders and middle-class 'progressives' much reduced, and reformist 'welfare' solutions widely questioned, the party appeared (briefly) to have mutated into a vehicle of the 'New Left'. In the 1990s, after a series of disastrous election defeats, another incarnation has been self-consciously proclaimed as the birth of 'New Labour'. Advancing a typology of twentieth-century Labour politics along these lines, Gareth Stedman Jones has argued that political parties should be seen, not as organisations with a continuous historical development, but as discursive 'sites' controlled by different social and political groupings at different times.[1]

However, whilst parties may indeed change radically over time, party activists have displayed a powerful need to believe in continuity –

Jon Lawrence

seeking to place themselves within an unfolding, seamless history of political commitment. Perhaps in consequence, they have proved to be assiduous consumers (and producers) of popular histories of the party. It is these popular histories that form the subject of the present chapter. Popular histories are not ephemeral and irrelevant to historical understanding. Quite the reverse: throughout the twentieth century the myths Labour activists have internalised about their party's past have done much to shape their understanding of its present, and its future. The more the party has reinvented itself, the more popular histories have helped to create a mythic sense of continuity with the past. 'Mythic' here must not be read as a synonym for 'untrue'. Rather, it refers to shared stories about the past – stories which, *regardless of their veracity*, have helped to shape political identities within the twentieth-century Labour Party. Of course all parties have their mythic histories (for generations Conservative politics were shaped by conflicting accounts of the split over protection in the 1840s), but there is little doubt that Labour activists have always had an especially strong sense of their party as a historic 'movement', which must know its past in order to envisage its future.

In recent years, there has been a growing interest in the role that myths play in the construction of identity and in social understanding. Where once historians sought merely to 'debunk' myths, there is now a much greater interest in explaining how they work – i.e. how they help shape social perception.[2] Historians have become more acutely aware of the partial and contested nature of their own 'knowledge' of the past. Just as history must necessarily offer an interpretation of the past shaped by present-day perspectives, so myth, despite appearances to the contrary, must be adaptable and 'relevant', rather than timeless and immutable. Indeed, myth's very survival depends on its ability to make sense of present circumstances: to re-work the past better to interpret the present. Thus whilst certain Labour myths can be said to recur throughout the century, they are not unchanging. Rather myths about the party's origins, or about the 'betrayal' of 1931, have been constantly re-worked to draw lessons of contemporary relevance that support the ideological perspective of the myth-maker/historian.

Interest in popular understandings of the party's past – its 'oral tradition' – is not new, but myth itself has seldom been central to such historical inquiries.[3] At the same time, autobiographies, the principal source for the present study, have rarely been read for the insights they can offer into party mentalities and party myths. Rather, they have either been read uncritically for 'facts' about past experiences and their meaning, or they have been dismissed as hopelessly subjective and unreliable. It is, of course, inevitable that autobiography (and biography more generally) will be profoundly partial in its reconstruction of the past as 'history', but once one recognises the importance of myth in shaping our social and political understanding it becomes clear that this is its great strength, not its weakness. Not only will events be selected and interpreted with the benefit of hindsight, but the whole project of trying to make sense of one's past life will necessarily be bound up with the desire to make sense of one's present 'self'.[4] Partly in consequence, there is also a strong tendency to turn to the certainties of myth to make sense of one's place in the past – to place oneself in the context of a 'shared' history. This tendency is especially strong when the story to be told impinges directly on public histories such as the 'rise of Labour'. But the mythic understandings woven into such a life-story will not be contemporary to the events described; they will be myths re-worked from the perspective of the present. It is for this reason that the present chapter makes little distinction between autobiography and popular biography; both are at heart imaginative reconstructions of a past life (hence the use of the term 'auto/biography' at several points).[5]

Of course, party mythology has taken many forms besides auto/biography. It has often been central to the rhetoric of internal political conflicts, and has sometimes played its part in electoral politics: notably in the 1920s, with the presentation of MacDonald as the charismatic 'new Gladstone' who had stood out against wartime jingoism, and in the 1950s and 1960s, when Labour's electoral appeal relied heavily on mythic accounts of the 1945–51 governments. However, the present study has chosen to focus exclusively on auto/biography for two reasons: firstly, because life-stories are especially rich in myth and, secondly, because, from the beginning of the century, people have been telling the story of their place in Labour history, and consuming stories of their leaders' 'lives for labour'. In contrast, 'official' histories, such as those commemorating the party's fiftieth anniversary (or the 1945 landslide), tend to be much less expansive in their use of myth.[6] Many offer little beyond a chronology of key events on Labour's 'march' to power,[7] while those that stray into the dangerous terrain of interpretation generally remain closed to the heterodox mythologies to be found in many autobiographies. As one would expect from a party that has always seen itself as a 'broad church', Labour mythology has not been monolithic and unchanging. At any one time, there have always been competing myths about the party's past, just as there have always been competing ideas about what it stands for in the present. Indeed, when one looks at autobiographical rather than 'official' histories, it becomes clear that even apparently universal myths, such as MacDonald's 'betrayal' of Labour in 1931, have been widely reinterpreted by activists determined to weave alternative stories about the party's past.

The following discussion examines four distinct types of mythology to be found within Labour auto/biographies. Firstly, it examines the ever-changing myths about the party's origins, since these 'foundation myths' have always played an important part in making party identities. Secondly, it picks up the theme of betrayal to examine the myths that have grown up around MacDonald's break with Labour in 1931 and the formation of the Social Democratic Party (SDP) fifty years later. Thirdly, it examines myths of division in the post-Second World War Labour Party, arguing that complex patterns of political disagreement have often been simplified to conform to mythic accounts of the party's past. Finally, the chapter examines Labour's myths of triumph by focusing on conflicting interpretations of the 1945 election. It is not suggested that these myths represent an exhaustive account of Labour mythology in the twentieth century. For instance, they exclude one of the most important and recurrent themes in Labour auto/biographies: the personal 'epiphany' of socialist conversion. Although strongly mythic in form, these tales of conversion have been considered too intensely personal for inclusion in a study concerned primarily with outlining Labour's contested mythic histories. For the intention of this chapter is essentially twofold: firstly, to demonstrate that myths matter in political history, and, secondly, to show that in the Labour Party mythic reworkings of the party's past have played a central part in the construction of conflicting party political identities throughout the century.

Foundation myths: the early days

Stories about origins represent a potent form of myth-making, and the Labour Party has been especially responsive to tales about the pioneers who shaped its early history. These 'foundation myths' serve simultaneously to legitimate the party's claim to represent all working people, and to reinforce the activists' sense of themselves as belonging to a 'chosen people' of true believers.[8] In politics there must always be a gulf between leaders and led, but in the early days of the socialist movement that gulf was especially keenly felt by would-be leaders who perceived the oppressed 'masses' to be either indifferent or actively hostile to their message. Before the First World War, socialist leaders such as Keir Hardie and Ramsay MacDonald portrayed themselves as locked in an unrewarding battle against working-class ignorance and prejudice. In his darker moments, Hardie in particular was prone to present himself as a man broken by the strain of ceaseless work on behalf of an ungrateful populace. In 1902, he apparently told the Durham miners that he was 'worn out in body, and very, very sad in spirit . . . If I were to die here and now, I would leave my wife and family a legacy of debt bigger than I care to think about.'[9] Four years later, on his fiftieth birthday, his lament focused more directly on the loneliness of the socialist pioneer forced to face '[h]owls, curses, execrations, peltings with mud and stones; one poor solitary figure knocked and buffeted about bodily and mentally'.[10]

Inter-war Labour auto/biographies mostly echoed this account of the 'wilderness years', though few writers followed Hardie in foregrounding their own martyrdom to 'the cause'. David Kirkwood, the wartime shop stewards' leader, recalled how church leaders in Glasgow had encouraged their followers to intimidate John Wheatley when he founded a Catholic Socialist Society before the First World War.[11] John Scanlon told the same tale of religious persecution, but made much more of Wheatley's physical bravery before the 'mob'. He wrote:

No one knew the psychology of the crowd better than Mr Wheatley. To have shown fear would have been fatal. Instead, he walked down the garden path quite unconcerned; then the mob, which had come to tear him limb from limb, opened their ranks, cowed. They made a passage for him and he made his way through the crowd unmolested. That was the last attempt at physical violence.[12]

As in Hardie's pre-war accounts, the 'masses' were portrayed as unruly and deeply ignorant, but these tales offered more than just the consolation of shared persecution. Firstly, 'the masses' were deliberately portrayed as the pawns of unscrupulous leaders, rather than as inherently 'bad' and thus irredeemable. Hence, in Kirkwood's version of the story, Wheatley's greatest victory is that he defies the church (rather than the masses) by continuing to attend Sunday mass. Secondly, the angry mob had been historicised; this was how things had been in the bad old days (the 'wilderness years'), before courageous socialists such as Wheatley and Hardie had spread 'the word'. Wheatley had faced the crowd as a lone socialist hero, and he had 'tamed' it by force of character alone. Such personal victories came to symbolise Labour's breakthrough; they were retold in the knowledge that many such communities had since been won for Labour (and in the belief that the remainder could be won). Joe Toole, the combative MP for Salford South, summed up this sentiment in retelling his own experience of confronting priest-led anti-socialism

Jon Lawrence

before the First World War. Having told how his first (unsuccessful) election contest had ended at the declaration with a hostile crowd threatening violence against him, Toole notes that within fifteen years he was representing the same people at Westminster.[13]

After his death in September 1915, Keir Hardie's followers were quick to present his life-story (and his tragic death) as symbolic of the heroic struggle to found an independent Labour politics. Ramsay MacDonald used the introduction to a 1921 biography of Hardie to conjure up a florid picture of the early socialist movement (and, by implication, of his, as well as Hardie's heroism). He wrote of the 1890s as 'days of fighting, of murmuring, of dreary desert trudging . . . a mere handful of men and women sustained the drudgery and the buffetings . . . those miraculous endurances of the men who defied hardship in the blank wilderness, the untangled forest, the endless snowfield'.[14] Hardie became the movement's great tragic hero: a man who had laid down his life that others might one day live lives less brutal and short. For a movement steeped in religious imagery the theme of sacrifice and redemption came almost as second nature. Labour MPs such as James Sexton, Philip Snowden, Tom Johnston and, of course, MacDonald, portrayed Hardie as dying from a 'broken heart'. Exhausted by years of selfless activism, they suggested that his despair at witnessing popular enthusiasm for the Great War had simply been too much to bear.[15] In turn, Hardie's tragic death served to legitimate the stance of fellow anti-war socialists such as Snowden, Lansbury and above all MacDonald, who had re-emerged as important Labour leaders after 1918. In the party mythology of the 1920s, these men were portrayed as something close to living martyrs. Like Hardie they had dared to stand out against the jingo tide, and had suffered greatly for their beliefs. Unlike Hardie, they had lived to see jingoism repudiated and the war itself widely questioned. Again, mythology offered more than the consolation of shared persecution – it proclaimed the idea of a public opinion open to the influence of individuals who upheld truth and morality. In 1923, a popular biography presented MacDonald as the only man who could save Britain from the bitter disillusionment that had followed the Armistice. The people, it suggested, were,

looking round desperately for some ideal that had not been bartered or betrayed, some man standing straight upon the truth, [and] they saw one man who had sacrificed everything for it. Now he seemed their only hope and stay. They might have joined once in stoning him; they knew now that the stones had come back against themselves . . . they felt that MacDonald was the one truthful man in a world of liars.[16]

346

After 1931 new myths would be woven around the character of MacDonald, but in the 1920s he, more than anyone, was held responsible for purging the 'jingo' mentality from the British working class. If Hardie was Labour's great martyr to the 'irrational' crowd, MacDonald was its conquering hero – the man who had emerged unbowed from years of press and public vilification to take office as the first Labour Prime Minister in 1924.[17] According to one euphoric account, it was MacDonald's wartime writings and speeches that had transformed popular attitudes in Britain: 'out of them has grown that new comprehension of foreign policy which surprises anyone who addresses a working-class audience to-day. He began sowing the seed at once, and was stoned for it.'[18] If anything, MacDonald was lauded above even Hardie in party mythology during the 1920s. In 1925 Mary Hamilton wrote that 'alone of the pioneers, MacDonald combines the attributes of fighter and builder, of enthusiasm and statesmanship'.[19] Indeed, it was precisely the strength of the MacDonald cult that made the 'betrayal' of 1931 so hard to bear. Party mythology had built MacDonald up as a new Gladstone – a popular hero who was nonetheless a moral and political colossus towering above mere mortals. Such men were betrayed, they were not betrayers.[20]

Foundation myths: 'the golden age'

In the 1930s, with MacDonald discredited, Keir Hardie re-emerged, unchallenged, as the central figure in the story of the 'rise of Labour'. The mythic Hardie became a yardstick against which contemporary leaders were compared, and found wanting. The 'wilderness years' before 1914 were now re-worked as a 'golden age' of socialist heroism – a period when Labour had been more than just another party.[21] With characteristic mischievousness, Lloyd George used the preface to James Sexton's autobiography to highlight how '[o]thers have since come in to gather the fruits of the harvest for which he [Sexton] and his fellow pioneers ploughed and planted, to seize on the high places to which they had cleared the road'.[22] Veteran Labour leaders made similar comments. Joe Toole, now former Salford MP, emphasised 'what we went through in those [early] days in order to get the Labour cause a place in the sun', noting that this was long before 'monied people and the intellectuals' became involved.[23] Similarly, the Glasgow socialist Martin Haddow recalled the financial hardship suffered by the movement's 'pioneers' and doubted whether 'there is such sacrifice in the movement today'. In Haddow's hands, the 'golden age' myth was also used to chastise working-class voters. According to Haddow, if the workers knew how

Jon Lawrence

much labour had accomplished since the 1890s, 'they would be more grateful, and appreciative of the men and women who devoted their time, and in some instances *their lives*, to the uplifting of their fellow men and women'.[24] After MacDonald's 'betrayal', Labour had had its fill of living heroes – at least for the present. It is noticeable that Edwin Jenkins's 1933 biography of Arthur Henderson avoids presenting its subject in heroic mode (despite being sub-titled a 'romantic life-story'). Ordinariness seemed a great virtue in the wake of MacDonald's 'defection', and in his foreword to the book J. R. Clynes insisted that Henderson possessed it in spades. Clynes, himself a former Labour leader, clearly thought it a great virtue that Henderson had 'displayed no gifts for dazzling rhetoric or fine flights of eloquence' and that he had seldom employed 'platform emotions' to win a point.[25] True, Jenkins himself detected nobility in Henderson's 'sense of duty towards the Trade Union movement' during the crisis of 1931, but his tone was very different from that deployed by the Labour hagiographers of the 1920s.[26] After his death, however, Henderson emerged as a safe subject for the role of mythic hero. Mary Hamilton's 1938 biography makes much of the 'mortal sickness' that fell upon Henderson after MacDonald announced that he had formed a National government. She claims that he was 'not only suddenly aged but broken', yet still he agreed to wear the 'crown of thorns' that was the party leadership.[27] A decade later, Margaret Cole went further, suggesting parallels between Henderson's final years and Hardie's decline after the outbreak of war in 1914. In her brief biographical sketch, Henderson emerges as a tragic figure: a man undone by the treachery of a trusted friend. Like Hardie in 1914–15, he is presented as having grown weary from endless struggle. With his last great hope, international disarmament, apparently doomed to failure, we are told '[h]is health began to deteriorate rapidly; his cheeks fell in, the pouches under his eyes grew heavier, and his ruddy complexion turned to yellow; he seemed to be dying along with the chances of peace'.[28]

Cole was writing in the wake of Labour's landslide victory at the 1945 general election. To many, the 'rise of labour' seemed complete (as it never had between the wars), and it became possible to weave the party's foundation myths into a much more confident, even triumphalist story of the 'forward march of labour'. Cole began her study of the *Makers of the Labour Movement* by declaring that Labour had won in 1945 'because, through long years of difficult and often tragic struggle, innumerable leaders and workers had built up a movement which was conscious of its own traditions and believed itself capable of carrying them on'.[29] Cole was acknowledging that a sense of the past – of the mythic struggles that had 'made' the movement – remained integral to its present strength and future purpose. Labour would continue on its 'forward march' because it knew well the lessons of the hard road already travelled. Even before the landslide victory of 1945 many Labour autobiographies had depicted the 'golden age' of socialist evangelism within a confident narrative that assumed, despite the debacle of 1931, that the labour movement was still marching to the 'promised land'. This was especially true of life-stories written against the backdrop of international crisis and war in the late 1930s and early 1940s, such as the autobiographies of Hannah Mitchell and Jennie Lee.[30] Concerned mainly to chronicle her battle to overcome sex prejudice and play an active part in public life, Hannah Mitchell's autobiography presents the early days of socialist evangelism as a glorious prelude to the rise of a mass socialist politics in Britain. We are shown, in effect, how Mitchell's life has intersected with this grand historical narrative, bringing her into intimate contact with politicians who would go on to assume roles of national prominence in the socialist movement.[31] Similarly Lee, though profoundly critical of the party's official leadership, clearly felt no need to chastise the modern movement by comparison with the past. She wrote within a left tradition that maintained a sharp distinction between the failures of the leadership and the virtues of the movement – past and present. Lee recalls the post-1918 period as one of '[i]dealism, ancestor worship and a happy feeling that we were the people who would one day revolutionize the world . . . Ours was a wonderful movement. All knights in shining armour.'[32] This was no longer a foundation myth as such – in Lee's 'golden age' the movement already possessed ancestors to worship – Hardie chief among them. What she offers instead is a personal account of her own initiation into the movement (which she compares to the early Scottish Covenanters), and her confidence that the spirit of the pioneers still enthuses the rank and file if not their leaders.

Writing after the 'noble' defeat of 1951 (Labour had polled more votes than the Tories but won twenty-six fewer seats), Clement Attlee offered a somewhat different version of the 'forward march of labour' story. He too recalled the 'exultation' of being part of 'a small fighting army' in the early days, but as one might imagine, Attlee acknowledged no abiding gulf between leadership and rank and file. His account is also notable for its affectionate portrayal of the poor working class. Gone are the harsh denunciations of working-class ignorance and jingoism found in earlier accounts, and instead one finds a celebration of the 'quiet heroism' of the Edwardian poor. For Attlee, socialism itself emerged out

Jon Lawrence

of the realisation that '[t]he slums were not filled with the dregs of
society', and that 'these people were not poor through any lack of fine
qualities'.[33] Powerfully influenced by the ethos of the settlement movement, and its strong sense of social service, Attlee would doubtless have
offered a similar appraisal of working-class qualities at any point
between 1910 and 1950. However, now his views reflected a general consensus within the labour movement. After the landslide victory of 1945
the so-called 'wilderness years' of the 1890s and 1900s needed further
re-working. In Attlee's version, a fundamentally decent working class
awaited its salvation from oppression by the emerging labour movement
– Labour's main problem was that it had to become strong enough, and
worthy enough, to win 'its people'.

Fenner Brockway's 1949 biography of the Bermondsey MP Alfred
Salter must stand as one of the most remarkable portrayals of a life dedicated to building the bond between party and people. As a young man,
Salter is shown turning his back on a glittering medical career in order to
live and work as a GP among the poor of Bermondsey. Later, we are told,
convinced that only socialism could cure the ills of the slums, Salter
shunned the prospect of becoming a Liberal MP in order to found a
local branch of the Independent Labour Party (ILP).[34] But such
sacrifices were nothing compared with the death of his only child from
scarlet fever – contracted, Brockway points out, because Salter and his
wife insisted that their daughter must not be shielded from the dangers
that faced other residents of Bermondsey. After this dreadful loss, Salter
is presented as finally understanding the lives of the poor from the
inside. No longer did he inadvertently 'talk down to them' from the platform, for now 'he and his audience were one. These men and women
loved and lost their children as he had lost Joyce, lost them unnecessarily
because of the social conditions to which they were condemned.'[35] In
this terrible story, it is perhaps significant that sacrifice transforms
Salter, the affluent convert to Labour, rather than the people he claimed
to represent. Through suffering, his life is brought closer to theirs, and,
in consequence, his politics are strengthened (in this post-1945 account
we are not asked to believe that Salter's symbolic 'sacrifice' was sufficient
to win the people).

Herbert Morrison, the former Home Secretary and leader of the
London County Council, also challenged conventional understandings
of the 'wilderness years' and the hardships endured 'for the people' by
socialist pioneers. Unlike many post-Second World War figures,
Morrison continued to emphasise the intense popular hostility that had
been directed against the early socialists, but unlike inter-war writers he

presented this hostility as understandable, even justified. Morrison claims that prior to the First World War he had gradually come to realise that the revolutionary rhetoric of many socialists, himself included, merely sent 'shivers down the spines of the stolid working-class men and women in our audiences'. In consequence, suggests Morrison, they were deterred from embracing a creed that could help banish the 'poverty, unemployment, ailing children [and] slums' that were all around them.[36] In this version the socialist pioneers inhabited a wilderness of their own making, and they would come into the promised land only when they broke with sterile political posturing and addressed the workers' very real and immediate needs. The contrast with earlier foundation myths was startling, but Morrison's revisionism is interesting less for its swipe at his own youthful ultra-leftism, than for its confident (post-1945) belief in an imminent mass working-class Labour constituency. This was a foundation myth forged out of certainty in the 'forward march of labour'.

Myths of 'betrayal': 1931

As the preceding discussion has indicated, the idea of 'betrayal' has played an important part in Labour mythology. Some within the party had always shown a tendency to accuse their leaders of betraying the working class and/or socialism – perhaps in order to legitimate their own faithfulness to class and ideology (hence the bitter disputes that racked the ILP before the First World War).[37] But there can be little doubt that the events of 1931 etched the idea of 'betrayal' into the party psyche. The shock with which MacDonald's cabinet greeted the news that he intended to head an all-party National government has become legendary. Henderson, we are told, left the cabinet room 'as white as a sheet; his face was drawn and heavily lined; his eyes dull and lightless. "In twenty-four hours . . . he had become an old man".'[38] That three cabinet members, Jimmy Thomas, Lord Sankey and the Chancellor, Philip Snowden, had agreed to stay in office and help MacDonald implement his package of 'emergency measures' (including cuts in unemployment benefit) merely compounded this sense of shock. In the 1920s, as we have seen, MacDonald's popularity depended in large measure on the idea that he had stood out against the 'betrayal' of the Great War, with its false promises of a war to end wars, and a land fit for heroes. Now, ironically, he was in turn to be pilloried, at least in Labour circles, as the great betrayer.

For a bold statement of the 'official' mythology of betrayal one need look no further than the autobiography of Clement Attlee: a man who

Jon Lawrence

many contemporaries argued owed his entire career as party leader and
Prime Minister to the fact that he was one of the few Labour MPs of
ministerial rank to survive the electoral debacle of 1931.[39] Commenting
on the formation of the National government, Attlee observes sharply:
'I had not . . . expected that he would perpetrate the greatest betrayal in
the political history of this country.' In a similar vein, he also comments
that, having already distributed the posts in his new all-party government, 'he would have been embarrassed if any Labour ministers had
wished to join'.[40] Herbert Morrison, for many years Attlee's great rival
for the Labour leadership, also had no qualms about reproducing the
'official' mythology – indeed his discussion of the crisis is simply called
'the 1931 betrayal'.[41]

By the time Attlee and Morrison wrote their autobiographies, the
events of 1931 had been processed into a fairly static, even ossified,
mythology in which MacDonald's perfidy had caused the only reverse in
Labour's otherwise relentless 'forward march'. As the men who had
'kept the faith', leaders such as Attlee and Morrison clearly had much to
gain from fuelling the betrayal myth, but even they were reluctant
simply to demonise MacDonald and his associates. On the contrary, they
always felt able to acknowledge the positive, inspirational influence that
Snowden and MacDonald had exerted over the early socialist movement, whilst stressing that both men had subsequently 'lost their way'.[42]
Similarly, Morrison had no difficulty acknowledging that many Labour
leaders, himself included, had misread the 1931 crisis and assumed that
MacDonald's programme of cuts would make the new government
deeply unpopular.[43] However, it is to the autobiographies of the 1930s
that one must turn to find sustained attempts to challenge the myth of
'betrayal'.

Jennie Lee, who began writing her biography in the late 1930s, offers
a self-consciously heterodox treatment of the 1931 crisis. Lee is scathing
about the hypocrisy of MacDonald's 'old henchmen' rushing forward to
burn him in effigy when they knew that his defection, far from being 'an
isolated and infamous act', was the logical conclusion of their shared
policy failures in office.[44] Writing as a long-time critic of the Labour
leadership, Lee insists that 'serious socialists are bound to ask, not what
was wrong with their [MacDonald, Snowden and Thomas's] morals, but
what was wrong with their political philosophy'. She concludes that
their failure was to remain wedded to 'most of the assumptions of nineteenth-century Liberalism', of which an abiding faith in 'gradual
progress' was the most heinous sin.[45] Fenner Brockway, who like Lee
followed the ILP out of the Labour Party in the early 1930s, offers a

similar analysis. Brockway had been abroad when the crisis broke, and he recalls being 'taken aback by the fury against MacDonald' on his return, pointing out that only weeks earlier these same people had called the ILP group 'traitors' for attacking the Prime Minister.[46]

If Lee saw the 'betrayal myth' as a right-wing plot to mask the bankruptcy of official Labour policy, many moderate Labour leaders sought to disown the myth out of distaste for its vulgar populism. In his 1938 autobiography, Henry Snell, the former under-secretary of state for India, set out to demolish both National government and Labour Party myths about the events of 1931. He proved as keen to acquit MacDonald of charges of 'personal vanity' as he was to deny that the former Labour ministers had been cowards who ran away in a crisis.[47] Interestingly, Snell was even prepared to admit that he had been tempted to accept MacDonald's offer of the chance to keep his ministerial post, arguing that only suspicion of Tory intentions on India persuaded him to leave office.[48] James Sexton, the dockers' leader, was equally candid, recalling that whilst at the time he had shared the hostile feelings of the rank and file, he now (in 1936) wished that the party had heeded Snowden's warning 'and decided to act loyally upon it'. Here was a startling inversion of the betrayal myth: Sexton was arguing that Labour activists (not their leaders) had failed to show loyalty. He added that: 'now, in calmer moments, I realize something of the difficulty in which my erstwhile colleagues were placed'.[49] Writing much later (in the early 1960s), Walter Citrine also acknowledges feeling 'bitter' towards the defectors in 1931, but he insists that he could not bring himself to dislike them. They might be 'mistaken', but they were at least 'sincere'.[50] In fact, Citrine's account of MacDonald's last years is remarkably sympathetic. Like Henderson, he is depicted as a man grown weary through years of political struggle. Tragically alone after 1931, Citrine tells how he was spurned by friends he had advised *not* to destroy themselves by following him into the National government. Alone and despised, we are told that he was forced to accept that 'power was steadily slipping from him'.[51]

By distancing himself from the betrayal myth Citrine underscored his status as first and foremost a trade unionist rather than a 'party man'. Conversely, for most Labour figures the events of 1931 came to define their sense of 'loyalty' and 'disloyalty' (so that articulating a 'sound' view of MacDonald's role in 1931 became part of defining oneself as a 'loyalist'). Writing in 1960, Herbert Morrison presented himself as the principal victim of 'the spiritual and psychological effects . . . of what became known as "the Great Betrayal"'. For at least a decade, he suggests, the

Jon Lawrence

party was racked by fears of new 'betrayals'; increasingly distrustful of leadership, party members were determined that 'there should be no more great men' (i.e. no Morrison).[52] Significantly, though Morrison claims that the role of Labour ministers in the wartime coalition helped expunge these feelings, he himself hides behind the 'betrayal' myth to justify his apparent bid to unseat Attlee after the 1945 election. According to Morrison, his plan to hold a vote among the newly returned Labour MPs to choose a party leader (and hence Prime Minister) stemmed from the anxiety of the parliamentary Labour Party to ensure that, after 'the salutary lesson [of] the MacDonald "betrayal"', the leadership should be made demonstrably accountable to the party's democratic procedures.[53] If Hugh Dalton is to be believed, Ernest Bevin also interpreted the plots against Attlee in the light of 'the 1931 tragedy', but drew a very different conclusion: Attlee must stay as a buffer against 'personal leadership like MacDonald's or Churchill's' (or, one assumes, Morrison's).[54] Here the role of party mythology as a force to legitimise current politics is especially clear, as is the essential mutability of myth. As Morrison and Bevin demonstrated, it could be re-worked to legitimate frankly contradictory positions.

As late as 1971, George Brown was still wheeling out the events of 1931 in order to justify his role in the murky squabbles of the Wilson governments of the 1960s. According to Brown, Wilson's actions during the financial crisis of March 1968 were no different from MacDonald's in 1931. Both had chosen to act alone, with a few ministerial allies, bypassing the proper procedures of cabinet government.[55] Later, after recounting a showdown with Wilson over the latter's determination to see 'his man' appointed general secretary of the party, Brown elaborates further on 'the lessons of 1931'. In doing so he offers a personal explanation for his belief that the power of the leader must remain tightly circumscribed: 'it is because I began active Party work in 1931 that the events of that period made such an impact on me . . . they have coloured so much of my thinking since'. Whether one should accept Brown's account at face value is, of course, debatable, but as evidence that the ghosts of 1931 had still not been fully exorcised four decades later it is nonetheless significant. Brown clearly felt his explanation would seem plausible to a Labour readership, regardless of whether it gets to the heart of his personal motivation.[56]

Myths of 'betrayal': the 'gang of four'

Given that the events of 1931 had been woven so densely into the mythology of Labour politics, it is perhaps surprising that they appear to play little part in auto/biographical accounts of an event that nearly tore the party apart half a century later: the formation of the SDP in 1981. True, Labour loyalists have not been slow to condemn the so-called 'gang of four' (Roy Jenkins, David Owen, Bill Rodgers and Shirley Williams) for breaking with the party, but even David Owen has generally escaped the vilification directed against MacDonald after 1931. Labour right-wingers appear to have faced the greatest difficulties integrating the 'gang of four' into their narratives of recent Labour politics. Some bullish leaders on the right, such as Denis Healey, have shown no inclination to condemn the SDP 'defectors' in order to legitimate their own loyalty. On the contrary, in his 1989 autobiography Healey openly acknowledges that he largely shared the views (and the frustrations) of the SDP's founder members. Moreover, whilst he claims that some 'defectors' voted for Michael Foot in the 1980 leadership ballot so that they would have an excuse for later jumping ship, he is adamant that Owen, Williams and Rodgers would not have responded to Jenkins's overtures if the events of 1980–81 had not been so badly mishandled within the party. In Healey's version the 'gang of three' did not jump, they were pushed.[57]

On the other hand, right-wing figures such as Denis Howell and the late John Smith have sought to distance themselves from the 'gang of four', presumably in an attempt to underscore their own loyalist credentials. Thus Howell has no qualms about criticising the 'gang of four' for 'deserting' the party, and for believing that they could 'crush the Labour Party' by their 'defection'. He, at least, is convinced that they should take the blame for Labour sliding to ignominious defeat in the elections of 1983 and 1987.[58] Similarly, in a biography published just before his death, John Smith recalls that he was 'scandalised' by the gang of four's behaviour, believing it 'dreadful and disloyal'.[59] In contrast, James Callaghan, Foot's predecessor as Labour leader, takes a middle course and offers a decidedly low-key account of the whole period. He describes the formation of the SDP as 'deeply disappointing' and chides the 'gang of four' for refusing to stay and fight, but there is little fire in his condemnation of their actions. Like Healey and the coming generation of 'New Labourites', he seems to see the SDP 'defectors' as a symptom of Labour's problems, rather than their cause – the real enemy was, of course, the 'Bennite Left'. Callaghan recalls how, after the fall of the government in 1979, he 'deeply resented the charges of "betrayal" made by the left and used as an excuse to fetter the parliamentary Party' (and to de-select good MPs).[60] Sharing the SDP's analysis of Labour's malaise, and reacting violently against the left's appropriation of the

Jon Lawrence

'betrayal' myth, it is perhaps hardly surprising that he declined to levy the same charge against 'the gang of four'.

Politicians on the left of the party have not been similarly handicapped; yet on the whole, they too decline to mobilise the betrayal myth against the 'gang of four' in their autobiographies.[61] Barbara Castle might scoff that the 'gang of four' should have known that party supporters would never be taken in by 'the vanities of a few middle-class intellectuals', but even she acknowledges feeling genuine regret at the loss of Shirley Williams.[62] Writing from the 'outside left', Eric Heffer records the same sentiment much more strongly. He tells of meeting Shirley Williams for lunch in September 1980, six months before the launch of the SDP, in a bid to persuade her to stay. Perhaps more remarkably, in acknowledging his failure to sway her, he admits that Williams was quite convinced that Labour had already swung too far towards Eastern European-style socialism for her to remain long within the party.[63]

All this naturally raises the question of why the 'gang of four' have not been demonised at least as much as MacDonald and his followers in the 1930s. After all, the SDP/Liberal Alliance certainly came closer to supplanting Labour's position on the left (or 'centre-left' in New Labour speak) than ever did MacDonald's flag of convenience, the 'National Labour Party' (or Mosley's equally ill-fated New Party). MacDonald's ultimate political failure must surely be judged at least as great as the Social Democrats', but it did not save him from vilification in party mythology. On the other hand, unlike MacDonald, the 'gang of four' could not be accused of desperately clinging onto office; indeed within a few years of the split it was fairly clear that none would ever enjoy high office again. This may go some way to explain the muted character of left-wing criticism – as may the fact that many felt that the 'gang of four' had at least had the honesty to acknowledge that their views had no place in a 'socialist' party. On the right of the party, however, the rehabilitation of the 'gang of four' owes more to the construction of new mythologies since the early 1980s, mythologies which are largely in harmony with the spirit of the SDP's rebellion. Labour leaders have had to legitimate their internal battles to expel the Militant Tendency, to discipline local left-wing parties, and ultimately to drop Clause Four (part 4) of the 1918 constitution. In the language of 'New Labour' mythology, the party found the will to take on the 'hard left' and to 'modernise' its policies, which is another way of saying that party leaders are now committed to a mythology couched in the battle cries of the social-democratic right *circa* 1979–81.[64] Equally important has been

the left's continued use of the 'betrayal myth' to oppose the 'modernisers'. The Liverpool Labour MP Bob Parry denounced Kinnock as
'the greatest traitor since Ramsay MacDonald' after his anti-Militant
speech at the 1985 Bournemouth conference, while others mockingly
labelled him 'Ramsay MacKinnock'.[65] Of course, it would be foolhardy
to suggest that there has ever been any realistic prospect of the former
SDP leaders rejoining Labour – their 'disloyalty' has always made them
political pariahs in party circles. Even New Labour sought to play down
Roy Jenkins's influence over Blair and the Prime Minister's inner circle
of policy advisers. But, on the other hand, by the late 1990s the 'gang of
four' were more likely to be portrayed as the tragic, if misguided,
victims of Labour's brief flirtation with ultra-leftism than as the 'traitors' who forced it into the political wilderness for a generation (an
equally plausible interpretation).

Myths of division: 'this is personal'

Labour, as the preceding discussion makes clear, has always been a party
divided against itself. But if the language of 'betrayal' was the most
emotive voice of political division, there were many other languages
available to the Labour politician keen to do down a fellow socialist.
There was, of course, the language of ideology, as in Jennie Lee's careful
dissection of right-wing versions of the 'MacDonald myth'. Much more
common, however, was the language she sought to challenge: the language of personalities. As one might imagine, in writing their autobiographies Labour leaders have often been keen to vindicate themselves at
the expense of their colleagues. In this respect, the language of personalities has a distinctly 'high politics' flavour, reflecting internecine struggles remote from the lives, or experience, of party activists. However,
perhaps because they view party activists as important arbiters of their
long-term reputations, Labour leaders have tended to imbue their
accounts of complex disagreements over policy and ideology at
Westminster with a bold, mythic quality that echoes dominant popular
understandings of the party's past. It is in this sense that they may be
thought of as 'myths of division'. Here the analysis will concentrate on
the post-war period, when the party's greater proximity to state power
increased the scope for powerful myths of division to be developed.

Few disputes within the Labour Party have been as intensely person-
alised as the 'Bevanite' left opposition movement of the 1950s. Many
accounts of the divisions that racked the party during its long years of
opposition after 1951 offer a crudely black-and-white picture of relations between Aneurin Bevan and his principal right-wing rival, Hugh

Gaitskell. Perhaps predictably, Barbara Castle and Ian Mikardo demonise Gaitskell in order to celebrate Bevan as the movement's great lost
leader. For instance, Castle denounces Gaitskell for his 'stubborn dog-
matism and his pedantic obsession with detail', while Mikardo dismisses
him as 'panicky' and weak in the wake of the 1959 election defeat.[66]
Perhaps not surprisingly, Jennie Lee is also sharply critical of Gaitskell
in her account of *My Life with Nye*, depicting the Labour leader as
authoritarian and paranoid in his determination to defeat the 'fellow
travellers' on Labour's left (though she is still fair-minded enough to
acknowledge that 'just as much as Nye he was fighting for what he
believed in').[67] Fenner Brockway brings out the personal and social
dimension of Labour's sectarian politics during the 1950s especially
well. He recalls how, after declaring his opposition to unilateralism in
1957, Bevan found himself shunned by his old associates on the left.
Often forced to sit alone in the Commons smoking room, Bevan, we are
told, felt deeply 'hurt' by the boycott.[68] Michael Foot, one of the few
who refused to spurn Bevan (though he strongly disagreed with him),
describes how 'all the mythology of pitiless Socialist sectarianism was
invoked' to argue that Bevan had set out 'to assist the Right at the
expense of the Left'.[69] Jennie Lee goes further, insisting that 'the
wounds inflicted by the unilateral disarmers in 1957 and 1958' hurt
Bevan deeply and caused his premature death from stomach cancer in
1960.[70] Perhaps unsurprisingly, this re-worked myth of Labour martyrdom has generally proved too divisive for most tastes. Rather, the tendency has been for politicians to play down their disagreements with
Bevan in order to celebrate him as the posthumous hero of 'true' socialism. Left-wingers say little about their vilification of Bevan over unilateralism in the late 1950s, while right-wing 'hard men' such as Healey
and Callaghan generally insist on distinguishing between Bevan and the
'Bevanites'. Thus Callaghan seeks to explain away the divisions of the
1950s by arguing that 'it was the use of his [Bevan's] reputation by
others that kept [Labour] divided'. Bevan himself, we are told, had long
since tired of dispute.[71] Similarly, Healey is happy to concede that Bevan
displayed a 'broad-minded tolerance and intellectual imagination' that
was foreign to his disciples, and that he was 'less guilty of "odium theo-
logicum" than his supporters'.[72] As Castle, Mikardo and others make
clear, it remains much more acceptable to criticise, if not vilify, Gaitskell,
but even here there are exceptions. Lee's fair-mindedness has already
been noted, but perhaps no less striking is Eric Heffer's frank admission
that when he met Gaitskell, shortly after an acrimonious Liverpool
meeting where he had helped to prevent the Labour leader from speak-

ing, he was genuinely impressed by his sincerity and political honesty.[73] In so doing, Heffer was able simultaneously to distance himself from the sectarian spirit of much internal Labour Party conflict and to imply that later right-wing leaders lacked Gaitskell's redeeming qualities.

The internal feuds that beset the Labour governments of the 1960s and 1970s have also generally been retold more as personal than as political confrontations. Even where the substantive political issues at stake are clearcut, most observers choose to highlight the personal dimension. This is the case with Barbara Castle's ill-fated attempt to introduce new laws governing trade unions in her 1969 White Paper *In Place of Strife*. For those involved, personalities loom large in the story of this ill-conceived initiative.[74] For Castle, in particular, this is clearly an intensely personal story. She is obviously conscious that, whilst many Labour figures were involved in devising and defending the White Paper (including Peter Shore, Tony Benn and Harold Wilson), in the party's mythic history she alone has been identified with its ignominious failure. Indeed, she concludes, probably rightly, that the episode destroyed any prospect that she might rise to the top in Labour politics. Perhaps understandably, therefore, her account is peppered both with accusations of base 'betrayal' and with evidence of 'contempt' for her 'vacillating colleagues'.[75] Denis Healey, by contrast, offers a rather detached account of the whole episode, offering no insights into his own position on trade-union reform. However, he too places personalities very much to the fore, arguing that Jim Callaghan's opposition to the reforms was entirely opportunist. According to Healey, Callaghan had been plotting to succeed Wilson for some time and saw that the controversy over *In Place of Strife* gave him the perfect opportunity to rally the trade unions behind his bid for the leadership.[76] Perhaps not surprisingly, Callaghan offers a very different account of events. He argues that Wilson and Castle deliberately by-passed cabinet discussion, and reneged on assurances that legislation would not be introduced until there had been a full debate on the reforms within the party. He then quotes extracts from his 1969 diary to 'prove' that there is no foundation to allegations that he hoped to exploit the controversy to unseat Wilson.[77] And so one could go on, but the point is made – Labour's myths of division have, for the most part, been intensely personal affairs.

Myths of 'triumph'

In the discussion of the constantly shifting character of Labour's 'foundation myths', it was suggested that an important function of mythology has always been to offer reassurance and comfort to the party faithful.

Jon Lawrence

Gradually, however, a new tone emerged, one that confidently assumed the 'progressive' character of history, and hence the inevitability of Labour's ultimate victory. Despite the reversal of 1931, the idea that Labour was marching in step with history was strong long before the landslide election victory of 1945. Most Labour auto/biographies from the 1930s display satisfaction at the extent of social progress since the formation of the Labour Party, and a quiet confidence that Labour has the power to complete the 'social reconstruction' of Britain.[78] However, this faith in history only assumed a genuinely triumphalist tone in the wake of the 1945 landslide, when the idea of the 'forward march of labour' suddenly appeared to be an objective fact of history, rather than just a hopeful battle cry. For this reason, autobiographical accounts of Labour's victory in 1945 are especially interesting.

Perhaps inevitably, most accounts of Labour's great breakthrough were written *after* the party had lost office in 1951, but even so, most remain strongly stamped with the imprint of the party's mythic 'forward march'. Perhaps wishing to show his detachment from electoral politics, Attlee makes little comment on the 1945 contest in his various memoirs, but other Labour leaders proved much less circumspect. For instance, in his 1957 autobiography, Hugh Dalton suggests that the electorate of 1945 appeared 'much more thoughtful and intelligent than before the war'. There was, he argues, 'much evidence of a serious mind among the electors', and in consequence the campaign proved unusually quiet.[79] Herbert Morrison presents a remarkably similar picture of the 1945 electorate. Recalling that audiences were often strangely silent at political meetings, he insists (rather inelegantly) that this was 'not the silence of lethargy but the quietness of thoughtfulness'. Like Dalton, Morrison suggests that 1945 witnessed the emergence of a new type of elector – a 'new sort of John Bull'. Indeed, he states (not wholly convincingly) that 'however he was to vote I liked him and was proud of him'.[80] In such accounts, Labour leaders can be seen almost consciously burying their long-held fears about the political instincts of the 'irrational' masses. More than that, given that both men were writing against the back-drop of successive Tory election victories in the 1950s, their story served to reassure Labour activists that the achievements of the 1945–51 governments remained safe. Labour's programme had been an articulation of the popular will (rather than party dogma), and the people remained true to the ideals of this programme even if (temporarily) many had forsaken the party at the polls.

The idea that the 1945 election finally brought Labour into harmony with 'its people' remains the dominant interpretation of this important breakthrough into majority government, but there are alter-native stories to be found in Labour autobiographies. Particularly striking is George Brown's account of the election – here the significance of 1945 is understood in purely personal terms. The story is not about the people 'coming home' to Labour, or about the party's inspiring vision of 'the New Jerusalem'. Rather, we are told how Brown braved the wrath of Ernest Bevin to win Transport and General Workers' Union sponsorship as a prospective parliamentary candidate, and how, had he not won the Derbyshire mining seat of Belper, he might well have ended up as the union's leader instead of serving in the cabinet.[81] Here the recapitulation of collective myths about 1945 loses out to the more important task of establishing Brown's credentials as the authentic voice of trade unionism among the Labour leaders of the 1950s and 1960s. In a similar vein, Tony Blair used the occasion of the fiftieth anniversary of the 1945 victory to remind Labour activists that '1945 was the exception and not the rule'.[82] Blair argued that 'with the possible exception of 1964, Labour has been unable to recreate the strong political consensus of 1945', and that 'the challenge of modernisation today' was to learn from this 'moment of greatest success' so that Labour might rebuild its fractured relationship with the 'people of Britain'.[83] Here was Labour's 'finest hour' reinterpreted to conform to a decidedly post-'forward march' mythology where Labour had never reached the 'promised land', even if it had glimpsed it briefly in the aftermath of the Second World War. It reminds us, of course, that mythologies are always with us, and always changing. The mythic histories of Labour's new 'finest hour' – its landslide victory in the May 1997 general election – are already forming. The Labour leadership clearly wish to see these myths of 'triumph' interwoven with fresh 'foundation myths' about the birth of 'New Labour' – presenting this ideological re-launch as the moment when the party finally came 'home to its people'.[84] If they succeed in this project it will be thanks more to the party's performance in the next, and subsequent, general elections, than to the activities of the would-be myth-makers of Millbank Tower. But there should perhaps be a word of warning here for Labour leaders: by relying so heavily on myths of 'newness' to define their project, they have largely conceded the terrain of the past – and its myths – to their embattled opponents within the party. Whilst Labour prospers at the polls they may have little to fear, but in adversity it seems likely that these opponents will seek to mobilise mythic accounts of Labour's past in order to challenge the modernising myths of 'New Labour'.

Jon Lawrence

Notes

1 Gareth Stedman Jones, *Languages of Class: Studies in English Working-Class History, 1832–1982* (Cambridge: Cambridge University Press, 1983), p. 243.

2 See especially Raphael Samuel and Paul Thompson (eds.), *The Myths We Live By* (London: Routledge, 1990), esp. pp. 1–22 and 49–60; cf. Eric Hobsbawm and Terence Ranger (eds.), *The Invention of Tradition* (Cambridge: Cambridge University Press, 1983), or the earlier Roland Barthes, *Mythologies*, trans. by Annette Lavers (London: Jonathan Cape, 1972).

3 H. M. Drucker, *Doctrine and Ethos in the Labour Party* (London: George Allen and Unwin, 1979); Daniel Weinbren, *Generating Socialism: Recollections of Life in the Labour Party* (Stroud: Sutton, 1997). However, see Tudor Jones, '"Taking Genesis out of the Bible": Hugh Gaitskell, Clause IV and Labour's socialist myth', *Contemporary British History* 11 (1997), 1–23.

4 For an introduction to these ideas on autobiography, myth and narratives of the self, see Liz Stanley, *The Auto/biographical I: The Theory and Practice of Feminist Auto/biography* (Manchester: Manchester University Press, 1992); Samuel and Thompson, *The Myths We Live By*; Karl J. Weintraub, 'Autobiography and historical consciousness', *Critical Inquiry* 1 (1974–5), 821–48; Agnes Hankiss, 'Ontologies of the self: on the mythological rearranging of one's life history', in Daniel Bertaux (ed.), *Biography and Society: The Life History Approach to the Social Sciences* (Beverly Hills: Sage, 1981).

5 See Stanley, *The Auto/biographical I* and N. K. Denzin, *Interpretive Biography* (Newbury Park, Calif.: Sage, 1989), pp. 17–26.

6 For instance, *Marching On, 1900–1950: Golden Jubilee of the Labour Party* (London: Labour Party, 1950); *The Rise of the Labour Party* (London: Labour Party, 1946); *A Pictorial History of the Labour Party 1900–1975 to Celebrate the Seventy-Fifth Anniversary of its Birth* (London: Labour Party, 1975).

7 The idea of the 'forward march of labour' was itself one of the most powerful myths of the mid-century labour movement: see especially Francis Williams, *Fifty Years' March: The Rise of the Labour Party* (London: Odhams, n.d., [1949]), esp. pp. 341, 376 and 378; also his *Magnificent Journey: The Rise of the Trade Unions* (London: Odhams, 1954).

8 See Jon Lawrence, *Speaking for the People: Party, Language and Popular Politics in England, 1867–1914* (Cambridge: Cambridge University Press, 1998), pp. 257–61.

9 Cited in Herbert Tracey (ed.), *The Book of the Labour Party: Its History, Growth, Policy and Leaders* (London: Caxton, n.d. [1925]), vol. III, p. 109.

10 Emrys Hughes (ed.), *Keir Hardie's Speeches and Writings: From 1888 to 1915*, 3rd edn (Glasgow: Forward Printing and Publishing, n.d. [1927?]), p. 124.

11 David Kirkwood, *My Life of Revolt* (London: G. G. Harrap and Co., 1935), p. 85.

12 John T. Scanlon, 'Rt. Hon. John Wheatley, MP: Labour's first Minister of Health', in Tracey (ed.), *Book of the Labour Party*, vol. III, p. 210.

13 Joe Toole, *Fighting through Life* (London: Rich and Cowan, 1935), pp. 100–1.

14 William Stewart, *J. Keir Hardie: A Biography*, 2nd edn (London: Independent Labour Party, 1925), p. xxii. On the sinners and saints approach to labour biography throughout the twentieth century, see Duncan Tanner, 'Socialist pioneers and the art of political biography', *Twentieth-Century British History* 4 (1993), 284–91.

15 James Sexton, *Sir James Sexton, Agitator: The Life of the Dockers' MP* (London: Faber, 1936), p. 239; Philip Snowden, *An Autobiography*, vol. I (London: Nicholson and Watson, 1934), p. 75; Tom Johnstone, 'James Keir Hardie: the founder of the Labour Party', in Tracey (ed.), *Book of the Labour Party*, vol. III, pp. 105, 115–16; Stewart, *J. Keir Hardie*, pp. xxvi (MacDonald's introduction) and 195, 198, 258, 346. See also, William M. Haddow, *My Seventy Years* (Glasgow: R. Gibson and Sons, 1943), p. 119; Margaret Cole, *Makers of the Labour Movement* (London: Longmans, 1948), p. 203; Emrys Hughes, *Keir Hardie: A Pictorial Biography* (London: Lincolns-Prayer, 1950), p. 78; Williams, *Fifty Years'*, p. 228.

16 'Iconoclast' [Mary Agnes Hamilton], *The Man of Tomorrow: J. Ramsay MacDonald* (London: Independent Labour Party, 1924), pp. 90–1.

17 H. Hessell Tiltman, *James Ramsay MacDonald: Labour's Man of Destiny* (London: Waverley, n.d. [1929]), esp. pp. 11–12, 162. Some on the socialist left were sceptical of his claims to heroic status even in the 1920s; for instance, see Joseph Clayton, *The Rise and Decline of Socialism in Great Britain, 1884–1924* (London: Faber and Gwyer, 1926), esp. pp. 120, 199, 212, though even Clayton accepts the sincerity of MacDonald's opposition to war in a life otherwise devoted to 'opportunism' (p. 199).

18 'Iconoclast', *Man of Tomorrow*, p. 111; see also Mary Agnes Hamilton, 'Rt. Hon. J. Ramsay MacDonald, M.P.: Labour's first Prime Minister', in Tracey (ed.), *Book of the Labour Party*, vol. III, pp. 132–4, and Hamilton's autobiography, written *after* the 1931 'betrayal', *Remembering My Good Friends* (London: Jonathan Cape, 1944), pp. 98, 130 and 254.

19 Hamilton, 'J. Ramsay MacDonald', p. 121.

20 For MacDonald as the new Gladstone, see 'Iconoclast', *Man of Tomorrow*, pp. 135 and 140.

21 This had always been the theme of Labour's left critics; see Clayton, *Rise and Decline*, pp. 197 and 212.

22 Sexton, *Agitator*, p. 8 (preface). Lloyd George clearly had a keen sense of Labour mythology, describing the book as an account of 'those years of struggle, hardship and injustice, of frequent setback and long-delayed success, through which those pioneers had to toil, who had vowed themselves to the task of securing fair play, better conditions and a more honourable status in the community for their fellow workers' (ibid., pp. 7–8).

23 Toole, *Fighting*, p. 88. This sentiment is echoed in his daughter's otherwise remarkably heterodox (and frank) portrait of her father as politician and wayward family man, Millie Toole, *Our Old Man: A Biographical Portrait of Joseph Toole by his Daughter* (London: J. M. Dent and Sons, 1948), pp. 28, 170, 184.

Jon Lawrence

24 Haddow, *Seventy Years*, pp. 31 and 117 (original emphasis).
25 Edwin A. Jenkins, *From Foundry to Foreign Office: The Romantic Life-Story of the Rt. Hon. Arthur Henderson, MP* (London: Grayson, 1933), p. viii.
26 Ibid., p. 264.
27 Mary Agnes Hamilton, *Arthur Henderson: A Biography* (London: Heinemann, 1938), pp. 386, 388 and 446; also p. 409 where she suggests that Henderson attributed Willie Graham's premature death from pneumonia to 'the heart-sickness of 1931'.
28 Cole, *Makers*, p. 265; cf. Hamilton, *Henderson*, p. 446. See also Williams, *Fifty Years'*, p. 229, where Hardie and Henderson are said to have shared the same unbending 'integrity' and lack of pretension, though apparently 'alike in so little'.
29 Cole, *Makers*, p. ix.
30 Jennie Lee, *This Great Journey: A Volume of Autobiography, 1904–45* (London: MacGibbon and Kee, 1963) (first published as *Tomorrow is a New Day* (London: Cresset Press, 1939)); Hannah Mitchell, *The Hard Way Up: The Autobiography of Hannah Mitchell, Suffragette and Rebel* (London: Virago, 1977) (first published by Faber, 1968).
31 For instance, Mitchell, *Hard Way Up*, pp. 86, 98, 107, 118, 206.
32 Lee, *Great Journey*, pp. 50–1.
33 Clement Attlee, *As It Happened* (London: Heinemann, 1954), pp. 20–1.
34 Fenner Brockway, *Bermondsey Story: The Life of Alfred Salter* (London: George Allen and Unwin, 1949), pp. 19–20, 32, and 33–42. Of the period after his break with liberalism, we are told, with a note of post-45 triumphalism, that Salter 'had entered the wilderness, but he had no doubt of the promised land' (p. 39).
35 Ibid., pp. 43–4.
36 Herbert Morrison, *An Autobiography* (London: Odhams, 1960), pp. 55–6.
37 See Duncan Tanner, *Political Change and the Labour Party, 1900–18* (Cambridge: Cambridge University Press, 1990), ch. 3; Logie Barrow and Ian Bullock, *Democratic Ideas and the British Labour Movement* (Cambridge: Cambridge: University Press, 1996), pp. 196–208; Dylan Morris, 'Labour or socialism? Opposition and dissent within the ILP, 1906–14: with special reference to the Lancashire division', unpublished Ph.D. thesis (University of Manchester, 1982), esp. chs. 6, 8, 12 and 13.
38 Hamilton, *Henderson*, p. 384. She is quoting 'an intimate friend' who met him in Downing Street. In a similar vein Manny Shinwell reports being told that Henderson had 'had to hold on to chair backs to reach the [cabinet room] door, he was physically shocked'; see Emmanuel Shinwell, *I've Lived Through It All* (London: Gollancz, 1973), p. 108.
39 For instance, Hugh Dalton, *Memoirs: The Fateful Years, 1931–1945* (London: Muller, 1957), pp. 19–20, 81–2; J. H. Thomas, *My Story* (London: Hutchinson, 1937), p. 226; John Parker, *Father of the House: Fifty Years in Politics* (London: Routledge and Kegan Paul, 1982), pp. 47–8; Shinwell, *I've Lived*, p. 124; Williams, *Fifty Years'*, p. 353; Woodrow Wyatt, *Confessions of an Optimist* (London: Collins, 1985), p. 116.

40 Attlee, *As It Happened*, p. 74.

41 Morrison, *Autobiography*, p. 126.

42 For instance, Morrison, *Autobiography*, p. 94 (Macdonald); Harold Wilson, *Memoirs: The Making of a Prime Minister, 1916–64* (London: Weidenfeld and Nicolson, 1986), p. 9 (Snowden); Margaret Bondfield, *A Life's Work* (London: Hutchinson, n.d. [1949]), p. 242 (Thomas); Walter Citrine, *Men and Work: The Autobiography of Lord Citrine* (London: Hutchinson, 1964), p. 63 (MacDonald and Snowden).

43 Morrison, *Autobiography*, p. 127; Ernest Thurtle, *Time's Winged Chariot* (London: Chaterson, 1945), p. 114 makes the same point – both men recall being surprised to lose their East London seats in the 1931 election.

44 Lee, *Great Journey*, p. 114.

45 Ibid., pp. 108–9. For an ideological explanation of the split from the trade-unionist right of the party, see Bondfield, *Life's Work*, pp. 305–7, which argues that the party was always an uneasy alliance of 'industrialists' and 'theoreti-cians', and that MacDonald represented the latter, and had no qualms about turning his back on the 'industrial' side in the crisis of 1931.

46 Fenner Brockway, *Towards Tomorrow* (London: Hart-Davis, MacGibbon, 1977), p. 86; see also comments in his biography of F. W. Jowett, *Socialism over Sixty Years: The Life of Jowett of Bradford, 1864–1944* (London: George Allen and Unwin for National Labour Press, 1946), pp. 292–3.

47 Henry Snell, *Men, Movements and Myself* (London: Dent, 1938), p. 251.

48 Ibid., p. 253. Shinwell, *I've Lived*, p. 109, tells a similar story, except that he insists he rejected the overture by declaring 'I must stand by the Party.'

49 Sexton, *Agitator*, pp. 280–1. Perhaps predictably, Jimmy Thomas offers a belligerent defence along these lines; see Thomas, *My Story*, pp. 189–99.

50 Citrine, *Men and Work*, p. 286.

51 Ibid., pp. 287, 290–2; also Thurtle, *Winged Chariot*, p. 113.

52 Morrison, *Autobiography*, pp. 131–2.

53 Ibid., p. 245.

54 Dalton, *Fateful Years*, p. 467.

55 George Brown, *In My Way* (London: Gollancz, 1971), p. 179.

56 Ibid., pp. 194–5.

57 Denis Healey, *The Time of my Life* (London: Michael Joseph, 1989), pp. 474–80.

58 Denis Howell, *Made in Birmingham: The Memoirs of Denis Howell* (London: Macdonald Queen Anne, 1990), pp. 272 and 360.

59 Andy McSmith, *John Smith: Playing the Long Game* (London: Verso, 1993), p. 82.

60 James Callaghan, *Time and Chance* (London: Collins, 1987), pp. 565–6. 'Kinnockite' biographies often took a similar line in the 1980s: see for instance, Michael Leapman, *Kinnock* (London: Unwin Hyman, 1987), p. 20.

61 Though Dennis Skinner certainly made great use of it as part of his sustained heckling campaign against the SDP 'defectors' in the House of Commons. See George Thomas, first Viscount Tonypandy, *George Thomas, Mr Speaker: The Memoirs of the Viscount Tonypandy* (London: Century, 1985), p. 189.

Jon Lawrence

62 Barbara Castle, *Fighting All the Way* (London: Macmillan, 1993), p. 531.
63 Eric Heffer, *Never a Yes Man: The Life and Politics of an Adopted Liverpudlian* (London: Verso, 1991), p. 190.
64 For instance, Jon Sopel, *Tony Blair: The Moderniser* (London: Bantam, 1995).
65 Leapman, *Kinnock*, p. 105.
66 Castle, *Fighting*, p. 322; Ian Mikardo, *Back-bencher* (London: Weidenfeld and Nicolson, 1988), pp. 162–3. Mikardo portrays Gaitskell as a lame duck sure to have given way to Bevan but for the latter's sudden death.
67 Jennie Lee, *My Life with Nye* (London: Jonathan Cape, 1980), pp. 205, 207, 217.
68 Brockway, *Towards Tomorrow*, p. 227.
69 Michael Foot, *Aneurin Bevan*, vol. II (London: Paladin, 1975), pp. 582–3; Brockway, *Towards Tomorrow*, p. 227 for Foot as one of the 'few faithfuls'.
70 Lee, *Life with Nye*, pp. 236–7, 252–3.
71 Callaghan, *Time and Chance*, p. 115.
72 Healey, *Time of my Life*, p. 151.
73 Heffer, *Never a Yes Man*, pp. 89 and 91.
74 'Non-combatants' such as the left-wing Eric Heffer offer a more impersonal, ideological account of the episode: see, *Never a Yes Man*, p. 135.
75 Castle, *Fighting*, pp. 415–25, esp. 419–21.
76 Healey, *Time of my Life*, p. 341.
77 Callaghan, *Time and Chance*, pp. 273–7.
78 For instance see, Ben Turner, *About Myself, 1863–1930* (London: Cayme Press, 1930), p. 352; Ben Tillett, *Memories and Recollections* (London: John Long, 1931), pp. 274–5; Kirkwood, *My Life*, pp. 264–9 (1935); Toole, *Fighting*, p. 232 (1935); Sexton, *Agitator*, p. 297 (1936).
79 Dalton, *Fateful Years*, p. 463; for his retrospective certainty in Labour's 'forward march' see his comments in Cole, *Makers*, p. vii; also 'official' post-1945 histories such as *Marching On, 1900–1950* and *Rise of the Labour Party*, and Williams, *Fifty Years'*.
80 Morrison, *Autobiography*, p. 236. See also Tom Driberg, *Ruling Passions* (London: Jonathan Cape, 1977), p. 184 (on the wartime Maldon by-election), and Toole, *Our Old Man*, pp. 89–90 (contrasting 1945 with the fiercer meetings of the 1920s, though as we have seen, many Labour politicians had made similar claims about the improved temper of the working-class electorate in the 1920s and 1930s).
81 Brown, *My Way*, pp. 42–3.
82 Tony Blair, *Let Us Face the Future: The 1945 Anniversary Lecture* (London: Fabian Society, 1995), p. 3.
83 Ibid., pp. 3, 6, 9.
84 See Steven Fielding, ch. 12 below.

12 | New Labour and the past
Steven Fielding

Anniversaries are times when parties, like people, reflect upon the past and look to the future; in doing this, they often reveal much about their present situation. Most Labour stalwarts approached their party's *fiftieth* anniversary confident of its identity, place in history and certain it would transform capitalism into what they termed socialism. At this time, the party saw itself as the consummation of a reforming tradition with antecedents stretching as far back as Magna Carta and the Peasants' Revolt, including, along the way, Puritans, Whigs, Nonconformists and Chartists. Few in Labour's ranks would have disagreed with the leading MP Emmanuel Shinwell's wartime claim that the party's birth 'marked one of the great stages in the political evolution' of Britain.[1] That 'evolution' was thought to have reached a critical stage when Labour won the 1945 general election and began, as promised in *Let Us Face The Future*, to build the 'Socialist Commonwealth'. Whilst the party's 'march', was incomplete by 1950, it had, according to its semi-official chronicler Francis Williams, become 'the greatest party in the State'. Firmly based in the working class and enjoying a 'deep-rooted identification of interest' with the trade unions, Labour's continued 'rise' was considered inevitable. As the editor of one commemorative pamphlet stated, his work 'proved . . . as nothing else could, that the Party is for always'. Even defeat in the 1951 general election could not temper this spirit: the future, it seemed, was already mapped out. To complete its mission all the party required of its members was hard work and true faith.[2]

In contrast, as Labour's centenary neared, many leading figures claimed that, despite the party's imposing Commons majority, there was little to celebrate. Tony Blair, they believed, had achieved the 1997 landslide by abandoning Labour's historic purpose. According to *Labour Left Briefing*, which advanced what contemporaries referred to as a 'hard' left agenda, Blair's government was 'Labour in name only'. Criticism from such quarters raised few eyebrows, but similar opinions were expressed by those normally hostile to the left. Roy Hattersley, Neil Kinnock's deputy and a longstanding member of the Labour right, believed Blair's circle were 'cuckoos in the nest' who wanted to create a new party from within. The Labour Prime Minister, he suggested, did not seek to modernise democratic socialism – Blair wanted to replace it with something entirely different. Moreover, having 'turned its back on history', he accused the leadership of knowing 'nothing of the indisputable truths on which the party was built'. As Hattersley's former antagonist Tony Benn complained, Blair talked about 'new Labour and old Labour, but never Labour, its traditions and aspirations'.[3]

There appeared good reason to accept these views. Blair described the party he had led since 1994 as 'New Labour'. In between becoming leader and Prime Minister he revised Clause Four of Labour's constitution, something many considered central to the party's identity. Blair also distanced himself from 'tax and spend', going so far as to accept the outgoing Conservative government's severely constrained budgetary plans. Labour's organisation was also recast. The sovereign role of the party's annual conference was compromised, activists were further marginalised and the trade unions' policy-making role reduced. Blair claimed he was not accountable to any class interest; in power he would treat employers and union leaders alike – 'fairness not favours' would be his watchword. In addition, whilst never taking the votes of manual workers for granted, his electoral strategy was tightly focused upon winning the support of suburban 'Middle England'. Blair consequently described Labour as the party, not of one class but, as the Conservatives had once been, of 'one nation'. Labour under his leadership had become, he claimed, 'literally a new party'.[4]

Some of Blair's assertions were overstated for electoral effect. The Labour leader wanted to distance his party from what pollsters confirmed was a harmful popular memory of the late 1970s and early

1980s. This was a time when Labour was considered economically incompetent, dominated by the unions and run by left-wingers antagonistic to the interests of the majority. If a distorted reflection of events, one encouraged by Conservative propaganda and a biased popular press, this was, none the less, a common view. Moreover, despite his best efforts, Kinnock had failed to shake off these associations. 'New Labour' was, in this regard, a rhetorical device. So, whilst Blair continued reforms initiated during the 1980s, for the benefit of Conservative-supporting *Sun* and *Daily Mail* readers, he gave the impression that his leadership marked a decisive break with the Kinnock years. This disingenuous tactic was part of a wider strategy in which, as one adviser put it, to court Conservative voters, Blair gave away 'a huge amount in language – but almost nothing in terms of policy'.[5] None the less, a substantial number of Labour members believed appearance *did* reflect reality: to their minds, New Labour was the antithesis of their party's history.

The purpose of this chapter is to assess New Labour's attitude to the past in the hope of establishing a rounded analysis of the party as it begins its second century. At the time of writing, Blair has been Labour leader for five years. Whilst this makes informed comment difficult, that has not prevented New Labour's many critics rushing to judgement. As will be suggested, a problem associated with such appraisals is that their authors have but fitfully studied what New Labour advocates have actually said. In particular, anyone who cared to listen would have heard a keen attempt to vindicate Labour's present course by relating it to the party's past. Yet, those antagonists serious enough to so bend their ears have still dismissed New Labour's understanding of party history as pitifully inaccurate. They see it as an attempt to further Blair's alleged strategy of transforming Labour into a 'cooler' version of the Gladstonian Liberal Party. Theirs is a view not exactly beyond reproach.

The uses of 'tradition'

Everybody is a historian: we all have some notion of what the past was like and how this connects with our present.[6] Yet, these individual beliefs usually only have a tangential relationship to what really happened. As any professional historian will confirm, it is often impossible to discover what occurred in times gone by. Moreover, even if the facts can be established, their interpretation will always be subject to revision as perspectives shift with the years. Thus, most beliefs or practices solemnly handed down from one generation to the next are often founded on deliberately constructed or unconsciously incomplete representations

Steven Fielding

of historic events. Contemporary images of the past may be even more misleading when organised in the form of a 'tradition', one of whose functions is to foster a sense of cohesion and identity. These misconceptions may be the creation of those searching for a vision of the past which would imbue their own interests with historic legitimacy. Fortunately, history is not always raided with the brutal cynicism memorably described in George Orwell's *1984*. Most traditions are based on real historic events and ideas, even if they have been rearranged and reinterpreted to best advantage. Moreover, inhabitants of the present can be as controlled by the past as in command of it: they may, for example, be the captives of a previously invented tradition.

By invoking the past against New Labour so as to suggest it has departed from party tradition, Blair's critics are, therefore, dabbling in the well-established practice of historical reconstruction. What is unusual about this attempt, however, is the extent to which that view of Labour's past to which it gives rise has prevailed over all others. What will be referred to, for convenience's sake, as this 'socialist' tradition is defined by two dates: 1918 and 1945. In 1918 Labour committed itself to the extension of public ownership through Clause Four of a constitution which marked the party's transformation into a national organisation. In 1945 Labour achieved its first working Commons majority which led, most notably, to a massive nationalisation programme and the pursuit of full employment through state planning and Keynesian demand management. The two dates are linked due to the belief that Labour won in 1945 *because* it had advanced the vision of socialism established in 1918. Consequently, these two moments came to be seen as encapsulating Labour's essential and eternal identity. Thus, when he stood for the leadership in 1994, John Prescott invoked the 'spirit of 1945', which he defined as a commitment to full employment and social justice, because 'that *has always* been our cry'. Two years later, historian and venerable Labour activist Royden Harrison claimed that the 'best' of the party's tradition was the 'settlement which followed victory in the Second World War: it was and *it will always be* the Party of full employment; comprehensive social services and extended common ownership with public accountability'.[7] It is as if, between 1918 and 1945, the party had discovered a transcendental truth to which future generations were obliged to remain committed.

It would be foolish to deny that Labour's formal commitment to the extension of public ownership and its post-war election victory both happened. However, the significance which the socialist tradition has invested in these events can be questioned. Some historians have, first,

370

emphasised the extent to which Clause Four was the result of a series of messy, tactical compromises resulting from a peculiar set of historical circumstances. Those who drafted the clause did not intend for it to become a principle that would echo through the ages like a secular version of the Ten Commandments. Secondly, others have suggested that Labour's commitment to state intervention should be seen as but one of many reasons for the party's 1945 landslide – and by no means the most important. Voters were, in any case, asked to support the extension of public ownership on a pragmatic basis – not because it was in accordance with socialist precepts.[8] It is, moreover, doubtful that even a majority of party members were much moved by Clause Four. When those in the safe midlands Labour seat of Newcastle-under-Lyme were asked about the matter in 1960 the result, according to those posing the questions, was 'somewhat surprising and disappointing'. They discovered that only 46 per cent had ever heard of the clause, meaning that, consequently, just over one-quarter of members actively championed it.[9] None the less, when leaders from Hugh Gaitskell onwards argued for the party to revise the clause, they were viewed as proposing treason – at least by those activists and trade-union delegates who attended Labour's annual conferences.

In the 1980s, those following Kinnock's lead in promoting change were, at their own prompting, referred to as 'modernisers'; their opponents were tagged 'traditionalists'. Whilst the former may have seen advantage outside the party's ranks in being so described, internally it had unfortunate consequences. For it only encouraged the view that changes which transformed the party's association with state intervention subverted Labour's established purpose. In the early 1990s, Claire Short, who became one of Blair's more sceptical cabinet colleagues, believed 'so-called modernisers' had 'very little understanding of Labour's traditions'. They wanted, she suggested, 'to rip lots of things up without realising they'd have nothing left'.[10] This perception was reinforced by a belief that advocates of change were motivated solely by pragmatism rather than principle. After all, Gaitskell's failed attempt to revise Clause Four had followed the party's third defeat in a row; Blair's successful assault was launched after four such reverses. Despite this widespread impression, both initiatives were presented as the application of established Labour values, albeit ones few 'traditionalists' wished to recognise. Moreover, in Blair's case, the call for change was accompanied by a confident exhortation for members 'to explore our own history' in light of a 'fresh understanding and an absence of preconditions'.[11] By invoking tradition Blair hoped to find one more justification for his reforms. His opponents mobilised tradition to thwart that change. Yet, whilst both sides advanced competing, if not contrary, versions of the party's past, neither was entirely false. Regardless of this, the general view remained that only New Labour's view of history was based, as one commentator put it, on 'caricature, exaggeration or plain untruths'.[12]

New Labour's tradition

There are two strands to New Labour's historical vision. The first, the one upon which most critics tend to alight, asserts that 1994 marked a 'scorched-earth, year zero'.[13] Philip Gould, pollster and strategist to Kinnock and Blair, is the most prominent figure to express this view. According to him, the seeds of Labour's post-war electoral problems were 'imbedded in its inception'. This was apparently because, 'Labour was born a conservative party', being 'too close to trade unionism; too obsessive about public ownership; too tied to myth; too rooted in the past'. Gould sees as weaknesses what 'traditionalists' would consider abiding strengths. Thus, Fabianism 'helped to ensure that Labour's dominant intellectual tendency was collectivist . . . leaving a progressive legacy that was unbalanced in favour of the state'. The unions were also 'sectional and inward-looking', promoting rigidity and opposition to change. This only reinforced the 'culture and psychology of the British working class' whose experience of exploitation made it 'cautious, defensive and backward-looking'. Even the influence of religion created a 'preference for glorious defeat, the fear that victory can be won only at the price of compromise'. As a consequence, Labour had to be 'reborn' if it was ever again to win power, and in 1994 it duly was.[14]

The second, effectively official, strand contends that New Labour embodies the most vital elements of the party's past. This version is articulated by New Labour's chief architects, Tony Blair and Gordon Brown. Whilst differences of detail can be discerned in the pictures they paint, accountable to their distinct party backgrounds, Blair and Brown share a fundamentally similar view.[15] What emerges from this is the belief that, whilst remaining true to its established values, Labour had to reject policies once considered appropriate to their realisation.[16] Thus, Blair described 'modernisation' as 'not about dumping principle', but actually, 'retrieving what the Labour Party is really about' and applying its 'enduring, lasting principles' to a new context. He considered his reforms were 'not destroying the Left's essential ideology' but 'retrieving it from intellectual and political muddle'. Accordingly, replacing Clause Four in 1995 was not about 'escaping' Labour's traditions but 'recapturing' them. In this paradoxical 'revolution', the party 'rejected the worst of our past, and rediscovered the best'. New Labour, then, should be seen as a vindication, not rejection, of history, 'liberating us from the terrible tyranny of confusing ends with means'. In the eyes of Brown and his co-author, the MP Tony Wright, New Labour's policies also manifested 'an underlying continuity of approach' with the past because they were underpinned by 'fundamental socialist values'. As Blair's first Secretary of State for Culture Chris Smith put it, the 'journey of "New Labour" is in fact a remarkably traditional journey'.[17]

The distinctive feature of Labour's socialism has always been, according to Brown, its morality: 'at root, more an ethic of society than an economic doctrine'. In Blair's many speeches the nature of Labour's ethical basis has varied, according to circumstances. He has sometimes described it as a dutiful 'concern' for the poor; on other occasions it was simply the 'spirit of solidarity' or a belief in 'community' and 'social equality'; alternatively, Blair has considered it to be adherence to a 'basic moral code'; and, more than once, it has become the promotion of democracy and liberty.[18] According to Brown, however, the socialist tradition was fundamentally a 'project of human emancipation', deriving from a belief in the 'equal worth of all individuals'. This stipulated that everybody 'should have the opportunity to realise their potential in full', to which end 'the strength of society' was 'essential'. As Blair noted, the history of workers' co-operatives, the friendly societies and the unions from which Labour sprang is 'one of individuals coming together for self-improvement and to improve people's potential through collective action'.[19]

In the Blair–Brown view, Labour's electoral difficulties after 1979 did not arise from the party's values; these remained popular even during Margaret Thatcher's heyday. Instead, the problem was Labour's reluctance to disassociate its basic convictions from a particular set of policies that had fallen into disrepute. Brown sees nationalisation and planning as the only means possible to promote the 'liberation of individual potential' after 1945. However, as Blair would point out, even then Labour supporters did not vote for 'some abstract notion of the public good'. Instead, they supported a 'collectivist government because that government was going to do good by them'. As it had done in the past and would do again in the future, under Clement Attlee Labour rightly represented 'society's ambition for improvement'. Popular affluence undermined the necessity for this type of collectivism. Moreover, as the public sector expanded it became a 'vested interest' which imposed an increasingly heavy tax burden on ordinary people. By the 1970s there was a perception, rightly or wrongly, that government impeded improvement. In addition, so far as Blair is concerned, Labour had developed a type of social individualism that confused 'liberation from prejudice with a disregard for moral structures'. At times, the party 'appeared indifferent to the family and individual responsibility'. This was simply another 'aberration peculiar to that period', of which the Attlee generation – comprising those who stressed 'responsibility, self-improvement and the family' – would never have been guilty. It was another 'aberration' that New Labour would rectify.

The Thatcher and Major governments' overreliance on the market led, Blair and Brown assert, to a greater appreciation of the need for the application of Labour values. Economic change had resulted in a skilled and educated labour force becoming central to national prosperity. By the 1990s, workers, rather than capital, were 'the driving force of the modern economy'. According to Brown, individual liberation could now arise from the 'enhancement of the value of labour', rather than, as in the past, 'the abolition of private capital'. State control of industry was no longer necessary to progress. Unfortunately for the Conservatives, economic success still entailed forms of collective endeavour they were ideologically incapable of embracing. As a result, by the last decade of the century, only Labour could take up the challenge. Thus, according to Blair, his party stood for more than running a 'Tory economy' with 'a bit of compassion added in', for the 'basic principle' which distinguished Labour from the Conservatives was the former's readiness 'to use the power of society in order to advance the individual'.[20]

Due to social and economic change, however, this 'power of society' could not be expressed in the same way as it had been in the past. Instead, Blair and Brown proposed taking Labour's historic principles and applying them 'anew and afresh to the world today'.[21] As the latter asserted, the 'era of big, centralised government is over': there was no hope of 'maintaining the old processes of mass production, of intervention and control' which had defined post-war Labour policy. Moreover, experience dictated there were disadvantages to a 'one-dimensional view of government' which assumed that 'where there is a public interest there must be a centralised public bureaucracy always directly involved in ownership of industry and services'. Indeed, one of the tasks of government was to redistribute power from the state to the individual. 'For a hundred years', Brown claimed, the socialist message was 'inevitably' that the state had to 'assume power on behalf of the people'. By the 1990s, however, it was 'time for the people to take power' from the state. For, whilst government was necessary to the promotion of freedom, the lesson of the previous fifty years had been that it could, in so doing, threaten liberty. To signify their appreciation of the validity of Labour's values, but also the potential danger they posed if not applied with care, Blair and Brown referred to their approach as 'liberal socialism'. This is a term they had appropriated, with due acknowledgement, from the turn-of-the-century New Liberals.

New Labour and New Liberalism

Mention of the New Liberals highlights the most intriguing feature of New Labour's tradition: its incorporation of elements from another party's past. This is largely due to a wistful regret that Labour's pre-1914 association with the Liberal Party had given way to full independence at the end of the First World War. Some, like Gould, see the parties' divorce as having had disastrous consequences. According to him, when Labour broke with the Liberals it cut itself off from Britain's 'other great radical movement' and 'stopped dead the possibility of building one united progressive party'. This led to 'divided intellectual traditions, separating Liberalism, with its emphasis on individualism and tolerance, from Labourism, which stressed solidarity and social justice'. Accordingly, Labour became a 'dogmatic, statist party' unable to cope with post-war change. The result was that the twentieth century became what some historians refer to as the 'Conservative century'.[22]

Presumably due to his desire to remain closer to a more familiar view of the party's roots, Brown has remained largely silent on this subject. Having described New Labour's outlook as liberal socialism, he has since assiduously selected antecedents only from within the party's bounds even when, in the case of the Clydesiders, they looked implausible candidates.[23] Blair, in contrast, appears to endorse Gould's perspective. Conceding that Labour was established because the Liberals rejected certain values and denied working people a voice he has, none the less, stressed the positive way New Liberals, such as the leading academic and journalist Leonard Hobhouse, responded to the emergent Labour Party.

As numerous historians have indicated, the New Liberals were thinkers who abandoned their party's strictly *laissez-faire* economics and adherence to a pure individualism abstracted from social relationships.[24] Instead, they sought to reconcile liberty with an activist state applying collectivist measures for the common good. Wanting to 'civilise', but not replace capitalism, New Liberals were still far too radical for their less innovative Liberal colleagues. They, none the less, promoted the

375

Edwardian Liberal government's establishment of what some see as the foundations of the welfare state. Later radical Liberals, such as William Beveridge and John Maynard Keynes, also influenced Labour policy after 1945. Thus, Blair has described Hobhouse's belief that collectivist measures were necessary to the development of individual freedom as an 'intellectual bridgehead' between Labour and the Liberals.

Before 1914 this 'bridgehead' looked as though it might become something more.[25] A Lib–Lab pact had seen the first Labour MPs elected to the Commons in 1906; the parties also fought the two general elections of 1910 under a common banner. New Liberals believed that, whilst Labour would never reach middle-class voters like their party, the Liberals were unable to mobilise workers as successfully as Labour. Both sides needed to continue to support each other within what they termed a 'progressive alliance'. This was not a purely pragmatic view. Hobhouse believed there was 'no division in principle or method' between most in Labour's ranks and Liberals of his persuasion. The practical collectivism of the majority of union leaders met with New Liberal approval, whilst they welcomed the influence of figures such as Ramsay MacDonald. As some historians argue, had it not been for the political and social consequences of the First World War, the progressive alliance might very well have continued. Even after 1918, Hobhouse looked upon the newly constructed organisational chasm which now divided the two parties with scepticism. During the early 1920s he still considered 'moderate' Labour leaders represented 'essential Liberalism' even better than the Liberal Party itself. By this point, many of Hobhouse's associates had joined Labour, despairing of the conservatism of other Liberals. Some later assumed leading positions in the two inter-war MacDonald governments.

There is, therefore, enough evidence to substantiate Blair's conviction that Labour should 'welcome the radical left-of-centre tradition outside our own party, as well as celebrating the achievements of the tradition within it'.[26] Labour's achievements in office – especially in 1945 – owed at least something to those who traced their antecedents back to New Liberalism. Such a view, of course, subverted the 'traditionalist' interpretation of the party's past.

Towards a new New Liberalism?

Blair's positive appraisal of New Liberalism was widely seen within the party as dictated by his desire to transform Labour into a latter-day Liberal Party. Such fears were fuelled by those, like the columnist Polly

Toynbee, who claimed that 'Liberalism is alive and rampant: it is New Labour'. Gould even urged a fusion of the two parties.[27] It was not a prospect which enthused all New Labour advocates. Chancellor Gordon Brown and Home Secretary Jack Straw were said to be especially unconvinced. Activists normally loyal to Blair wanted Gould to be 'thrown in the dust-bin of history as a genuine enemy of the party' for suggesting a formal Lib–Lab union.[28] However, despite these misgivings, after the 1997 election, Blair announced he wanted Labour to become 'as the Liberal Party was in the 19th Century'.[29] He invited Liberal Democrats to sit on a consultative cabinet sub-committee to discuss most policy areas. The Prime Minister also established a commission under the Liberal Democrat peer Roy Jenkins to recommend a more proportional electoral system. Blair intended to put this proposal to the people in a referendum – a longstanding Liberal demand.

Whilst seen as dangerously innovative, Blair's respect for liberalism was not without precedent. Most parties which formed West European social democracy were intellectually or organisationally indebted to liberalism, whether they liked to admit it or not. This was especially the case in Britain, at least partly because of the absence of a significant Marxist presence within the indigenous labour movement.[30] Thus, warily perhaps, Labour figures in the past had often paid tribute to liberalism. The left-wing intellectual Harold Laski, who chaired Labour's National Executive Committee in 1945, conceded that liberalism constituted part of the 'great tradition' which was Labour's 'parent'. Laski even believed there were some Liberal members 'on the very verge of the Socialism we profess'. However, he still saw no place for the Liberal Party in contemporary politics as it could only 'cloud the issue by the fragmentation of an electorate that ought to be divided into two parts'.[31]

Laski's view, that Labour was superior to liberalism, had long been party orthodoxy. MacDonald had written as early as 1905 that, 'Socialism, the stage which follows Liberalism, retains everything of value in Liberalism by virtue of its being the hereditary heir of Liberalism.'[32] Blair's attitude was more enigmatic. In one 1995 speech he followed convention, describing Labour as 'the political heir of the radical Liberal tradition'. Yet, within the same sentence Blair portrayed democratic socialism and progressive liberalism as cousins, a description which implied neither was any further up the evolutionary chain than the other. If Blair believed such creeds equal that was because he considered them very similar. As he declared when Prime Minister: 'we're all modern social democrats, [and] a large part of the Liberal Democrats are in that position'.[33]

One reason for Labour members' hostility to Blair's desire for a closer working relationship with the Liberal Democrats was their conviction that he was an 'old fashioned Liberal', Gladstonian in his belief in free trade and balanced budgets. The liberalism critics assumed appealed to Blair was the one committed to *laissez-faire*: it was another way of saying he was 'Thatcherite'.[34] Yet this was not the doctrine of contemporary Liberal Democrats. They consciously advanced an outlook which owed much to New Liberalism – and incorrectly accused Blair of being ignorant of Hobhouse.[35] Liberalism in the 1990s was, however, as much a heterogeneous creed as earlier in the century: those believing liberty was more precious than equality continued to argue with adherents of the opposite view. Yet, as he made clear in a private letter to the philosopher Isaiah Berlin, Blair favoured that liberalism which advocated 'positive' rather than 'negative' liberty. This meant he considered it necessary for the state to act so as to create conditions appropriate for the advancement of liberty for all. Advocates of the latter concept preferred leaving individuals to their own devices. Indeed, Liberal Democrats were warned, on that interpretation, 'liberalism is inimical to Tony Blair'. Other prominent champions of negative liberty also made plain their suspicions of what they considered New Labour's preference for intervention.[36]

In most other respects, Blair's attitude to liberalism was unremarkable. In wanting Labour to be like Gladstone's party, he and his advisers merely sought to emulate the Grand Old Man's success in creating a 'broad coalition of those who believe in progress and justice' and a party 'founded on clear values, whose means of implementation change with the generations'.[37] Blair simply drew attention to the demonstrable fact that both Labour and Liberals, in the present as in the past, shared a common outlook on a number of issues. This was done, at least in part, to assure doubtful voters that Labour under his leadership was no longer an extreme left-wing party, but was located firmly on the centre ground of politics.

Despite fervent denials, politicians have to respond to the same economic and social forces with what are only a limited range of intellectual tools. As a result, there has often been considerable doctrinal overlap and cross-fertilisation between political parties. This is especially so in the case of liberalism and socialism. In an almost literal sense, Labour grew out of liberalism; the latter then helped stimulate the development of New Liberalism, some of whose ideas and personnel were grafted back on to Labour. In fact, whilst not publicly acknowledging their debt, forty years before New Labour there had been another group in the party profoundly influenced by New Liberalism. Described by one authority as the 'central example' of socialist–liberal 'intermingling', they were Labour's post-war social democrats or 'revisionists'.[38]

Revisionist echoes

Roy Jenkins is said to be the only living leading figure from Labour's past to enjoy Tony Blair's respect. The author of a number of works on Liberal subjects – Asquith, the 1906–14 governments and Gladstone – Jenkins has been described as Blair's 'personal history tutor'.[39] It would be interesting to know what lessons the old man has sought to inculcate in his pupil, for Jenkins's own past, which involves membership of three political parties, is intriguing enough. The son of a Labour MP, he entered the Commons in 1948 and soon associated with self-styled revisionists, most notably the future leader Hugh Gaitskell and Anthony Crosland, author of *The Future of Socialism* (1956). In the 1960s and 1970s Jenkins held high office under Harold Wilson, becoming Chancellor and deputy leader. During this time he was, retrospectively at least, a self-confessed 'closet Liberal'.[40] As a result, Jenkins's place within the party was sometimes uneasy. After a desultory showing in the 1976 leadership election, he took the hint, left the cabinet and became president of the European Economic Community. When Jenkins returned to Britain in 1980 it was to establish, along with other disillusioned revisionists, the Social Democratic Party (SDP). At the 1983 general election, he led the SDP into an alliance with the Liberals which came within 700,000 votes of overtaking Labour. That, however, was the summit of SDP support and in 1988 it merged with the Liberals, forming what became known as the Liberal Democrats. Jenkins remained to lead the new party in the Lords. Other social democrats returned to a Labour Party which, under Kinnock, appeared once more hospitable to their views, a process accelerated by Blair's leadership.

Revisionists believed the Labour Party had, as their journal *Socialist Commentary* put it in 1951, to 'look beyond the old gospel of more and more nationalisation, "workers' control" or class appeals to "soak the rich"'. The Attlee governments had, they thought, established 'a decent material basis of life, and a sense of social security for every citizen'. However, Labour's future progress would be assured only if it examined 'what is needed for creating not only an equal society, but a good and rich one'.[41] Most crucially, they advanced the view that, despite 1918, Labour's purpose had never been exclusively defined by the extension of state ownership. Yet Gaitskell for one believed Clause Four had encouraged the widespread belief that public control was 'the be all and end all, the ultimate first principle and aim of socialism'. This, he claimed, arose 'from a complete confusion about the fundamental meaning of socialism and, in particular, a misunderstanding about ends and means'.[42]

The party's ultimate ends were, in the revisionist schema, the furtherance of freedom and equality, the latter being a precondition of the former. The pursuit of greater equality was, according to Crosland, 'the strongest ethical inspiration of virtually every socialist doctrine' and remained 'the most characteristic feature of social thought'. In fact, he argued, it was 'these ethical ideals, and not some particular economic theory or arid dogma, which constitute the essence of democratic Socialism'.[43] This equality was, however, qualified. Inequality was certainly considered a problem: Crosland believed the 'distribution of rewards and privileges' in society was 'highly inequitable, being poorly correlated with the distribution of merit, virtue, ability, or brains'. Yet, like Gaitskell, he did not support equality of outcome, as that might undermine merit and reduce incentives. Gaitskell sought the eradication of 'feelings or attitudes of superiority or inferiority between groups' rather than the abolition of the groups themselves. In other words, he wanted 'equal opportunity for all to develop'. Whilst this would only be possible if privately owned wealth was 'fairly evenly distributed', he thought a higher rate of tax on the inheritance of large fortunes would largely accomplish that end.[44] Like his leader, Crosland believed further public ownership was marginal to achieving equality. Taking the unprecedented post-war boom as permanent, Crosland thought economic growth would provide government with ample tax revenues to finance welfare spending. This, he considered, would be the primary means of overcoming the problem. Economic expansion also meant funding welfare would be relatively painless for taxpayers: even if the proportion of income taken by tax remained constant, in absolute terms government revenues would increase. Labour could, therefore, reduce inequality at little political cost.[45]

Revisionists were also sceptical about other aspects of what some took to be Labour's defining characteristics. Jenkins, for example, responded to Labour's 1959 general election defeat by suggesting it should 'watch out for the dangers of the union links and not rule out an association with the Liberals'. Douglas Jay even proposed changing the party's name.[46] Despite this, they were keen to demonstrate the extent to which revisionism was true to Labour's past. This was illustrated by the manifesto of the Campaign for Democratic Socialism (CDS), formed in 1960 to advance their cause within the party. Heavily indebted to Crosland, the document claimed loyalty to Labour's 'central tradition', defined as a

New Labour and the past

'non-doctrinal, practical, humanitarian socialism – a creed of conscience and reform rather than of class hatred'. The CDS wanted Labour to be 'a broadly-based national party of all the people, as the early pioneers saw it'. It argued:

To their vision we wish to return. A democratic socialist party must be based predominantly on working people. But a purely sectional, one-class party would face electoral suicide; more importantly, it would be a betrayal of the ideal of a classless society . . .

We interpret socialism not as an arid economic dogma, but in terms of freedom, equality, social justice and world co-operation. We believe that the British people, who rightly mistrust doctrinaire utopianism, will always respond to an idealistic appeal to remedy real evils by practical and radical reform.[47]

Not all were convinced. They believed that, without a firm commitment to advancing public ownership, Labour had no distinctive purpose. Aneurin Bevan spoke for many on the left when he stated that, should Clause Four be revised along Gaitskell's lines, Labour 'would not differ in any important respect from the Tory Party'. 'Such an outlook', he declared, 'would take us back to the situation as it existed when the Liberal Party was in its heyday.' According to Bevan, those proposing revision believed that 'private enterprise should still remain supreme but that its worst characteristics should be modified by liberal ideas of justice and equality'. If they succeeded, he believed, Labour might as well merge with the Liberals.[48]

In the face of such views – and lacking support from many large trade unions – Gaitskell accepted that a thoroughgoing modification of party doctrine was beyond his grasp. He died having failed to revise the clause. Whilst despised by most Gaitskellites, Harold Wilson, elected leader in 1963, applied the revisionist approach with more cunning than his predecessor. Wilson's 1964–70 governments still came to grief, as would have any led by Gaitskell, for, confounding Crosland's expectations, economic growth proved inadequate. Whilst the assault on poverty stalled, Wilson was forced to raise taxes and curb wage increases. This not only antagonised the unions and alienated party members but also lost Labour the 1970 election. After this, revisionism's critics successfully advanced the argument within the party that Labour needed to get back to what they considered its basics. In opposition, Labour increased its commitment to direct state ownership and emphasised its working-class identity.

Forced to accept a programme in which few believed, revisionist ministers in Labour's 1974–9 governments confronted a bleak vista: postwar expansion had given way to recession.[49] In this context, welfare

381

Steven Fielding

spending could only be financed by increasing relative levels of tax: the painless road to equality was blocked. Rising unemployment also led some to question the efficacy of demand management.[50] Prime Minister James Callaghan stated that inflation, rather than unemployment, was now the main enemy. If mounting job losses were to be reversed, low wage costs and high productivity were the key – not state intervention.[51] In the face of such dire circumstances, some social democrats re-thought their attitude to the market, the state and the unions. A few had always viewed the influence enjoyed by unions in a full employment economy with misgivings. By the late 1960s the former minister Christopher Mayhew considered union power as 'less an instrument of social justice than a means by which one section of the workers promotes its own interests at the expense of others'.[52] A group of younger revisionists, like David Marquand, hoped a series of speeches delivered by Jenkins in 1972 would persuade workers to support equality through accepting low wage increases and high tax levels.[53] After union leaders declined the offer, the MP John Mackintosh argued that the state itself had become an impediment to growth: the private sector needed liberation from a tax burden grown too heavy.[54] It seemed to many that, as the cabinet minis-ter Shirley Williams noted, by the late 1970s popular opinion had moved against 'the typical product of social democratic government' which she listed as government intervention in the economy, high public-sector expenditure, the welfare state, a substantial public sector and the pursuit of equality.[55] Thus, still viewing the reduction of inequality as their primary goal, an increasing number of social democrats stressed that this could only be achieved through a greater role for the market and the decentralisation, if not contraction, of government power.[56]

Whilst revisionists moved further from the state, the rest of the party embraced public ownership with unprecedented fervour, especially after Margaret Thatcher entered Downing Street in 1979. By 1981 the tension was too much for some social democrats who asserted that Labour was no longer the party they had joined. The object of the SDP was to be, according to Jenkins, to revive the 'old Labour Party of Attlee and Gaitskell' and resurrect the 'coalition of liberal social democrats and industrially responsible trade unionists' which had formed its basis. The new party would, he claimed, represent 'the best part of the non-dog-matic Labour spirit of conscience and reform'. Indeed, four years after its creation, the SDP debated a motion calling on members to reaffirm their commitment to 'traditional Labour values'. Whilst defeated, it was voted down by delegates who themselves asserted the centrality of 'social justice'.[57]

An inheritance of problems

Given the extent to which New Labour echoed key revisionist themes, it is no wonder Gould described the likes of Gaitskell as the party's 'first modernising tendency'; that Blair viewed his Third Way as 'modernised social democracy'; or Brown thought he followed in Crosland's footsteps. The revisionists had, after all, distinguished between time-bound means and fundamental ends; asserted that public ownership was not necessary to achieving equality; broadly accepted the market; and disavowed class appeals.[58]

Due to its contentious recent past, however, highlighting New Labour's revisionist debt was much more hazardous than paying compliments to New Liberalism. Within Labour's ranks, revisionism was tainted by the SDP secession, even though the likes of Hattersley and Denis Healey had remained loyal. That former leading SDP members became advisers to Blair affronted those who looked on them as traitors. It was also another big stick with which to beat the new leader.[59] Consequently, there could only be an unspoken affinity with the 'social market' approach of Callaghan's Foreign Secretary David Owen. As SDP leader after 1983, Owen had embraced 'market realism' and 'social compassion' in a search for a 'new synthesis, a combination of what are wrongly assumed to be incompatible objectives' to which a more equal society remained central. Despite Owen's anticipation of much that would seem indubitably New Labour, no moderniser dared publicly claim this difficult and deeply antagonistic figure for their own. At least Hobhouse was safely dead and buried.[60]

More importantly, revisionism was historically linked to policies which embarrassed New Labour due to their association with the party's popularly discredited past. The Labour cabinets which contained the likes of Crosland and Jenkins had taken for granted what were, for the 1990s, high levels of public ownership and taxation. Along with *laissez-faire*, it was their 'old style Government intervention' embodied in the 'corporatism' of '1960s social democracy' against which Blair defined his Third Way.[61] Thus, in *The Blair Revolution* (1996), Blair's confidant Peter Mandelson, who at least thought about joining the SDP, and policy adviser Roger Liddle, a founder member of the party, mentioned Crosland only twice – so as to criticise him.[62] Indeed, having disavowed the redistribution of income through direct taxation, higher benefits and demand management, some venerable social democrats questioned how Blair could claim any link with revisionism. Marquand, having returned to Labour in 1995, went so far as to claim that Blair's party did not embody 'social democratic values'. Crosland's latter-day disciple Hattersley even asserted New Labour had committed 'apostasy' by abandoning the pursuit of a 'more equal society'.[63]

By employing the revisionist method of distinguishing between means and ends, New Labour should have been safe from such attacks. Crosland had not been confronted with endemic unemployment; government spending devoted to this matter was, in his day, negligible. He had also not lived in a world economy which made demand management on a national scale virtually impossible. It was, therefore, at least debatable whether Crosland would have been a Keynesian in the utterly changed circumstances of the 1990s.[64] Moreover, Brown asserted that – like Crosland – he sought to increase equality of opportunity through government, helping people 'bridge the gap between what they are and what they have it in them to become'.[65] The object was, according to Blair, that 'everyone must have the chance to fulfil their potential, whatever their background, age, sex or race' so there would be 'ladders of opportunity' for all, 'no more ceilings that prevent people from achieving the success they merit'.[66] As others like Mandelson and Smith suggested, New Labour remained committed to achieving a 'more equal society'.[67] Yet, instead of macro-economic demand-side intervention, Labour's 'Welfare to Work' policies were designed to help the unemployed into work by providing them with appropriate skills and motivation. This initiative reflected government's responsibility to 'promote real opportunities' adapted to meet the needs of the contemporary economy.[68] David Blunkett, charged with the brief for education and employment, thought that simply paying out more in benefits would achieve little: recipients would remain poor. Far better, he claimed, to invest directly in education, training and health provision to help the disadvantaged cultivate themselves. By 'developing greater equality in circumstances', he argued, government would 'enable those who are able to earn their own living to have the opportunity to escape poverty themselves'.[69]

The Third Way and 'timeless' values

New Labour's attempt to construct a tradition which challenged the dominant view of the party's past was a political act. It was one more example of how history can be the servant of the present. It was, nonetheless, based upon verifiable facts whose interpretation was, at the very least, plausible. Perhaps the most surprising aspect of New Labour's search for a suitable past was that it was ever considered worthwhile. For, as some prominent historians, sociologists and others have concluded, the twentieth century ended on a very particular note. Rapid change had forced a 'snapping of the links' between past and present, making history an increasingly irrelevant guide to the future. In addition, an emergent 'post-traditional order' had undermined the power of history to legitimise, especially in politics where party structures were collapsing with the evaporation of the social loyalties which had once sustained them.[70]

If such views were often overly dramatic, Blair was undoubtedly influenced by them – they were advanced by some of his closest advisers.[71] Thus he believed that 'the rate of economic, political, industrial and social change is quicker than at any time in our history', as a result of which 'traditional values' had been displaced by a 'rampant' mass culture. In this increasingly formless world, government lacked its previous powers. There was now a 'myriad of individual choices' making up economic and social activity, most of which were beyond the ability of government to control. Globalisation and technological change had also reduced government's competence to run its domestic economy free of external influences. Moreover, the electorate was 'tired of dogma', mistrustful of politicians 'pretending to have a monopoly on the answers'. Consequently, Blair declared that the day of 'all-embracing theories of politics – religious in nature, whose adoption would solve all human problems' was over. Other modernisers took up this theme. Mandelson stated that 'the era of pure representative democracy' was coming to an end. Voters, he asserted, no longer deferred to political elites but wanted to be more directly involved in politics through mechanisms such as the internet and referenda.[72] Some believed that, as political allegiances were weaker than ever before, parties had to be able to perpetually 'recreate' themselves to match the shifting public mood.[73] As the cabinet minister John Reid warned party members, no matter how popular the party might be, 'the absence of a continual self-critical re-evaluation would inevitably see us gradually lapse into the Labour Party of 15 years ago . . . outdated, irrelevant and spurned by the electorate'.[74] No wonder another New Labour enthusiast proclaimed that Blair's was a 'revolution that never stops'.[75]

Amidst such apparent end-of-the millennium flux, Blair still considered the values of democratic socialism 'timeless' in their relevance.[76] In an ever-changing world, he declared, it was especially vital for those on the left to remain absolute in their adherence to these values, otherwise they would have no compass to guide them. That said, he added, 'we should be infinitely adaptable and imaginative in the means of applying these values'. There could be, Blair stated, 'no ideological preconditions, no pre-determined veto on means'.[77] This outlook underpinned Blair's Third Way, his response to the challenges of the globalised economy.

If, as the century ended, Labour policy was based on 'timeless' values, it also faced what must have seemed to party strategists like an ageless electoral predicament. One of the disappointments of Labour's first century was that on only three occasions did it win a working majority in the Commons. To Blair, the crucial reason for this failure was the Labour–Liberal split, as that had prevented progressives combining against the Conservatives. As he bluntly told Isaiah Berlin, his urgent need was to find a way of 'appropriating the great aspects of the liberal tradition' so that Labour could occupy the centre ground. Whilst Gould recommended that Labour merge with the Liberal Democrats, he also thought it possible for Blair to simply annex the latter's ideological territory. In this way, Labour could consolidate its support amongst the 'new middle class' of white-collar workers and aspirational skilled manual workers and ensure that the following hundred years would become the 'progressive century'.[78]

Whilst viewed, within Labour's ranks, as an alarming innovation, this was the most antediluvian of strategies. As Blair and Gould recognised, they were merely addressing what David Marquand – ex-Labour MP, ex-SDP and Liberal Democrat thinker and, for the time being, a critical Labour member – described as the 'progressive dilemma'. Marquand posed the question: how could the traditions represented by Labour and the Liberals be harnessed so as to construct an electoral coalition sufficient to maintain a long-term hold on office?[79] Like other European social-democratic parties, Labour had tried to appeal to those beyond the manual working class. Yet the party's efforts usually met with a pitiful response. Ironically, the creation of Clause Four in 1918 had been an attempt to mobilise middle-class support; its 1995 revision was another. In that sense, Blair was taking Labour full circle.

What is still referred to as New Labour has not yet assumed its final form: Blair's is, as he has admitted, still a 'work in progress'. Moreover, to his mind, Labour remains 'a young party' being a 'product of the modern world'.[80] Predicting the party's precise direction as Labour enters its second century is, therefore, more than usually foolish. Over and above the potentially decisive influence of 'events', even modernisers remain undecided as to how best to proceed. On the vital matter of direct taxation, for example, Brown and Blair have had their differences; the former also seems to believe more in the power of government to promote equality than the latter.[81] Adherence to a tradition of values, no matter how 'timeless' they may be, is no guarantee of agreement as to their interpretation, nor how and when it is opportune to implement them. Such vital decisions are at the heart of all politics which, as the cliché has it, is after all the art of the possible. New Labour has not changed that. Indeed, if, as Blair believes, infinite adaptability is necessary when applying the party's values, for New Labour politics is a more uncertain craft than it ever was.

Some may wish to exchange this uncertainty for the assurance of those members who celebrated the party's first fifty years of existence. Then, as was noted at the beginning of this chapter, the past seemed to provide a blueprint for the future. It is certainly comforting to believe that history, interpreted correctly, can perform such a role. If such nostalgia is aroused, it should be discouraged by sober reflection upon the way that too close an adherence to the supposed lessons of the past allowed the Conservatives to dominate most of Labour's first hundred years of existence.

Steven Fielding

Notes

The author wishes to thank Andrew Adonis, Stefan Berger, Duncan Tanner and Nick Tiratsoo for their comments on earlier versions of this chapter.

1 *Daily Herald*, 15 February 1946; *Listener*, 4 July 1947; John Parker, *Labour Marches On* (Harmondsworth: Penguin, 1947), pp. 13–15; Emmanuel Shinwell, *When the Men Come Home* (London: Victor Gollancz, 1944), p. 66.
2 Francis Williams, *Fifty Years' March. The Rise of the Labour Party* (London: Odhams, 1950), p. 377; Williams, *Magnificent Journey. The Rise of the Trade Unions* (London: Odhams, 1954), p. 426; R. B. Stucke (ed.), *Fifty Years' History of the Woolwich Labour Party, 1903–53* (Woolwich Labour Party, 1953); Steven Fielding (ed.), *The Labour Party since 1951. 'Socialism' and Society* (Manchester: Manchester University Press, 1997), pp. 27–30.
3 'Editorial', *Labour Left Briefing* (September 1997), 3; *Guardian*, 14 May and 8 June 1998; Roy Hattersley and Trevor Fisher, 'Real Labour and Labour reality', *Labour Review* (Autumn 1998), 7–10; *Times Higher Education Supplement*, 19 February 1999.
4 Steven Fielding, 'Labour's path to power', in Andrew Geddes and Jonathan Tonge (eds.), *Labour's Landslide. The British General Election 1997* (Manchester: Manchester University Press, 1997), pp. 23–35; Stephen Driver and Luke Martell, *New Labour. Politics after Thatcherism* (Cambridge: Polity, 1998).
5 Derek Draper, *Blair's Hundred Days* (London: Faber and Faber, 1997), p. 78.
6 This paragraph relies on Eric Hobsbawm, 'Introduction: inventing traditions', in Eric Hobsbawm and Terence Ranger (eds.), *The Invention of Tradition* (Cambridge: Cambridge University Press, 1983), pp. 1–15 and E. H. Carr, *What is History?* (Harmondsworth: Penguin, 1964).
7 Colin Brown, *Fighting Talk. The Biography of John Prescott* (London: Simon and Schuster, 1997), pp. 279–80; *Guardian*, 27 May 1994; Royden J. Harrison, *New Labour as Past History* (Nottingham: Socialist Renewal, 1996), pp. 26–7.
8 For Clause Four, see Ross McKibbin, *The Evolution of the Labour Party, 1910–24* (Oxford: Oxford University Press, 1974), pp. 91–106 and Tudor Jones, *Remaking the Labour Party* (London: Routledge, 1996); for the context of Labour's 1945 triumph, see Steven Fielding, Peter Thompson and Nick Tiratsoo, *'England Arise!' The Labour Party and Popular Politics in 1940s Britain* (Manchester: Manchester University Press, 1995).
9 Frank Bealey, J. Blondel and W. P. McCann, *Constituency Politics. A Study of Newcastle-under-Lyme* (London: Faber and Faber, 1965), pp. 283–4.
10 Quoted in John Rentoul, *Tony Blair* (London: Little, Brown, 1995), p. 274.
11 Tony Blair, *New Britain. My Vision for a Young Country* (London: Fourth Estate, 1996), pp. 7, 13.
12 *Spectator*, 2 January 1999.
13 Paul Richards, 'The permanent revolution of New Labour' in Anne Coddington and Mark Perryman (eds.), *The Moderniser's Dilemma. Radical Politics in the Age of Blair* (London: Lawrence and Wishart, 1998), p. 37.

New Labour and the past

14 Philip Gould, *The Unfinished Revolution. How the Modernisers Saved the Labour Party* (London: Little, Brown, 1998), pp. 24–6, 392.

15 For more on their backgrounds see Rentoul, *Blair*, and Paul Routledge, *Gordon Brown. The Biography* (London: Simon and Schuster, 1998).

16 Unless otherwise stated the account contained in the following six paragraphs is based on Blair, *New Britain*; Tony Blair's introduction to Tony Wright and Matt Carter, *The People's Party. A History of the Labour Party* (London: Thames and Hudson, 1997); Gordon Brown, 'The politics of potential: a new agenda for Labour' in David Miliband (ed.), *Reinventing the Left* (Cambridge: Polity, 1994); and Gordon Brown and Tony Wright, 'Introduction' in Gordon Brown and Tony Wright (eds.), *Values, Visions and Voices. An Anthology of Socialism* (Edinburgh: Mainstream, 1995).

17 Chris Smith, *New Questions for Socialism* (London: Fabian Society, 1996), p. 2.

18 *Guardian*, 15 May 1998.

19 Ibid., 25 May 1994.

20 *Financial Times*, 11 June 1994.

21 Tony Blair's speech to the Institute for Public Policy Research, 14 January 1999. All speeches cited in this chapter are available on the internet at www.number-10.gov.uk.

22 Gould, *Unfinished Revolution*, pp. 27 and 397.

23 *Observer*, 10 January 1999.

24 Peter Clarke, *Liberals and Social Democrats* (Cambridge: Cambridge University Press, 1978), and Michael Freeden, *The New Liberalism. An Ideology of Social Reform* (Oxford: Oxford University Press, 1978).

25 This paragraph is based on Clarke, *Liberals*, pp. 111–12, 139–40 and 237–8; James Meadowcroft's introduction to L. T. Hobhouse, *Liberalism and Other Writings* (Cambridge: Cambridge University Press, 1994), pp. ix–xxvi; Blair, *New Britain*, pp. 7, 14–17; Frank Bealey and Henry Pelling, *Labour and Politics, 1900–1906* (London: Macmillan, 1958); P. F. Clarke, *Lancashire and the New Liberalism* (Cambridge: Cambridge University Press, 1971); and Duncan Tanner, *Political Change and the Labour Party, 1900–1918* (Cambridge: Cambridge University Press, 1990).

26 Blair, *New Britain*, pp. 7, 11, 12.

27 *Guardian*, 18 November 1998; Gould, *Unfinished Revolution*, p. 398.

28 *Independent*, 1 January 1999.

29 Blair's speech on the 150th anniversary of the Associated Press, 15 December 1998.

30 For more on this issue see John Breuilly, *Labour and Liberalism in Nineteenth Century Europe* (Manchester: Manchester University Press, 1992); Donald Sassoon, *One Hundred Years of Socialism. The West European Left in the Twentieth Century* (London: Fontana, 1997); and Ross McKibbin, 'Why was there no Marxism in Great Britain?' in his *Ideologies of Class. Social Relations in Britain, 1880–1950* (Oxford: Oxford University Press, 1991), pp. 1–41.

31 Labour Party, *Report of the 45th Annual Conference of the Labour Party* (London: Labour Party, 1945), pp. 143–4.

32 David Marquand, *Ramsay MacDonald* (London: Richard Cohen, 1997), p. 92.

33 Blair, *New Britain*, p. 12; *Guardian*, 3 October 1998.

34 *Daily Telegraph*, 13 January 1995; *Guardian*, 1 June 1998; *Economist*, 20 June 1998; *Observer*, 3 January 1999; *Independent*, 13 January 1999; Trevor Fisher, 'Forward to the past', *Labour Review* (Spring 1999), 8–9.

35 Richard Grayson (ed.), *Liberal Democrats and the Third Way* (London: Centre for Reform, 1998), p. 18.

36 *Observer*, 15 November 1998; *Times Higher Education Supplement*, 6 November 1998; *Identity and Politics. A Discussion with Michael Ignatieff and Sean Neeson* (London: Centre for Reform, 1998), p. 13; Samuel Brittain, *Essays, Moral, Political and Economic* (Edinburgh: Hume Papers on Public Policy, 1998).

37 Blair's Associated Press speech. See also Andrew Adonis, 'Byzantium and Liverpool', *Times Literary Supplement*, 9 February 1996, 12–13.

38 Michael Freeden, *Ideologies and Political Theory. A Conceptual Approach* (Oxford: Oxford University Press, 1996), pp. 470–1.

39 Draper, *Hundred Days*, p. 76; *Observer*, 14 June 1998.

40 Roy Jenkins, *A Life at the Centre* (London: Macmillan, 1991), p. 367.

41 'Editorial', *Socialist Commentary* no. 11 (1951), 246–7.

42 *Report of the 58th Annual Conference of the Labour Party* (London: Labour Party, 1959), pp. 107–9.

43 Jones, *Remaking Labour*, pp. 25–40.

44 C. A. R. Crosland, *The Future of Socialism* (London: Jonathan Cape, 1956), p. 116; Hugh Gaitskell, 'Public ownership and equality', *Socialist Commentary* no. 19 (1955), 165–7; and Gaitskell, *Socialism and Nationalisation* (London: Fabian Society, 1956), p. 3.

45 Crosland, *Socialism*, p. 89.

46 Tony Benn, *Years of Hope. Diaries, Papers and Letters 1940–1962* (London: Hutchinson, 1994), pp. 317–19.

47 Manifesto of the Campaign for Democratic Socialism, Anthony Crosland papers, 6/1, British Library of Political and Economic Science, London.

48 *Tribune*, 11 December 1959. See also, Ralph Miliband, *Parliamentary Socialism. A Study in the Politics of Labour* (London: Merlin, 1972), pp. 344–6.

49 Ivor Crewe and Anthony King, *SDP. The Birth, Life and Death of the Social Democratic Party* (Oxford: Oxford University Press, 1995), pp. 20–4.

50 Denis Healey, *The Time of My Life* (Harmondsworth: Penguin, 1990), pp. 378–9.

51 *Report of the 75th Annual Conference of the Labour Party* (London: Labour Party, 1976), pp. 188–9.

52 Christopher Mayhew, *Party Games* (Hutchinson: London, 1969), pp. 94–5.

53 Roy Jenkins, *What Matters Now* (London: Fontana, 1972).

New Labour and the past

54 J. P. Mackintosh, 'Has social democracy failed in Britain?', *Political Quarterly*, 49 (1978), 266–7.
55 Shirley Williams, *Politics is for People* (Harmondsworth: Penguin, 1981), pp. 28–9.
56 Crewe and King, *SDP*, pp. 36–8, 93, 125–7.
57 Roy Jenkins, *Partnership of Principle* (London: Secker and Warburg, 1985), pp. 11, 26, 29, 35; Crewe and King, *SDP*, pp. 335–7.
58 Gould, *Unfinished Revolution*, pp. 30–1, 33; Tony Blair, *The Third Way. New Politics for the New Century* (London: Fabian Society, 1998), p. 1; Gordon Brown, 'Equality – then and now', in Dick Leonard (ed.), *Crosland and New Labour* (London: Macmillan, 1999), pp. 35–48; Routledge, *Brown*, p. 331.
59 *Tribune*, 21 July 1995.
60 David Owen, *A Future That Will Work* (Harmondsworth: Penguin, 1984), pp. 7–29; Crewe and King, *SDP*, pp. 332–5; *New Statesman*, 17 May 1999.
61 *European*, 19 January 1998.
62 Donald MacIntyre, *Mandelson. The Biography* (London: HarperCollins, 1999), pp. 62–7; Peter Mandelson and Roger Liddle, *The Blair Revolution. Can New Labour Deliver?* (London: Faber and Faber, 1996), pp. 10, 26.
63 Raymond Plant, 'Crosland, equality and New Labour', in Leonard (ed.), *Crosland*, pp. 33–4; *Guardian*, 26 July 1997; *The Times*, 16 August 1997; David Marquand, 'The Blair paradox', *Prospect* (May 1998), 19–24; *New Statesman*, 26 February 1999.
64 David Lipsey, 'Revisionists revise', in Leonard (ed.), *Crosland*, pp. 13–15; Raymond Plant, 'Social democracy', in David Marquand and Anthony Seldon (eds.), *The Ideas That Shaped Post-War Britain* (London: Fontana, 1996), p. 166; Brown, 'Equality', pp. 37–9.
65 *Guardian*, 2 August 1997.
66 Speech to the Institute of Public Policy Research.
67 Peter Mandelson, *Labour's Next Steps: Tackling Social Exclusion* (London: Fabian Society, 1997), p. 7 and Smith, *New Questions*, p. 5.
68 *Getting Welfare to Work: A New Vision for Social Security* (London: Labour Party, 1996); *New Deal for a New Britain. Labour's Proposals to Tackle Youth and Long-Term Unemployment* (London: Labour Party, 1997); *Observer*, 11 May 1997; *Guardian*, 26 June 1997; *Independent*, 16 July 1997.
69 *Guardian*, 29 July 1997.
70 For example, see Eric Hobsbawm, *Age of Extremes. The Short Twentieth Century, 1914–1991* (London: Abacus, 1995); Anthony Giddens, *Beyond Left and Right. The Future of Radical Politics* (Cambridge: Polity, 1994); and Geoff Mulgan, *Politics in an Anti-Political Age* (Cambridge: Polity, 1994).
71 Unless otherwise stated, this paragraph is based on Blair, *New Britain*, pp. 15, 46–7, 55, 203–5, 213.
72 Paul Routledge, *Mandy. The Unauthorised Biography of Peter Mandelson* (London: Simon and Schuster, 1999), pp. 277–8.
73 *New Statesman*, 25 July 1997.
74 John Reid, 'Tough choices, great rewards', *Inside Labour* (July 1999), 14.

75 Richards, 'Permanent revolution', p. 46.
76 Foreword in Christopher Bryant (ed.), *Reclaiming the Ground. Christianity and Socialism* (London: Spire, 1993), p. 11.
77 Blair's speech to the French National Assembly, 24 March 1998.
78 Gould, *Unfinished Revolution*, pp. 394–9.
79 David Marquand, *The Progressive Dilemma* (London: Heinemann, 1990), pp. 5–25.
80 Blair, *Third Way*, p. 2; Wright and Carter, *People's Party*, p. 8.
81 For examples of these different emphases, *New Statesman*, 13 and 20 March 1998; Neal Lawson, 'New Labour's field of dreams', *Renewal* 7 (1999), 1–7.

Appendix 1 | Labour and the electorate 1900–1997

Election year	Number of candidates	Votes cast	% of vote	MPs elected
1900	15	62,698	1.3	2
1906	51	329,748	5.9	30
1910 (Jan)	78	505,667	7.6	40
1910 (Dec)	56	371,802	6.4	42
1918	361	2,245,777	20.8	57
1922	414	4,237,349	29.7	142
1923	427	4,439,780	30.7	191
1924	514	5,489,087	33.3	151
1929	569	8,370,417	37.1	287
1931	516	6,649,630	30.9	52
1935	552	8,325,491	38.0	154
1945	603	11,967,746	48.0	393
1950	617	13,266,176	46.1	315
1951	617	13,948,883	48.8	295
1955	620	12,405,254	46.4	277
1959	621	12,216,172	43.8	258
1964	628	12,205,808	44.1	317
1966	622	13,096,629	48.0	364
1970	625	12,208,758	43.1	288
1974 (Feb)	623	11,645,616	37.2	301
1974 (Oct)	623	11,457,079	39.2	319
1979	623	11,532,218	36.9	269
1983	633	8,456,934	27.6	209
1987	633	10,029,807	30.8	229
1992	634	11,559,857	34.4	271
1997	639	13,517,911	43.2	418

Source: Harry Harmer, The Labour Party 1900–1998 (London: Longman, 1999), pp. 29–41.

Appendix 2 | Labour Party membership

Year	Individual members[a]	Trade-union members	Socialist and co-operative societies	Total membership
1900	–	353,000	23,000	376,000
1901	–	455,000	14,000	469,000
1902	–	847,000	14,000	861,000
1903	–	956,000	14,000	970,000
1904	–	855,000	15,000	900,000
1905	–	904,000	17,000	921,000
1906	–	975,000	21,000	998,000
1907	–	1,050,000	22,000	1,072,000
1908	–	1,127,000	27,000	1,159,000
1909	–	1,451,000	31,000	1,486,000
1910	–	1,394,000	31,000	1,431,000
1911	–	1,502,000	31,000	1,539,000
1912	–	1,858,000	31,000	1,895,000
1913[b]	–	–	33,000	–
1914	–	1,572,000	33,000	1,612,000
1915	–	2,054,000	33,000	2,093,000
1916	–	2,171,000	42,000	2,220,000
1917	–	2,415,000	47,000	2,465,000
1918	–	2,960,000	53,000	3,013,000
1919	–	3,464,000	47,000	3,511,000
1920	–	4,318,000	42,000	4,360,000
1921	–	3,974,000	37,000	4,010,000
1922	–	3,279,000	32,000	3,311,000
1923	–	3,120,000	36,000	3,156,000
1924	–	3,158,000	36,000	3,194,000
1925	–	3,338,000	36,000	3,374,000

Labour Party membership

Year	Individual members[a]	Trade-union members	Socialist and co-operative societies	Total membership
1926	–	3,352,000	36,000	3,388,000
1927	–	3,239,000	55,000	3,294,000
1928	215,000	2,025,000[c]	52,000	2,292,000
1929	228,000	2,044,000	59,000	2,331,000
1930	277,000	2,011,000	58,000	2,347,000
1931	297,000	2,024,000	37,000	2,358,000
1932	372,000	1,960,000	40,000	2,372,000
1933	366,000	1,899,000	40,000	2,305,000
1934	381,000	1,858,000	40,000	2,278,000
1935	419,000	1,913,000	45,000	2,378,000
1936	431,000	1,969,000	45,000	2,444,000
1937	447,000	2,037,000	43,000	2,528,000
1938	429,000	2,158,000	43,000	2,630,000
1939	409,000	2,214,000	40,000	2,663,000
1940	304,000	2,227,000	40,000	2,571,000
1941	227,000	2,231,000	28,000	2,485,000
1942	219,000	2,206,000	29,000	2,454,000
1943	236,000	2,237,000	30,000	2,503,000
1944	266,000	2,375,000	32,000	2,673,000
1945	487,000	2,510,000	41,000	3,039,000
1946	645,000	2,635,000	42,000	3,322,000
1947	608,000	4,386,000	46,000	5,040,000
1948	629,000	4,751,000	42,000	5,422,000
1949	730,000	4,946,000	41,000	5,717,000
1950	908,000	4,972,000	40,000	5,920,000
1951	876,000	4,937,000	35,000	5,849,000
1952	1,015,000	5,072,000	21,000	6,108,000
1953	1,005,000	5,057,000	34,000	6,096,000
1954	934,000	5,530,000	35,000	6,498,000
1955	843,000	5,606,000	35,000	6,484,000
1956	845,000	5,658,000	34,000	6,537,000

Appendix 2

Year	Individual members[a]	Trade-union members	Socialist and co-operative societies	Total membership
1957	913,000	5,644,000	26,000	6,583,000
1958	889,000	5,628,000	26,000	6,542,000
1959	848,000	5,564,000	25,000	6,437,000
1960	790,000	5,513,000	25,000	6,328,000
1961	751,000	5,550,000	25,000	6,326,000
1962	767,000	5,503,000	25,000	6,296,000
1963	830,000	5,507,000	21,000	6,358,000
1964	830,000	5,502,000	21,000	6,353,000
1965	817,000	5,602,000	21,000	6,440,000
1966	776,000	5,539,000	21,000	6,336,000
1967	734,000	5,540,000	21,000	6,295,000
1968	701,000	5,364,000	21,000	6,087,000
1969	681,000	5,462,000	22,000	6,164,000
1970	680,000	5,519,000	24,000	6,223,000
1971	700,000	5,559,000	25,000	6,284,000
1972	703,000	5,425,000	40,000	6,169,000
1973	665,000	5,365,000	42,000	6,073,000
1974	692,000	5,787,000	39,000	6,518,000
1975	675,000	5,750,000	44,000	6,469,000
1976	659,000	5,800,000	48,000	6,507,000[d]
1977	660,000	5,913,000	43,000	6,616,000
1978	676,000	6,260,000	55,000	6,990,000
1979	666,000	6,511,000	58,000	7,236,000
1980	348,000	6,407,000	56,000	6,811,000
1981	277,000	6,273,000	58,000	6,608,000
1982	274,000	6,185,000	57,000	6,516,000
1983	295,000	6,101,000	59,000	6,456,000
1984	323,000	5,844,000	60,000	6,227,000
1985	313,000	5,827,000	60,000	6,200,000
1986	297,000	5,778,000	58,000	6,133,000
1987	289,000	5,564,000	55,000	5,908,000

Labour Party membership

Year	Individual members[a]	Trade-union members	Socialist and co-operative societies	Total membership
1988	266,000	5,481,000	56,000	5,804,000
1989	294,000	5,335,000	53,000	5,682,000
1990	311,000	4,922,000	54,000	5,287,000
1991	261,000	4,811,000	54,000	5,126,000
1992	280,000	4,634,000	51,000	4,965,000
1993	279,530	nfa	nfa	nfa
1994	266,270	nfa	nfa	nfa
1995	305,189	nfa	nfa	nfa
1996	365,110	nfa	nfa	nfa
1997	400,465	nfa	nfa	nfa
1998	405,238	nfa	nfa	nfa
1999	387,776	nfa	nfa	nfa

Notes:

[a] Officially there was no individual membership until 1918. No count of individual members was made until 1928. For the period to 1917, members of the Co-operative and Women's Labour League were included in the 'total membership' column, which therefore exceeds the sum of the previous columns.

[b] The Osborne judgement prevented the compilation of membership figures in 1913.

[c] From 1928 to 1946 inclusive, trade-union members of the Labour Party had to 'contract in' to party political funds.

[d] This total differs from Butler and Butler's since in this book and in the original source the arithmetic is in error.

nfa no figures available.

Sources: For the period before 1992, David Butler and Gareth Butler, *British Political Facts 1900–94* (London: Macmillan, 1994), pp. 146–7. For the period 1993 to 1999, Labour Party NEC reports.

Index

Abel-Smith, Brian 106, 109, 111
abortion law reform 110, 209, 210, 211
academics, post-war Labour 30
Addison, Christopher 160, 165
AES (Alternative Economic Strategy)
    67–8
affluence
    and the Conservatives 60–1
    and Labour's political thought 32
    and New Labour's tradition 373
Africa, colonial reform programme 135
Aims for Industry 293, 294
ALP (Australian Labor Party) 311,
    312, 313–14
Ammon, Charles 268
Amnesty International 123
Anglo-American Council on
    Productivity 59
Anti-Apartheid Movement 123
appeasement 120, 127
Applegarth, Robert 224
Arab nationalism 135
Aristotle 16
arts, Labour support for the 110
Asquith, Herbert 153
Attlee, Clement 26, 29, 124, 160, 185,
    186, 261
    autobiography of 349–50, 351–2, 360
    governments (1945–51)
        and constitutional reform 161–6
        and consumption 207–8
        and the economy 57–60, 61
        and international affairs 126,
            130–6, 138
        and revisionists 379
        and trade unions 230–1
        and the welfare state 4, 28–9, 60,
            97–103
        and women 198, 207–8, 209

governments of, (1945–51) 2, 3
    and internationalism 317
    and Labour mythologies 343, 354
    and New Labour's tradition 373,
        374
    plans for welfare reform (1930s)
        95–7
    and the Second World War 97
    on the trade union block vote 238
    austerity, and the Attlee government
        58, 207, 209
    Australian Labor Party (ALP) 311,
        312, 313–14
    auto/biographies see mythologies

Bacon, Alice 193
Bagehot, Walter 162
    English Constitution 167
Ball, Sidney 16, 22
Balogh, Thomas 36
Bank of England 332
Barker, Sara 269
Barnes, George 87
Beales, H. L. 283
Bebel, August 309
Beer, Max 312
Belloc, Hilaire 86
Benn, Anthony Wedgwood (Tony)
    169, 207, 213, 234, 264, 266,
    297, 300, 359
    on New Labour 368
Berlin, Isaiah 378, 386
Bernstein, Eduard 317
Bevan, Aneurin 17, 29, 98, 101, 102
    and the Bevanite left opposition
        movement (1950s) 357
    and Clause Four 381
    and foreign policy 130, 134, 138,
        144

Index

Index

Index

Index

Index

Index

Index

Index

Index

Marxism
attacks on the Labour Party 1
and Crossland's *The Future of
Socialism* 34
and the economy 48, 49
and international affairs 119, 120,
121, 136–7
and Labour's social and political
thought 9, 10
and the Second World War 129–30
and the Wilson government 36
maternity benefit 86
maternity leave 112
Mayhew, Christopher 382
Mays, John Barron 288
means-tested benefits 100–1
Meet the Challenge, Make the Change
172
Meir, Golda 190
membership (Labour Party) 248–73,
394–7
activists 249, 259–66, 270
and campaigning 297–300
campaigns in the 1990s 271–2
figures 249, 250, 256, 257–8, 285
in the inter-war years 250–6
Labour clubs 255
and the Labour left 270–1
leaders and members 267–73
and New Labour 266, 271–3
and one member, one vote (OMOV)
266
and parliamentary candidates
253–4, 270
post-war patterns of 256–9
regional variations in 251, 252–3,
256–7
social composition of 259
and the trade unions 240, 249–50,
253, 259, 384, 395
values and ideas of party members
post-war 263–6
pre-war 259–63
and women 192, 196, 248, 250–1,
255–6, 258, 259, 261, 262

youth movement 255, 256
men
male breadwinner idea 73–4, 204
male manual workers 191, 207, 212
and representations of masculinity
211–13
Michael, Alun 272
middle class
and the 1997 general election
301–2
activists 299, 329
culture and lifestyle 31, 32
electorate
and Labour campaigning 296
and popular conceptions of
politics 288–9, 290
and Labour MPs 244–5
and Labour Party membership 262,
264, 270
'progressives' 341
and support for Labour 57
and the welfare state 102
women
and consumption 207
and feminism 203, 205, 206
as Labour Party members 192
Middle East, Labour's foreign policy
in the 132, 133, 134–5, 138,
139
'Middle England', and New Labour
368
Middleton, James 159
Mikardo, Ian 170, 358
Militant Tendency 120, 265, 356
military affairs 124, 140–1
miners' strikes 206, 289
Mitchell, Hannah 349
Mitchell, Isaac 313
modernisation, Labour and the
economy 58–9, 61–3
Montefiore, Dora 315
morality, public enforcement of
private 22
Morgan, Ken 310
Morgan, Rhodri 272

409

Index

410

Index

and social welfare 84, 106, 111
working families tax credit 114
Temperance movement 22
Temple, Archbishop William 19
Tenfelde, Klaus 310
Thatcher, Margaret 201
governments of
and electoral support for Labour
284, 293, 373
and European social democracy
329
and the Labour left 266
and New Labour 374
and the press 294
and the SDP 382
and trade unions 233–5, 236, 242
and Labour economic policy 69
and public spending 66
'third force' advocates 137
Thomas, George 214
Thomas, Jimmy 126, 130–1, 158, 351,
352
Titmuss, Richard 104, 106
Tomlinson, Jim 102
Toole, Joe 345–6, 347
town planning 108
Townsend, Peter 109
Toynbee, Polly 376–7
trade
and the AES 68
free trade 54, 56, 68, 121
versus protection 47–8
Trade Boards Act (1909) 85
Trade Disputes Act (1927) 17, 226
Trade Union Act (1913) 226
trade unions 3, 14, 221–45
in the 1970s 64, 67
block votes at the Labour Party
conferences 236–41, 269, 271
constructing a governing
partnership with Labour
241–5
and European social democracy
328–9, 333
and evolutionary socialism 9, 13

funds 83
and international affairs 127
and Labour MPs 244–5
and Labour Party membership 240,
249–50, 253, 259, 394, 395
and Labour Party policy
(1900–50) 228–31
(1950–2000) 231–6
and New Labour 235, 241, 368
and New Liberalism 376
and the 'new realism' 234–5
in the nineteenth century 83
and the origins of the Labour Party
222–5
and party finances 225–8, 237
and personal liberty 21
and pluralism 221–2
and the politics of planning 24
and the post-war economic boom
221
and the role of the state 17, 22
and state control 22
and the Thatcher governments
233–5, 236
and welfare 83, 87–8, 100
and the Wilson government 63,
232–3
and women 196, 198
see also TUC (Trades Union
Congress)
tradition
Labour Party 369–72
and New Labour 273–5
Tribune group 33
TUC (Trades Union Congress) 224,
225
and the 1932 Club 268
affiliated organisations 241
and international affairs 127
and Labour Party finances 226, 227
and party policy 229–30, 233
and the 'Social Contract' 64, 233

UDC (Union of Democratic Control)
125, 128, 138

415

Index

women (*cont.*)
  working class (*cont.*)
    Labour Party members 192, 206
    representations of 213–15
    and welfare 204–5
    younger women 214
    see also feminism; motherhood; sex
      discrimination
Women's Labour League *see* WLL
    (Women's Labour League)
Women's Trade Union League 85
Woolf, Leonard 124
work
  attitudes of pre-war party members
    259
  and employment legislation 200
  Labour's emphasis on 73–4
  Right to Work 49–50, 73, 80–1, 85,
    91, 115
  and welfare 80–2, 96, 112, 114, 115
working-class
  and the deproletarianisation of
    Western Europe 325
  electorate 285, 286, 329–30
    and popular conceptions of
      politics 286–8

and Labour Party membership 255
male manual workers 191, 207, 212
popular culture 209, 260
and sexuality 211
women
  and birth control 210–11
  and feminism 205–6
  housewives 203, 208
  Labour Party members 192, 206
  representations of 213–15
  and welfare 194, 204–5
working families tax credit 114
workmen's compensation 84
Wright, Tony 373
Wrigley, Chris 314
WS (women's sections in the Labour
    Party) 93–4, 192, 194, 195, 251,
    262

Young, Michael 103
Young, Sir Robert 162
Yugoslavia (former), conflicts in 121,
    122, 143

Zweig, Ferdinand 289–90